T.M.

RELIGION IN VICTORIAN SOCIETY

A Sourcebook of Documents

Edited by

Richard J. Helmstadter
Department of History, University of Toronto

and

Paul T. Phillips
Department of History, St. Francis Xavier University
Antigonish, Nova Scotia

UNIVERSITY
PRESS OF
AMERICA

LANHAM • NEW YORK • LONDON

Copyright © 1985 by

University Press of America,® Inc.

4720 Boston Way
Lanham, MD 20706

3 Henrietta Street
London WC2E 8LU England

Library of Congress Cataloging in Publication Data
Main entry under title:

Religion in Victorian society.

    1. England—Church history—19th century—Sources.
2. Church and social problems—England—History—19th
century—Sources. I. Helmstadter, Richard J.,
1934-   . II. Phillips, Paul T., 1942-
BR759.R45   1986   274.2'081   85-20241
ISBN 0-8191-4994-2 (alk. paper)
ISBN 0-8191-4995-0 (pbk. : alk. paper)

All University Press of America books are produced on acid-free
paper which exceeds the minimum standards set by the National
Historical Publications and Records Commission.

This book is dedicated to the memory of Brian Heeney, a much cherished colleague and a distinguished contributor to the history of Victorian religion.

Contents

Foreword

Many years ago, a clerical friend heard an elderly clergyman preach in Westminster Abbey on Genesis 26:18: "And Isaac digged again the wells of water, which they had digged in the days of Abraham his father." Identifying the physical desert of biblical times with the spiritual desert of the mid-twentieth century and drawing the parallel of remembered wells, the preacher urged his hearers to return to the great age of the Church — by which he meant the reign of Queen Victoria — and ended his sermon, to my friend's astonishment, with a plea for the revival of family prayers.

That the Victorian era encompassed one of the great religious eras in history scarcely anyone would deny, and those who experienced its power — whether through conviction or repulsion — saw everything within its perspective, as did the preacher in fondly recalling a typical religious practice dead beyond hope of resurrection. The spell was strong among historians and particularly among historians who were Englishmen. Churchmen and Dissenters looked back on their eighteenth-century forbears with something like horror at their worldliness, at their lack of missionary spirit, and at a style of preaching and devotion far different from what so moved Victorian worshippers. The titanic religious struggles of the Reformation or the seventeenth century were seen by Protestants and Roman Catholics alike as mirrors of the ecclesiastical and political battles of the nineteenth century, and even the Fathers of the Church were brought forward in shovel hats and gaiters to serve as allies of Victorian clerics in their strenuous battles. Anti-clericals and free thinkers searched the past for anticipations of their own liberalisms, while Levellers and Diggers came to do yeoman service as protosocialists.

Apologetic or pious history is with us still, long surviving in the changed intellectual climate that emerged throughout Western culture early in this century. The English contribution to the new dispensation was strongest in the field of comparative religion, dominated but not exhausted by *The Golden Bough*, by the great Scottish anthropologist J.G. Frazer, which began to appear in 1890. Just after the turn of the century, the American psychologist and philosopher William James insisted to a Scottish audience that religion was a phenomenon worthy of serious study and proved it in his lectures, *The Varieties of Religious Experience* (1902), still an unsurpassed exercise in scientific, and empathetic, understanding. In these same years, with Emile Durkheim in France and Ernst Troeltsch in Germany, the sociology of religion was established as a discipline, especially concerned with the civic and structural characteristics of religion, but its influence was late in arriving in Britain, and even the most important of the historians of religion of the time, the French scholar Elie Halévy, was not really domiciled in English awareness until his great *History of the English People*, and especially its first volume with its central emphasis on Methodism and Evangelical religion, began to appear in translation in the 1920s.

The effort to see nineteenth-century English religion as it really was, and not as what the Victorians or their Victorianizing successors thought it should be, began in earnest in the 1930s. It is not invidious to mention two names. In *Church and State in the XVIII Century* (1934), Norman Sykes rescued the Church of England during what was, in its way, also a great religious age from Victorian condescension; also at Cambridge, G. Kitson Clark exerted a wide influence, not only through a succession of his own books in the 1950s and 1960s, but also through his students and admirers. The reinterpretation of Victorian religion was, then, no small part of the re-evaluation of the Victorian age as a whole that has taken place so impressively in the generation or so since the end of World War II. Nineteenth-century Britain has attracted students and scholars alike as the first industrial nation, a laboratory of economic, social, political, and administrative experiment under unprecedented conditions of technological and imperial growth, of wealth and poverty, of profoundly influential theorizing and of hard-headed (or muddle-headed) empiricism. And because no aspect of English life was untouched by religion, Victorian religious history offers a sweep and drama and relevance that can be matched in few other countries or times.

The immense monographic literature on Victorian religion is threatening to escape the mastery of any one scholar, though surveys of general or social history make many of its conclusions available to students. What has been singularly lacking is a means of access to crucial and revealing documents that will permit students to share in original materials familiar to scholars but beyond ordinary availability or fitting the time constraints that students and teachers alike must feel. This collection provides a sensitive and wonderfully unhackneyed sample of an immense literature: inescapable, central texts (like Gladstone on church and state) are here, and so are many little-known but revealing documents that give a sense of the range of religious concerns and styles. The selection deliberately emphasizes religion in society: family prayers, deathbeds, devotional poetry, learned and popular theology other than in connection with science, all those private or technical aspects of religion have had to be sacrificed, on good Victorian pragmatic grounds. But Victorian churchmen, of whatever stripe, were agreed that the private side of religion was more than matched in importance by its public face. It is the mosaic of a Christian society, an ideal that surprisingly often came close to reality, that Professors Helmstadter and Phillips allow us to experience in the making.

R.K. Webb
University of Maryland,
Baltimore County

Preface

Religion played a major role in the lives of many Victorians. Organized religion was an important element in Victorian society. These are unassailable assertions, but their specific meanings are not obvious. The religious life of nineteenth-century England was richly varied. Even among those Protestant Christians who constituted the great majority of the church-going public, there was little uniformity in thought or practice. Christianity in an Oxford common room or a catherdral close bore little resemblance to that in a Primitive Methodist community or a Salvation Army meeting. Victorian religion reflected the diversity of Victorian society, and it was shaped, as well, by the complex religious heritage from the past. Some religious institutions, particularly those associated with politically militant members of nonconformist denominations, represented the aspirations and interests of particular social classes. Other institutions, particularly those identified with the Church of England, involved a number of social groups and cut across class lines. It is dangerous to generalize about the social role of religion in Victorian England.

As English society was transformed under the impact of industrialization in the late eighteenth and early nineteenth centuries, organized religion seemed, to some, a critically important force for stability. When older agencies of social control seemed to be crumbling, especially in the increasingly large and democratic cities, some looked to the internal disciplines inculcated by religion for the salvation of the social order. Others, newly prosperous and looking for liberation from the constraints of the old aristocratically dominated society, found their dissenting religious institutions to be convenient agencies for pressing forward their political and social ambitions. For these militant nonconformists, typically

Congregationalists, Baptists or Unitarians, religion seemed a force for change, a focus for social conflict. The documents in this volume illustrate both positions, that of the conservative churchman and the radical nonconformist, as well as the heavily populated ambiguous ground between them.

The place of religion in the lives of the urban working classes was a troubling issue for members of the Established Church and nonconformists alike. Why did the churches not attract the working classes? Was this a new failure? How could more prosperous Christians reach the working classes in order to improve their social and spiritual lives? These questions called forth inventive responses, some of which are illustrated by documents in this volume. Middleclass nonconformists were among those most concerned with civilizing the poor and dangerous classes. There is some irony in the situation of those politically militant dissenters, intent on battle when they looked towards the Church and the aristocracy, committed to peace and harmony when they looked towards the poor.

By the fourth quarter of the century the power of the aristocracy was obviously in decline, and the future clearly belonged to democracy. The well being of the poor, the democratic majority, assumed, at this time, a greater importance, stimulating a heightened sense of urgency within a new generation of well to do Christian social reformers. Partly in reaction to the impact of science, the theological orientation of the major Protestant denominations shifted in the late nineteenth century. The increase in the concern of the churches for social reform is bound up with that shift in theology. That complex change is documented in this book.

The documents in Chapter I are drawn from the first third of the century, a period of dramatic social and political change. The chapter concentrates on three themes: the idea that religion, especially Anglicanism, was a powerful support for social stability; the ambiguous role of Methodism; and the attack by radicals and nonconformists on the Church of England as a pillar of the embattled aristocratic constitution.

Chapter II deals with ideas about the nature of the relation between the Anglican Church and the state, and more broadly, with ideas about the role of religion in the national life. The documents are drawn from the 1830s, a decade particularly fertile for theories about the connection between the Church and the state. More than any other time in the century it seemed possible then that the constitutional revolution which centred on the Reform Act of 1832 would involve a fundamental change in the legal and political base of the Established Church. Represented here are three quite different points of view, each associated with one of the three "parties" in the Church, the Evangelical, the Broad and the Tractarian.

Chapter III presents a range of comments on the new industrial economy from leading churchmen and dissenters of the 1830s and 1840s. These comments display a variety of viewpoints: they indicate the difficulty which the churches experienced in working out a distinctively Christian position on industrial capitalism. The chapter demonstrates the connection between agressive nonconformity and the anti-corn law league, and exemplifies the Evangelical Lord Ashley's concern with factory reform. The early manifestation of the Christian Socialist Movement is documented here.

Chapter IV, with documents from the 1830s and 1840s, includes evidence of some of the early efforts of the churches to identify and come to grips with the problems of life in the new industrial cities. This chapter documents the pessimistic view that there was something in urban life that was antagtonistic to religion, and also the optimistic, Liberal view that the growth of cities was an important factor in the progress of English society towards a more free and more enlighted future.

Chapter V contains documents from the 1830s and 1840s which reflect the extremely high hopes entertained for the gains to be derived from the primary education of the poor at the time when the state was just beginning to support the rudiments of a public education system. The widespread assumption that religion was a necessary part of effective public education, and the equally widely held suspicion of state control, are clearly articulated in this chapter. The *Report* from the Rev. Henry Moseley, a school inspector, represents the disillusionment with earlier optimism that began to emerge at mid century.

Chapter VI contains documents from the second half of the century which explore the reasons why the churches did not attract the urban working classes. Some of the steps taken to reach the masses are illustrated, including the Moody-Sankey missions and the Salvation Army. These were two of the more spectacular efforts to cast the net of organized religion over more people from the lower middle classes and the working classes through the use of techniques rooted in popular culture or derived from the world of commercial entertainment.

Chapter VII is focussed on three areas of sectarian conflict, each of which served to colour the lives of many Victorians through much of the nineteenth century, and each of which had an impact on politics at the parliamentary level over a long period of time. In this chapter the very important struggle of protestant nonconformity for social and legal equality is represented by documents drawn from the late 1860s and early 1870s, the time of Gladstone's first Liberal administration. The tension between the High Church and Low Church parties within the Anglican establishment is represented by the debate on the Public Worship Regulation Bill in 1874. Anti-Catholicism is included through documents related to the restoration of the Roman Catholic hierarchy in England in 1850.

Chapter VIII continues the theme begun in Chapter VI, the attempt on the part of the churches to exercise some influence over the lives of the working classes. The documents, from the second half of the century, indicate something of the range of concern of religiously inspired urban philanthropy. Embodied in the tracts selected for this chapter are the main lines of that middle class strategy which associated religion, morality and social discipline and attempted to persuade the poor to become more respectable by adopting all three.

Chapter IX is focussed on the impact of Darwin and the idea of evolution. One document illustrates the pre Darwinian accommodation of religion and science in natural theology, but the bulk of the chapter is concerned with several immediate responses to Darwin's *On the Origin of Species*. The sense of warfare between science and religion engendered by the controversies over evolutionary theory is emphasized here in full awareness of the current scholarly view that it is important not to exaggerate the degree and extent of that conflict. Also included here are two documents which draw connections among science, secularization and social progress.

Chapter X, through documents for the 1880s, concentrates on the increased sensitivity of many in the churches to the intolerable conditions of life among the poor in the slums of large cities. This awareness, and the strengthened impulse towards Christian socialism in a variety of forms, had a complex web of causes, including the emergence of political democracy and the accumulated experience of city missionaries who were affronted by what they discovered in the slums. The Christian socialism of the late nineteenth century represents, albeit in extreme form, an important general change in orientation on the part of many leading figures in the churches, particularly the clergy. By the end of the century political leaders no longer thought of the churches as major institutions of social control. As they ceased to be considered major bulwarks of the social order, the churches were much more ready than they had been early in the century to emphasize the social obligations enjoined by the idea of the fatherhood of God and the brotherhood of man.

We wish to express our gratitude to the Royal Historical Society for permission to reproduce selections from the correspondence of Jabez Bunting. Thanks also go to the Research Council of St. Francis Xavier University for a grant that defrayed the cost of some of the research, and to Chris and Barbara Johnson who skilfully prepared the manuscript for publication.

July 1985
R.J.H.
P.T.P.

Chapter I

The Old Order Crumbling

Introduction

During the last quarter of the eighteenth century and the first half of the nineteenth, momentous changes in the shape of the English economy, in the character of English society and in the structure of the English constitution transformed English life. This is the period to which the Industrial Revolution is conventionally assigned, the period in which social class came to dominate the organization of society, and the period in which the great Reform Act of 1832 served as a symbol for constitutional and political transformation.

Between the Glorious Revolution of 1688 and the accession of George III in 1760, the growth of prosperity and social stability was reflected in a quiet style of politics in which power and influence were shared among the Crown, the aristocracy and a small group of wealthy merchants. The American Revolution, however, and more clearly and forcefully the French Revolution encouraged in England the re-emergence of radical demands for democratic changes in the constitution. Furthermore, the Industrial Revolution created groups of men who turned to radical politics in search of social justice because they thought the state had granted them insufficient protection against loss of social status and harsher living conditions brought about by changes in commerce and industry.

On the whole the men who favoured modernization or worked for radical constitutional reform perceived the Church of England, the Established Church, as part of the old order, as an institution embedded in traditional, aristocratically dominated society, and as an enemy of change. This view, as is the case with any such stereotype, was exaggerated, too simple, and inapplicable to the many liberal and forward looking churchmen. Nevertheless, from the bishops in the House of Lords, all but one of whom voted against the Reform Bill, to the parish clergy who often served as magistrates upholding law and order in the countryside, the Established Church, for many, became identified with the conservative effort to preserve for the future as much as possible of the England that was passing.

To some extent organized religion itself was associated with the old order, but, unlike the case in Continental Europe, there was not a very widely spread predilection in England to identify Christianity with conservatism. This was so partly because the Church of England was not the only church in England. There were, during this period Roman Catholics in England, and, more importantly, a large and growing number of Protestant Dissenters, principally Congregationalists, Baptists, Presbyterians and their Unitarian successors, Quakers, and Methodists. The Methodist and evangelical revivals of the eighteenth century were certainly in part responsible for the increase in the following which the nonconformists commanded, and the popular imagination was so stirred by these developments that some historians have been very interested in their political ramifications. Some argue that Methodism in particular may have subdued support for French-style revolution, either by teaching political submission or by providing popular religious alternatives to revolutionary democracy. Other historians see Methodism as essentially liberating and progressive, authoritarian in structure but with a deeply democratic theology.

Protestant dissenters tended to support the struggle for constitutional reforms partly because they wanted to improve their own legal position. The repeal of the Test and Corporation Acts in 1828 and Catholic Emancipation in 1829 clearly demonstrated that England had become a religiously pluralistic society. The presence of dissenters on the political left, therefore, added religious content to the struggle between those who favoured and those who opposed the great changes taking place in England, while at the same time their presence prevented religion itself from being identified with those who would maintain the old order.

Guide to Further Reading

Harold Perkin, *The Origins of Modern English Society, 1780-1880* (1969), is the most stimulating synthetic account of the changes in English society during the period of the Industrial Revolution. The most recent and most comprehensive work on the central event in the movement for constitutional reform is Michael Brock, *The Great Reform Act* (1973). Geoffrey Best provides an excellent picture of the social and constitutional situation of the Established Church in *Temporal Pillars* (1964); particularly valuable is Chapter IV, "Church, State and Society, 1770-1840." The political predicament of the Established Church and its changing place in the constitution is very clearly discussed by Olive Brose in *Church and Parliament: The Reshaping of the Church of England, 1828-1860* (1959), and in G.I.T. Machin, "Resistance to the Repeal of the Test and Corporation Acts, 1828," *Historical Journal* (1979). The Dissenters' Campaign to repeal the Test and Corporation Acts, the symbols of their legal inferiority under the unreformed constitution, is dealt with by R.W. Davis in *Dissent in Politics, 1780-1830: the Political Life of William Smith M.P.* (1972). G.I.T. Machin provides a general survey of the relation between politics and the churches in the period between the first and second reform acts in *Politics and the Churches in Great Britain, 1832-1868* (1977). Norman Gash's highly regarded *Reaction and Reconstruction in English Politics 1832-1852* (1965) includes a thorough discussion of religious issues in politics after the passing of the reform act. The best account of the growth of radicalism in the late eighteenth and early nineteenth centuries is E.P. Thompson's classic study, *The Making of the English Working Class* (1963). The central interpretation of Methodism as a stabilizing force is found in Elie Halevy, *England in 1815* (1924) and in the recent collection of his early articles, *The Birth of Methodism in England* (1971), edited by Bernard Semmel. In *The Methodist Revolution* (1974), Bernard Semmel argues that Methodism, and evangelicalism generally, were essentially modernizing, liberalizing movements. Semmel sees Methodism as a substitute for revolution. The relations among social class, politics and denomination are explored by W.R. Ward in *Religion and Society in England 1790-1850* (1972).

Reflections on the Revolution in France (1790), by Edmund Burke. Selections.

Edmund Burke (1729-1797), author and politician, is best remembered as the conservative defender of traditional government and society in the face of fears raised by the French Revolution. A Whig and reformer for most of his career, he broke with his party in 1791 and gave his support to the Tory administration of the younger William Pitt. The *Reflections* appeared in 1790 in response to the sermon, *A Discourse on the Love of Country*, by the radical dissenter Richard Price, an advocate of religious equality and constitutional change. The *Reflections* was an immediate success, and eleven editions were published within a year. In the *Reflections* Burke argued against revolution and celebrated the value of tradition. He portrayed society as an organism with a multitude of essential links with the past and he stressed that social and political change should be gradual. The *Reflections* provided conservatives with a storehouse of arguments against radical change. In spite of the fact that Burke's argument was more polemical than philosophical, and in spite of his ill-informed comments on the French Revolution, the *Reflections* has remained a classic statement of a conservative vision of society.

  In the following selection, Burke portrays religion as an important civilizing force, and the Church of England as an historic national institution whose tradition was inseparably interwoven with that of the state. The *Reflections* are addressed to a citizen of France

---

We know, and it is our pride to know, that man is by his constitution a religious animal; that atheism is against, not only our reason, but our instincts; and that it cannot prevail long. But if, in the moment of riot, and in a drunken delirium from the hot spirit drawn out of the alembic of hell, which in France is now so furiously boiling, we should uncover our nakedness, by throwing off that Christian religion which has hitherto been our boast and comfort, and one great source of civilization amongst us, and among many other nations, we are apprehensive (being well aware that the mind will not endure a void) that some uncouth, pernicious and degrading superstition might take place of it.

  For that reason, before we take from our establishment the natural, human means of estimation, and give it up to contempt as you have done, and in doing it have incurred the penalties you well deserve to suffer, we desire that some other may be presented to us in the place of it. We shall then form our judgement.

On these ideas, instead of quarrelling with establishments, as some do, who have made a philosophy and a religion of their hostility to such institutions, we cleave closely to them. We are resolved to keep an established church, and established monarchy, an established aristocracy, and an established democracy, each in the degree it exists, and in no greater. I shall show you presently how much of each of these we possess.

It has been the misfortune (not as these gentlemen think, the glory) of this age, that everything is to be discussed, as if the constitution of our country were to be always a subject rather of altercation than enjoyment. For this reason, as well as for the satisfaction of those among you (if any such be among you) who may wish to profit of examples, I venture to trouble you with a few thoughts upon each of these establishments. I do not think they were unwise in ancient Rome, who, when they wished to new-model their laws, set commissioners to examine the best constituted republics within their reach.

First, I beg leave to speak of our church establishment, which is the first of our prejudices, not a prejudice destitute of reason, but involving in it a profound and extensive wisdom. I speak of it first. It is first, and last, and midst in our minds. For, taking ground on that religious system, of which we are now in possession, we continue to act on the early received, and uniformly continued sense of mankind. That sense not only, like a wise architect, hath built up the august fabric of states, but like a provident proprietor, to preserve the structure from profanation and ruin, as a sacred temple, purged from all the impurities of fraud, and violence, and injustice, and tyranny, hath solemnly and forever consecrated the commonwealth, and all that officiate in it. This consecration is made, that all who administer in the government of men, in which they stand in the person of God Himself, should have high and worthy notions of their function and destination; that their hope should be full of immortality: that they should not look to the paltry pelf of the moment, not to the temporary and transient praise of the vulgar, but to a solid, permanent existence, in the permanent part of their nature, and to a permanent fame and glory, in the example they leave as a rich inheritance to the world.

Such sublime principles ought to be infused into persons of exalted situations; and religious establishments provided, that may continually revive and enforce them. Every sort of moral, every sort of civil, every sort of political institution, aiding the rational and natural ties that connect the human understanding and affections to the divine, are not more than necessary, in order to build up that wonderful structure. Man: whose prerogative it is, to be in a great degree a creature of his own making; and who, when made as he ought to be made, is destined to hold no trivial place in the creation. But whenever man is put over men, as the better nature ought ever to preside, in that case more particularly, he should as nearly as possible be approximated to his perfection.

The consecration of the state, by a state religious establishment, is necessary also to operate with a wholesome awe upon free citizens; because, in order to secure their freedom, they must enjoy some determinate portion of the power. To them therefore a religion connected with the state, and with their duty towards it, becomes even more necessary than in such societies, where the people, by the terms of their subjection, are confined to private sentiments, and the management of their own family concerns. All persons possessing any portion of power ought to be strongly and awfully impressed with an idea that they act in trust; and that they are to account for their conduct in that trust to the one great Master, Author and Founder of society.

****

But one of the first and most leading principles on which the commonwealth and the laws are consecrated, is lest the temporary possessors and life-renters in it, unmindful of what they have received from their ancestors, or of what is due to their posterity, should act as if they were the entire masters; that they should not think it amongst their rights to cut off the entail or commit waste on the inheritance, by destroying at their pleasure the whole original fabric of their society; hazzarding to leave to those who come after them a ruin instead of a habitation — and teaching these successors as little to respect their contrivances, as they had themselves respected the institutions of their forefathers. By this unprincipled facility of changing the state as often, and as much, and in as many ways, as there are floating fancies or fashions, the whole chain and continuity of the commonwealth would be broken. No one generation could link with the other. Men would become little better than the flies of a summer.

And first of all, the science of jurisprudence, the pride of human intellect, which, with all its defects, redundancies, and errors, is the collected reason of ages, combining the principles of original justice with the infinite variety of human concerns, as a heap of old exploded errors, would no longer be studied. Personal self-sufficiency and arrogance (the certain attendants upon all those who have never experienced a wisdom greater than their own) would usurp the tribunal. Of course, no certain laws, establishing invariable grounds of hope and fear, would keep the actions of men in a certain course, or direct them to a certain end. Nothing stable in the modes of holding property, or exercising function, could form a solid ground on which any parent could speculate in the education of his offspring, or in a choice for their future establishment in the world. No principles would be early worked into the habits. As soon as the most able instructor had completed his laborious course of institution, instead of sending forth his pupil, accomplished in a virtuous discipline, fitted to procure him attention and respect, in his place in society, he would find everything altered; and that he had turned out a poor creature to the contempt and derision of the world, ignorant of the true grounds of estimation. Who would insure a tender and delicate sense of honour to beat almost with the first pulses of the heart, when no man could know what would be the test of honour in a nation, continually varying the standard of its coin? No part of life would retain its acquisitions. Barbarism with regard to science and literature, unskillfulness with regard to arts and manufactures, would infallibly succeed to the want of a steady education and settled principle; and thus the commonwealth itself would, in a few generations crumble away, be disconnected into the dust and powder of individuality, and at length dispersed to all the winds of heaven.

To avoid therefore the evils of inconstancy and versatility, ten thousand times worse than those of obstinacy and the blindest prejudice, we have consecrated the state, that no man should approach to look into its defects or corruptions but with due caution; that he should never dream of beginning its reformation by subversion; that he should approach to the faults of the state as to the wounds of a father, with pious awe, and trembling solicitude. By this wise prejudice we are taught to look with horror on those children of their country, who are prompt rashly to hack that aged parent in pieces, and put him into the kettle of magicians, in hopes that by their poisonous weeds, and wild incantations, they may regenerate the paternal constitution, and renovate their father's life.

Society is indeed a contract. Subordinate contracts for objects of mere occasional interest may be dissolved at pleasure — but the state ought not to be considered nothing better than a partnership agreement in a trade of pepper and coffee, calico or tobacco, or some other such low concern, to be taken up for a little temporary interest, and to be dissolved by the fancy of the parties. It is to be looked on with other reverence; because it is not a partnership in things subservient only to the gross animal existence of a temporary and perishable nature. It is a partnership in all science; a partnership in all art; a partnership in every virtue, and in all perfection. As the ends of such a partnership cannot be obtained in many generations, it becomes a partnership not only between those who are living, but between those who are living, those who are dead, and those who are to be born. Each contract of each particular state is but a clause in the great primeval contract of eternal society, linking the lower with the higher natures, connecting the visible and invisible world, according to a fixed compact sanctioned by the inviolable oath which holds all physical and all moral natures, each in their appointed place. This law is not subject to the will of those, who by an obligation above them, and infinitely superior, are bound to submit their will to that law. The municipal corporations of that universal kingdom are not morally at liberty at their pleasure, and on their speculations of a contingent improvement wholly to separate and tear asunder the bands of their subordinate community, and to dissolve it into an unsocial, uncivil, unconnected chaos of elementary principles. It is the first and supreme necessity only, a necessity that is not chosen, but chooses, a necessity paramount to deliberation, that admits no discussion, and demands no evidence, which alone can justify a resort to anarchy. This necessity is no exception to the rule; because this necessity itself is a part too of that moral and physical disposition of things, to which man must be obedient by consent of force: but if that which is only submission to necessity should be made the object of choice, the law is broken, nature is disobeyed, and the rebellious are outlawed, cast forth, and exiled, from this world of reason, and order, and peace, and virtue, and fruitful penitence, into the antagonist world of madness, discord, vice, confusion, and unavailing sorrow.

                              ****

It is on some such principles that the majority of the people of England, far from thinking a religious national establishment unlawful, hardly think it lawful to be without one. In France you are wholly mistaken if you do not believe us above all other things attached to it, and beyond all other nations; and when this people has acted unwisely and unjustifiably in its favour (as in some instances they have done most certainly) in their very errors you will at least discover their zeal.

This principle runs through the whole system of their polity. They do not consider their church establishment as convenient, but as essential to their state: not as a thing heterogeneous and separable; something added for accommodation; what they may either keep or lay aside, according to their temporary ideas of convenience. They consider it as the foundation of their whole constitution, with which, and with with every part of which, it holds an indissoluble union. Church and state are ideas inseparable in their minds, and scarcely is the one ever mentioned without mentioning the other.

Our education is so formed as to confirm and fix this impression. Our education is in a manner wholly in the hands of ecclesiastics, and in all stages from infancy to manhood. Even when our youth, leaving schools and universities, enter that most important period of life which begins to link experience and study together, and when with that view they visit other countries, instead of old domestics whom we have seen as governors to principal men from other parts, three-fourths of those who go abroad with our young nobility and gentlemen are ecclesiastics; not as austere masters, nor as mere followers; but as friends and companions of a graver character, and not seldom persons as well born as themselves. With them, as relations, they most commonly keep up a close connexion through life. By this connexion we conceive that we attach our gentlemen to the church; and we liberalize the church by an intercourse with the leading characters of the country.

So tenacious are we of the old ecclesiastical modes and fashions of institution, that very little alteration has been made in them since the fourteenth or fifteenth century: adhering in this particular, as in all things else, to our old settled maxims, never entirely nor at once to depart from antiquity. We found these old institutions, on the whole, favourable to morality and discipline; and we thought they were susceptible of amendment, without altering the ground. We thought that they were capable of receiving and meliorating, and above all preserving, the accessions of science and literature, as the order of Providence should successively produce them. And after all, with this gothic and monkish education (for such it is in the groundwork) we may put in our claim to as ample and as early a share in all the improvements in science, in arts, and in literature, which have illuminated and adorned the modern world, as any other nation in Europe: we think one main cause of this improvement was our not despising the patrimony of knowledge which was left us by our forefathers.

It is from our attachment to a church establishment, that the English nation did not think it wise to entrust that great, fundamental interest of the whole to what they trust no part of their civil or military public service, that is, to the unsteady and precarious contribution of individuals. They go further. They certainly never have suffered, and never will suffer, the fixed estate of the church to be converted into a pension, to depend on the treasury, and to be delayed, withheld, or perhaps to be extinguished by fiscal difficulties; which difficulties may sometimes be pretended for political purposes, and are in fact often brought on by the extravagance, negligence, and rapacity of politicians. The people of England think they have constitutional motives, as well as religious, against any project of turning their independent clergy into ecclesiastical pensioners of state. They tremble for their liberty, from the influence of a clergy dependent on the crown; they tremble for the public tranquility from the disorders of a factious clergy, if it were made to depend on any other than the crown. They therefore made their church, like their king and their nobility, independent.

From the united considerations of religion and constitutional policy, from their opinion of a duty to make a sure provision for the consolation of the ignorant, they have incorporated and identified the estate of the church with the mass of *private property*, of which the state is not the proprietor, either for use or dominion, but the guardian only and the regulator. They have ordained that the provision of this establishment might be as stable as the earth on which it stands, and should not fluctuate with the Euripus of funds and actions.

The men of England, the men, I mean, of light and leading in England, whose wisdom (if they have any) is open and direct, would be ashamed, as of a silly, deceitful trick, to profess any religion in name, which, by their proceedings, they appear to contemn. If by their conduct (the only language which rarely lies) they seemed to regard the great ruling principle of the moral and the natural world, as a mere invention to keep the vulgar in obedience, they apprehend that by such a conduct they would defeat the political purpose they have in view. They would find it difficult to make others believe in a system to which they manifestly gave no credit themselves. The Christian statesmen of this land would indeed first provide for the *multitude*; because it is the *multitude*; and is therefore, as such, the first object in the ecclesiastical institution, and in all institutions. They have been taught that the circumstance of the Gospel's being preached to the poor was one of the great tests of its true mission. They think, therefore, that those do not believe it, who do not take care it should be preached to the poor. But as they know that charity is not confined to any one description, but ought to apply itself to all men who have wants, they are not deprived of a due and anxious sensation of pity to the distresses of the miserable great. They are not repelled through a fastidious delicacy, at the stench of their arrogance and presumption, from a medicinal attention to their mental blotches, and running sores. They are sensible that religious instruction is of more consequence to them than any others; from the greatness of the temptation to whch they are exposed; from the important consequences that attend their faults; from the contagion of their ill example; from the necessity of bowing down the stubborn neck of their pride and ambition to the yoke of moderation and virtue; from a consideration of the fat stupidity and gross ignorance concerning what imports men most to know, which prevails a courts, and at the head of armies, and in senates, as much as at the loom and in the field.

The English people are satisfied, that to the great the consolations of religion are as necessary as its instructions. They too are among the unhappy. They feel personal pain and domestic sorrow. In these they have no privilege, but are subject to pay their full contingent to the contributions levied on mortality. They want this sovereign balm under their gnawing cares and anxieties, which, being less conversant about the limited wants of animal life, range without limit, and are diversified by infinite combinations in the wild and unbounded regions of imagination. Some charitable dole is wanting to these, our often very unhappy brethren, to fill the gloomy void that reigns in minds which have nothing on earth to hope or fear; something to relieve the killing languor and over-laboured lassitude of those who have nothing to do; something to excite an appetite to existence in the palled satiety which attends on all pleasures which may be bought, where nature is not left to her own process, where even desire is anticipated, and therefore fruition defeated by mediated schemes and contrivances of delight; and no interval, no obstacle, is interposed between the wish and the accomplishment.

The people of England know how little influence the teachers of religion are likely to have with the wealthy and powerful of long standing, and how much less with the newly fortunate, if they appear in a manner no way associated to those with whom they must associate, and over whom they must even exercise, in some cases, something like an authority. What must they think of that body of teachers, if they see it in no part above the establishment of their domestic servants? If the poverty were voluntary, there might be some difference. Strong instances of self-denial operate powerfully on our minds; and a man who has no wants has obtained great freedom, and firmness, and even dignity. But as the mass of any description of men are but men, and their poverty cannot be voluntary, that disrespect, which attends upon all lay poverty, will not depart from the ecclesiastical. Our provident constitution has therefore taken great care that those who are to instruct presumptuous ignorance, those who are to be censors over insolent vice, should neither incur their contempt not live upon their alms; nor will it tempt the rich to a neglect of the true medicine of their minds. For these reasons, whilst we provide first for the poor, and with a parental solicitude, we have not relegated religion (like something we were ashamed to show) to obscure municipalities, or rustic villages. No! we will have her to exalt her mitred front in courts and parliaments.We will have her mixed throughout the whole mass of life, and blended with all classes of society. The people of England will show to the haughty potentates of the world, and to their talking sophisters, that a free, a generous, an informed nation honours the high magistrates of its church; that it will not suffer the insolence of wealth and titles, or any other species of proud pretension, to look down with scorn upon what they look up to with reverence; nor presume to trample on that acquired personal nobility, which they intend always to be, and which often is, the fruit, not the reward (for what can be the reward?) of learning, piety, and virtue. They can see, without pain or grudging, an archbishop precede a duke. They can see a bishop of Durham, or a bishop of Winchester, in possession of ten thousand pounds a year; and cannot conceive why it is in worse hands than estates to the like amount in the hands of this earl, or that squire; although it may be true that so many dogs and horses are not kept by the former, and fed with the victuals which ought to nourish the children of the people. It is true, the whole church revenue is not always employed, and to every shilling, in charity; nor perhaps ought it; but something is generally so employed. It is better to cherish virtue and humanity, by leaving much to free will, even with some loss to the object, that to attempt to make men mere machines and instruments of a political benevolence. The world on the whole will gain by a liberty, without which virtue cannot exist.

When once the commonwealth has established the estates of the church as property, it can, consistently, hear nothing of the more or the less. Too much and too little are treason against property. What evil can arise from the quantity in any hand, whilst the supreme authority has the full, sovereign superintendence over this, as over any property, to prevent every species of abuse; and, whenever it notably deviates, to give it a direction agreeable to the purposes of its institution.

In England most of us conceive that it is envy and malignity towards those who are often the beginners of their own fortune, and not a love of the self-denial and mortification of the ancient church, that makes some look askance at the distinctions, and honours, and revenues, which, taken from no person, are set apart for virtue. The ears of the people of England are distinguishing. They hear these men speak broad. Their tongue betrays them. Their language is the *patois* of fraud; in the cant and gibberish of hypocrisy. The people of England must think so, when these praters affect to carry back the clergy to that primitive, evangelic poverty, which, in spirit, ought always to exist in them (and in us too, however we may like it), but in the thing must be varied, when the relation of that body to the state is altered; when manners, when modes of life, when indeed the whole order of human affairs has undergone a total revolution. We shall believe those reformers then to be honest enthusiasts, not, as we now think them, cheats and deceivers, when we see them throwing their own goods into common, and submitting their own person to the austere discipline of the early church.

With these ideas rooted in their minds, the commons of Great Britain, in the national emergencies will never seek their resource from the confiscation of the estates of the church and poor. Sacrilege and proscription are not among the ways and means of our committee of supply. The Jews in Change-alley have not yet dared to hint their hopes of a mortgage on the revenues belonging to the see of Canterbury. I am not afraid that I shall be disavowed when I assure you, that there is not *one* public man in this kingdom whom you would wish to quote; no not one, of any party or description, who does not reprobate the dishonest, perfidious, and cruel confiscation which the National Assembly has been compelled to make of that property, which it was their first duty to protect.

It is with the exultation of a little national pride I tell you, that those amongst us who have wished to pledge the societies of Paris in the cup of their abominations have been disappointed. The robbery of your church has proved a security to the possessions of ours. It has roused the people. They see with horror and alarm that enormous and shameless act of proscription. It has opened, and will more and more open, their eyes upon the selfish enlargement of mind, and the narrow liberality of sentiment of insidious men, which, commencing in close hypocrisy and fraud, have ended in open violence and rapine. We are on our guard against similar conclusions.

The Address of the Conference to the Methodist Societies in Great Britain, in the Connexion Established by the Late Rev. John Wesley, A.M. (1819), by Richard Watson.

Richard Watson (1781-1833) was one of the great men in early nineteenth-century Methodism. The son of a Lincolnshire saddler, he was well educated at Lincoln grammar school, and he began preaching at age fifteen. He became a full time Methodist itinerant minister in 1801. From 1808 to 1812 he was editor of a conservative newspaper, the *Liverpool Courier*. He reentered the Wesleyan ministry in 1812, became deeply involved with the Wesleyan missionary movement, and from 1816 until his death he lived almost continuously in London working at the headquarters of the Wesleyan missionary society. During this period he became one of the most prominent Wesleyan ministers, and through his preaching, his many publications, and his widespread personal connections, he exerted a powerful influence for both piety and political conservatism.

From 1913, when Elie Halevy published *England in 1815* (translated from the French in 1924), historians have given serious consideration to his thesis that Methodism was the principal factor which prevented revolution in England during the critical thirty years following the fall of the Bastille in 1789. No historian denies that Methodism, which achieved considerable growth during those years, and principally among the upper levels of the working class, was a force for political quietism. Some historians, J.L. and Barbara Hammond, *The Skilled Labourer*, for example, take issue with Halevy indirectly by arguing that there was no serious threat of revolution in England at the time. Others follow the lead of Edward Thompson, *The Making of the English Working Class*, who argues that Methodism constituted an other-worldly escape from political frustration, a symptom rather than the cause of the failure of radical politics.

The following pastoral address was issued in 1819 by Richard Watson on behalf of the Conference, the governing body of the Wesleyan Methodists. It illustrates the general official political position which the Wesleyans inherited from John Wesley himself, and which they preserved until nearly the middle of the nineteenth century. The year 1819 was one which saw high prices for food and a high rate of unemployment, and consequently a high level of radical demand for constitutional change. Just nine days after Watson issued his pastoral address, a mass meeting in support for parliamentary reform took place on St. Peter's Fields in Manchester. The meeting was dispersed by mounted troops, eleven people were killed and several hundred were injured, and Peterloo, as the incident quickly came to be called, passed into liberal mythology as one of the key events in the history of class conflict in England.

DEARLY BELOVED BRETHREN,

IN pursuance of a resolution passed at our recent meeting, that an Address from the Conference to the societies in Great Britain shall annually be written and printed, we now affectionately solicit your attention. Our object in the adoption of this measure, is to draw still closer the bond of spiritual connexion between us and you, which is so dear to our hearts; and to afford to you, dear brethren, from time to time, such advices and encouragements as the events of the year — presented to us from every quarter, when assembled in Conference — may suggest.

Never can you or your interests be absent from our minds when engaged in the business of this solemn assembly. The sole object of our labours is to preserve that form of sound doctrine, and that body of discipline, under which we have all been made wise unto salvation, and nourished up to the enjoyment of a spiritual life, and intercourse with God; and it is our greatest anxiety that, "as you have received the Lord Jesus, you may walk in him; adorning the Gospel of God our Saviour in all things;" and that you may thus diffuse through the land the knowledge of Christ, and the influence of religion.

We rejoice to state to you, that the increase in our societies during the past year, including Ireland, is six thousand seven hundred and nine. For this success you will join us in thanksgivings to God, to whom alone the praise of turning men from darkness to light is due. But we would not fail to remind you that, although the conversion of men from the errors of their ways is the great work of God, he himself has made it, in all cases, to depend greatly upon the faithfulness and zeal of his people. We exhort you, therefore, dear brethren, as you wish the prosperity of the cause of God, to "pray for us, that the word of the Lord may have free course, and be glorified." Be yourselves the examples of a regular and conscientious attendance on the ordinances of his house; let your light shine before men. Remember the high designation given you by your Lord: "Ye are the salt of the earth." "Be blameless and harmless, the sons of

God without rebuke, in the midst of a crooked and perverse generation, among whom shine ye as the lights of the world." Let the holiness of your conduct, the gravity and seriousness of your speech, your kind and faithful admonition of others, the religious order of your families, and the exact discharge of every relative and social duty, bear full testimony to the truth and excellency of your piety, and give its evidence all around you, that "you have not received the grace of God in vain."

A long experience has proved that such effects are intimately connected with the observance of every part of our salutory discipline in all our societies. We do not enjoin this upon you as a burden; we invite you to it as a privilege. Preserve that simplicity of heart, and that sense of the importance of experimental religion, which will induce you not only to a regular attendance upon your classes, but to enter their spirit and intention. Seek from them the knowledge you most want, — the work of God in the heart. Strive together, that you may "apprehend all for which you are apprehended of God in Christ Jesus;" and solemnly record it in your spirits, that the true kingdom of God is not the existence of its visible forms among any people, but "righteousness, peace, and joy in the Holy Ghost."

We deeply sympathize with those of you, dear brethren, who, from the pressure of the times, and the suspension of an active commerce, are, in common with thousands of your countrymen, involved in various and deep afflictions; we offer up our prayers to God for you in this dark season of your distress, "that you may not be tempted above that you are able to bear;" and that he who "comforteth the distressed" may comfort you. "Cast all your care on God, for he careth for you;" and fail not to remember, and to comfort one another with these words, "That in heaven you have a better and enduring substance." In the present changeful scene of things, one event happeneth to the righteous and the wicked; but you are, nevertheless, still under the care and the eye of your Father in heaven. Such afflictive events he will sanctify to those who trust in him: His promises cannot fail, because he changeth not. "He knoweth the way that you take; and when he hath tried you, he will bring you forth as gold." Never fail, dear brethren, to commit your cause to him who has a thousand ways to "deliver the godly out of temptation," or to render their temptations the over-ruled instruments of putting them in possession of a good which shall remain their portion and their joy, when their spirits shall be for ever beyond the reach of the joys or sorrows of this present state. "In patience possess ye your souls;" and remember him who hath said, "I will never leave you nor forsake you."

As many of you to whom this measure of national suffering has been appointed reside in places where attempts are making, by unreasonable and wicked men, to render the privations of the poor the instruments of their own designs against the peace and the Government of our beloved country, we are affectionately anxious to guard all of you against being led astray from your civil and religious duties by their dangerous artifices. Remember you are Christians, and are called by your profession to exemplify the power and influence of religion by your patience in suffering, and by "living peaceably with all men." Remember that you belong to a religious society which has, from the beginning, explicitly recognized as high and essential parts of Christian duty, to "fear God, and honour the King; to submit to Magistrates for conscience' sake, and not to speak evil of dignities." You are surrounded with persons to whom these duties are the objects of contempt and ridicule: Show your regard for them, because they are the doctrines of your Saviour. Abhor those publications in which they are assailed, along with every other doctrine of your holy religion; and judge of the spirit and objects of those who would deceive you into political parties and associations, by the vices of their lives, and the infidel malignity of their words and writings. "Who can bring a clean thing out of an unclean?"

Be it your care, beloved, who are exposed to this trial, "to serve God in all good conscience;" to preserve your minds from political agitations; to follow your occupations and duties in life in peaceful seclusion from all the strife and tumults; and God will, in his own time, appear by his providence to your relief. We trust our country to his gracious favour, and doubt not "that he will speak good concerning us."

Whilst this period of suffering continues, we affectionately and earnestly exhort the opulent members of our societies and congregations, to afford as ample a relief as possible to their brethren

in distress. This, we are sure, "they are forward to do." The liberal
and active benevolence of our friends in every place, and on every
charitable occasion, is our "glory and joy;" we speak this, therefore,
only to "put them in remembrance." Many of the suffering household
of faith now need their special liberalities; and the kind affection which
exists in all our societies towards each other, is a sufficient pledge
to us, that this suggestion will lead to those acts of sympathizing
kindness, which will at once call forth and strengthen that sentiment
of brotherly love, which is the distinguishing character of the disciples
of Jesus Christ. "Remember them that are in affliction, as being
yourselves also in the body."

****

We are now about to depart to our respective scenes of labour
for the ensuing year. We met in the spirit of the kindest affection,
and are about to separate with increased attachment to each other,
to you, and to the work of Christ. We have renewed our pledges of
zeal and faithfulness in the strength of Him, without whom "nothing
is strong;" and we cast ourselves on his mercy, and your prayers.
Beloved brethren, join with us in this renewed dedication of ourselves
"to God and to the church by the will of God." Why do we live, but
to do his will, and spread his praise? Let all our thoughts rest in God;
to him let us open our spirits for richer supplies of his sanctifying
grace and clearer demonstrations of his presence and love. In
simplicity of heart let us follow our Lord, copy his example, walk as
he walked, follow his steps of active charity, breathe his calm and
loving mind, die like him to all earthly good, and hasten to the end
of our course. "The time is short." O let us fill it with all the fruits
and acts of Christian love and zeal, that our last moments may be
peace, and that, through the meritorious passion of our divine Saviour,
we may be accounted worthy to renew our fellowship in his
unsuffering kingdom, and be eternally one with Christ as he is one
with the Father.

Signed in behalf and by order of the Conference.

BRISTOL, *Aug. 7th,* 1819.

The Early Correspondence of Jabez Bunting, 1820-1829 (1972), edited by W.R. Ward.
1. From Robert Pilter, 23 October 1819.   2. From James Briggs Holroyd, 23 December 1819.

Jabez Bunting (1779-1858), third president of the Wesleyan Methodist Conference, was the most important leader of Methodism after Wesley himself. Bunting's early experience as a minister and church administrator was mainly in the north of England. In 1820 he was elected Conference president for the first time, and resided permanently in London after 1833. Bunting guided the organization of the new administrative structures which helped the transition from sect to full church status. Though a strict disciplinarian and deeply conservative in social and political views, Bunting allowed for more democracy in Methodism itself than was the case under John Wesley. The laity were given a greater role in church affairs. Bunting also defended in the abstract religious and political freedom, though his actions often seemed to contradict his views. Like Richard Watson, Bunting carried on and reinforced political conservatism as the official Wesleyan position.

The following two letters from circuit superintendants in the industrial north — North Shields is near Newcastle and Haslingden is near Manchester — illustrate the existence of a democratic, radical element at the local level. A number of historians have noticed that Methodism provided a valuable education in public speaking and organizational techniques for some radical leaders in the early nineteenth century. And Bernard Semmel has recently argued in his important and provocative book, *The Methodist Revolution*, that Methodism was a liberalizing, modernizing force, with an essentially democratic theology. In any event there is no doubt that there were many radicals among the Methodists, and their radicalism stimulated the official leadership towards increased conservatism. Radicalism and the conservative reaction were both pronounced in 1819, a year of high social tension particularly in the industrial districts of the north.

Pilter and Holroyd wrote the following letters to Bunting in the aftermath of Peterloo, and both are deeply concerned about the rising level of radicalism in their districts.

---

1. *From Robert Pilter*   North Shields, October 23, 1819
I take the liberty of addressing you on a subject which appears to myself and friends of very great importance. I shall impartially state

the case, and leave you to judge of the propriety of laying it before you brethren in town or calling together the Committee of Priviledges.

On Monday the 11th instant a meeting of reformers was held at Newcastle for the purpose of expressing their opinion on the Manchester Murders as they call them. 50 or 60,000 people attended, amongst whom were a great number of our people, several of our Leaders and some of our Local Preachers. One of the latter William H. Stephenson, a young man who teaches a school at Burton Colliery in this Circuit went upon the hustings and made a speech, condemning in strong terms the conduct of the Manchester magistrates: this has given very great offence to most of the Travelling Preachers and respectable friends in this neighbourhood and to none more than myself, and I have been advised at all events to *put him off the plan.* I have had repeated interviews with him and *advised him as a friend on public grounds to give up his plan.* He replied that he would never give up his plan until he was compelled, that he would be *tried by his peers* and did not fear the result, that if they expel him he will publish the cause to the world, that I had better let it quietly pass as three quarters of our people are radical reformers, that if he be tried so must hundreds more, that he only went to plead the cause of suffering humanity, that he believed it his *duty* to go, that he never joined himself to the reformers, nor attended any of their private meetings. I fixed on Friday the 22nd as the day of his trial. I will tell you in a parenthesis how I acted in the interim. (Conceiving that the *Body* might be seriously implicated and not feeling disposed to push matters to extremities on my own responsibility I wrote to the President for his advice. After stating the case as above I asked him the following questions — 'Shall I do all I can to influence the meeting to expel him? Or if the meeting resolve that his offence is not of a nature so atrocious as to justify his expulsion, shall I by my own authority leave him off the plan; and look to a District [Meeting] for an act of indemnity (this I am advised to do by our chairman) or shall I act according to the decision of the meeting?' And I also stated what might probably be the consequences of his being expelled etc. The substance of Mr. President's reply is as follow[s]. 'I do not believe that we are called either to pull down Governments or to prop them up. Our business is of a higher and more spiritual nature. We are called to promote the salvation of souls. We should, therefore, as far as possible avoid exasperating or hardening any description of men against us, and especially on grounds merely political. It was Mr. Wesley's opinion and advice, that the Methodists should never appear in politics as a body. The doing this in the affairs of America had like to have ruined Methodism there. I do not see why we should *volunteer* our services in support of the Government, more than any other body of people, whether Dissenters or Churchmen. I do not hear of any of these expelling or punishing their people on account of their politics. Respecting the case of your local preacher, I think as he said nothing but what related to the Magistrates of Manchester, so much ado need not have been [made] about it, more specially as he never did join himself to the reformers. My opinion and advice is this, that you give him a serious admonition, including in this your thoughts on his recent conduct, and your advice that he keep out of such matters in future. I verily believe this will be the best line of conduct you can pursue. If you expell such men, the Kilhamites and Ranters will greedily gather them up. In politics I think our present duty is neutrality. In *stillness and quietness will be our strength.* Stand still and see the salvation of the Lord. Such is my opinion and advice to obtain which you wrote. You must, however, do as you think best.' My writing to the President was a profound secret and I did not inform any person, except my worthy colleague of the reply). Last night the meeting was held, and the trial or altercation lasted from 7 to halfpast 10 o'clock. We positively interdicted the discussion of politics, the question whether reform was a good or bad thing abstractly considered was not the business of the meeting, but whether Brother Stephenson as a Methodist preacher had done right in attending and speaking at the Meeting. He insisted on arguing the necessity of a radical reform, contended that he had done right as a Christian and a preacher in speaking, that his conscience impelled him to the duty, that immense mishchief would result from his expulsion and that he relied on the justice of his Brethren for his acquittal. The question was then proposed whether it was expedient for Brother S. as a Methodist preacher to attend and speak at those meeting[s]. The consequence[s] to the Circuit and the Connexion were mentioned, particularly his being called in the London papers 'The Rev. G. Stephenson who we understand is a preacher in the Methodist Connexion'. Two thirds of the meeting pronounced it inexpedient but 4 Brethren thought he was justified in so doing. I then asked if he would promise his brethren never to attend another public meeting? But he said he would not *pledge* himself. He was an Englishman and would not give up his liberty and his conscience. I then submitted it to the meeting, how I could especially after such an avowal plan the Brother. Several however thought that expulsion were too severe a punishment and that such an act would be fatal to the interests of the circuit. They laboured in vain to extort a promise for him. It was then proposed 'that as our decision might on the one hand *injure* the whole *connexion,* or on the other ruin the circuit and subject themselves, but especially ME, to *assassination* it would be well to pause and consult you gentlemen at the fountain head of information before we came to a final decision. We accordingly agreed to adjourn the meeting until Friday the 5th November.

Now my dear Brother what must I do? If my own Circuit alone was concerned, I should know how to act. But Mr. Grindrod and others think we shall, unless we exclude him, bring down the vengeance of government upon the whole connexion. But is it probable that the government would attend more to the conduct of one insignificant individual, than to the loyal address of Conference and the loyal conduct of the Body at large? If so I think he should at all events be expelled. If he be expelled we have reason to apprehend the following consequence. Many of our members will leave the Society, 20 in one place have resolved this. Some of our Local Preachers will give up their plans. A great and general ferment (will be) excited as he is already considered a persecuted man. A (col)league and I will be in no small danger of being mu(rdered). You are in no doubt apprized of the state of the public (m)ind in these parts. During a riot at Sheilds on the 14th instant a man was shot. The jury after sitting 4 days brought in their verdict 'Justifiable Homicide'. Some of the people were so exasperated that they assailed the houses of three of the jurymen and actually fired into their parlour windows. However no personal considerations shall deter me from the performance of my duty. But amidst so many conflicting considerations and interests, I am at a loss how to act. I would just observe that the Brother is a great stickler for law and right and some of our local Brethren are jealous of their prerogatives. Anxiously awaiting your reply . . .

****

2. From J.B. Holroyd   Haslingden, December 23, 1819

I cannot refrain from acknowledging the gratitude I feel for the timely encouragement afforded by the address from the committee for guarding our privileges. The state of the public mind in these parts exceeds all description. The country for a few miles around here may with propriety be called the hot-bed of radicalism. I believe I shall be within compass in saying that two-thirds of the population in this circuit are reformers, and having no magistrate or chief constable within 8 miles, every man seems as if left to do that which is right in his own eyes. We have had them parading the streets almost every night by the 200 or 300 together, singing their favourite songs of Hunt and Liberty, with lighted torches, flags and a Cap of Liberty hoisted upon a high pole with a lanthorn suspended with it. At the houses of the Radicals they stop and salute them with three cheers, and at the houses of the *marked kings-men* they give three horrible groans. They make no hesitation at calling by name the *marked* ones, who are to be killed the first day the orders come for them to break out. There are five in this town openly spoken of. The church minister and myself are of the number. They have regular organized societies that meet weekly, where they read the *Manchester Observer*, Cob[b]ett's *Register, Black Dwarf*, etc., the leader asks them personally if they are resolved to observe the resolutions of the *Union* and then receives their subscriptions, part of which goes to support the general cause of reform, and part to purchase pikes and pistols. There have been great numbers of pikes made in this town. One evening a few weeks since, just as I came out of my door to go into the chapel, the procession was just drawing up in front of the house, I did not judge it prudent to go through the crowd but stood inside the garden gate; they gave three of the most horrid groans I ever heard, and with each groan a young man brandished a pike within a yard of my breast accompanied with such dreadful oaths, enough to make one's blood run chill. I believe there is no part of the kingdom where the distresses of the poor are more general than in this neighbourhood. They are principally cotton weavers, who by working hard six days cannot earn above 7s. or 8s. per week, for the support of a family, this having been the case for sometime past they now seem quite impatient for relief and are ready to adopt the most desperate means to obtain it. It is with grief that I say that our society is not free from the contagion. Some have left us this quarter, and assign this as their reason. They do not think it right to give anything towards the support of those who encourage and pray for a number of tyrants.

The Address is very unpopular in some parts of the circuit, the sentiments of the *Manchester Observer* are preferred where I am informed they charge the committee with assuming an authority they were never invested with. The above are not the sentiments of our leading friends in Haslingden, quite the reverse, but they can render the preachers no efficient support in opposing the general impetus.

I fear we shall have a considerable decrease both in numbers and collections this year. It is painful in the extreme to see the change which this spirit of reform has made in some places where a few months back they were all alive to God, and the work spreading, but now you can scarcely prevent them introducing reform into the House of God. On Sunday last I had but just got out of the Chapel before I was attacked by 3 Leaders, 2 Local Preachers, 1 Steward and several private members on t(he) subjects of Lord Castlereagh's bills, and the Address from the Committee, when they told me in plain terms that (the) Methodist Preachers were as bad as the Church ministers in supporting government, but it was asked, 'Will Lord Castlereagh support you?' To the troubles without I have some severe family affliction . . . if we are spared till the ensuing Conference I shall beg the indulgence of having an appointment some w(h)ere in the South . . . .

The Black Book: An Exposition of Abuses in Church and State
(1835), by John Wade. Selections.

John Wade (1788-1875), publicist and reformer, was the author of
numerous articles and books ranging in subject matter from legal
reform to women's role in society. He is best known for his widely
circulated *Black Book*, first published in 1820-23, a work which
enjoyed considerable success in reform agitation over the next twenty
years. The *Black Book* was reissued with only minor variations in
1831, 1832 and 1835. Very much a tract for its times, the *Black Book*
fell into obscurity by the middle of the nineteenth century. The central
theme of the *Black Book* is the corruption and inefficiency of the
aristocratic government and the Church of England. Wade paid little
attention to the social changes that are associated with the industrial
revolution, and he was not interested in the wider implications of the
progress of parliamentary democracy. For him, reform meant
purification. The following selection illustrates how the unreformed
Church of England was seen as an integral part of the unreformed
state.

CHURCH OF ENGLAND.

RELIGION and the institution of property, the pursuits of
science, literature, and commerce have greatly benefited the human
race. Christianity is peculiarly the worship of the people: among them
it originated, and to the promotion of their welfare its precepts are
especially directed. Under the influence of its dogmas the pride of
man is rebuked, the prejudices of birth annihilated, and the equal
claim to honour and enjoyment of the whole family of mankind
impartially admitted.

Men of liberal principles have sometimes shown themselves
hostile to the Gospel; forgetting, apparently, that it has been the
handmaid of civilization, and that for a long time it instigated, and,
finally, greatly aided in breaking the yoke of feudality. They are
shocked at the corruptions of the popular faith, and hastily confound
its genuine principles with the intolerance of Bigotry, the oppression
of tithes, the ostentation of prelacy, and the delinquencies of its
inferior agents, who pervert a humble and consoling dispensation into
an engine of pride, gain, and worldliness. In spite, however, of these
adulterations, the most careless observer cannot deny the generally

beneficial influence of the Christian doctrine, in promoting decorum and equality of civil rights, in spreading a spirit of peace, charity, and universal benevolence.

As education becomes more diffused, the ancillary power of the best of creeds will become less essential to the well-being of society. Religions have mostly had their origin in our depravity and ignorance; they have been the devices of man's primitive legislators, who sought, by the creations of the imagination, to control the violence of his passions, and satisfy an urgent curiosity concerning the phenomena by which he is surrounded. But the progress of science and sound morals renders superfluous the arts of illusion; inventions, which are suited only to the nursery, or an imperfect civilization, are superseded; and men submitting to the guidance of reason instead of fear, the dominion of truth, unmixed with error, is established on the ruins of priestcraft.

Even now may be remarked the advance of society towards a more dignified and rational organization. The infallibility of popes, the divine right of kings, and the privileges of aristocracy, have lost their influence and authority: they once formed a sort of secular religion, and were among the many delusions by which mankind have been plundered and enslaved. Superstition, too, is gradually fading away by shades; and it is not improbable it may entireley vanish, ceasing to be an object of interest, further than as a singular trait in the moral history of the species. Formerly, all sects were bigots, ready to torture and destroy their fellow-creatures in the vain effort to enforce uniformity of belief; now, the fervour of all is so far attenuated, as to admit not only of dissent, but equality of claim to civil immunities. The next dilution in pious zeal is obvious. Universal toleration is the germ of indifference; and this last the forerunner of an entire oblivion of spiritual faith. Such appears the natural death of ecclesiastical power; it need not to be hastened by the rude and premature assaults of Infidelity, which only shock existing prejudices, without producing conviction; while the priesthood continue to aid the civil magistrate, their authority will be respected; but when, from the diffusion of science, new motives for the practice of virtue and the maintenance of social institutions are generally established, the utility of their functions will cease to be recognized.

Sensible men of all ages have treated with respect the established worship of the people. If so unfortunate as to disbelieve in its divine origin, they at least classed it among the useful institutions necessary to restrain the passions of the multitude. This was the predominant wisdom of the Roman government. Speaking of this great empire, in its most triumphant exaltation, GIBBON says, "The policy of the emperors and the senate, as far as it concerned religion, was happily seconded by the reflections of the enlightened, and by the habits of the superstitious part of their subjects. The various modes of worship which prevailed in the known world were all considered by the people as equally true; by the philosophers as equally false; and by the magistrate as equally useful. And thus toleration produced not only mutual indulgence, but even mutual religious concord." Further on he continues, "Notwithstanding the fashionable irreligion which prevailed in the age of the Antonines, both the interests of the priests and the credulity of the people were sufficiently respected. In their writings and conversation, the philosophers asserted the independent dignity of reason; but they resigned their actions to the command of law and custom. Viewing with a smile of pity the various errors of the vulgar, they diligently practised the ceremonies of their fathers, devoutly frequented the temple of the gods, and, sometimes condescending to act a part on the theatre of superstition, they concealed the sentiments of the atheist under the sacerdotal robes. Reasoners of such a temper were scarcely inclined to wrangle about their respective modes of faith or of worship. It was indifferent to them what shape the folly of the multitude might choose to assume; and they approached with the same inward contempt and the same external reverence the altars of the Libyan, the Olympian, or the Capitoline Jupiter."

Can it be supposed the statesmen and teachers of the nineteenth century are less adroit and sagacious than those of pagan Rome? Can it be supposed those whose minds have been enlightened by foreign travel, who have witnessed the conflict of opposite creeds, and who have escaped the mental bondage of cloisters and colleges in the freedom of general intercourse, are less penetrating than the magnates of the ancient world? Like them too, they will be equally politic in maintaining an outward respect for the errors of the vulgar.

In the prevailing worship they recognize an useful auxiliary to civil government; prosecuting no one for dissent, it can as little offend the philosopher as politician; and the topics of all-absorbing interest it holds forth to every class, divert the vast majority from too intense a contemplation of sublunary misfortunes, or from painful contrast of their privations with the usurpations and advantages of their superiors.

The policy of governing nations by enlightening the *few* and hoodwinking the *many* is of very old standing. It is strongly inculcated by Machiavelli in his *Prince*, and Dugald Stewart remarks, that public men of the present day mostly hold the *double-doctrine*; that is, they have one set of principles which they openly profess in complacence to the multitude, and another, comprising their real sentiments, which they keep to themselves, or confide to intimate friends. The result of this sinister policy may be constantly remarked in the proceedings of legislative assemblies: in the discussion of questions bearing on the social interests, especially such as involve the principles of government, the theory of morals, or population, there is invariably maintained a conventional latitude, beyond which if anyone trespass, it is deemed more creditable to his sincerity than understanding. It is only the vain and superficial who unreservedly assail popular opinions, and prophane with invective and ribaldry the sanctities of religion. Such rash controversialists are ignorant of the *points d'appui* upon which the welfare and harmony of society depend; and though it may happen that honour, philanthropy, or patriotism be sufficient guarantees for the discharge of social duties by some, there are others whose turpitude can only be restrained by the fear of Tyburn or Tartarus. Hence theological inquiries have lost much of their interest, and are, in fact, placed beyond the pale of discussiuon. The mysteries of religion are well understood by the intelligent of all classes; it is considered for the good of society that some should "believe and tremble," while others enjoy, in private, the consciousness of superior light; and to those who impugn and to those who dogmatise in matters of faith, the same indulgence is extended as to well-meaning disputants, who utter, as new discoveries, commonplace or self-evident truths.

Having made these general observations on the utility of religion, considered as a civil institution for the government of mankind during a period of ignorance, we shall proceed to our more immediate object an exposition of the Established Church of this country.

In our elucidations of this important inquiry, it is not our intention to interfere with the doctrines of the national religion. We have heard that there are more than one hundred sects of Christianity: so it would be highly presumptuous in mere laymen to decide which of these multifarious modes of worship is most consonant to the Scripture. A certain Protestant Archbishop said, "Popery was only a religion of *knaves* and *fools*;" therefore, let us hope the Church of England, to which the Right Reverend Prelate belonged, comprises the honest and enlightened. The main purpose of our enquiries, is not the dogmas, but the temporalities of the Church. To us the great possessions of the clergy have long appeared an immense *waste,* which wanted surveying and enclosing, if not by act of parliament, by the act of the people. Like some of our public institutions, the excellence of our religious establishment has been greatly over-rated; it has been described as the most perfect in Europe; yet we are acquainted with none in which abuses are more prevalent, in which there is so little real piety, and in which the support of public worship is so vexatious and oppressive to the community.

Most countries on the Continent have reformed their church establishments: wherever a large property had accumulated in the hands of the clergy, such property has been applied to the service of the nation; and we are now the only people who have a large mass of ecclesiastical wealth appropriated to the maintenance of an indolent and luxurious priesthood. Even in papal Rome the church property has been sold to pay the national debt; so that far more property belonging to the clergy is to be found in any part of England of equal extent than in the Roman state. The cardinals of Rome, the bishops, canons, abbotts, and abbesses, have no longer princely revenues. A cardinal who formerly had thousands has now only *four* or *five hundred* pounds a-year. Residence is strictly enforced, and no such thing as *pluralities* is known; the new proprietors of the Church estates live on them and improve them to their best advantage. In France, there has been a still greater ecclesiastical reformation. Before the Revolution the clergy formed one fifty-second part of the population. The total number of ecclesiastics, in 1789, was estimated at 460,000 and their revenues at £7,400,000. At present the total number of ecclesiastics of all ranks, Protestant and Catholic, is about 40,000, and their total incomes £1,460,000. Throughout Germany and Italy there have been great reforms in spiritual matters; the property of the church has been sold or taxed for the use of the state, and the enormous incomes of the *higher* have been more equally shared among the *lower* order of the clergy. In the Netherlands, the charges for religion, which supply the wants of the whole community, except those of a few Jews, do not, in the whole, exceed £252,000, or 10d. per head per annum, for a population of six millions. Even in Spain, under the most weak and bigotted government, ecclesiastical reform has made progress. A large portion of the produce of tithe is annually appropriated to the exigencies of the State, and the policy adopted of late has dispossessed the clergy of their wealth; and this body, formerly so influential, is now lightly esteemed, and very moderately endowed.

Wherever these reforms have been made, they have been productive of the most beneficial effects; they have been favourable to religion and morality, to the real interests of the people, and even to the interests of the great body of the clergy themselves; they have broken the power of an order of men at all times cruel and tyrannical, at all times opposed to reform, to the progress of knowledge, and the most salutary ameliorations; they have diffused a spirit of toleration among all classes, removed the restrictions imposed by selfish bigotry, and opened an impartial career to virtue and talent in all orders; they have spread plenty in the land by unfettering the efforts of capital and industry, they have been gratefully received by the People, and well they might; for with such changes their happiness is identified, liberty and intelligence diffused.

To England, however, the spirit of ecclesiastical improvement has not yet extended; though usually foremost in reform, we are now behind all nations in our ecclesiastical establishment; though the Church of England is ostentatiously styled the *reformed* church, it is, in truth, the most *unreformed* of all the churches. Popery, in temporal matters at least, is a more reformed religion than Church of Englandism. There is no state, however debased by superstition, where the clergy enjoy such prodigious wealth. The revenues of our priesthood exceed the public revenues of either Austria or Prussia. We complain of the poor-rates, of superannuation charges, of the army and navy, of overgrown salaries and enormous sinecures; but what are all these abuses, grievous as they are, to the abuses of our church establishment, to the sinecure wealth of the bishops, dignitaries, and aristocratical rectors and incumbents? It is said, and we believe truly, that the clergymen of the Church of England and Ireland receive, in the year, more money than the clergymen of all the rest of the Christian world put together. The clergy of the United Church cost at least seven times more than the whole clergy of France, Catholic and Protestant, while in France there is a population of 32,000,000; whereas, of the 24,000,000 of people comprising the population of our islands, less than *one-third*, or 8,000,000, are hearers of the Established Religion.

Such a system, it is not possible, can endure. While reform and reduction are in progress in other departments, it is not likely the clergy should remain in undisturbed enjoyment of their possessions. To protect them from inquiry, they have neither prescriptive right nor good works to plead. As a body they have not, latterly, been remarkable for their *learning*, nor some of them for exalted notions of *morality*. It would be unfair to judge any class from individual examples; but it is impossible to open the newspapers without being struck by the repeated details of clerical delinquency. When there is an instance of magisterial oppression, or flagrant offence, it is almost surprising if some father in God, some very reverend dean, or some other reverend and holy person, be not accused or suspected. In this respect they resemble the clergy of the Church of Rome before the Reformation. It is known that the catholic priesthood in the fourteenth century exceeded all other classes in the licentiousness of their lives, their oppression, and rapacity; it is known, too, that their vices arose from the immense wealth they enjoyed, and that this wealth was the ultimate cause of their downfall.

It is not to the credit of the established clergy, that there names have been associated with the most disastrous measures in the history of the country. To the latest period of the first war against American independence, they were, next to George III, its most obstinate supporters; out of twenty-six English Bishops, Shipley was the only prelate who voted against the war faction. To the commencement and protracted duration of the French revolutionary war, they were mainly instrumental; till they sounded the ecclesiastical drum in every parish, there was no disposition to hostilities on the part of the people; it was only by the unfounded alarms they disseminated, respecting the security of property and social institutions, the contest was made popular. In this, too, the episcopal bench was pre-eminent. Watson was the only bishop who ventured to raise his voice against the French crusade, and he, finding his opposition to the court fixed him in the poorest see in the kingdom, in the latter part of his life appeared to waver in his integrity. In supporting measures for restraining the freedom of discussion, and for interdicting to different sects of religionists a free participation in civil humanities, they have usually been foremost.

Uniformly in the exercise of legislative functions, our spiritual lawmakers have evinced a spirit hostile to improvement, whether political, judicial, or domestic, and shown a tenacious adherence to whatever is barbarous, oppressive, or demoralizing in our public administration. The African slave-trade was accompanied by so many circumstances of cruelty and injustice, that it might have been thought the Bishops would have been the most forward in their endeavours to effect its abolition. Yet the fact is quite the contrary. They constantly supported that infamous traffic, and so marked was their conduct in this respect, that Lord Eldon was led, on one occasion, to declare that the commerce in human bodies could not be so inconsistent with Christianity as some had supposed, otherwise it would never have been so steadily supported by the right reverend prelates. The efforts of Sir Samuel Romilly and others to mitigate the severity of the Criminal Code never received any countenance or support from the Bishops. But the climax of their legislative turpitude consists in their conduct on the first introduction of the Reform Bill. Setting aside the political advantages likely to result from this great measure, one of its obvious consequences was the destruction of the shameless immoralities and gross perjuries committed in parliamentary elections. Yet the Heads of the Church, in their anti-reform speeches, never once adverted to this improvement; their fears appeared chiefly to centre on the ulterior changes in our institutions which might flow from the Bill, and which might involve a sacrifice of their inordinate emoluments, and under this apprehension they voted against the people and reform.

Public education is a subject that appears to have peculiar claims on the attention of the clergy; unless indeed, as instructors of the people, their functions are extremely unimportant, and certainly, in this world, do not entitle them to much remuneration. Yet this is a duty they have generally neglected. Had not a jealousy of the Dissenters roused them into activity, neither the Bell nor Lancaster plans of instruction would have been encouraged by them. A similar feeling appears to have actuated them in the foundation of King's College, in which their object is not so much the diffusion of knowledge, as the maintenance of their influence, by setting up a rival establishment to the London University. In short, they have generally manifested either indifference or open hostility to the enlightenment of the people, and, in numerous instances of eleemosynary endowments, they have appropriated to their own use the funds bequeathed for popular tuition.

So little connexion is there between the instruction of the people and the Church establishment, that it may be stated as a general rule that the ignorance and degradation of the labouring classes throughout England are uniformly greatest where there are the most clergy, and that the people are most intelligent and independent where there are the fewest clergy. Norfolk and Suffolk, for instance, are pre-eminently parsons' counties; Norfolk has 731 parishes, and Suffolk 510. Yet it has been publicly affirmed, by those well-informed on the subject, that so far as instruction goes, the peasantry of these two counties are as ignorant as "Indian savages." The same observation will apply to the southern and midland counties, which have been the chief scene of fires and popular tumults, and where the people have ben debased by the maladministration of the poor-laws. Compare the state of these districts with that of the north of England, in which it is generally admitted the people are best instructed and most intelligent, and where, from the great extent of parishes, they can have little intercourse with the parsons. Cumberland has 104 parishes, Durham 75, Northumberland 88,

Westmoreland 32, Lancaster 70, West-Riding of Yorkshire 193, Chester 90. It appears that Norfolk alone has a great many more parsons than all these northern counties, containing about one third of the population of the kingdom. In Lancashire there are only 70 parsons for a million and a half of people; yet so little detriment have they suffered from the paucity of endowed pastors, that barristers generally consider the intelligence of a Lancashire common jury equal to that of a special jury of most counties.

A feeling of charity is the great beauty of Christianity; it is, indeed, the essence of all virtue, for, if real, it imports a sympathy with the privations of others divested of selfish considerations. The rich and prosperous do not need commiseration; if they are not happy, it is their own fault, resulting from their artificial desires and ill-regulated passions. But the poor, without the means of comfortable subsistence, have scarcely a chance of happiness, though equally entitled with others to share the enjoyments of life. It is the especial duty of the clergy to mitigate extreme inequalities in the lot of their fellow-creatures. Yet it is seldom their labours are directed to so truly a Christian object; though wallowing in wealth, a large portion of which is the produce of funds originally intended for the destitute and unfortunate, they manifest little sympathy in human wretchedness. As a proof of their ordinary callousness, it may be instanced that, at the numerous public meetings to relieve the severe distress of the Irish, in 1822, not a single Irish bishop attended, when it was notorious the immense sums abstracted by that class from the general produce of the country had been a prominent cause of the miseries of the people.

The clergy might be usefully employed in explaining to popular conviction the causes of the privations of the people, and in enforcing principles more conducive to their comfort and independence. In the agricultural districts, where their authority is least disputed, and where the sufferings of the inhabitants are greatest, such a course might be pursued under peculiar advantage. Their remissness in this respect is less excusable, since they are relieved from cares which formerly engaged anxious attention. In the time of Headley, Barrow, and Tillotson, much of the zeal and talent of the church was consumed in theological controversy; the removal of civil disqualifications has tended to assuage the fervour of ecclesiastical disputation, and the clergy have only tithes, not dogmas, to defend. This tendency to religious tranquility has been also promoted by the indifference of the people, who discovered that little fruit was to be reaped from polemical disquisitions, which, like the researches of metaphysicians, tended to perplex rather than enlighten. Men now derive their religions as they do parochial settlements, either from their parents or birth-place, and seldom, in after life, question the creed, whether sectarian or orthodox, which has become planted in infancy. The all-subduing influence of early credulity is proverbial. Once place a dogma in the catechism, and it becomes stereotyped for life, and is never again submitted to the ordeal of examination.

> By education most have been misled,
> So they believe because they were so bred;
> The priest continues what the nurse began,
> And thus the child imposes on the man! — *Hind and Panther.*

It is the inefficiency of the clergy as public teachers, the hurtful influence they have exerted on national affairs, and their inertness in the promotion of measures of general utility, that induce men to begrudge the immense revenue expended in their support, and dispose them to a reform in our ecclesiastical establishment. To the Church of England, in the *abstract*, we have no weighty objection to offer; and should be sorry to see her spiritual functions superseded by those of any other sect by which she is surrounded. Our dislike originates in her extreme oppressiveness on the people, and her unjust dealings towards the most deserving members of her own communion. To the enormous amount of her temporalities, and abuses in their administration, we particularly demur. It is unseemly, we think, and inconsistent with the very principles and purposes of Christianity, to contemplate lofty prelates with £20,000 or £40,000 a-year, elevated on thrones, living sumptuously in splendid palaces, attended by swarms of menials, gorgeously attired, and of priests to wait upon their persons, emulating the proudest nobles, and even taking precedence of them in all the follies of heraldry. Beneath them are crowds of sinecure dignitaries and incumbents, richly provided with worldy goods, the wealthiest not even obliged to reside among their flocks; and those who reside not compelled to do any one act of duty beyond providing and paying a miserable deputy just enough to keep him from starving. Contrasted with the preceding, is a vast body of poor laborious ministers, doing all the work, and receiving less than the pay of a common bricklayer or Irish hodman: but the whole assemblage, both rich and poor, paid so as to be a perpetual burthen upon the people, and to wage, of necessity, a ceaseless strife with those whom they ought to comfort, cherish, and instruct.

Motion for Repeal of the Test and Corporation Acts, proposed in the House of Commons, 26 February, 1828, by Lord John Russell, and a reply from Sir Robert Inglis. *Hansard's Parliamentary Debates.* Selections.

The division between Protestant Dissent on the one hand and the established Church of England on the other had a major impact on society and politics in nineteenth-century England. Dissent, or nonconformity as it came to be called in the nineteenth century, included those protestant denominations which were separated from the Church of England in the seventeenth century — the Congregationalists, Baptists, Presbyterians and Quakers — the Methodists, who formally separated from the established Church in 1795 and gradually drifted into the nonconformist camp, the Unitarians, who were in many cases successors to the Presbyterians, and, in addition, a host of new and smaller sects, including a number of splinter groups which left Wesleyan Methodism. The evangelical revival enormously increased the number of dissenters in the late eighteenth and early nineteenth centuries, particularly in the industrial towns of the midlands and north. Led by their middle class elite — who surprisingly often were Unitarians — and gaining political influence with the general advance of democracy, dissenters worked towards freedom from specific legal disabilities, and, eventually, towards full civil equality with members of the established Church.

During the eighteenth and early nineteenth centuries, dissenters considered as the chief symbols of their second class citizenship the Test Act (1673) and the Corporation Act (1661), which, strictly interpreted, prevented conscientious dissenters from holding office under the Crown or in municipal corporations. The following motion proposed by Lord John Russell began the debate which resulted in the repeal of the Test and Corporation Acts in 1828, the first great step towards civil equality for dissenters since the Toleration Act of 1689. The story of the nonconformist campaign leading up to the debate on repeal of the Test and Corporations Acts has been very well told by Richard W. Davis in *Dissent in Politics, 1780-1830: The Political Life of William Smith, M.P.* So well laid was the groundwork for repeal, that in the end the debate was short; there was no serious opposition to repeal from political leaders on either the Tory or the Whig side of the house.

Lord John Russell (1792-1878), younger son of the 6th Duke of Bedford, was a leading figure among the progressive Whigs. He introduced the Reform Bill in 1831, and was twice prime minister (1846-52; 1865-66).

Sir Robert Inglis (1786-1855), an extremely conservative

politician and old fashioned churchman, opposed to change and reform, was a popular figure among Tory back benchers.

———————•—•————————

Lord John Russell rose and said:

I rise, Sir, in consequence of the notice which I some time ago gave upon the subject, for the purpose of submitting to the consideration of the House, a motion which, although it has not, for many years, been submitted to the House, will, I am sure, not be esteemed less worthy of their attention, either on that account, or on account of the weakness of the advocate by whom it is about to be supported. I am satisfied that the great number of petitions in favour of civil and religious liberty, which are now upon your table, will, at least, induce the House to take the question into their most serious consideration; and if they do dismiss it, at least not do so until after the investigation which its importance demands.

****

So great has been the improvement in knowledge and liberality, particularly among the middle classes, that the successors of those who most warmly opposed the motion of 1790 are, in 1828, its most zealous supporters. For instance, let us look to what has taken place in the common-council of London. It is notorious, as has been mentioned by an hon. alderman, that in the year 1790, the corporation passed some strong resolutions against the repeal of the Test and Corporation acts, and voted thanks to those members of the city who had opposed the repeal in this house; but so great has been the change in men's minds on the subject since that time, that the corporation has recently agreed to resolutions declaring those acts hostile to the principles of religious liberty. Another circumstance which I look upon as favourable to my motion is, that the powerful antagonist of Mr. Fox, in 1790, Mr. Pitt, as is now well known, did in a few years after his opposition to the measure, completely change his mind on the subject, and express a wish that the Test and Corporation acts be repealed. He saw, as every man of enlarged and enlightened mind must have seen, that all things around him were changed since the passing of those acts; that the religious questions which had been the subject of the world's debate at the time of their enactment had given place to divisions purely political; that the dispute for power no longer lay between Catholic, Lutheran, and Calvinist, but between the adherents, of despotism, representative monarchy, and democracy; that he could only defend the constitution by rallying around it the victims of an extinct quarrel, and calling on men of different religious opinions to defend the same form of political government.

****

I now come to the great principle involved in the numerous petitions before the House; petitions signed by the whole body of Dissenters, by Roman Catholics, and by many members of the established church. The principle is, that ever man ought to be allowed to form his religious opinions by the impressions on his own mind, and that, when so formed, he should be at liberty to worship God according to the dictates of his own conscience, without being subjected to any penalty or disqualification whatever; that every restrainst or restriction imposed on any man on account of his religious creed is in the nature of persecution, and is at once an affront to God, and an injury to man. This is the just and noble principle on which the Dissenters claim the repeal of the Test laws. But I will fairly admit, that there be an exception to its application, and I will illustrate it by reference to the general principle of non-interference by one state in the internal affairs of another. It may be stated, that one state would not generally be justified in interfering in the internal concerns of another; but if some of the internal regulations or political institutions of one state are of such a nature as to tend directly to the injury of another, then the interference properly commences on the part of the state making such regulations, and not on the part of the state which complains of them. I will say the same of religion: if the religion of any body of men be found to contain political principles hostile to the state, or militating against that allegiance which is due from every subject of the Crown, in that case the questions ceases to be a religious question; and you have the right to interfere and impose such restrictions as you may deem necessary, because you do not impose them on religious opinions; you impose them only on political doctrines (hear, hear!).

****

It is said, however, "after all, the grievances of which you

complain are only theoretical — they no longer exist in practice —
Dissenters are not in fact kept out of office." I will say, in the first
place, that if the case be so, that is not a sufficient argument in
support of these acts. Statutes imposing penalties and restrictions
on men on account of religious belief can be justified on no other
ground than that of necessity. When that ground is taken away, the
acts remain exposed in all their naked deformity of principle, and
that principle is religious persecution. But it is not a fact that no
practical grievance is suffered by the Dissenters. Indeed the fact is
far otherwise — the real practical grievance is a great deal more than
the legal grievances which appear on the face of the statute. Though
it be true that by later statutes indemnity was given to those who
omitted to qualify, yet that indemnity was given on the ground that
the omission was occasioned by ignorance, absence, or unavoidable
accident. Those words evidently do not apply to those persons who
had omitted to qualify from grounds of religious scruple. The situation
in which the Dissenters at present stand is evidently considered one
of practical grievance by the best and ablest defender of the acts,
I mean Lord North, who said, speaking of those Dissenters who took
advantage of the indemnity, "This sort of mental fraud did not
recommend these persons to the indulgence of the legislature; it was
an evasion and an abuse of an act of parliament." With such a round
declaration as this staring them in the face, how can it be expected
that men whose nice scruples are the cause of their dissent will submit
to the stigma — will render themselves liable to the imputation —
of acting fraudulently in order to obtain offices and emoluments which
the Church would allow them to obtain in no other way? That they
will not do so, I know for a fact. A great portion of the Dissenters
say among themselves, "we will not accept of office on these
conditions: if we cannot hold office without the degradation of being
liable to an imputation which we scorn, we will refrain from office
and emolument altogether." What is the consequence? The state is
deprived of the service of men who would be amongst her bravest
defenders in military achievement, and the most illustrious of her
servants in civil capacity. The individuals thus shut out will always
retain — I will not say a bitterness — but — a soreness of feeling
against the church which excludes them, and the state which makes

their admission to office a reproach to them.

Not only this; it should also be recollected, that it is in the power of any corporation, actuated by bigotry, or personal animosity, to carry the Corporation act into effect against Dissenters. I have in my possession a statement of cases which have occurred in the course of the last few years, in which persons who had a minority of votes in elections for corporation offices have been declared duly elected, because a previous notice had been given that the individuals who had the majorities could not act from being Dissenters. If there are so many cases of this kind that appear in the records of a court of law, how many other cases must there be in which the Dissenters will not come forward to expose themselves to the risk of such an objection? More than this: persons admitted to office ought, under the Test act, to produce their certificates. Dissenters do not like to expose themselves to the chance of those certificates being demanded. Rather than that, they well consent to forego office. The consequence is, that not one tenth part of the Dissenters who ought, in proportion to their numbers, at present hold office.

I have now stated, Sir, some of the practical grievances under which the Dissenters labour, but I am aware, whilst I am proving that these acts operate to the exclusion of Dissenters, I am only confirming many persons in the belief that it is necessary to continue them. I allude to those persons who use the argument of the security of the Church, and who think that in proportion as the number of Dissenters excluded is large, it is so much better for the Church, that the establishment is so much safer. I however, cannot admit that the security of the Church is founded on any such exclusion. I think with bishop Kennet, and I believe the security of the establishment consists in its moderation, its fair temper, and in its decent worship being conformable to the wishes, sentiments, and consciences of the majority of the people; and if it were not so — if it were not agreeable to the people — can it be imagined that any Test, any exclusive laws, will save the Church, and prevent its being destroyed by the overwhelming mass of its enemies?

"But," says a learned prelate of the present day, "the property of the Church will be liable to be affected by the various classes of Dissenters, if you admit them all to office." I think that argument is the most impolitic that could be advanced; for if those who use it ostentatiously declare they cannot admit the numerous millions — I will not say how many — of Protestant and Catholic Dissenters, to the enjoyment of civil rights of Englishmen, because such enjoyment necessarily tends to the destruction of church property, in the minds of all those Dissenters the enjoyment of civil rights and the division of church property are sure to be confounded. I consider it most impolitic to use such an argument, and I likewise consider it quite unfounded.

* * * * * * * * *

I have heard with considerable pain, that it is the intention of the new ministry to make this what is called a government question, to array all the power which their influence can muster against it. I am sorry to learn this; not on account of the question itself, whose progress they may retard, but never can prevent — I am sorry to hear it, because it is an indication, on the part of the government, of a determination to resist the liberality which is daily gaining ground in the great mass of society. Whatever kings or parliaments may think of their power, they must more or less submit to be influenced by the spirit of the times in which they live. The history of the last few years speaks aloud this undeniable truth. — Of Lord Liverpool, his warmest admirers must admit that the country governed him at least as much as he governed the country. It was conformity to this spirit that constituted all of hope and fame that attached to the political character of Mr. Canning — his name was great because he went along with the spirit of the times. Even the most illustrious person now at the head of his majesty's government must consult the same voice, and conform to the same standard. That illustrious person is justly hailed as the preserver of Portugal, the deliverer of Spain, the conqueror of Waterloo, — as one of the greatest military chiefs his country has ever produced — that country, to whose gratitude and admiration he is entitled by a list of services never to be forgotten. But even he, with all his fame, standing in such a position as few men have ever stood in, with the patronage of the church, and the state, and the army in his hands, — an army of one hundred and ten thousand men, attached to him not merely by their interests or their professional hopes, but by the memory of past dangers — possessing

the confidence, I had almost said the authority, of his Sovereign —
yet even he, with all his character, with all his patronage, with all
his power, must modify the exercise of those several qualities, and
in the tone and features of his government, if he would have it last,
conform to the spirit of the times in which he lives. No matter how
great his achievements or his glory, to the spirit of improvement
which has gone abroad he must bow. It is wisdom to do so without
waiting for the dictation of a necessity, or allowing a meritorious body
of individuals to stand, year after year, at the doors of parliament,
asking for what it is a disgrace to have so long refused. Such is the
line of conduct that would best become the government; but, whether
adopted by the government or not, the House is interested in
observing it, and by agreeing with the motion with which I shall
conclude, they will but discharge their duty, and render an act of
justice to three millions of their fellow-subjects. I move, Sir, "That
this House will resolve itself into a Committee of the whole House,
to consider of so much of the Acts of the 13th and 25th of Charles
2nd, as requires persons, before they are admitted into any office
or place in Corporations, or having accepted any office, civil or
military, or any place of trust under the Crown, to receive the
Sacrament of the Lord's Supper according to the Rites of the Church
of England."

* * * * * * * * *

Sir R.H. Inglis rose and said:

I approach, Sir, the consideration of this great question with the
same distrust of myself, but with the same confidence in my cause,
which, on his part, the noble lord — my noble friend, if I may so call
him — has felt and expressed in submitting his motion to you. I shall
be very happy, if I can carry to the discussion of it the same talent
and temper which he has displayed.

* * * * * * * * *

I proceed, then, at once, to the consideration of the real question:
Are the restrictions, the repeal of which is now required, restrictions
on the natural rights of man? The passage in the noble lord's speech,
in which he insisted on this position, was much cheered by the House,
or rather by those who sat more immediately around him; and, in
fact, it is on this ground that much of what we hear elsewhere, or

see in the petitions, much of what the hon. gentleman who last addressed you, have urged, mainly rests. On this ground, therefore, I will first meet the question. Let me say, in the first instance, that, on this, as on a somewhat similar subject, I should feel ashamed to resist, on the mere ground of expediency, a claim which any man, or any body of men, could urge as a matter of right and justice. It is because I do not see any such right or justice in the present case, that I resist the motion of my noble friend. Sir, the question of power is one of pure unmixed expediency: no man has an abstract right to it: power, as Burke has stated it, is the creature of society: when once established, indeed, its sanctions are from a higher source: but, in the beginningit is not like the right of life, or of liberty, original and absolute, but it is the arbitrary and artificial arrangement of men, modified and distributed in different ages and countries by every possible variety of combination. No one can, by nature, independently of the conventions of society, claim a right to govern his fellow men. The question, therefore, whether any man or any body of men, ought to be eligible to power is a question of pure expediency, not of justice; and such power may be regulated by sex, by age, by property, or by opinions, without any wrong to any one's natural claims. Sir, it is the highest right, and the first duty of every man, to worship God according to his own conscience; and God forbid that any man should be compelled to worship in one way, or be prohibited from worshipping in another, by any deposition of society: but I repeat it, a man's opinions may just as reasonably as the measure of his property exclude him from power: and, therefore, the question is still left one of mere policy, upon which men equally conscientious may well arrive at different conclusions.

Some established opinions every government, in every age, and in every country, with one single and late exception, has recognized and enforced. Some established form of religion there has ever been in every other civilized state:— all reason, all experience, all history, ancient and modern, the United States of America alone excepted, justify such a measure on the part of every government. Now, the very idea of an authorized religion implies some preference. I cannot conceive how an establishment can exist without some special protection and preference. The question then follows, what preference of those belonging to the establishment, what exclusion of others, may be necessary to its preservation?

* * * * * * * * *

The Dissenters of the present day enjoy the fullest rights of conscience: and I am willing to admit that there is nothing in their overt acts from which I apprehend any danger. With some of them I am intimate, for many more I have the highest respect; but it is perfectly clear, that the principles of Dissenters conscientiously opposed to the Church, can never give the same undivided allegiance to the constitution in church and state which a churchman does. The principles, if carried to the same extent as formerly, would produce the same results. The laws which restrain Dissenters are, and will ever be, left inoperative, so long as those principles slumber also: but I think that they should be retained for the purpose of being exerted in extreme cases, if such should ever arise. In fact, a richly-endowed Church, with all its privileges and immunities, will always be an object of jealousy to those who differ from it: but, connected as it is with the constitution, the state is bound to protect it against any dangers from any quarters. Dangers will always exist: and, if the present disabilities were removed, and Dissenters placed on the fullest equality as to power with the Church, some new question, perhaps of property, would immediately be started, on which new struggles and new dangers would arise. The question of tythes would probably come: and, as we should have followed the example of America in giving no preference to any Church, we should be called upon to follow it further, and to enact that no man should pay any thing to any pastor but his own (hear, hear). I accept the cheer of the hon. member for Montrose as a proof that my inference is correct; that there are those who would go so far. — No, Sir, differences must always exist; and the removal of the present matter of grievance will only bring the discontent one step nearer. I therefore prefer that the contest shall still continue about the out-works, and that we should not surrender them, because I am too sure that, in that case, we should have to fight for the citadel.

Chapter II

Church and State

Introduction

During the period of political crisis and constitutional reform in the first half of the nineteenth century, the Church of England, the church by law established, was seen as one of the pillars of the constitution. There had developed since the Reformation such a web of connections between the Church of England and the state that, after three centuries, the Church was considered by most Englishmen to be part of the apparatus of government. Church and state were intertwined in many ways, some formal and some informal. The highest officers of the Church, the bishops, were chosen by the Crown, on recommendation from the prime minister. The bishops, who sat in the House of Lords, looked upon matters of state as a major portion of the responsibilities, and some bishops became important political figures. Parliament from time to time granted money to the Church, and the Church was empowered by law to collect tithes and local taxes (church rates) for the upkeep of the local church. The basic theological posture of the Church, enshrined in the thirty nine articles of religion adopted in the reign of Elizabeth, was sanctioned by parliament, and parliament approved the Prayer Book and controlled its revision. The Church performed a number of functions which subsequently passed to the state. Until 1837, for example, there was no civil marriage, and only the priests of the Church of England could perform marriages. There was no civil registration of births or deaths; the only official records were the parish registers kept by the Church of England. Oxford and Cambridge and the most eminent secondary schools in England were intimately associated with the Church. Because they were often the best educated men in the area, the clergymen of the established church, deployed in nearly 15,000 parishes throughout the country, played a significant role in local government. In rural areas, in the early nineteenth century, clergymen frequently served as justices of the peace, thus symbolizing the role of the Church as an agency of social control whose function in society was to keep the peace.

The three major eighteenth-century writers on the theory of the church establishment, Bishop William Warburton, Edmund Burke and William Paley, all assumed without discussion that the principal civil role of the Church was to maintain social order. William Wilberforce, the great Evangelical enemy of the slave trade, put it thusly: "The necessity of religion among the bulk of the people, i.e. the lower orders, is the greater because that great principle of honour, which it would scarcely be too strong to term the religion of the higher orders, does not exist among them. Consider then what the former would be without the restraint of honour, and estimate what the latter without religion." [Geoffrey Best, *Temporal Pillars*, p.152]

The assumption that social order depended on the personal morality of the people was widely held in the nineteenth century, particularly in the early nineteenth century before the creation of effective police forces. And morality was widely assumed to be the product of religion. Samuel Taylor Coleridge gave elaborate voice to a common contemporary idea when he wrote, in his influential book *On the Constitution of Church and State According to the Idea of Each* (1829), "the English Constitution results from the harmonious opposition of two institutions, the State, in the narrower sense, and the Church. For as by the composition of the one provision was alike made for permanence, and progression in wealth and personal freedom; to the other was committed the only remaining interest of the State in its larger sense, that of maintaining and advancing the moral cultivation of the people themselves, without which neither of the former could continue to exsist."

In several important ways, however, eighteenth-century ideas of establishment were questioned in the early nineteenth century. As the numbers and political power of protestant dissenters and Roman Catholics increased, the religious pluralism of the nation could not be ignored. The repeal of the Test and Corporation Acts in 1828 and Catholic Emancipation in 1829 helped to stimulate new interest in the nature of the relationship between church and state. Along with these measures, the great reform of parliament in 1832, which seemed at the time as if it might open the way to continuing constitutional reform, encouraged men holding widely different religious views to reexamine the meaning of establishment and to reconsider the role of the church in both its spiritual and social spheres.

Guide to Further Reading

The best general introductions to the relations of church and state in the early nineteenth century can be found in the first four chapters of the first volume of Owen Chadwick, *The Victorian Church*(1966), the first three chapters of *Church and Society in England 1770-1970* (1976) by E.R. Norman, in Part I of Desmond Bowen, *The Idea of the Victorian Church* (1968), the fourth chapter of Geoffrey Best, *Temporal Pillars* (1964), and the first three chapters of G.I.T. Machin, *Politics and the Churches in Great Britain 1832-1868* (1977). R.A. Soloway has written a good study of Anglican social thought in *Prelates and People, Ecclesiastical and Social Thought in England 1783-1852* (1969). Along with Best's *Temporal Pillars*, the most helpful works on the organizational modernization of the Church of England are W.L. Mathieson, *English Church Reform 1815-1840* (1923), K.A. Thompson, *Bureaucracy and Church Reform — the Organizational Response of the Church of England to Social Change 1800-1965* (1970), and the stimulating book by Olive Brose, *Church and Parliament: the Reshaping of the Church of England 1828-1860* (1959). Two important articles by Geoffrey Best deal with the politics of the establishment at the time of its perceived crisis, "The Evangelicals and the Established Church in the early Nineteenth Century," *Journal of Theological Studies* (1958), and "The Whigs and the Church Establishment in the Age of Grey and Holland," *History* (1960). Norman Gash includes an extended discussion of the place of the establishment in parliamentary politics in *Reaction and Reconstruction in English Politics 1832-52* (1965). John Prest's study of the early career of *Lord John Russell* (1972) is the fullest account of the Whig leader's erastian church policies. Norman Gash, in *Sir Robert Peel* (1972), deals with Peel's crucial role in the administrative reform of the church.

The most satisfactory general study of the Oxford Movement is Marvin O'Connell, *The Oxford Conspirators: A History of the Oxford Movement 1833-1845* (1969). Still valuable is *The Oxford Movement 1833-1845* (1891) by R.W. Church. John Henry Newman's *Apologia Pro Vita Sua* (1864), an autobiographical view of the Oxford Movement, has great literary merit; as historical evidence it must be treated with caution.

C.R. Sanders, *Coleridge and the Broad Church Movement* (1942) is the fullest survey of early broad churchmen. It includes a good essay on Thomas Arnold. The best study of Arnold remains Arthur Penrhyn Stanley, *The Life and Correspondence of Dr. Arnold* (2 vols., 1844). There is a useful introduction by Michael Jackson and John Rogan in their edition of Thomas Arnold's *Principles of Church Reform* (1962).

The best biography of Gladstone is now Richard Shannon, *Gladstone*, the first volume of which was published in 1982. Perry Butler's *Gladstone: Church, State and Tractarianism* (1982), is a first rate study of Gladstone's religious views through the middle of the century. Deryck Schreuder examines the relation between Gladstone's early book on church and state and his later liberalism in a provocative chapter, "Gladstone and the Conscience of the State," in Peter Marsh, ed., *The Conscience of the Victorian State* (1979). H.C.G. Matthew puts Gladstone's book into perspective in the excellent introduction to Volume III of his edition of *The Gladstone Diaries*.

A charge to the Clergy of the Diocese of Lincoln at the Triennial Visitation in 1831 (1831), by John Kaye. Selections.

John Kaye (1783-1853), was bishop of Lincoln from 1827 until his death. He had previously been bishop of Bristol (1820-27), master of Christ's College, Cambridge (1814-30), and from 1816 he was Regius Professor of Divinity at Cambridge. In politics Kaye played no prominent role. He was, however, an active ecclesiastical reformer at both Bristol and Lincoln where he worked hard to stimulate his clergy towards a more conscientious, reverent and energetic fulfilment of their duties. He was one of the original members of the Ecclesiastical Commission which Sir Robert Peel appointed in 1835. The Ecclesiastical Commission, under the direction of Charles James Blomfield, irrepressible bishop of London, was the most important agency in the modernization of the administration of the Church. The Ecclesiastical Commission did much to limit sinecures, to prevent pluralism and non residence, and to promote discipline and activity among the clergy. Kaye pressed forward the reform of the Church because he recognized that a reformed and invigorated clergy would be more effective ministers of Christ, and also because he recognized that the unreformed Church, like the unreformed state, presented a vulnerable target to men whom he considered destructive radicals.

In the first of his triennial charges to the clergy of Lincoln, Kaye shows symptoms of the alarm which gripped so many friends of the old order in the early 1830s. The constitution was in process of momentous change. With repeal of the Test and Corporation Acts in 1828 a religiously pluralistic society seemed clearly the way of the future. The Roman Catholic Relief Act of 1829, a very much more contentious measure than repeal of the Test and Corporation Acts, cleared the way for Catholics to sit in Parliament and hold office under the crown. Its passage seemed to ultra Tories to put the protestant constitution in dire danger. Early in 1831 the new Whig government under Lord Grey brought in the Reform Bill, and its impending passage convinced many that a constitutional revolution was under way. Some feared and others hoped that the pace of constitutional change would continue unabated until the Church of England was disestablished, shorn of its privileged place in the constitution. Kaye, whose theology tended towards evengelicalism, in 1831 saw disestablishment as a serious possibility for the near future. While he deplored this possibility, Kaye, like many other evangelicals, tended to think of the structure of the Church in utilitarian rather than sacred terms. His emphasis upon the central spiritual mission of the Church permitted him to look upon the connection between Church and state as a secondary matter, important of course, but not as important as saving souls.

———————•◦•———————

MY REVEREND BRETHEREN,

We live in times of no ordinary character. In making this assertion,
I run no hazard of committing an error into which it is natural to
man to fall — the error of overrating the magnitude of the
transactions which have occurred while he has himself been an actor
in the scene of life. In the interval of three years which have elapsed
since we last met, events have taken place important in themselves,
but still more important in their probable influence on the future
fortunes of the civilized world. It is unnecessary for me to specify
them in detail. They will immediately suggest themselves to your
recollections; and supply my justification when I repeat, that we live
in times of no ordinary character.

If we attempt to carry our view onward into futurity, we can
discover little that is cheering in the prospect; little to encourage the
hope that we are drawing near to a state of permanent tranquillity
and peace. It may be that the fury of the tempest has for a while
subsided; but we must not too hastily infer from this interval of quiet
that all will be in future calm and serene. There is still a distant
murmur of the wind, a lowering of the sky, a heaving of the wave,
to warn us that the danger is not passed, and that we must continue
to watch. He must be an inattentive observer of the state of public
opinion and feeling who does not discern in it the elements of future
struggles and collisions. There is a disposition to search out blemishes
and faults in all that is established — to regard all existing institutions
as impediments in the way of the prosperity and well-being of the
country. So long as this disposition prevails, a desire of change, and
its necessary accompaniment, a restless and discontented spirit, must
also prevail. To little purpose do we urge that, with our present
institutions, notwithstanding the defects, real or imaginary, which
are imputed to them, our country has risen to an astonishing height
of power, and its inhabitants have enjoyed a larger share of prosperity
and happiness than usually falls to the lot of nations. It is easy to
reply, that these beneficial results have been obtained, not by the
operation of our present system, but in spite of it; or that the system

might be suited to ignorant and unenlightened times; but that its various irregularities and anomalies, as they cannot stand the test of rational examination, can no longer be tolerated, and must give way to a system better suited to the increased and increasing intelligence of the age.

If this is a correct account of the state of public feeling at the present moment, we cannot be surprised that the Established Church shares the fate of all other institutions; that it is the object of frequent attack; that it is denounced, not merely as useless, but as positively injurious; as obstructing instead of advancing the interests of true religion. We cannot be surprised at being told, as we repeatedly are, that its days are already numbered, and that it is destined to sink at no distant period before the irresistible force of enlightened public opinion. When in former times the Clergy spoke of the dangers impending over the Church, they were charged with exciting a cry of which they know the falsehood from interested motives; but now that its adversaries declare it to be in danger, and exultingly tell us that it is tottering to its fall, we cannot be accused of childish proneness to alarm, if we suspect that these confident anticipations are not merely the suggestions of their wishes, but that they intend their prediction to work its own accomplishment.

At the Revolution, when the principle of toleration was first recognised by the law, it was nevertheless thought necessary for the security of the Established Church that none but members of it should be admitted to the possession of political power. The sacramental test was in consequence retained; but though retained, it soon ceased to be enforced: and when three years ago it was formally abolished, they who pressed the abolition did not so much complain of any practical grievance resulting from it, as that the continuance on the statute-book of the enactments by which it was required was regarded by our dissenting brethren as implying an offensive and groundless distrust of their attachment to the constitution. With the repeal, however, of the sacramental test, the principle that political power should be lodged exclusively in the hands of members of the Established Church was abandoned. The following year produced a still wider deviation from the principles on which the union of the Established Church with the State had previously been supposed to rest. At the revolution the attempts of the last misguided monarch of the Stuart race, to make his own religion that of the State, were too fresh in the recollections of Protestants to permit them to pronounce temperately and dispassionately on the case of their Roman Catholic fellow-subjects; who were, in consequence, excluded from the benefits of the Act of Toleration, and during the greater part of the last century performed their acts of public worship only under connivance. These restraints, however, on the public exercise of their religion, which ought, in my opinion, never to have been imposed, had, during the reign of George III., been gradually removed, and in the session of 1829, the civil disabilities affecting them were also done away. All offices, some few excepted, were thrown open to them, and they were admitted to seats in Parliament; in other words, the principle that the legislature of this country should be exclusively Protestant was abandoned. Last year, a further change was attempted, though unsuccessfully; it was proposed to remove the civil disabilities affecting the Jewish subjects of the realm. Had that attempt succeeded, the legislature would have ceased to be exclusively Christian.

To turn from the measures themselves to the principle on which many of their advocates urge their adoption: — the principle is, that it is unjust to subject men to civil disabilities on account of religious opinions. The ends of civil and religious society are said to be totally distinct — that of the former being the temporal — of the latter, the eternal happiness of men. The State, therefore, has no concern with the religion of its subjects; its concern is not with opinions, but with actions; and with them only so far as they affect the frame or well-being of society. Doubts may reasonably be entertained respecting the soundness of the principle so confidently put forth. The relations in which man stands to his fellow-men, and consequently the duties arising out of those relations, originate in the appointment of God. That broad line of distinction which it is attempted to draw between man in his religious and in his civil character cannot be drawn. Moral and social is necessarily connected with religious obligation; it is equally, though less directly, to be referred to God as author. In proportion as men take a more enlightened and comprehensive view of their relation to their Maker, they will be better qualified and more anxious faithfully to discharge their social duties; and the State has consequently a deep interest in the soundness of the religious opinions of its subjects. My object, however, is not to combat, but to state the opinions prevalent at the present moment, concerning the course which the civil magistrate ought to pursue with respect to religion; and I state them in order to point out their bearing on the interests of the Established Church. If the advocates of these opinions are consistent, they cannot be favourable to an Established Church, Finding it in existence, they may apprehend greater mischief from attempting to remove it, than from suffering it to remain; but they must still consider its existence as an evil. According to them, the State ought to be of no religion; it ought to protect all modes of faith, but to prefer none, — the system, which still, I believe, exists in the States of New England; and according to which every member of the community is bound to contribute towards the support of the ministers of the Gospel, but may select the particular religious society, to the minister of which his contribution shall be paid. This system is too narrow for the enlarged conceptions of the age in which we live. It establishes Christianity; but as to believe is an act, not of the will, but of understanding, to compel men to contribute towards the support of the ministers of a religion, with the evidences of which their understandings are not satisfied, is said to be an indirect violation of their right of private judgement.

Looking, then, at the feeling with which all existing institutions are regarded, and at the growing indifference, I should not perhaps use too strong a term were I to say dislike, to civil establishments of religion, we should wilfully close our eyes did we not recognise the probability that attempts will be made to dissolve the union at present subsisting between the Church and the State in this kingdom. That such attempts, if successful, will be productive of great evil — that they will tend to the general decay of religion and morality throughout the land — and that their baneful effects will be felt not least sensibly in those religious communities which dissent from the Established Church; these are assertions which the past history of our country fully warrants: though, when they proceed from me, they will perhaps be imputed to the personal interest which I have in the maintenance of the existing order of things. But the point to which

I wish particularly to call your attention is, in what manner ought the present state of public feeling and opinions to operate on the minds and conduct of the Clergy? Surely it ought to stimulate them to increased diligence in the discharge of their pastoral duties; to render them more earnest and assiduous in ministering both to the temporal and spiritual wants of their flocks; more circumspect in their conversation and deportment; more pure and holy in the whole tenor of their lives. Let not those who scruple not to resort to any mode of attack when the object is to injure the Established Church — let them not be enabled to give weight to the objections which they urge against the system, by appealing to the negligence or misconduct of the individuals by whom it is administered. A single vicious, or frivolous, or even careless minister of religion produces a more mischievous impression on the minds of all classes of society, and adds greater number to the ranks of infidelity or dissent, than the most ingenious arguments which can be advanced against the evidences of Christianity, or the particular doctrines and discipline of our own Church.

* * * * * * * * *

It may be thought, from the tenor of my remarks, that I undervalue the assistance which the civil power can render to the cause of religion. Far from it. I know that, in their glowing anticipations of the future glories of the Visible Church, the prophets, among other marks of its prosperity, announce, that kings shall be its nursing fathers, and queens its nursing mothers. But the effect of the protection afforded by the State to the Church, ought to be to increase the vigilance of the ministers of religion. Has this always been the effect upon ourselves? Or has not our reliance upon the support which we derived from our connexion with the State, rather caused us to remit something of our diligence in the work of the ministry?

It may be thought too, that in representing an attempt to dissolve the union between the State and the Established Church as a probable event, and in even hinting at the possibility of the success of the attempt, I am speaking the language of despondency — a language calculated to paralyze instead of invigorating the energies of the Clergy, by causing them to think that at last their labours will be fruitless. It would be a more pleasing task, a task more congenial to my feelings, to address you in a different tone; to use the language only of joyful and confident anticipation. But he is the worst of flatterers, who speaks peace when there is no peace. I have felt, therefore, that I should best discharge my duty by placing before you, without reserve, my opinion of our present situation. To close our eyes against its difficulties would be foolish, if it were possible. Our true wisdom is to prepare to meet the danger while it is still at such a distance that we can contemplate it calmly, and accurately estimate its magnitude. If we wait till it comes nearer, the season of deliberation will be passed, and we shall take counsel only from fear or rashness.

If, however, my language implies apprehension respecting the permanence of the connexion of the Established Church with the State, let it not be supposed that I doubt of the permanence of the Established Church, *as a congregation of faithful men, in the which the pure Word of God is preached, and the sacraments are duly ministered according to Christ's ordinance.* On that point, we are not permitted to doubt — for we have the promise of Christ Himself, *as an anchor of the soul, sure and stedfast.* To the work of the ministry, in that branch of his visible Church which has long been known and reverenced throughout Protestant Christendom, by the title of the Church of England, we have dedicated ourselves. No change in its external circumstances can affect the relation in which we stand to it, or release us from the obligation to labour for its welfare. Though, unhappily for the country, its connexion with the State should be dissolved, we shall not want either an ample field to call forth our exertions, or a fertile soil to repay them. What if some of its professed adherents regard it only as useful political instrument; it numbers amongst its followers thousands whose attachment originates in high and noble motives; who regard it as a powerful instrument, in the hand of God, for the salvation of the souls of men. They adhere to it, because they cordially assent to its scriptural creed; because they love its simple yet impressive ceremonies, and the strain of warm yet sober devotion, which pervades its services; because they admire the long list of illustrious and venerable names which grace its annuals. Whatever be its temporal fortunes, prosperous or adverse, their affection towards it, their zeal for its interests, will suffer no abatement. To minister to the spiritual well-being of this chosen congregation of Christ, to maintain it in the unity of the faith and in the bond of peace, will still be our delightful office; an office, in the faithful discharge of which we may be assured of the Divine support and blessing. No, my brethren — that pure branch of the Catholic Church in which we exercise our ministry, will not fail. It will still shine as a light from heaven, to direct the footsteps of the Christian traveller; it will still stand as a city on a hill, to which he may flee, as a place of refuge from the perils, of rest from the toils of his way. *Therefore, my beloved brethren, be ye stedfast, unmoveable, always abounding in the work of the Lord; forasmuch as ye know that your labour is not in vain in the Lord.*

Principles of Church Reform (1833), by Thomas Arnold. Selections.
Thomas Arnold (1795-1842) is best remembered as headmaster of
Rugby (1828-1842). His great success at Rugby, immortalized in
Arthur Penrhyn Stanley's *Life and Correspondence of Dr. Arnold*
(1844) and Thomas Hughes' *Tom Brown's School Days* (1857), caused
him to be considered the principal shaper of the Victorian public
schools. Arnold's reaction to the emergence of religious pluralism and
democracy in the constitutional changes of 1828-1832 was very
different from that of either the Tractarians or of Evangelicals like
Bishop Kaye. Arnold believed that the Church of England was in
imminent danger of disestablishment in the early 1830s, but more
than the Oxford men or Bishop Kaye, Arnold thought
disestablishment would be a great national disaster. Arnold was
deeply influenced by Samuel Taylor Coleridge — the principal
intellectual inspiration for many liberal Churchmen — and by German
romantic thought. He looked upon the Church of England as a great
national institution, as both guardian and embodiment of the best
in English civilization. Impelled by his commitment to national
culture, Arnold proposed in *Principles of Church Reform* a grand and
bold scheme of reunion with protestant dissent, a comprehensive,
national English church that would embrace English protestantism.

Arnold's scheme of comprehension was sympathetically received
by only a few liberal intellectuals within the Church. The Evangelicals
distrusted Arnold's liberal approach to dogma, while the budding
Oxford Movement reacted with horror and scorn. The leaders of the
Oxford Movement viewed the political crisis of the Church from a
perspective opposite to Arnold's. The Oxford men de-emphasized the
national character of the Church, and turned instead to its Catholicity,
its divine and ancient origin, its authentic traditions and its ultimate
independence of political authority. Arnold tended to identify the
Church and the nation, and therefore he de-emphasized Catholicity
and antiquity and placed a great deal of importance on maintaining
intimate association between Church and state. Arnold's proposal for
comprehension produced no practical results, but for historians it is
a document which helps to clarify the temper of its time.

This evil of religious dissent is so enormous, — is so fraught with
danger at this moment to our highest interests, national and spiritual,
— and has been to my mind so unfairly and unsatisfactorily treated
by men of all parties, that I shall make no apology for entering fully
upon the consideration of it. Unless it be duly appreciated, and in

some measure remedied, it is perfectly needless to talk of Church Reform.

Whoever is acquainted with Christianity, must see that differences of opinion amongst Christians are absolutely unavoidable. First, because our religion being a thing of the deepest personal interest, we are keenly alive to all the great questions connected with it, which was not the case with heathenism. Secondly, these questions are exceedingly numerous, inasmuch as our religion affects our whole moral being, and must involve, therefore, a great variety of metaphysical, moral, and political points; — that is to say, those very points which, lying out of reach of demonstrative science, are, through the constitution of man's nature, peculiarly apt to be regarded by different minds differently. And thirdly, although all Christians allow the Scriptures to be of decisive authority, whenever their judgment is pronounced on any given case, yet the peculiar form of these Scriptures, which in the new Testament is rather that of a commentary than of a text; — the critical difficulties attending their interpretation, and the still greater difficulty as to their application: — it being a constant question whether such and such rules, and still more whether such and such recorded facts or practices, were meant to be universally binding; — and it being a farther question, amidst the infinite variety of human affairs, whether any case, differing more or less in its circumstances, properly comes under the scope of any given Scripture rule; — all these things prevent the Scriptures from being in practice decisive on controverted points, because the contending parties, while alike acknowledging the judge's authority, persist in putting a different construction upon the words of his sentence.

Aware of this state of things, and aware also with characteristic wisdom, of the deadly evil of religious divisions, the Roman Catholic Church ascribed to the sovereign power in the Christian society, in every successive age, an infallible spirit of truth, whereby the real meaning of any disputed passage of Scripture might be certainly and authoritatively declared; and if the Scripture were silent, then the living voice of the Church might supply its place, — and being guided by that same spirit which had inspired the written word, might pronounce upon any new point of controversy with a decision of no less authority.

With the same view of preventing divisions, the unity of the Church was maintained, in a sense perfectly inteligible and consistent. Christians wherever the lived, belonged literally to one and the same society, — they were subject to the same laws and to the same government. National and political distinctions were wholly lost sight of; the vicar of Christ and his general council knew nothing of England or of France, of Germany or of Spain; they made laws for *Christendom* — a magnificent word, and well expressing those high and consistent notions of unity, on which the Church of Rome based its system. One government, one law, one faith, kept free from doubt and error by the support of an infallible authority — the theory was in perfect harmony with itself, and most imposing from its beauty and apparent usefulness; but it began with assuming a falsehood, and its intended conclusion was an impossibility.

It is false that there exists in the Church any power of office endowed with the gift of infallible wisdom; and thererore it is impossible to prevent differences of opinion. But the claim to infallibility was not only false, but mischievous; because it encouraged the notion that these differences were to be condemned and prevented, and thus hindered men from learning the truer and better lesson, how to make them perfectly compatible with Christian union. Doubtless it were a far happier state of things if men did not differ from each other at all; — but this may be wished for only; it is a serious folly to expect it. For so, while grieving over an inevitable evil, we heap on it aggravations of our own making, which are far worse than the original mischief. Differences of opinion will exist, but it is our fault that they should have been considered equivalent to differences of principle, and made a reason for separation and hostility.

Our fathers rightly appreciated the value of church unity; but they strangely mistook the means of preserving it. Their system consisted in drawing up a statement of what they deemed important truths, and in appointing a form of worship and a ceremonial which they believed to be at once dignified and edifying; and then they proposed to oblige every man, by the dread of legal penalties or disqualifications, to subscribe to their opinions, and to conform to their rites and practices. But they forgot that while requiring this agreement, they had themselves disclaimed, what alone could justify them in enforcing it the possession of infallibility. They had parted with the weapon which would have served them most effectually, and strange were the expedients resorted to for supplying its place. At one time it was the Apostles' Creed; at another, the general consent of the primitive Church, which formed an authoritative standard of such truths as might not be questioned without heresy. But though the elephant might still rest upon the tortoise, and the tortoise on the stone, yet since the claim to infallibility was once abandoned, the stone itself rested on nothing. The four first councils were appealed to as sanctioning their interpretation of Scripture by men who yet confessed that the decisions of these councils were only of force, because they were agreeable to the Scripture. Turn which ever way they would, they sought in vain for an *authority* in religious controversies; infallibility being nowhere to be found, it was merely opinion against opinion; and however convinced either party might be of the truth of its own views, they had no right to judge their opponents.

With regard to the ceremonies and practices of the Church, a different ground was taken. It is curious to observe the contradictory positions in which the two parties were placed: — the Church of England enforcing a tyranny upon principles in themselves not liberal and most true; — the Dissenters accidentally advocating the cause of liberty, while their principles were those of the most narrow minded fanaticism. One feels ashamed to think that the great truths so clearly and so eloquently established by Hooker, in the earlier books of his ecclesiastical polity, should have served in practice the petty tyranny of Laud and Whitgift, or the utterly selfish and worldly policy of Elizabeth. The Church of England maintained most truly, that rites and ceremonies, being things indifferent in themselves, might be altered according to the difference of times and countries, and that the regulation of such matters was left wholly to the national Church. But inasmuch as the government of the national Church was a mere despotism — the crown having virtually transferred to itself the authority formerly exercised by the popes — its appointments were made with an imperious stiffness, which was the more offensive from the confessed indifferent nature of the matters in question; and while one ritual was inflexibly imposed upon the whole community, in direct opposition to the feelings of many of its members, and too simple and unattractive to engage the sympathies of the multitude, this fond attempt to arrive at uniformity, inflicted a deadly blow, according to Lord Falkland's most true observation on the real blessing of Christian union.

I am well aware that if it be a mere question of comparative faultiness, the opponents of the Established Church in the sixteenth and seventeenth centuries are at least as much to be condemned as its rulers. That coarse-minded ignorance, which delighted to isolate itself from all the noble recollections of past times, and confounded all the institutions and practices of the Christian Church during several centuries, under the opprobrious names of superstition and idolatry; that captious superstition which quarrelled with the form of a minister's cap, or the colour of his dress, deserved indeed little consideration, if the principles of government are to be made dependent on the merits of paricular parties or individuals. But the cause of truth, and the welfare of mankind, have been forever sacrificed to the paltry triumphs of personal argument: — if a party can show that its opponents have been more blameable than itself, it looks upon itself as standing clear in the judgment of posterity and of God. The provocation given may indeed lessen our estimate of the guilt of individuals; but it ought not to affect our sentiments of the wisdom or evil tendency of their conduct; and though the virulence and ignorance of the puritans may dispose us to excuse Whitgift and Laud, as individuals, yet their system is not the less to be condemned, as in itself arbitrary and schismatical, and tending to aggravate and perpetuate the evils which it professed to combat.

Thus within fifty years of the overthrow of the Roman Catholic religion in England, the spirit of Protestantism, followed up only in one half of its conclusions, had divided the nation into two hostile parties, each careless of union, and looking only to victory. The religious quarrel blending itself with the political struggle at which society in its progress had then arrived, became thus the more irreconcileable; each party boasted of its martyrs, and exulted in the judgments which had befallen its enemies; the royalist churchmen consecrated the 29th of May as a day of national thanksgiving; the puritan, who had deemed popery and prelacy crushed for ever by the arms of God's saints, now bewailed the new St. Bartholomew of 1662, and the vindictive oppression of the Five Mile Act.

There succeeded an age of less zeal, but scarcely of more charity. Time had reconciled men to the monstrous sight of a large proportion of a Christian people living in a complete religious separation from their fellow-Christians; of a numerous portion of the children of the State, living as aliens from the national worship. And the means hitherto adopted for preventing such a division were so odious in themselves, and had so signally failed to effect their object, that none could wish them to be continued any longer. Hostilities were accordingly suspended, and the Toleration Act was passed; — a strange measure, by which the nation sanctioned the non-observance of its own institutions, and relaxed by one half the bond of national communion. Yet at the very same period an attempt to effect, not a peace, but an union with the Dissenters, totally failed: those true Christians who wished to make the national Church more comprehensive, were unable to carry their point: persecution first — toleration afterwards — any thing seemed preferable to Christian charity and Christian union.

Then followed one of those awful periods in the history of a nation, which may be emphatically called its times of trial. I mean those tranquil intervals between one great revolution and another, in which an opportunity is offered for profiting by the lessons of past experience, and to direct the course of the future for good. From our present dizzy state, it is startling to look back on the deep calm of the first seventy years of the eighteenth century. All the evils of society were yet manageable; while complete political freedom, and a vigorous state of mental activity, seemed to promise that the growth of good would more than keep pace with them, and that thus they might be kept down for ever. But tranquility, as usual, bred carelessness; events were left to take their own way uncontrolled; the weeds grew fast, while none thought of sowing the good seeds. The Church and the Dissenters lived in peace; but their separation became daily more confirmed. Meanwhile the uniformity, and the strict formality, which the Church had fondly adopted in order to extinguish Dissent, now manifestly encouraged it. As the population increased, and began to congregate into large masses in those parts of the country which before had been thinly inhabited, the Church required an enlarged machinery, at once flexible, and powerful. What she had was both stiff and feeble; her ministers could only officiate in a church, and were compelled to confine themselves to the prescribed forms of the liturgy; while the Dissenters, free and unrestricted, could exercise their ministry as circumstances required it, whether in a mine, by a canal side, or at the doors of a manufactory; they could join in hymns with their congregations, could pray, expound the Scriptures, exhort, awaken, or persuade, in such variety, and in such proportions, as the time, the place, the mood of the hearers, or their own, might suggest or call for.

Thus, by the very nature of the case, the influence of the Dissenters spread amongst the poorer classes. It was a great good, that the poor and ignorant should receive any knowledge of Christianity; — but it was a mixed good, because the evil of sectarianism was at hand to taint it. The minister at the meeting-house rejoiced to thin the church; — the minister of the church rejoiced in his turn, if he could win back hearers from the meeting. As if their great common cause had not required all their efforts, much of their zeal was directed against each other; and if there was not hostility, there was an increase of rivalry and of jealousy. It might have been thought that the many good and active men who were now daily rising up amongst the ministers of the Establishment, would have been struck by the evils of their position, and have laboured to remove them. But some had been so used to the existence of Dissent, that they were insensible to the magnitude of its evils; — others, with the old party spirit of the High Churchmen, imagined that all the blame of the separation rested with the Dissenters; they talked of the sin of schism, as if they were not equally guilty of it; they would have rejoiced in the conformity of the opposite party, that is to say, in their own victory; but they had no notion of any thing like a fair union. Others, again, fully occupied with their own individual duties, and feeling that they themselves were usefully employed, never directed their attention to the inadequacy of the system to which they belonged, considered as a whole; while a fourth set argued against reforming the Church now, from the fact of its having gone unreformed so long; and because the crisis was not yet arrived, they were blind to the sure symptoms of its progress, and believed that it would only be brought on by the means used to avert it.

But the population outgrew the efforts both of the Church and of the Dissenters; and multitudes of persons existed in the country who could not properly be said to belong to either. These were, of course, the most ignorant and degraded portion of the whole community, — a body whose influence is always for evil of some sort, but not always for evil of the same sort, — which is first the brute abettor and encourager of abuses, and afterwards their equally brute destroyer. For many years the populace hated the Dissenters for the strictness of their lives, and because they had departed from the institutions of their country; for ignorance, before it is irritated by physical distress, and thoroughly imbued with the excitement of political agitation, is blindly averse to all change, and looks upon reform as a trouble and a disturbance. Thus the populace in Spain and in Naples have shown themselves decided enemies to the constitutional party; and thus the mob at Birmingham, so late as the year 1791, plundered and burnt houses to the cry of "Church and King," and threatened to roast Dr. Priestley alive, as a heretic. But there is a time, and it is one fraught with revolutions, when this tide of ignorance suddenly turns, and runs in the opposite direction with equal violence. Distress and continued agitation produce this change; but its peculiar danger arises from this, that its causes operate for a long time without any apparent effect, and we observe their seeming inefficiency till we think that there is nothing to fear from them; when suddenly the ground falls in under our feet, and we find that their work, though slow, had been done but too surely. And this is now the case with the populace of England. From cheering for Church and King, they are now come to cry for no bishops, no tithes, and no rates: from persecuting the Dissenters, because they had separated from the Church, they are now eagerly joining with them for that very same reason; while the Dissenters, on their part, readily welcome these new auxiliaries, and reckon on their aid for effecting the complete destruction of their old enemy.

This being the state of things, it is evident, that the existence of Dissent has divided the efforts of Christians, so as to make them more adverse to each other than to the cause of ungodliness and wickedness; it has prevented the nation from feeling the full benefits of its national Establishment, and now bids fair to deprive us of them altogether. Dissent, indeed, when it becomes general, makes the Establishment cease to be national; there being so large a portion of the nation whose religious wants it does not satisfy. Yet we have seen, on the other hand, that differences of religious opinion, and of religious rites and ceremonies, are absolutely unavoidable; and that since there exists on earth no infallible authority to decide controversies between Christians, it is vain for any one sect to condemn another, or in its dealings with others to assume that itself is certainly right, and its opponents as certainly in error.

Is it not, then, worth while to try a different system? And since disunion is something so contrary to the spirit of Christianity, and difference of opinion a thing so inevitable to human nature, might it not be possible to escape the former without the folly of attempting to get rid of the latter; to constitute a Church thoroughly national, thoroughly united, thoroughly Christian, which should allow great varieties of opinions, and of ceremonies, and forms of worship, according to the various knowledge, and habits, and tempers of its members, while it truly held one common faith, and trusted in one common Saviour, and worshipped one common God?

The problem then is, to unite in one Church different opinions and different rites and ceremonies; and first, let us consider the case of a difference of religious opinions.

Before such an union is considered impracticable, or injurious to the cause of Christianity, might we not remember what, and how many, those points are, on which all Christians are agreed?

We all believe in one God, a spiritual and all-perfect Being, who made us, and all things; who governs all things by His Providence; who loves goodness, and abhors wickedness.

We all believe that Jesus Christ, His Son, came into the world for our salvation; that He died, and rose again from the dead, to prove that His true servants shall not die eternally, but shall rise as He is risen, and enjoy an eternal life with Him and with His Father.

We all believe that the volume of the Old and New Testaments contains the revelation of God's will to man; that no other revelation

than what is there recorded has been ever given to mankind before
or since; that it is a standard of faith and a rule of practice; so that
we all acknowledge its authority, although we may often understand
its meaning differently.

We all have, with very few exceptions, the same notions of right
and wrong; or, at any rate, the differences on these points do not
exist between Christians of different sects, but between sincere
Christians of all sects, and those who are little better than mere
Christians in name. We all hold that natural faults are not therefore
excusable, but are earnestly to be struggled against; that pride and
sensuality, are among the worst sins; that self-denial, humility,
devotion, and charity, are amongst the highest virtues. We all believe
that our first great duty is to love God; our second, to love our
neighbour.

Now, considering that on these great points all Christians are
agreed, while they differ on most of them from all who are not
Christians, does it seem unreasonable that persons so united in the
main principles of man's life, in the objects of their religious
affections, and of their hopes for eternity, should be contented to live
with one another as members of the same religious society.

National Apostasy, a sermon delivered 14 July 1833 by John Keble.
Selections.

Thoughts on the Ministerial Commission (1833), by John Henry
Newman. Tract No. 1 in *Tracts for the Times*.

The Anglo-Catholic revival, which Newman dated from Keble's
sermon on *National Apostasy*, had, and continues to have, an
enormous impact on the Anglican Church. Because it began and
flourished for a time in the university, the revival is called the Oxford
Movement; it is also called the Tractarian Movement because its
leaders published their views in a series of pamphlets, the *Tracts for
the Times*, between 1833 and 1840. By calling attention to the Catholic
tradition and spiritual foundation of the Church, the Tractarians
helped to bring about a spiritual regeneration within the Church of
England, and helped to raise permanently the level of dignity, order
and beauty in public worship. The Movement was, in part, a reaction
to the dry rationalism and utilitarianism of the eighteenth-century
Church, and in this it parallels the Wesleyan revival. In part, as well,
the Oxford Movement was a response to the preceived crisis in the
constitutional relationship between the Church and the state in the
late 1820s and early 1830s. Keble's sermon on *National Apostasy*
and Newman's first tract were written in general response to the
repeal of the Test and Corporation Acts, to Catholic Emancipation,
and to the Reform Act of 1832 which many conservatives feared
would open Parliament to increased democratic pressure from
dissenters, Catholics, Jews and Godless radicals. Newman's tract and
Keble's sermon were immediately inspired by the Whig government's
proposal to reform radically the established Church of Ireland, a
protestant episcopal church whose endowments seemed, to some,
greater than its needs.

In both the sermon and the tract the characteristic view of the
Church taken by the Oxford Movement is clearly announced. The
Church is considered a divine institution whose authority is rooted
in the commission of Christ to His apostles. Thus the authority of
the Church is seen as entirely independent of the state. The priests
of the Church are seen as the successors of the apostles, deriving
their privileged status through episcopal ordination.

While the immediate occasion for its emergence was political,
Tractarianism itself was not a political movement. Its emphasis was
essentially religious, and it served to promote piety and personal
spirituality far more than political action.

John Keble (1792-1866), along with John Henry Newman and
Richard Hurrell Froude, was one of the founders of the Oxford
Movement. He was a poet of some distinction; his long meditative

poem, *The Christian Year* (1827) was one of the most successful pieces of religious poetry written in the nineteenth century. After a distinguished career at Oxford where he was a fellow of Oriel College from 1811 and Professor of Poetry (1831-1841), Keble lived a quiet life as vicar of a country parish, Hursley in Hampshire.

John Henry Newman (1801-1890), one of the eminent Victorians, was a great man in the history of English religion and literature. He was the leading figure in the Oxford Movement until he converted to Roman Catholicism in 1845. Thereafter he had a prominent career as a Catholic priest. He was created cardinal in 1879. His *Apologia Pro Vita Sua* (1864), in which he recounts his role in the Oxford Movement and his conversion to Rome, remains one of the classics of English literature.

NATIONAL APOSTASY
1 SAMUEL xii. 23

As for me, God forbid that I should sin against the Lord in ceasing to pray for you; but I will teach you the good and the right way.

On public occasions, such as the present, the minds of Christians naturally revert to that portion of Holy Scripture, which exhibits to us the will of the Sovereign of the world in more immediate relation to the civil and national conduct of mankind. We naturally turn to the Old Testament, when public duties, public errors, and public dangers, are in question. And what in such cases is natural and obvious, is sure to be more or less right and reasonable. Unquestionably it is a mistaken theology, which would debar Christian nations and statesmen from the instruction afforded by the Jewish Scriptures, under a notion that the circumstances of that people were altogether peculiar and unique, and therefore irrelevant to every other case. True, there is hazard of misapplication, as there is whenever men teach by example. There is peculiar hazard, from the sacredness and delicacy of the subject; since dealing with things supernatural and miraculous as if they were ordinary human precedents, would be not only unwise, but profane. But these hazards are more than counterbalanced by the absolute certainty, peculiar to this history, that what is there commended was right, and what is there blamed, wrong. And they would be effectually obviated, if men would be careful to keep in view this caution: — suggested every where, if I mistake not, by the manner in which the Old Testament is quoted in the New: — that, as regards reward and punishment, God dealt formerly with the Jewish people in a manner analogous to that in which He deals now, not so much with the Christian nations, as with the souls of individual Christians.

* * * * * * * * *

What are the symptoms, by which one may judge most fairly, whether or no a nation, as such, is becoming alienated from God and Christ?

And what are the particular duties of sincere Christians, whose lot is cast by Divine Providence in a time of such dire calamity?

The conduct of Jews, in asking for a king may furnish an ample illustration of the first point: the behaviour of Samuel, then and afterwards, supplies as perfect a pattern of the second, as can well be expected from human nature.

I. The case is at least possible, of a nation, having for centuries acknowledged, as an essential part of its theory of government, that, as a Christian nation, she is also a part of Christ's Church, and bound, in all her legislation and policy, by the fundamental rules of that Church — the case is, I say, conceivable, of a government and people, so constituted, deliberately throwing off the restraint, which in many respects such a principle would impose on them, nay, disavowing the principle itself; and that, on the plea, that other states, as flourishing or more so in regard of wealth or dominion, do well enough without it. Is not this desiring, like the Jews, to have an earthly king over them, when the Lord their God is their King? Is it not saying in other words, "We will be as the heathen, the families of the countries," the aliens to the Church of our Redeemer?

To such a change, whenever it takes place, the immediate impulse will probably be given by some pretence of danger from without, — such as, at the time now spoken of, was furnished to the Israelites by an incursion of the children of Ammon; or by some wrong or grievance in the executive government, such as the malversation of Samuel's sons, to whom he had deputed his judicial functions. Pretences will never be hard to find; but, in reality, the movement will always be traceable to the same decay or want of faith, the same deficiency in Christian resignation and thankfulness which leads so many, as individuals, to disdain and forfeit the blessings of the Gospel. Men not impressed with religious principle attribute their ill success in life, — the hard times they have to struggle with, — to any thing rather than their own ill-desert: and the institutions of the country, ecclesiastical and civil, are always at hand to bear the blame of whatever seems to be going amiss. Thus, the discontent in Samuel's time, which led the Israelites to demand a change of constitution, was discerned by the Unerring Eye, though perhaps little suspected by themselves, to be no better than a fresh development of the same restless, godless spirit, which had led them so often into idolatry. "They have not rejected thee, but they have rejected Me, that I should not reign over them. According to all the works, which they have done since the day that I brought them up out of Egypt even unto this day, wherewith they have forsaken Me, and served other gods, so do they also unto thee."

The charge might perhaps surprise many of them, just as, in other times and countries, the impatient patrons of innovation are surprised, at finding themselves rebuked on religious grounds. Perhaps the Jews pleaded the express countenance, which the words of their Law, in one place, seemed, by anticipation, to lend to the measure they were urging. And so, in modern times, when liberties are to be taken, and the intrusive passions of men to be indulged, precedent and permission, or what sounds like them, may be easily found and quoted for every thing. But Samuel, in God's name, silenced all this, giving them to understand, that in His sight the whole was a question of motive and purpose, not of ostensible and colourable argument; — in His sight, I say, to Whom we, as well as they, are nationally responsible for much more than the soundness of our deductions as matter of disputation, or of law; we are responsible for the meaning and temper in which we deal with His Holy Church, established among us for the salvation of our souls.

These, which have been hitherto mentioned as omens and tokens of an Apostate Mind in a nation, have been suggested by the portion itself of sacred history, to which I have ventured to direct your attention. There are one or two more, which the nature of the subject, and the palpable tendency of things around us, will not allow to be passed over.

One of the most alarming, as a symptom, is the growing indifference, in which men indulge themselves, to other men's religious sentiments. Under the guise of charity and toleration we are come almost to this pass; that no difference, in matters of faith, is to disqualify for our approbation and confidence, whether in public or domestic life. Can we conceal it from ourselves, that every year the practice is becoming more common, of trusting men unreservedly in the most delicate and important matters, without one serious inquiry, whether they do not hold principles which make it impossible for them to be loyal to their Creator, Redeemer, and Sanctifier? Are not offices conferred, partnerships formed, intimacies courted, — nay, (what is almost too painful to think of,) do not parents commit their children to be educated, do they not encourage them to intermarry, in houses, on which Apostolical Authority would rather teach them to set a mark, as unfit to be entered by a faithful servant of Christ?

I do not now speak of public measures only or chiefly; many things of that kind may be thought, whether wisely or no, to become from time to time necessary, which are in reality as little desired by those who lend them a seeming concurrence, as they are, in themselves, undesireable. But I speak of the spirit which leads men to exult in every step of that kind; to congratulate one another on the supposed decay of what they call an exclusive system.

* * * * * * * * *

II. But here arises the other question, on which it was proposed to say a few words; and with a view to which, indeed, the whole subject must be considered, if it is to lead to any practical improvement. What should be the tenor of their conduct, who find themselves cast on such times of decay and danger? How may a man best reconcile his allegiance to God and his Church with his duty to his country, that country, which now, by the supposition, is fast becoming hostile to the Church, and cannot therefore long be the friend of God?

Now in proportion as any one sees reason to fear that such is, or soon may be, the case in his own land, just so far may he see reason to be thankful, especially if he be called to any national trust, for such a complete pattern of his duty, as he may find in the conduct of Samuel. That combination of sweetness with firmness, of consideration with energy, which constitutes the temper of a perfect public man, was never perhaps so beautifully exemplified.

****

After all, the surest way to uphold or restore our endangered Church, will be for each of her anxious children, in his own place and station, to resign himself more thoroughly to his God and Saviour in those duties, public and private, which are not immediately affected by the emergencies of the moment: the daily and hourly duties, I mean, of piety, purity, charity, justice. It will be a consolation understood by every thoughtful Churchman, that let his occupation be, apparently, never so remote from such great interests, it is in his power, by doing all as a Christian, to credit and advance the cause he has most at heart; and what is more, to draw down God's blessing upon it. This ought to be felt, for example, as one motive more to exact punctuality in those duties, personal and official, which the return of an Assize week offers to our practice; one reason more for veracity in witnesses, fairness in pleaders, strict impartiality, self-command, and patience, in those on who decisions depend; and for an awful sense of God's presence in all. An Apostle once did not disdain to urge good conduct upon his proselytes of lowest condition, upon the ground, that, so doing, they would adorn and recommend the doctrine of God our Saviour. Surely, then, it will be no unworthy principle, if any man be more circumspect in his behaviour, more watchful and fearful of himself, more earnest in his petitions for spiritual aid, from a dread of disparaging the holy name of the English Church, in the hour of peril, by his own personal fault or negligence.

As to those who, either by station or temper, feel themselves most deelply interested, they cannot be too careful in reminding themselves, that one chief danger, in times of change and excitement, arises from their tendency to engross the whole mind. Public concerns, ecclesiastical or civil, will prove indeed ruinous to those, who permit them to occupy all their care and thoughts, neglecting or undervaluing ordinary duties, more especially those of a devotional kind.

These cautions being duly observed, I do not see how any person can devote himself too entirely to the cause of the Apostolical Church in these realms. There may be, as far as he knows, but a very few to sympathise with him. He may have to wait long, and very likely pass out of this world before he see any abatement in the triumph of disorder and irreligion. But, if he be consistent, he possesses, to the utmost, the personal consolations of a good Christian: and as a true Churchman, he has that encouragement, which no other cause in the world can impart in the same degree: — he is calmly, soberly, demonstrably, SURE, that, sooner of later, HIS WILL BE THE WINNING SIDE, and that the victory will be complete, universal, eternal.

TRACTS FOR THE TIMES

THOUGHTS on THE MINISTERIAL COMMISSION

Respectfuly Addressed to the Clergy

I am but one of yourselves, — a Presbyter; and therefore I conceal my name, lest I should take too much on myself by speaking in my own person. Yet speak I must; for the times are very evil, yet no one speaks against them.

Is not this so? Do not we "look one upon another," yet perform nothing? Do we not all confess the peril into which the Church is come, yet sit still each in his own retirement, as if mountains and seas cut off brother from brother? Therefore suffer me, while I try to draw you forth from those pleasant retreats, which it has been our blessedness hitherto to enjoy, to contemplate the condition and prospects of our Holy Mother in a practical way; so that one and all may unlearn that idle habit, which has grown upon us, of owning the state of things to be bad, yet doing nothing to remedy it.

Consider a moment. Is it fair, is it dutiful, to suffer our Bishops to stand the brunt of the battle without doing our part to support them? Upon them comes "the care of all the Churches." This cannot be helped; indeed it is their glory. Not one of us would wish in the least to deprive them of the duties, the toils, the responsibilities of their high Office. And, black event as it would be, for the country, yet, (as far as they are concerned,) we could not wish them a more blessed termination of their course, than the spoiling of their goods, and martyrdom.

To them then we willingly and affectionately relinquish their high privileges and honours; we encroach not upon the rights of the SUCCESSORS OF THE APOSTLES: we touch not their sword and crosier. Yet surely we may be their shield-bearers in the battle without offence; and by our voice and deeds be to them what Luke and Timothy were to St. Paul.

Now then let me come at once to the subject which leads me to address you. Should the Government and country so far forget their GOD as to cast off the Church, to deprive it of its temporal honours and substance, *on what* will you rest the claim of respect and attention which you make upon your flocks? Hitherto you have been upheld by your birth, your education, your wealth, your connexions; should these secular advantages cease, on what must CHRIST'S Ministers depend? Is not this a serious practical question? We know how miserable is the state of religious bodies not supported by the State. Look at the Dissenters on all sides of you, and you will see at once that their Ministers, depending simply upon the people, become the *creatures* of the people. Are you content that this should be your case? Alas! Can a greater evil befall Christians, than for their teachers to be guided by them, instead of guiding? How can we "hold fast the form of sound words," and "keep that which is committed to our trust," if our influence is to depend simply on our popularity? Is it not our very office to *oppose* the world? can we then allow ourselves to *court* it? to preach smooth things and prophesy deceits? to make the way of life easy to the rich and indolent, and to bribe the humbler classes by excitements and strong intoxicating doctrine? Surely it must not be so; — and the question recurs, on *what* are we to rest our authority, when the State deserts us?

Christ has not left His Church without claim of its own upon the attention of men. Surely not. Hard Master He cannot be, to bid us oppose the world, yet give us no credentials for so doing. There are some who rest their divine mission on their own unsupported assertion; others, who rest it upon their popularity; others, on their sucess; and others, who rest it upon their temporal distinctions.This last case has, perhaps, been too much our own; I fear we have neglected the real ground on which our authority is built, — OUR APOSTOLICAL DESCENT.

We have been born, not of blood, nor of the will of the flesh, nor of the will of man, but of God. The Lord JESUS CHRIST gave His Spirit to His Apostles; they in turn laid their hands on those who should succeed them; and these again on others; and so the sacred gift has been handed down to our present Bishops, who have appointed us as their assistants, and in some sense representatives.

Now every one of us believes this. I know that some will at first deny they do; still they do believe it. Only it is not sufficiently practically impressed on their minds. They *do* believe it; for it is the doctrine of the Ordination Service, which they have recognised as truth in the most solemn season of their lives. In order, then, not to prove, but to remind and impress, I entreat your attention to the words used when you were made Ministers of CHRIST'S Church.

The office of Deacon was thus committed unto you: "Take thou authority to execute the office of a Deacon in the Church of God committed unto thee: In the name,"&c.

And the priesthood thus:

"Receive the HOLY GHOST, for the office and work of a Priest, in the Church of God, now committed unto thee by the imposition of our hands. Whose sins thou dost forgive, they are forgiven; and whose sins thou dost retain, they are retained. And be thou a faithful dispenser of the Word of GOD, and of His Holy Sacraments: In the name," &c.

These, I say, were words spoken to us, and received by us, when we were brought nearer to GOD than at any other time of our lives. I know the grace of ordination is contained in the laying on of hands, not it any form of words; — yet in our own case, (as has ever been usual in the Church,) words of blessing have accompanied the act. Thus we have confessed before GOD our belief, that through the Bishop who ordained us we received the HOLY GHOST, the power to bind and to loose, to administer the Sacraments, and to preach. Now *how* is he able to give these great gifts? *Whence* is his right? Are these words idle, (which would be taking GOD'S name in vain,)or do they express merely a wish, (which surely is very far below their meaning,)or do they not rather indicate that the Speaker is conveying a gift? Surely they can mean nothing short of this. But whence, I ask, his right to do so? Has he any right, except as having received the power from those who consecrated him to be a Bishop? He could not give what he had never received. It is plain then that he but *transmits*; and that the Christian Ministry is a *succession*. And if we trace back the power of ordination from hand to hand, of course we shall come to the Apostles at last. We know we do, as a plain historical fact; and therefore all we, who have been ordained Clergy, in the very form of our ordination acknowledged the doctrine of the APOSTOLICAL SUCCESSION.

And for the same reason, we must necessarily consider none to be *really* ordained who have not *thus* been ordained. For if ordination is a divine ordinance, it must be necessary; and if it is not a divine ordinance, how dare we use it? Therefore all who use it, all of *us*, must consider it necessary. As well might we pretend the Sacraments are not necessary to Salvation, while we make use of the offices of the Liturgy; for when GOD appoints means of grace, they are *the* means.

I do not see how any one can escape from this plain view of the subject, except, (as I have already hinted,) by declaring, that the words do not mean all that they say. But only reflect what a most unseemly time for random words is that, in which Ministers are set apart for their office. Do we not adopt a Liturgy, in *order* to hinder inconsiderate idle language, and shall we, in the most sacred of all services, write down,subscribe, and use again and again forms of speech, which have not been weighed, and cannot be taken strictly?

Therefore, my dear Brethren, act up to your professions. Let it not be said that you have neglected a gift; for if you have the Spirit of the Apostles on you, surely this *is* a great gift. "Stir up the gift of GOD which is in you." Make much of it. Show your value of it. Keep it before your minds as an honourable badge, far higher than that secular respectability, or cultivation, or polish, or learning, or rank, which gives you a hearing with the many. Tell *them* of your gift. The times will soon drive you to do this, if you mean to be still any thing. But wait not for the times. Do not be compelled, by the world's forsaking you, to recur as if unwillingly to the high source of your authority. Speak out now before you are forced, both as glorying in your privilege, and to ensure your rightful honour from your people. A notion has gone abroad, that they have given and can take it away. They think it lies in the Church property, and they know that they have politically the power to confiscate that property. They have been deluded into a notion that present palpable usefulness, produceable results, acceptableness to your flocks, that these and such like are the tests of your office, as being ordained by them to take part in their Ministry.

But, if you will not adopt my view of the subject, which I offer to you, not doubtingly, yet (I hope) respectfully, at all events, CHOOSE YOUR SIDE. To remain neuter much longer will be itself to take a part. *Choose* your side; since side you shortly must, with one or other party, even though you do nothing. Fear to be of those, whose line is decided for them by chance circumstances, and who may perchance find themselves with the enemies of CHRIST, while they think but to remove themselves from worldly politics. Such abstinence is impossible in troublous times. HE THAT IS NOT WITH ME, IS AGAINST ME, AND HE THAT GATHERETH NOT WITH ME SCATTERETH ABROAD.

The State In Its Relations With The Church (2 vols., 4th ed., 1841), by W.E. Gladstone. Selections.

William Ewart Gladstone (1809-1898) was one of the great figures in Victorian politics. He was prime minister four times (1868-1874; 1880-1885; 1886; 1892-1894) and a member of parliament from 1832. From 1859 he was a member of the Liberal party, and each of his four governments was Liberal. In the earlier portion of his political career, however, he was a Tory, an admirer of Sir Robert Peel. From his childhood until his death, Gladstone was a deeply religious man with a strong personal commitment to the Church of England. He was reared in a devoutly Evangelical family, but at Oxford, where he was brilliantly successful as an undergraduate, he began to move towards the Anglo Catholicism of Edward Pusey, John Henry Newman and John Keble. Gladstone entered parliament intending to take as his principal political role the protection and advancement of the Church of England. His first book, *The State In Its Relations With The Church*, published in 1838, was a lengthy discussion of a theory of establishment which he never entirely abandoned. In his book, Gladstone emphasized the social role of the Church, the concomitant moral role of the State, and the importance of the establishment. While he later became a powerful proponent of concessions to protestant dissenters and Irish catholics, at this early point in his career Gladstone paid little attention to religious minorities. His book was in some ways surprisingly old fashioned. It drew heavily on the traditional ideas of establishment that had been developed in England from the end of the sixteenth century, when Richard Hooker published his *Laws of Ecclesiastical Polity* (1594). Gladstone's book, indeed, might be considered the last major work in that tradition in which the Church was seen as the moral tutor to the nation, the conscience of the state.

The other form of universal association, which I would couple with the family in respect of its extensive range of influences upon the characters and destinies of men, and of its high moral characteristics, is that of the nation or the state.

****

Some writers have indeed mischievously exaggerated the office of the state, and even under the Christian revelation have represented it either as the fountain of morality, or at least as supremely charged with the regulation of the large province of relative duty; that province so comprehensive and important that the Redeemer has honoured it more than once with a distinct enunciation of the law of moral obligation, although of course in the highest and ultimate sense it is comprehended within the yet larger commandment that enjoins upon us love to God as the universal principle of action. Thus they have superseded the paramount principle of our private responsibility. Even these exaggerations, however, may serve for a sign of that real grandeur and comprehensiveness in the functions of the state, upon which they have been built.

* * * * * * * *

Still more remarkable is the State in that which it symbolises. Independent of the will of man alike in the origin and in the exercise of its power, it both precedes and survives the individual; and it perpetually presents to him the images and associations of duty, of permanency, of power, of something greater and better than himself. It claims to represent to us, in that relative sense which alone the conditions of our earthly sojourning will admit, the principles of the Divine nature, inclusively of the power to assert them; to set before us, hand in hand with resistless power, unlimited duration, uniform right, unrespect of persons, the harmony of degree, the law of discipline and retribution. So far as respects the rewards and penalties of this world, it is the only general minister of Divine government, treading unequally in its steps, no more than a shadow of its glory, yet a shadow truly projected from the substance.

I have here, it is true, spoken of the State in its idea, rather than of a particular country or constitution. Yet these considerations have practical application to the historical forms of the State, which, in falling below its own standard, has merely resembled the individual; both are still bound to the pattern which they have never exemplified. However much particular actual States may fall short of the absolutely true, all that has ever been recorded of human society testifies to this at the least, — that in the State, considered both as an active and as a permissive power, we find the index both of the characters and of the conditions of the men within its pale; in its peculiar modifications we discover an effect, which is also the most fruitful of social causes, as estimated by its results upon individual being and well-being. Therefore it is that the civil history of man has

ever been, under the sanction of that example which is afforded by
the inspired writings of the Old Testament, the history of States, from
the time when first the family had expanded into this its larger
development.

It is very easily seen, upon a review of what has now been
propounded respecting the abstract idea of the State, that it fulfils
the same grand conditions which have been enumerated as descriptive
of the family. Like the family, it is of universal, or, at the least, of
general application. Its agency is permanent and annexed to the whole
of our life. It is natural, as opposed to what is spontaneous and
conventional. There is no limit of quantity to the obligations of the
individual towards it. It is moral, and not merely economical,
inasmuch as its laws and institutions, and the acts done under them,
are intimately connected with the formation of our moral habits, our
modes of thought, and the state of the affections, and inasmuch as
its influences pervade the whole scheme and system of our being,
mingling with the first instincts of boyhood; it may be, even attracting
the last lingering look of age on the threshold of its departure;
inasmuch as that which we are individually, we have come to be, in
a very considerable degree, through and by means of that which we
are nationally.

Of all the qualities that have here been predicated of the State,
there is but one on which I propose to dwell a little in detail; it is
this, that the State is properly and according to its nature, moral.
In a lower sense this is likely to be admitted on all hands. Every man
will perceive that there must be such things as public faith and justice,
or that political society would become an universal and intolerable
curse. But the morality of the State means much more than this. It
means that the general action of the State is under a moral law, is
conversant with moral subject-matter, is fruitful of moral influences.
Now, as regards the second of these in particular, the lawgiver,
proposing to himself as his idea the establishment of peace and order
and the security of property,immediately finds that he impinges upon
the subject-matter of moral science; that the same acts which are
favourable to politic designs are the acts that general morality
approves; that the same acts which are hostile to these designs are
the acts that general morality condemns, and that upon a scale which,

though there are partial exceptions, ordinarily very much conforms to his. Thus his law and his subject-matter are in relations of the closest proximity, although not identical, with those of moral science. He is to consider how far it may be in his power to encourage, and, on the other hand, by what means most effectually to repress, through prevention or punishment, classes of acts which he must estimate mainly by the standard of that science; although he may be compelled in certain particulars to qualify that criterion by regard to those lower purposes, without the regular attainment of which he cannot proceed to such as are higher. So that law travels over much of the same ground as ethics, and guides its course nearly according to their dictates.

If this be the case, then it is clear that (while we may reserve for another place the consideration of the preventive function of civil rule) the lawgiver has the same need to be ethically instructed as the individual man. The philosophy which holds that the latter will do best to choose his actions by a consideration of their general consequences, and which maintains that presumed advantage is to the human mind the best and most available criterion of right, may propound the same doctrine for the lawgiver. But most men revolt from this position, and maintain that the intrinsic nature of acts is in itself generally accessible to the understanding, as well as the calculation of their results; that it is usually the easier and safer rule; above all, that, according to the Divinely ordained canon, right is intended to be employed as the criterion of advantage, much more than advantage as the test of right. They, therefore, will also hold that the deviser of public law, because it deals (in great part) with subject-matter of right and wrong, and deals with it for the public well-being, must like the private person, read the guarantees of that well-being in the nature of the acts, and take this nature as a guide to their results, as well as measure his enactments by the results which he is thus enabled to estimate. The lawgiver then, that is, the legislative mind of the nation, must be ethically instructed; which implies that it must be enlightened by religion, upon the basis of which alone it is, that moral science can be effectually reared.

And, indeed the circumstance that the State has primary regard to certain external conditions of well-being, peace and order, so far from overthrowing, corroborates the necessity for guarding its acts by the forms of religion. Nothing could be more dangerous to moral health than the habits which would be engendered by continually estimating action, of which the subject-matter is admitted to be moral, with exclusive reference to these external results, and with no regard whatever therefore to their intrinsic nature. The practice proceeds upon a false opinion, that we are at liberty to deal with truth upon considerations of simple convenience, and its sure effect would be the general induration of the human heart. But it is a practice to which the State is continually tempted, for the very reason that the law of its being compels it to have some, and that no inconsiderable, regard to these exterior results; and thus it lies under a peculiar need or the influences of religion, in order that a healthy tone of disinterestedness and of public virtue may pervade its action, and hold up an example for private imitation rather than avoidance.

A reflective agency, then, conversant with moral subject-matter, involves of necessity a conscience, which is, *ex vi termini*, the regulator of moral offices.

In an earlier part of this chapter the case of the family has been alleged to be in the main analogous to that of the State. The application of the principle of collective religion is, in the smaller sphere, it has been admitted, more palpable and less disputed. But of the reality of the analogy between the two we may be persuaded, among other means, by this remakable circumstance: that the school of reasoners, which alone in this country has employed the methods of logic in its attacks upon the principle of national religion, and which, therefore, holds out to us the best promise of a certain self-consistency, has likewise proceeded to assail the principle of family religion, and to contend that it is a capital offence against the laws of truth to communicate any bias to the minds of the young, or to inculcate belief antecedently to comprehension. In this very sense, Mr. James Mill has written his essay on ' The Principles of Toleration.'

This idea of conscience in the State is supported, as I contend, by the impartial and weighty testimony of human language, which continually applies the phraseology of duty to its acts, and predicates of them all the moral qualities and their opposites. And I think every man must feel that injustice embodied in law, that bad faith in the inobservance of national engagements, imply something quite beyond the guilt of the individuals who may have been the instruments of the offence, although undoubtedly including it. Further, is it not true that the inward experience of conscientious men, who have been engaged in the discharge of public functions would yield us a similar witness? Such a man will surely feel, in entering even on the routine of his duties, that he has come under a new set of conditions of action, involving elements quite distinct from those merely personal; that he is impelled to do one act and to avoid another, upon reasons, justified indeed by reference to his own moral obligations as a private man, but felt to have infinitely greater force, and to assume a far higher form, than any such reference singly can supply. He will be sensible, that in yielding to any suggested temptation, in doing or procuring to be done any unjust action (as, for example, in using means to carry a partial and oppressive billl), he is dragging along with himself, not merely into dishonour but into guilt, not merely by reputation, but the positive, subjective, character of the State. He will feel that this great idea of State duty is as true and stringent as the kindred idea of individual duty, and is only capable of being explained away by sophistry of the same kind as that which, from the days of the Cyrenaics and Epicureans, with intervals, until now, has laboured to destroy the principle on which private rectitude depends, and to resolve it into a pure calculation of consequences: thus, as Coleridge remarks, making that which is the absolute, the one thing needful in every man alike, to depend upon the faculty which of all others is most unequally distributed among the human race.

I will propose another reason, which seems to me to prove with clearness that the responsibilities of the nation are not satisfied by the individual piety of its members. The national conscience, or, if this phrase be too alarming, that sense of duty which ought to regulate public acts, should be as far as possible formed upon a pure and comprehensive idea of right and wrong, and as little as possible coloured with idiosyncracy, or individual peculiarity. The statesman should feel that his office demands this larger rule of action, while his conscience must remind him of the difficulty of separating his own opinions, and even caprices, form those conditions of truth and justice which he is to apply to the national service. Even those who hold the loftiest doctrine of the rights of government will admit that it must commonly harmonise in its proceedings with the national character and will. The statesman, then, must resolve to lay aside in his public function a part of his individuality, and very commonly, in all matters that are not of conscience, must act more as impelled than as impelling, more upon the convictions of others than his own. Still the acts so done are acts which may be fraught with most serious, even with highly moral results. At least, they are acts which ought to be, like all others, commended to God. Yet these are acts done, so to speak, without an agent, unless the nation, the moral person of the State, be that agent. They are not the acts of the statesman in any sense, except that he is their instrument; he is, with respect to these, as the soldier in the ranks. He will shift the responsibility for them from himself in proportion as they are less the genuine offspring of his individual judgment; he will feel, and with a degee of justice, that morally, though not constitutionally, it rather lies elsewhere. But what is its true and proper seat? The persons, whose will he is anticipating, are busy each with his farm and his merchandise, with personal interests or duties. This responsibility, however, which has an aspect so indefinite while we look only at individual men, has, in fact, a legitimate subject, which can consistently and adequately refer all these acts to the Almighty Ruler. There are qualities in a combination which arise out of the union of its parts, and are not to be found in those parts when they have been separated and are singly examined. In the government and laws of a country we find not a mere aggregation of individual acts but a composite agency, the general result yielded by a multitude of efforts, each of which in part modifies, in part is absorbed amid the rest. This composite agency represents the personality of the nation; and, as a great distinct moral reality, demands a worship of its own, namely, the worship of the State, represented in its living and governing members, and therefore a public and joint worship.

To sum up then in a few words the result of these considerations, religion is applicable to the State, because it is the office of the State in its personality to evolve the social life of man, which social life is essentially moral in the ends it contemplates, in the subject-matter on which it feeds, and in the restraints and motives it requires; and which can only be effectually moral when it is religious. Or, religion is directly necessary to the right employment of the energies of the State as a State.

Chapter III

The New Industrial Economy

Introduction

The aristocracy and most men of influence in the Established Church distrusted and opposed the drift toward democracy in the first half of the nineteenth century. Because the aristocracy, and to a considerable extent the Church as well, depended upon agricultural rents as a principal source of income, they tended also to oppose those movements in the economy which threatened to undermine agrarian prosperity. But the aristocracy and the Church were not enemies of the Industrial Revolution. On the whole, they and the parliament which they controlled generally supported commercial values and movement towards modernization in the economy. That is why they were accused of abdicating their proper role as a governing class by men, such as the Luddites, who conceived their own well being as bound to a social order that was disappearing without influential defense.

That the governing classes generally accepted the new economic order is illustrated by their acceptance of political economy as a science which could help men towards a better understanding of social change. The mainstream of clergy, whose opinion on such matters was taken seriously in the early nineteenth century, supported the new economics in the belief that the economists were discovering the laws which God had ordained for the organization of society. Some clergymen, T.R. Malthus, for example, or Archbishop Sumner, themselves undertook serious and original work in economics. But most ministers of religion who wrote about economic questions wrote as popularizers of theories developed by Adam Smith, David Ricardo, and other leading secular economists.

The most important developments in popular theology at this time, moreover, helped to reinforce the thrust of political economy and to strengthen the support granted capitalism by the churches. The evangelical movement which was sweeping through Nonconformity and making great progress in the Church as well, provided a theological substructure well suited to support capitalist society. Evangelicalism, through its stress on individualism and the ability of each individual to achieve salvation outside the corporate society of the church, provided a religious parallel to the emphasis on untrammeled individual enterprise and the free market in labour which suffused the writing of the economists.

Confidence in political economy, opposition to monopoly and general suspicion of "state intervention", as the Victorians put it, were attitudes widely shared by Englishmen without necessary reference to political party or religious denomination. In the struggle for repeal of the Corn Laws, however, these attitudes came to seem peculiarly liberal and political economy itself was given politically partisan and religiously sectarian colouration.

The Corn Laws against which the free trade movement was directed were passed in 1815 to inhibit importation of foreign grown grain in order to maintain high prices for English producers who had enjoyed prosperity during the previous twenty years and more of war with France. Modified several times before they were repealed in 1846, the Corn Laws appeared to violate the principle of free competition stressed by the English economists. The Anti-Corn Law League was formed in Manchester in 1838 by merchants and manufacturers in the cotton industry who believed the tariffs on grain made it more difficult for them to market cotton abroad and also more difficult to maintain low wages. The League succeeded in giving this economic question the character of a moral crusade against taxing the bread of the poor. They were able to enlist the support of many Nonconformist ministers and journalists because the Church of England was traditionally identified with the landed interests, while Nonconformists believed that their own strength and their future lay with the industrial towns. Because so many Nonconformist chapels were controlled and financed by families whose money and place in society flowed from commercial and industrial firms, Nonconformists may have been even more enthusiastic than Churchmen in preaching the virtues that men of business most admire.

The League achieved an extraordinary amount of public notice with Richard Cobden and John Bright as their star speakers. Their success as political propagandists helped to dramatize, perhaps exaggerate, the confrontation between city and countryside, Liberals and Conservatives, Dissenters and Churchmen, which they saw as bound up in the debate over the Corn Laws. Those Liberal Nonconformists who thought that free trade in religion would follow naturally from free trade in grain, clearly believed that repeal of the Corn Laws in 1846 marked the beginning of a new era of social justice. For the remainder of the century, free trade served as a sacred liberal principle and the struggle itself attained the status of a legend which inspired many liberal pressure groups. "Monopoly" became a term of abuse invoked against traditional institutions, and the free trade analogy was argued in support of the liberal position on a variety of questions, including temperance, education, and disestablishment of the Church of England.

Guide To Further Reading

The relationships among English Protestantism, individualism and the commercial spirit are discussed in parts of Geoffrey Best, *Mid-Victorian Britain* (1971), W.L. Burn, *The Age of Equipoise* (1964) and Walter Houghton, *The Victorian Frame of Mind* (1957). Questions involving the interplay of social and economic status and religious behaviour are explored in A.D. Gilbert, *Religion and Society in Industrial England* (1976). W.G. Rimmer in the *Marshalls of Leeds, Flax-spinners* (1960) has produced an excellent portrait of a provincial industrial family concretely displaying these associations. Harold Perkin, *The Origins of Modern English Society, 1780-1880* (1969), is the most stimulating account of the changes in English society during the period of the Industrial Revolution.

Karl Polanyi's controversial and interpretative essay, *The Great Transformation* (1944), argues that the development of a free market in labour was the key to the economic and social changes which comprised the Industrial Revolution in England. S.E. Finer, in his study of *The Life and Times of Sir Edwin Chadwick* (1951), shows how a Benthamite social engineer attempted to build up a state bureaucracy in order to hasten the development of a society based on a free labour market.

The best history of the free trade movement, although it suffers from a narrow focus, is Norman McCord, *The Anti-Corn Law League* (1958). Donald Read, *Cobden and Bright* (1967) is a good comparative account of the two most powerful figures in the League, while his book on *The English Provinces* (1964) discusses the development of powerful centres of liberal public opinion in the new industrial towns. Rhodes Boyson illustrates the links between free trade and provincial Dissent in *The Ashworth Cotton Enterprise* (1970). Several liberal pressure groups, politically and culturally similar to the League, are studied in *Pressure From Without* (1974), edited by Patricia Hollis. Aspects of the free trade movement and its general impact on mid nineteeth-century society are treated in G.S.R. Kitson Clark's, *The Making of Victorian England* (1962).

Richard Soloway in *Prelates and People* (1969) traces the acceptance of modern commercialism and industrial capitalism by many Anglican bishops in the first half of the nineteenth century. Soloway also notes their increasing concern for the plight of the working classes. J.M. Goldstrom discusses "Richard Whately and Political Economy in School Books, 1833-1880", in *Irish Historical Studies* (1966-67). John Kent, in his article "The Victorian Resistance: Comments on Religious Life and Culture, 1840-1880", *Victorian Studies* (1968), argues, perhaps too strongly, that most Victorian Christian thinkers resisted the forces of modernization including industrial growth. Howard W. Fulweiler in "Tractarians and Philistines: The Tracts for the Times vs Middle-Class Values", *Historical Magazine of the Protestant Episcopal Church* (1962) illustrates the distaste of Tractarians for middle-class Protestant commercial attitudes.

Geoffry Best in *Shaftesbury* (1964) provides an excellent portrait of a leading lay crusader for factory reform. John C. Gill's *The Ten Hours Parson* (1959) traces the Reverend G.S. Bull's fight for the poor in industrial Yorkshire. J.M. Ludlow, F.D. Maurice and other early Christian Socialists are ably discussed by Torben Christensen in his *Origin and History of Christian Socialism* (1963).

The most interesting treatment of the religious aspects of the Chartist crisis is Eileen Yeo "Christianity in Chartist Struggle, 1838-1842", *Past and Present* (1981). The struggle of the churches to come to grips with this working class movement is also explored in the much older account by H.U. Faulkner, *Chartism and the Churches: A Study in Democracy* (1916).

Easy Lessons on Money Matters (1835), by Richard Whately. Selections.

Richard Whately (1787-1863) was Anglican Archbishop of Dublin from 1831, and Drummond Professor of Political Economy at Oxford, 1829-1831. A prolific writer, Whately published extensively on philosophy, economics, ecclesiastical politics and the leading social problems of his time. He was a liberal in both parliamentary and ecclesiastical politics, without sympathy for the Evangelicals and openly hostile to the Tractarians. Whately had a very active interest in the primary education of the mass of the people, and he wrote *Easy Lessons on Money Matters* for use in primary schools. Whately's *Money Matters* is representative of a considerable body of literature produced in the 1830s and 1840s and designed to present the principles of political economy to school children. Popularized political economy constituted an attempt to counter, through education, the radical social ideas developing among the trade unionists and Chartists and others among the working classes who were unhappy with their economic situation.

THE LESSON ON WAGES

Some labourers are paid higher than others. A carpenter earns more than a ploughman, and a watchmaker more than either; and yet, this is not from the one working harder than the other.

And it is the same with the labour of the mind, as with that of the body. A banker's clerk, who has to work hard at keeping accounts, is not paid so high as a lawyer or a physician.

You see, from this, that the rate of wages does not depend on the hardness of the labour, but on the *value* of the work done.

But on what does the value of the work depend?

The value of each kind of work is like the value of anything else; it is greater or less, according to the *limitation of its supply*; that is the *difficulty* of procuring it. If there were no more expense, time, and trouble, in obtaining a pound of gold than a pound of copper, then gold would be of no more value than copper.

But why should the supply of watchmakers and surgeons be more limited than that of carpenters and ploughmen? That is, why is it more difficult to make a man a watchmaker than a ploughman?

The chief reason is, that the education required costs a great deal more. A long time must be spent in learning the business of a watchmaker or a surgeon, before a man can acquire enough skill to practise. So that unless you have enough to support you all this time, and also, to pay your master for teaching you the art, you cannot become a watchmaker, or a surgeon. And no father would go to the expense of breeding up his son a surgeon or watchmaker, even though he could well afford it, if he did not expect him to earn more than a carpenter, whose education costs much less.

But sometimes a father is disappointed in his expectation. If the son should turn out stupid or idle, he would not acquire skill enough to maintain himself by his business; and then, the expense of his education would be lost. For it is not the expensive education of a surgeon that *causes* him to to paid more for setting a man's leg, than a carpenter is for mending the leg of a table; but the expensive education causes fewer people to become surgeons. It causes the supply of surgeons to be more *limited*; that is, confined to a few; and it is this limitation that is the cause of their being better paid.

So that, you see, the value of each kind of labour is higher or lower, like that of all other things, according as the supply is limited.

Natural genius will often have the same effect as the expensiveness of education, in causing one man to be better paid than another. For instance, one who has a natural genius for painting, may become a very fine painter, though his education may not have cost more than that of an ordinary painter; and he will then earn, perhaps, ten times as much, without working any harder at his pictures than the other. But the cause why a man of natural genius is higher paid for his work than another, is still the same. Men of genius are *scarce*; and their work, therefore, is of the more value, from their being more limited in supply.

Some kinds of labour, again, are higher paid, from the supply of them being limited by other causes, and not by the *cost* of learning them, or the natural *genius* they require. Any occupation that is *unhealthy*, or *dangerous*, or *disagreeable*, is paid the higher on that account; because people would not otherwise engage in it. There is this kind of limitation in the supply of house-painters, miners, gunpowder-makers, and several others.

Some people fancy that it is unjust, that one man should not earn as much as another who works no harder than himself. And there certainly would be a hardship, if one man could *force* another to work for him at whatever wages he chose to pay. This is the case with those slaves, who are forced to work, and are only supplied by their masters with food and other necessaries, like horses. So, also, it would be a hardship, if I were to force any one to sell me *any*thing, — whether his labour, or his cloth, or cattle, or corn, — at any price I might choose to fix. But there is no hardship in leaving all buyers and sellers free: the one, to ask whatever price he may think fit; the other, to offer what he thinks the article worth. A labourer is a seller of labour; his employer is a buyer of labour, and both ought to be left free.

If a man chooses to ask ever so high a price for his potatoes, or his cows, he is free to do so; but then it would be very hard that he should be allowed to force you to buy them at that price, whether you would or no. In the same manner, an ordinary labourer may *ask* as high wages as he likes; but it would be very hard to *oblige* others to employ him at that rate, whether they would or not. And so the labourer himself would think, it the same rule were applied to him: that is, if a tailor, and a carpenter, and a shoemaker, could oblige him to employ them, whether he wanted their articles or not, at whatever price they chose to fix.

In former times, laws used to be often made to fix the wages of labour. It was forbidden, under a penalty, that higher or lower wages should be asked or offered, for each kind of labour, than what the law fixed. But laws of this kind were found never to do any good. For when the rate fixed by law, for farm-labourers, for instance, happened to be *higher* than it was worth a farmer's while to give for *ordinary* labours, he turned off all his workmen, except a few of the *best* hands; and employed these on the best land only: so that less corn was raised, and many persons were out of work, who would have been glad to have it at a lower rate, rather than earn nothing. Then, again, when the fixed rate was *lower* than it would answer to a farmer to give the *best* workmen, some farmers would naturally try to get *these* into their service, by paying them, privately, at a higher rate. And this they could easily do (so as to escape the law,) by agreeing to supply them with corn at a reduced price; or in some such way; and then the other farmers were driven to do the same thing, that they might not lose all their best workmen. So that laws of this kind come to nothing.

The best way is, to leave all labourers and employers, as well as all other sellers and buyers, free, to ask and to offer what they think fit: and to make their own bargain together, if they can agree, or to break it off, if they cannot.

But labourers often suffer great hardships, from which they might save themselves by looking forward beyond the present day. They are apt to complain of others, when they ought rather to blame their own imprudence. If, when a man is earning a good wages, he spends all, as fast as he gets it, in thoughtless intemperance, instead of laying by something against hard times, he may afterwards have to suffer great want, when he is out of work, or when wages are lower. But then he must not blame others for this, but his own improvidence. So thought the Bees in the following fable.

"A Grasshopper, half starved with cold and hunger at the approach of winter, came to a well-stored beehive, and humbly begged the Bees to relieve his wants with a few drops of honey. One of the Bees asked him how he had spent his time all summer, and why he had not laid up a store of food, like them? 'Truly,' said he, I spent my time very merrily, in drinking, dancing, and singing, and never once thought of winter.' — 'Our plan is very different,' said the Bee; 'we work hard in the summer, to lay by a store of food against the season when we foresee we shall want it; but those who do nothing but drink, and dance, and sing, in the summer, must expect to starve in the winter.' "

****

THE BEE

"How doth the little busy bee
Improve each shining hour,
And gather honey all the day
From ev'ry op'ning flow'r.

How skilfully she builds her cell,
How neat she spreads the wax:
An labours hard to store it well
With the sweet food she makes.

In works of labour or of skill
I would be busy too,
For Satan finds some mischief still
For idle hands to do.
In books, or works, or healthful play,

Let my first years be past;
That I may give for every day
Some good account at last."

****

"Observe the Ant, for she instructs the Man,
And preaching labour, gathers all she can;
Then brings it to increase her heap at home,
Against the winter, which she knows will come,
And when that comes, she creeps abroad no more,
But lies at home, and feeds upon her store."

Report of the Conference of Ministers of All Denominations on
the Corn Laws held in Manchester, August 17, 18, 19, 20, 1841
(1841). Selections.

The Conference of Ministers was sponsored by the Anti Corn Law
League as part of their campaign to secure the abolition of tariffs
on imported grain. The Anti Corn Law League was organized in
Manchester in 1838 by cotton merchants and manufacturers. In their
struggle against the corn laws the leaders of the League associated
tariffs with aristocratic privilege and their own cause with popular
progress. To a considerable degree the League grounded its call for
free trade on moral arguments. This is one reason why the Conference
was useful to the League; another is the generally high status as
leaders of opinion which ministers enjoyed in the early nineteenth
century. Only two of the nearly seven hundred ministers at the
Conference were Anglican. This reflects the association of the
Anglican Church with the traditional rural forces in English society.
The nonconformists who dominated the Conference were identified
with the liberal, urban and progressive posture of the Anti Corn Law
League. F.A. Cox, president of the Conference on 19 August, was
a prominent Baptist minister from a London suburb. Benjamin
Parsons, who moved the second resolution that day, was a well known
Congregationalist.

———————•———————

THURSDAY, AUGUST 19.
From nine to half-past nine o'clock, the hall became gradually filled
with ministers; and, in the part alloted to the public, with ladies and
gentlemen.

   At twenty minutes before ten o'clock, the Rev. F.A. Cox, D. D.
LL.D., of Hackney, the president of the day, took the chair; and,
shortly afterwards, the proceedings commenced.

   The CHAIRMAN, in opening the proceedings, said, — Gentlemen
and Christian ministers, I am fully sensible of the distinguished
honour of being called upon to preside, on this occasion, over one of
the most remarkable, one of the most important, meetings that ever
was convened in our country — *remarkable* for the number of
ministers of religion assembled from every quarter — for the sublime
spirit of philanthropy which is displayed — and for the sobriety,
harmony, and dignity of its proceedings; (cheers;) *important* for the
moral influence it must exert through its individual members, who

will carry the sparks of holy fire from this central conference to their respective localities; important for the moral force with which it will push forward the settlement — the inevitable, (cheers,) the satisfactory, and the speedy settlement, of one of the greatest questions before the country; (cheers;) the practical exemplification it will afford in the eye of mankind of the might of principle — (cheers;) in its self-denying, self-sacrificing, and potent effects, when wrought into benevolent combination; and for the influence which it cannot fail of exerting over the present generation and far distant times. (Loud applause.) Gentlemen, if such an assembly as the present were to fail of producing great and good effects, then I should begin to despair of my country. (Hear, hear.) I should begin to think that despotism, in that case, was likely to restore the darkness of the middle ages — that society would be on the eve of retrocession, and the bright era of the nineteenth century likely to suffer an eclipse. (Cheers.) Depend upon it, that the period of a nation's decline must be at hand, whenever the popular voice cannot be heard in high places — whenever the public sentiment and private feeling are disregarded — whenever legislation *dares* to be indifferent to the woes and the wailings of a suffering people. (Applause.) It is fearfully ominous when the lightnings of a nation's indignation begin to glare, and when the thunders of a troubled, tormented, united, but afflicted people begin to roll. (Cheers,) We have been asked the reason why we are here. Why, gentlemen, we are here at the call of groaning humanity; at the voice of afflicted patriotism; at the cry of outraged religion. (Cheers.) The monster monopoly stalks through the length and breadth of the country — bleeding millions are trodden down by the giant foot, and are perishing by the iron gripe that digs into the very soul. (Hear, hear.) Abject misery, starvation, and vice, in every hideous form and multiform variety, compose the train; and shouts of agony and shrieks of woe attend the direful march over our desolated land. Gentlemen, why should we be here? I ask why should we *not* be here? (Loud cheers.) Is any priciple sacrificed? (No.) Is any duty neglected? (No.) Are the mere interests of a party, political or theological, subserved? (No.) Our *principle* is to love God supremely, and our neighbours as ourselves. Our *duty* is to do good, by whatever mode we can accomplish it. Our *party* is our country.

(Applause.) "I see," as Lord Fitzwilliam said, "my countrymen in distress, and my country in danger." (Cheers.) We are all sufficiently convinced of this, that misery exists. The cause of the misery it is important for us to ascertain, in order that we may, if possible, remove it. The fact is, that Providence gives the people bread, and monopoly gives the people a stone. (Hear, hear.) It is easy enough to sit in the aristocratic chair, or move heedlessly along the avenues of splendour, and indulge in the carpeted magnificence of superior life, and amidst luxury to forget poverty; but starvation prevails — there is the horror — it meets us on every side. (Hear, hear, hear.) This is a question, therefore of the utmost importance to our country. The details we have already heard tend to show, not only the danger of the state, when men are driven to desperation by their sufferings, but the true character of the present meeting. And what is it? It is a *shield* — a shield against the encroachment of aristocratic power on the one hand, and the faction and fury of mob-democracy on the other. (Cheers.) We say on the one hand, from this great meeting, that the aristocracy *shall not* oppress the people. (Prolonged cheering.) We say, on the other, that the people *shall not* rebel against the constituted authorities, nor act inconsistently, if we can prevent it, with the great principles of the constitution. (Renewed cheering.) We say to the aristocracy, "You must *come down* to a right state of feeling and sympathy with the condition of the poor of the land;" and we say to the poor, "You must *come up* to right sentiments — to just views — to a feeling of submission to the inscrutable dispensations of Providence — and cherish a serious, solemn, and pious concern to do your duty to God and to man." (Cheers.) At present, gentlemen, a great portion of the higher classes have stood aloof in their eminences — a great gulf has been between them and the people; but it is our object to link them together — to bind them by common sympathies. The predjudices and the passions of both have kept them asunder for ages. Wrong views, petty self-interests, and mutual aggression, have separated them. (Hear.) The laws that have been enacted have been inapplicable to the actual condition of society, hostile to the interests, and aggravating to the feelings of the people. (Here a loud and prolonged cheer announced the entrance of Earl Ducie.) Gentlemen, I hesitate not to say — and I say it with peculiar pleasure, now in the presence of one of our illustrious aristocracy, (cheers,) that it is most obvious a moral revolution is at hand. (Hear, hear.) A moral revolution has begun — we must direct it. (Cheers.) We are the intercessors for the people. We seek their confidence; and we will plead their cause. (Cheers.) Gentlemen, when hostile arms were opposed to our countrymen in former days, one of our most illustrious admirals — indeed, the most distinguished that ever belonged to this country — on the eve of battle said, "England expects every man to do his duty." I say, gentlemen, that England, and the poor of England especially, expect every minister to do his duty. (Cheers.) We must not blind our eyes to the fact, that we have a great contest to maintain; but, trusting in the power of the Most High, and the grace he shall dispense to us in answer to our fervent prayers and supplications, I look to the period as not far distant when we shall return from the contest crowned with victory, and having inscribed on our banners, "Monopoly has fallen," (applause,) "Britain has risen." (Cheers.) Britain's queen, not coming from afar, like the queen of Sheba, to contemplate the magnificence of Solomon, shall pass through the length and breadth of her own blessed isle, to contemplate a glory far greater than that of Solomon — the land filled with plenty — the cottages with joy, (cheers,) gratitude in every poor man's heart, (cheers,) and a *cheap loaf* in every poor man's hand. (Loud, continued cheers.) Gentlemen, permit me to state, that Mr. M'Kerrow will now introduce a certain deputation, who are about to present themselves to this meeting; after which, individuals wishing to address the meeting will be called on to hand up their names to the chairman. They will address the meeting in the order in which their names are handed in, and give such statements of facts as they may have collected in the different districts from which they have come. We shall hear them until those measures are ready for introduction, which the committee are preparing to bring under our notice. Memorials, petitions, and addresses are in the adjoining room; and gentlemen who are about to leave town before the conference concludes its sittings, are requested to sign them before their departure. I hope all will be over tomorrow, at the farthest. Those gentlemen who may leave town this evening are requested not to transfer to any one their cards of admission. It is hoped that the memorials, etc. alluded to will be read to the meeting this day. (Applause.)

* * * * * * * * *

The Rev. B. Parsons, of Ebley, near Stroudwater, Gloucestershire, moved the second resolution in a speech replete with facts and observation. He said — Before he left his congregation he called together some of their more experienced labourers and manufacturers, men working in the various departments of the cloth manufacture for the last forty years, and thus, from their lips, he obtained facts which he should state. The powerloom there had been generally used. He inquired about wages, and found them to be only half what they were years ago, before the corn laws came into operation. Wages had been reduced 50 per cent. Then, if they took into consideration that at the present time bread was more than double the price that it was in 1835 — if it is taken into consideration, that these men, many of them, have not 4s. a week to live upon, then according to a calculation placed before them yesterday, here was a reduction again upon the poor man's income of 50 per cent; so that the wages of these operatives are many times worse than they were a few years ago. (Hear, hear.) These were facts elicited from the people, and he wished those people were in this place that the conference might hear the moderation and the sense with which they gave their opinions when stating these facts, on the laws in question. Many industrious ablebodied men were walking about the streets in absolute idleness, and but for the children of some of them bringing home a few shillings a week, they would be in a state of starvation. Had not some of them been of frugal habits they must have been in their grave long ago. Some of them, he might say, were in the deepest distress, and these, too, were men who were tee-totallers, and therefore it could not be laid to their charge that improvidence had any thing to do with their condition. One of his congregation told him on Saturday evening last, that he went to visit three families in his neighbourhood, and found them without fire, and without bread, and without a penny to purchase even soap to clean themselves to go to the house of God on the Sunday. There were also in his neighbourhood a great number destitute of clothes. He had missed them at the Sabbeth morning worship; but they would wrap themselves up in the evening, and come out under cover of darkness when they were ashamed to come out in the daylight. Nor were these feelings to be despised. They were modest, though suffering people, and ought not to be less cared for than the bold pauper who cried out his wants to every one. (Hear, hear.) There were those who said that it was political to take part in a conference like this; but he told them that there was this difference between them and some others he could mention — that while they were what was called politically religious, those who came to the conference were only religiously political. (Cheers and laughter.) The day in which we lived was the day of scarecrows (Laughter.) He often smiled when he saw a scarecrow hanging in a field, to think that if the crows really know what it was, how little they would be frightened at it. (Laughter.) Well, their moral opponents wanted to frighten them from this conference, and they put up this scarecrow of "political ministers." (Laughter.) And the political ministers who had no souls had been frightened. (Laughter, and loud cheers.) Those who had souls, however, only smiled at the trick; and they would continue in the path of right and benevolence, be the consequences what they might. (Cheers.) Why, if it was political to take part in this question, it was political to eat; (Laughter.) and, then, if it was political to eat, perhaps it would be said that it was political to be hungry. (Great laughter.) He was looking, before he came in, at Johnson's Dictionary, for the meaning of the word, and he said that it was "prudent, artful, cunning." But he (Mr. Parsons) did not find that Johnson any where said that it was political to be hungry. (Laughter.) According to this notion, it was political to be humane. (Hear.) According to this doctrine, Christ was political when he fed the five thousand. (Cheers.) The following is the resolution: —

"That, in the judgment of this conference, the prevailing distress painfully tends to arrest the progress of education, to prevent the exercise of domestic and social affections, to induce reckless and immoral habits, to prevent attendance on religious worship, and to harden the heart against religious impressions."

The British Churches In Relation to the British People (1849), by
Edward Miall. Selections.

Edward Miall (1801-1881) (*q.v.*), journalist, Congregationalist minister
and radical politician was a leading spokesman of militant Dissent.
As editor of an influential newspaper, the *Nonconformist*, which he
founded in 1841, Miall played an important role in shaping
Nonconformist opinion on social and political questions. His book, *The
British Churches In Relation to the British People*, first appeared as
a series of articles in the *Nonconformist*.

About to enter upon an examination of the depraving influence of
the trade spirit upon religious life in the British Churches, I deem
it expedient, in order to prevent any misapprehension of my object,
to state, as clearly as I am able, the views I hold on the relationship
of trade to religion. Trade, then — employing the term in the broadest
sense of which it is susceptible — is not only not antagonistic in its
own nature to the main object of Christianity, but is eminently
auxiliary to it. It constitutes one of the principal schools, ordained
by the wisdom of Providence, for eliciting, training, exercising, and
maturing, the spiritual principle implanted in the heart of man by
the gospel. It opens to us one of the most accessible, and one of the
largest spheres in which to develop the new and heavenborn
character. Affectionate sympathy with truth, rightness, temperance,
benevolence, forbearance, meekness — in a word, with all the moral
attributes the love of which divine revelation is adapted to inspire
and nourish — may here find ample scope for exerting, proving, and
invigorating its strength. Trade multiplies our relations with our
fellow-men. It puts us into close contact with others, at innumerable
points. It furnishes us with a quick succession and an endless variety
of occasions for the action of the governing principle begotten in our
souls. It shifts our position with every passing hour, calling incessantly
for new manifestations of the spiritual life, correspondent with every
change. The scenes into which it introduces us, and in which it
requires us to take a part, rapidly vary, and call out, consequently,
a vigilance of spirit, a promptitude of judgment, and a repeated
reference to first principles, not needed elsewhere. It increases almost
indefinitely the number of ties by which man is linked to man, and

through which mind may transmit influence to mind. It creates countless grades of mutual dependence, and necessitates mutual trust in all its stages. It places our earthly lot so far within our own reach as to hold out an almost certain reward to diligence and frugality — and yet its issues are so far beyond our individual control, and its vicissitudes so incapable of being accurately foreseen, as to throw us most sensibly upon the overruling providence of God. It accustoms us to subordination — for "method," as is proverbial, "is the soul of business." It raises us to posts of responsibility and government — for few men can prosecute trade through a lifetime without occupying, occasionally or statedly, a position of authority. It offers all kinds of facilities for pushing the spirit of the gospel into notice — an intricate and all-prevading ramification of channels, along which to propel the waters of eternal life. It gives us, at one and the same time, scope, means, opportunities, and motives, for the lively exemplification of every characteristic of the spiritual man. Suppose trade to be annihilated, and every individual of our teeming population sustained by simple labour upon his own spot of land — and the monotony of social life, so far from favouring the development of Christian virtues, would necessarily impart to them very much of its own insipidity and listlessness. I can scarcely conceive of a high cultivation of spiritual life in this world — a rich growth of Christian character — an intelligent manhood of religion in the soul — save by means and arrangements partaking very closely of the nature of trade. If our present state of existence is emphatically one of education — if what we are to be hereafter, in mind, morals, and spirit, is to result from what we are now — I can imagine no arrangement of such exquisite contrivance for subjecting all our powers to salutary discipline, for breathing our young capabilities, and giving to right principles such meet and daily exercise, as that which passes under the generic name of trade. It is as much God's ordination as is the culture of the soil. It bears upon it the unequivocal marks of his wisdom and his benevolence. Intrinsically, and in its own nature, it is the handmaid of Christianity; a humble but useful helpmate to religion — smiled upon by it, and greatly promotive of it.

It will be manifest, however, even to momentary reflection, that trade can only be ancillary to spiritual life, when made subordinate to a dominant spiritual purpose. Its use to us, religiously, depends upon the end to which we are determined to turn it to account. It may be entered upon as a sphere for the discipline of character, or as one for the attainment of a much lower order of gratification. It is quite possible to traverse it — in company, too, with moral principles of a high grade — without the remotest moral intention. It displays numberless attractions to men, viewed simply in their relation to the present life. It is occupation — and that alone is desirable to active and energetic spirits. The variety of it is pleasing. The excitement it quickens soon becomes grateful — in many cases, necessary. The facilities it furnishes for the indulgence of social tendencies are alluring. It stimulates intelligence — gives scope for the exercise of ingenuity, contrivance, forethought, calculation. It is an excellent stage for the observation of human nature. To many it is a pastime of the graver sort. To most it is a necessity, between which and ruin there is no other alternative. It is the condition exacted form the large proportion of our fellow countrymen for their livelihood — it is the only means to a numerous class of compassing the gratification of their passions and their tastes. Trade, resorted to for any of these purposes exclusively, is an impediment to spiritual life. Whether the end be bare subsistence, decent comfort, extravagant display, pleasurable excitement, or the love of money, there is the same absence of Christian morality from it. The object aimed at falls short of spiritual good — is acquisition, not development — the gain of somewhat external to us, not the ripening of somewhat inherent in us — and, inasmuch as the means to that object are in no sense religious, all activity, all self-sacrifice, all expenditure of our powers, in that direction, must be set down, in relation to the divine life, as constituting so much dead loss. And this is what I mean by the trade spirit. The phrase, in the sense I attach to it, does not necessarily imply a reigning desire of wealth, a hard-hearted, mean-spirited, all-grasping cupidity, although it comprehends them. But under this term I wish to expose and condemn, as fatally suppressive of religious vitality, the disposition to pursue trade with an exclusive, or even a predominant view to the worldly advantage to be got by it — making it its own end, or at least proposing in it something distinct and apart from, and infinitely inferior to, the nourishment of our sympathies with God and his government. I believe this to be the greatest and most pernicious practical error of the present day. Partly from misapprehension, partly from habit, and partly from motives which conscience must condemn, the sphere of trade is frequented by Christian men, as one in which they are to serve themselves mainly, and their Divine Master incidentally only, and by the way. This is supposed to be their own ground, on which, if the character exemplified must be in some measure accordant with their spiritual profession, the end pursued is chiefly their own temporal good. They seem to have no notion that business is allotted to them as one of the means of grace, and one that might be rendered most efficient. At least, they do not resort to it as such. They speak of it sometimes as a hindrance, sometimes as a snare — often as a trying necessity — occasonally as an instrument of gratification — never, hardly, as a school for the education of their spiritual nature. They can understand communion with God in direct religious exercises, in the sanctuary, in the outspread works of his hands — but not in trade. They go to the house of God to seek him there — to their factories, counting-houses, and shops, they repair for no such purpose. In this direction, few, indeed, look for him — some, it is to be feared, do not even take him there. Much of what they know of him they forget within these precincts of secular engagement — to learn more of him in such places, they do not expect. Their Christianity is rather of the nature of a branch of occupation, than a principle of life and action. They may be honest — they may be diligent — they may be truthful — they may be frugal — they may economize their time — but their purpose in business is distinct from their purpose in the place of worship. Hence the double pursuit is sometimes bemoaned as if antagonistic; whereas the only thing wanting in order to render their trade a means to their religion, is their own determination to make it so. Business as well as nature yields fruits after the kind of seed we sow. The results we reap will correspond with the objects we desire. Things are secular or spiritual as we make them such. The difference originates in our own intention.

Religious life in this country is peculiarly liable to the unfriendly action upon it of the trade spirit. Without imputing to British people generally a more selfish or sordid spirit than may be found elsewhere, there can be no doubt that devotion to the pursuits of trade is our national characteristic. Gain, in one shape or another is "the great goddess" most assiduously worshipped in these realms. Business is everything with us — the power to which all others are secondary. The phenomenon may, perhaps, be fairly accounted for. Something may be set down to the score of race — something to climate — something to geographical position. Our political history may have done much to mould our character into the form it has taken — possibly our religious faith may have exerted some influence upon it. But the intensity of the trade spririt has, I think, been much increased by an artificial pressure upon its energies — and, just as population in the presence of poverty multiplies in a higher ratio than in the enjoyment of ease and abundance, so, I apprehend, restrictions of one sort and another upon our industrial commercial energies, have forced them to re-act with unnatural vigour. For many years a monopoly of food — to this day an enormous weight of taxation, and a population expanding so rapidly as to fell the terrible inconveniences resulting to them from the law of primogeniture and entail — the land, as it were, too strait for its inhabitants, and every profession, every trade, every industrial pursuit overcrowded with hands — the sharpest competition, consequently, in every branch of employment, and the absolute necessity, in order to achieve moderate success, of great diligence, promptitude, and, in some cases, pushing — the increased value, in such a struggle for a livelihood, of minutes and of pence, and the absorption of undivided attention by details, by means of which only can a man hope to realize a tolerable income — these are causes in daily operation well calculated to stimulate into excessive development the trade spirit. And, certainly, it has been raised to a pitch which it is scarcely possible to sustain without great moral deterioration. The national wear and tear under this high pressure system of business is frightful. As a people, it is clear we are living too fast. Ours is the rush of railway life. We see nothing by the way. Health, comfort, affections, intellectual culture, reflection, devotion, — they scarcely fill a more important space in our plans, scracely detain our attention longer, than the trees and churches, the homesteads and meadows, which seem to dance past us as we gaze through the window of a carriage in an "express train."

And we are always on the line. True! we stop at appointed stations — most of which, however, are simply for convenience, not for refreshment. We are whirled along from early youth in most cases to the hour of death, with no other pause or break than the weariness of exhausted nature absolutely requires. The march of trade is like the irresistible career of a locomotive — and even they who most delight in rapid movement are compelled to ask themselves, at times, "Can such speed as this be safe?"

It must in fairness be admitted, I think, that the religious life involved in this incessant whirl and scramble, has done something to check the progression of the evil. I am far from believing that Christian principle has exerted no retarding effect upon it, or that, had it been entirely wanting or inoperative, the mischief would not have grown to still more appalling proportions. Much as the gentleness, the truthfulness, the righteousness, and the high spirituality of the gospel may be ignored within the trade sphere — often as they may be repudiated as having no authority there, and as being out of place, there can hardly be a question, that even within the ungenial precincts of trade, they have made their civilizing and modifying influence felt. The maxims of the counting-house, and the habits of the shop, would be found, upon close examination, to have been partially improved, at least by the influence of revealed truth, sometimes directly, more frequently by reflex operation, brought to bear upon the customary manifestations of the trade spirit. Whither we might have been dragged in this direction but for the moderating power of Christianity it is vain to conjecture — but, in justice to the gospel, and even to our imperfect exemplifications of it, we are bound, I think, to admit that religion has not been without beneficent results even here — and its conservative tendencies have done not a little to prevent the machinery of trade from acquiring a velocity which must in the end have been fatal to the preservation of social order, and, to a great extent, of individual morality.

****

Speaking generally, the toil of workpeople in this country, both in manufacturing and agricultural districts, is excessive, and is exacted from them, for the most part, precisely as if they were unconscious machines. The laws of political economy, equally unchangeable, at least under an exclusively competitive system, as the laws of nature, and equally incapable of violation with impunity, have, unhappily, been permitted to operate beyond their own proper sphere, and to destroy amongst employers, to a great extent, the sense of responsibility, and the feelings of compassion. The relation to the employed is regarded very much as the relation of an engineer to the mechanism which works his will. Because there are some things affecting the remuneration of labour which no individual benevolence can control, the conclusion is too often adopted and acted upon, that there is nothing which it should attempt to meddle with. Because the rate of wages rises or falls with the demand or supply of labour in the market, it is too generally taken for granted, that the condition of his workpeople is in no respect a matter of special concern to their employer. And yet, surely, they who make their wealth by the unceasing industry of other men, might, without any transgression of economical laws recognise in those men the rights and claims of humanity. A soul duly impressed with a sense of reponsibility, might determine upon, a sympathizing heart might plan, a vigilant eye and a liberal hand might execute, not a few projects of systematic benevolence, calculated to smooth the rugged path of toil, to enlarge the circle of its enjoyments, to aid it in misfortune, to reward persevering merit, and to diffuse through the factory, the workshop, the mine, or the farm, a sentiment of oneness in nature between the master and the men. Christian principle has here a most favourable opportunity for displaying itself to advantage — and occasionally it does so. I have witnessed instances of it — heart-cheering instances — and hence I am not to be told that it is the mere dream of an amiable enthusiasm. I believe, too, such instances are fast multiplying — but as yet, it must, I fear, be conceded, they are comparatively rare. I am fully aware, indeed, that this habit of looking at workpeople through the medium simply of economical laws, and with a reference to commercial profit and loss, to the entire exclusion of Christian impulses, does not necessarily spring from or imply individual hard-heartedness. Experience, as well as charity, I think, teaches us to ascribe it chiefly to an entire misunderstanding by employers of the relation they sustain to those by whose toil they live, and of the duties which that relation imposes upon them. The trade spirit, rather than the genius of Christianity, kindles the light by which such subjects are studied. Accordingly, many men who take the lead in our religious institutions, who give princely sums to evangelical societies, and whose names are identified in their several localities with this or that denomination of Christians, are observed to be as ready as others to act almost exclusively upon the hard, inflexible, inexorable maxims of commercial economy. They pay their workmen the wages which happen to rule — they take on, and dismiss, hands as business requires — they do all that they engage to do as the employers of labour — but beyond this, they recongnise no responsibility. Nothing is set on foot tending to show that the heart of the master is interested in the condition of his workpeople. If his eye is upon them, it is not to mark their wants. If sickness overtakes them, his is not the hand foremost in extending relief. He knows nothing of their sorrows. He makes no attempts to win their confidence. They are not thought of as his brethren. The wear and tear which they sustain in his service elicit scarcely a single expression of sympathy.

* * * * * * * * *

Before I pass away from these illustrations of the power of the trade spirit over the British Churches, it affords me lively gratification to record some symptoms of decided improvement. I verily believe we have seen the worst of it, and that the tide is already on the turn. The force of religious principle operates, as yet, chiefly upon the relationship of masters to dependents, or, at least, it is in that quarter that it has made itself most conspicuous. There is a powerful reaction against the cruelty of Mammon worship, in the progress of which every feeling heart must take a lively interest. An abridgment of the hours of labour, the cheering success of the Early-closing Association, both in the metropolis and in the provinces, the determined hostility offered to Government against all increase of Sunday employment, the interest exhibited in the diffusion of education, the growing concern felt in the social condition of the masses, cheap baths and wash-houses, model lodging-houses, people's colleges, public libraries, and many projects and movements of a similar character, prove that Christianity, in one form and another, is fairly grappling with the trade spirit of the age, and give assurance that, when thoroughly roused, she will be competent to put it down.

Lord Ashley on the Ten Hours Bill. *Hansard's Parliamentary Debates,* 29 January 1846.

Lord Ashley (Anthony Ashley Cooper), seventh Earl of Shaftesbury from 1851 (1801-85), was one of the most famous nineteenth-century Evangelical philanthropists. Educated at Harrow and Oxford he entered Parliament in 1826 as Tory M.P. for Woodstock, a "pocket borough". Instead of using his considerable family connections to advance to high cabinet posts he devoted himself to various social causes including better treatment of the mentally ill, factory reform, education of the poor, housing, working women and child labour. He was the driving force behind the passage of the Factory Act of 1847 which limited the working hours of women and young persons to ten per day in textile factories. Ashley's commitment to social reform was inseparable from his evangelicalism. His larger social vision, however, his Toryism and his Anglicanism, made him a reformer whose particular objectives were often in conflict with those of the Anti Corn Law League and liberals generally. He was not a champion of the new industrial economy, but, rather, a friend of its victims.

Lord ASHLEY presented petitions from various places in Scotland in favour of a measure for limiting the hours of labour of young persons in factories to ten hours.

Lord ASHLEY, on rising to move for leave to bring in a bill to effect this object, said: Sir, it has so often been my duty to solicit the indulgence of the House, that I may seem to be acting merely in conformity with ceremonial when I prefer my earnest entreaty for its patient attention on this occasion; but at no time have I felt it more neccessary to make this request. I am about to revive the discussion of a proposition oftentimes propounded in this House, and as oftern rejected; one upon which I can offer no novel arguments.

****

Let me just point out to the House what are the general results of our factory regulations on the moral, physical, and financial condition of our operatives. I request the particular attention of the House to this subject, for I believe that the results in question offer a complete contradiction to all the opinions put forward in the year 1833, against the measure which I introduced at that period. Let the House see what were the predictions then made, as compared with the actual results of our legislation. I recollect that in the year 1833, when I first brought forward a Bill for a limitation of the hours of labour, there were four predictions, which were constantly ringing in our ears, which were repeated at every meeting, and were transcribed into every journal adverse to the measure. The first of these predictions was, that the great cotton trade would be destroyed by any limitation of the hours of labour; the second was, that the wages of the protected parties would be diminished; the third was, that the wages of children would be reduced to a mere fraction; and the fourth was, that the children would be dismissed, and that great suffering would universally ensue. Now, let the House permit me to state the actual results, as compared with those predictions. It has been said, in the first place, that our great cotton trade would be destroyed by any diminution of the hours of labour. In answer to that prediction, I need only refer to the state of our cotton trade in the years 1835 and 1836, and during the last three years; and it is not, I believe, necessary that I should dwell any further upon that part of the question. But it was predicted, in the second place, that the wages of the protected paties would be diminished. Now, there were two classes who were at that time protected by our legislation. There were, first, persons under the age of thirteen, who were called "children;" and there were, secondly, persons between the ages of thirteen and eighteen, who were called "young persons." The law enacted that young persons between the ages of thirteen and eighteen should not be exposed to a longer duration of work than twelve hours in the day. Now, before the year 1833, the average wages of those young persons were 5s. 4d. per week, while their average wages since that period have been 6s. 11d. per week; thus showing an increase of 30 per cent. in the average drawn from the four great towns of Manchester, Bolton, Preston, and Oldham. Let us next pass to the third prediction, that the wages of children would be reduced to a mere fraction. The average wages of children under thirteen years of age, for twelve or more than twelve hours labour a day, were, before 1833, 3s.1d. per week; and since 1833, their average wages for six hours labour a day have been 2s. 2d. per week. But although there has been in that case an apparent abatement of wages, the families have not, in many instances, suffered in consequence;

because, by that admirable provision restricting the labour of children to six hours a day, a great demand has been created for the labour of those children; and many families which could formerly obtain employment for one child only, now find employment for two children; so that the aggregate wages are at present frequently greater than the wages received under the old system. Let us look at the fourth prediction, which was that the children would be dismissed and that much physical suffering would ensue. It is very difficult to obtain statistical returns with respect to children under thirteen years of age employed before the year 1833. But this we know — that very few of them indeed were receiving any education at all; whereas, I have grounds for asserting that there are now 30,000 children, under thirteen years of age, working six hours a day, and receiving education during three hours, that education being in many instances of a very excellent description, and having been much improved during the last two or three years. I have also been informed that in the towns of Manchester, Bolton, and Preston, the increase of children at school has been, since the year 1833, as eight to one, exclusive of those who attend night schools; while the increase of those above thirteen years (who labour twelve hours a day), in places for teaching persons of that age, has been little or none. Let me add the remarks of the Committee of Operative Spinners upon that point — remarks which ought to carry with them great weight for they had been extremely opposed to the clause which limited the labour of children to half time. They have written to me as follows:—

"We also instituted an inquiry into the moral and physical condition of piecers and young persons now, as compared with the same class in 1833, and from every quarter we learn that it is much improved; and since the Bill of 1833, which restricted the hours of labour to eight in the day, and that of 1844 to six in the day, with enactments for education, their physical and moral condition has been improved to such an extent that they do not appear to be the same race of beings. We have recently conversed with a large number of the operatives, and those men especially who have devoted a large portion of their time and much of their means to the promotion of this question, and they all declare that the benefits which have arisen to themselves and their children are more than sufficient to repay them for their time and sacrifices, and that sooner than go back to their old system they would part with the last shilling they have in the world in defence of the restrictive system of factory labour."

I have felt great satisfaction in reading that statement, for it not only justifies my past conduct, but gives me great assurance of future success in my efforts upon this subject. I hope I am not assuming too much for our efforts, when I ascribe to them the collateral advantage of the half-holiday system for warehousemen in Manchester, and other great towns, at one time so energetically opposed, but now as warmly approved by the employers. I have reason to know that the system has been attended with the most beneficial results; and I believe that the hon. Member for Durham will bear me out in that statement. Among all the alterations that have been effected since the year 1833, I am sorry to perceive that nothing has been done for the benefit of young persons between the ages of thirteen and eighteen. Those young persons are exposed under the existing law to twelve hours' actual labour per day; now a very large portion of them are females, and I think I may appeal to the House to say, whether it is not cruel to take a young female on the very day on which she has passed the age of thirteen, at the most tender period of her life, and to demand of her precisely the same work in duration, and frequently the same in intensity, which is demanded from ripe and vigorous manhood? Observe the results to which this practice must lead. I believe every one will admit that it is a matter of vital importance to the peace and welfare of society, and to the comfort and well-being of the working classes, that females should be brought up with such a knowledge of domestic arts and household concerns as may enable them efficiently to discharge the various duties of wives and mothers. but how can it be possible that young women, whose labour has been so heavy and so prolonged, that they are in many cases unable to cook their own suppers, or even to eat the suppers prepared for them — how is it possible that they should learn the details of domestic life which constitute the comfort of the working man's home, and contribute so powerfully to the morality of the rising generation, because women must have and ought to have, almost undivided influence on children during the earliest and most impressible years of their existence? I am not expressing my own opinions merely upon that point, because the comissioners appointed in the year 1840 to inquire into the employment of young persons, went so far as to state, that it was the universal opinion of clergymen, medical men, teachers, and others that the condition of the women was one great and universally prevailing cause of the distress among the working classes.

****

Sir, it would really be well, for all parties, both master and operative, if this long-agitated question could be finally set at rest. If you will not concede the whole that we require, concede at first some part of it, and let the success or the failure of the experiments determine the further progress or revocation of the measure. Nothing, you may be assured, will be easier than to repeal such a law should its results prove injurious; the operatives will, themselves, be the first to cry out if their condition be seriously affected; should the results be beneficial, we shall trust to your willingness to accomplish our desires, and give us the remainder of our present prayer. We are ready, at any rate, to try that issue. But without some such arrangement as this, the manufacturing population will never desist from their efforts for redress; vain is the hope to weary them out by perpetual refusals; they gather resolution under defeats; and at no period have they been more unshaken and courageous than in this present hour, in which I am urging, for the tenth time, I believe, their just and reasonable demands. You cannot wonder at their perseverance, it is natural and praiseworthy; they feel the pressure of intolerable and all-absorbing toil, they perceive the success of experiments towards the alleviation of it in their own department of industry; they perceive too the contemporaneous efforts, arising in no small degree out of their own, to obtain the half-holiday system and the early closing of shops, both of which, whenever practicable, have proved highly beneficial. Their growing intelligence shows to them the moral and physical advantages of abridged labour; and their claims, when stated in this House, always meet with respect, and sometimes with considerable support. Sir, in stating these claims, I have abstained from a repetition of evidence adduced, at various times, to exhibit the amount of moral and physical suffering endured by these young persons. This has been a disadvantage to my argument; but I was fearful of wearying the House. I have abstained also from repeating the several calculations made by experienced operatives themselves, on which we maintained that either there would be no abatement of wages, or that, if there were any, they would be enabled, under a reduced period of labour, to establish such economies as would more than compensate for a diminished income. Be this as it may, I do say on their behalf, that they are fully prepared — and I did not, when I proposed the question to them, hear a dissentient voice — to submit to any contingency, in return for this concession to their prayers. Sir, we have reason to thank this House, that its successive interpositions in behalf of the factory population have produced most beneficial results, and specially by its enactments which enjoin that certain hours in every day should be set apart for the education of the younger workers; but the education of a people requires something more than this one provision: you must give them time, not only for the acquisition of the necessary elements, but time to retain and practise them. You give to the children, by your present system, a certain amount of literary teaching until the age of 13; they are then, at that period, when the acquisition and experience of whatever is practical would begin, advanced to the full extent of labour, and debarred by their unceasing occupation from the attainment of knowledge, useful — we may say indispensable — to their welfare in after life. This is especially true of the females, who form so large a proportion of the manufacturing population. Their accomplishments, though few and simple, yet unspeakably important to society at large, must be learned in the daily detail of household affairs. They are unsexed in nature and habits by such constant abstraction from domestic duties — duties which they alone can perform — and the community suffers in their toilsome devotion to employments which demand the powers and habits of men. It can find no compensating circumstances in any system which hinders the peace, the comforts, or the honours of the working man's home; but these things will rise or fall with the character and condition of the females; and all statesmen of every age, and all the maxim mongers have never surpassed the concentrated wisdom of Madam Campan, who, in answer to a question of the Emperor Napoleon, "What shall I do for the benefit of France?" replied without hesitation, "Give us, Sire, a generation of mothers."

* * * * * * * *

Sir, we must not shut out of our view the wide surface of society to be affected by our decision. It is the concern of many thousands.

This single class has been selected out of many to bear the forefront of the battle; but the vote of this evening will affect them all alike, for it may fairly be taken as a representative of the whole; it will be a fatal night whenever you decide adversely, for you will have closed all hopes of moral, and even of secular improvement to multitudes of the young and helpless. And will not this tend to widen the interval — already a deep and yawning gulf — that separates the rich from the poorer sort? The rise of the more affluent classes is very observable; numberless luxuries of mind and sense, hitherto attainable by none but the wealthy, are brought within the reach of much smaller people — they are elevated proportionally in the scale of society. The overtoiled operatives, both as children and as adults, are alone excluded from the common advantage; a few, it is true, of special genius, may triumph over every opposing obstacle; but the mass are abandoned to a state of things in which moral and intellectual culture, forethought and economy, and the resources of independent action, are far beyond their means, and not even in their contemplation. This, surely, is an unsound and fearful position; the contrast is seen, felt, and resented; it revives and exasperates the ancient feud between the House of Want and the House of Have; and property and station become odious, because they seem founded on acquirements from which multitudes are excluded by the prevailing system. Sir, I cannot fail to perceive that to weary the House with repetitions of these things would be useless, and, therefore, disrespectful. I will persist, nevertheless, to anticipate success, though I must, perhaps remember that the array of capitalists, backed by the weight of the Ministry, will present an obstacle almost insuperable by persons of far greater power and station than myself. By my course in the last few years, I have accumulated such an amount of public and official odium and distrust, that I cannot but feel I am addressing many whose minds are already averted from the proposition. Should I be defeated, I shall wait for fairer times, and more propitious hearts, conscientiously resolved never to abate one iota of my principles; and fully convinced that if this now mighty nation be destined to sustain its independence, and glory, and power, the counsels of thinking and unselfish men, for the social and religious improvement of all classes of the realm, must eventually and abundantly prosper.

Politics For The People (May-July, 1848), edited by F.D. Maurice
and J.M. Ludlow. Selections.

Politics For the People (1848) was the first organ of Christian
Socialism, a movement founded in 1848 by Maurice and Ludlow and
Charles Kingsley. The Christian Socialists criticized capitalist society
for its emphasis on individualism and competition. They stressed the
value of co-operation and the preeminence of the community. The
movement, which flourished for a little less than ten years, constituted
the most comprehensive Christian critique of industrial society in the
period before the 1880s.

F.D. Maurice (1805-1872) was an eminent Anglican theologian and
a leader of the Broad Church party. He wished the Church of England
to become sufficiently flexible in its theology so that it might
comprehend the various protestant denominations and become the
Church of the entire community.

J.M. Ludlow (1827-1911), lawyer and devout laymen, was educated
in France and familiar with French socialist theories. The plight of
the London poor led him into association with Maurice and Kingsley.
He vigorously promoted co-operative schemes among working men.

MAY 6, 1848

Prospectus.

It is proposed in this Paper to consider the questions which are most
occupying our countrymen at the present moment, such as the
Extension of the Suffrage; the relation of the Capitalist to the
Labourer; what a Government can or cannot do, to find work or pay
for the Poor. By *considering* these questions, we mean that it is not
our purpose to put forth ready-made theories upon them, or vehement
opinions upon one side or the other. We think that whatever a great
number of our countrymen wish for, deserves earnest reflection. It
should be studied in the light of present experience and past history.
There is leisure for deliberation now, — a year hence there may not be.

To speak of these questions calmly is a duty; to speak of them
coldly is a sin; for they cannot be separated from the condition of
men who are suffering intensely. If we do not sympathize with their
miseries we are not fit to discuss the remedies which they propose
themselves, or which others have proposed for them. That sympathy
we desire to cultivate in ourselves and in our countrymen. It will be
strongest when it is least maudlin. The poor man wishes to be treated

as a brother, not to be praised as an angel. Those who flatter him do not love him.

Politics have been separated from household ties and affections — from art, and science, and literature. While they belong to parties, they have no connexion with what is human and universal; when they become POLITICS FOR THE PEOPLE, they are found to take in a very large field: whatever concerns man as a social being must be included in them.

Politics have been separated from Christianity; religious men have supposed that their only business was with the world to come; political men have declared that the present world is governed on entirely different principles from that. So long as politics are regarded as the conflicts between Whig, and Tory, and Radical; so long as Christianity is regarded as a means of securing selfish rewards, they will never be united.

But POLITICS FOR THE PEOPLE cannot be separated from Religion. They must start from Atheism, or from the acknowledgment that a Living and Righteous God is ruling in human society not less than in the natural world. Those who make that acknowledgment from their hearts will not proclaim it for the sake of bringing home the charge of infidelity to other men; but that they may apply the highest and severest test to their own thoughts, and words, and actions. The world is governed by God; this is the rich man's warning; this is the poor man's comfort; this is the real hope in the consideration of all questions, let them be as hard of solution as they may; this is the pledge the Liberty, Fraternity, Unity, under some conditions or other, are intended for every people under heaven.

WORKMEN OF ENGLAND,

We who have started this Paper are not idlers in the land, and we have no great sympathy with those that are. But we do not work with our hands; we are not suffering hardships like many of you. Therefore you may think that we shall not understand you. Possibly we shall not altogether at first, but you can help us. Many of you write clearly and nobly; you can tell us what you are thinking and wherein we have mistaken you.

Many people try to convince you that it is your interest not to injure the richer classes, and to convince you that it is their interest to redress your wrongs. We, who do not, properly speaking, belong to your body or theirs, shall not try to make out that our interests are in commmon with either. But we believe that we have a DUTY to both, and that you have a DUTY to you own class, to every other, to God. We believe that every true Englishman had rather a thousand times hear his sense of duty spoken to than his self-interest; if any are of a different mind we shall not humour them, for we will not degrade a man in order to get his good will.

We hope not to forget your different occupations; but we wish above all things to remember that you are MEN. To be husbands, fathers, brothers, dwellers on the English soil, children of God, is the inheritance of all classes. Whatever knowledge is fit for men, as men, is fit for you. You have hearts and heads which can take it in, and can give back more than they receive. You are in contact with the realities of life; you can help to make all our studies and thoughts more real.

FRATERNITY.

The three words which from the motto of the new French Republic are — FRATERNITY, LIBERTY, EQUALITY. We shall hope to speak of each in turn; we begin to-day with Fraternity. It is needful that we should speak of it at the beginning of our paper, for the first question which our readers have a right to ask is, On what grounds do you who address us, fraternize? How shall we know which of us you will acknowledge as part of your brotherhood, which of us you will disclaim?

The French spoke of Fraternity in their first revolution, and the word went to the heart of many brave men in England, Scotland, and Ireland. They were not quite unprepared for it. They had become weary of conventions in politics and literature. The American Republic had given a new direction to the thoughts of some. The Methodists had broken down a great many barriers; they had treated the colliers of Cornwall, and the thieves of Kingswood, as sharers in the same nature with themselves.

But in seeking to gain something new, our fathers found that they had parted with something that was old. In seeking to embrace the Universe, they had lost their English feelings and their domestic feelings; these they must recover. It seemed worth while to cast away all large dreams, that they might secure such precious realities. For some time, therefore, you might trace a strong reaction in England against the notion of universal brotherhood; we were to be very national; that we might be so, we must also give great heed to the boundaries and divisions of classes; we must define very accurately the opinions of the sect or party to which we attached ourselves. Literature took the same tone. We had our novels for the aristocracy, our novels for the middle class, our novels about low life, each affecting to give glimpses of what passed within a world quite unknown to those who lay beyond it. Religion justified the habit. The most exalted Christianity seemed to be that which could exclude most.

But this state of things could not last. It has been breaking up on all sides of us for a long time. People discovered that their wish to be national was not promoted by cutting up the nation into sections. Parties in the Houses of Parliament went to pieces with a great crash; they were soldered up for a time; we have seen how loose the workmanship was; they have split again, and everybody is anxiously inquiring where he is to stand — with whom he is to ally himself. The fashionable novels, and the whole tribe that belonged to them, vanished from the stage, not without some hissing and laughter; their place was taken by Mr. Dickens, as the head of a company, which, whatever may be its merits or faults, has been most earnest and pertinacious in asserting a common humanity with every dweller in St. Giles's. Every recent religious movement, whether in a Protestant or a Romish direction, or any other, has been for the purpose of putting an end to parties and asserting a more general fellowship.

And now the French say again that men are all meant to be brothers. We cannot disregard the words. They are mighty words. Do the French know what they signify? We cannot find that they do. We find that they are divided into republicans of yesterday, of to-day, or the morrow; that there are among them communists and socialists of all kinds, and anti-communists and anti-socialists. We find that Paris is ruled by opposing clubs; that the members of the Provisional Government are continually at war with each other. Is this Fraternity — is it anything like Fraternity?

But because they have not found the secret, is it impossible that we should? We profess that we have found it long ago. We pretend to think that an Everlasting Father has revealed Himself to men in an elder Brother, one with him and with us, who died for all. We may believe this to be true or false. We believe it to be true, therefore we can feel to each other as brothers; we can look upon all of you whom we address in this paper, nobles, shopkeepers, labourers, mechanics, beggars, aristocrats, democrats, people of every class and party, as brothers.

The workmen of England should especially consider this point. If a working age of the world is, as some say, beginning, this must be one of its chief differences from that which has preceded it. Men cannot be merely joined together in the support of certain plans, or in opposing them. They must learn to act and feel together as men; so they will be able fairly and hopefully to discuss a great number of questions which are of great importance to them. At present, members of the working class, like those of the other classes, are often unnaturally bound together, not in the pursuit of great ends, but of certain means which they suppose, on the authority of others, must lead to those ends. They are asked to swear to the five, or six, or twelve points of the Charter — to declare themselves for this or that theory of Government — for this or that arrangement of wages and profits. There is no fair discussion whether these schemes will lead to the great objects, bodily or intellectual, which the workmen ought to desire; there is no steady inquiry what these objects are. The Chartist, just like the Conservative, or Whig, or Radical, in the House of Commons, is told that he must "follow the leader" over hedge and ditch, through ploughed fields, and quagmires, into rivers, fordable or unfordable. He runs till he is tired, then the party takes some strange jump, and makes the leader follow them.

The consequence is the same in every case. In the Conservative party there are men of the noblest hearts, who fear God with no slavish fear, who love the land they dwell in and its history — who wish to maintain only that which they think to be needful for the poorest man as much as themselves — who would gladly give up anything that is dearest to them for his sake. And there are, in the same party, men who care for nothing but their ease and luxury, who mean by Conservatism the preservation of their self and their game

— who one hour will cant with the holy name of God to secure an election, and will use it (not more profanely) to curse their servants with, the next. There are Radicals who have the most intense and righteous abhorrence of whatever is corrupt and false, and wish it to be cast out of the land as well as of their own hearts, because it is hateful to man and to God; there are Radicals who wish only to get rid of what stands in the way of their own advancement, their own lusts, their own tyranny. There are Whigs who form a most admirable link to bind the Conservative and Radical together; to make them understand each other; and there are Whigs who avoid what is good in both, not having the sense and courage of either, looking upon the whole question of Government as one between families or clubs. So it is, we are convinced, with the Chartists. There are among them generous, noble-hearted men who wish injustice to none, but desire that all should have a free play for their minds and hearts, as well as enough to feed their bodies — men who would gladly die to get this good for the whole land, that it should be righteously governed; and there are those who think of nothing but getting power and money for themselves, and who, for the sake of these ends, besides trampling down laws, would run the risk of inflicting more tremendous injuries upon the working men of England than upon all other classes together.

Is it not time that the better men in all these parties should cast off alliances which are only delusions from beginning to end? They do not mean the same things as those with whom they are acting; they mean the most opposite things. What signifies it that they are agreed about certain measures, if they seek by these measures to produce the most different results? It is not the old case of two men going as far as Brentford together, though one of them knows that his fellow is determined upon reaching Hounslow; the good man wants to go just as far as the bad, but in another direction. Why then should not the men who are pursuing the same objects, try to understand one another, and bring in their different lights as to the ways of attaining them?

This is what we wish to aim at in our *Politics for the People*. We disavow at once any fraternization on the ground of coincidence in conclusions about certain measures. There may be those among us who think the Reform Bill went far enough, or too far; those who think the middle class as yet inadequately represented; those who think even the poorest ought to have a share in the government. There may be those who believe a Repeal of the Union would be fatal to Ireland, and those who think it is becoming necessary for both countries. There may be those who rejoice in the victories of Free Trade; those who look back with a lingering love on Protection; those who do not find in the formulas of either that which is adequate to our present necessities. There may be those who think that the present relations of Capital and Labour are not incompatible with the well-being of the poor, and those who seek for a quite new adjustment of them. There may be those who look to Government for the direction both of labour and education; those who think that it may profitably interfere with either — not with the other; those who believe that it can in no case meddle with the free action of individuals and voluntary societies, except to do hurt.

We do not exact uniformity on any points of this kind; we promise and desire a conflict of opinions. We are as liable as all other men to set up our different opinions, and make them objects of worship; we are in danger of separating from our dearest friends in consequence of disagreements, which we do not pretend to consider trifling or insignificant. But we believe we shall not make the danger greater by being aware of it, by calling to mind continually the grounds of sympathy which we have one with another, in spite of these diversities, by seeking to hold converse with our readers of all classes, as fellow-men and fellow-workmen, by labouring strenuously in God's strength, that we may realize the true Fraternity of which this age has dreamed, and without which we believe it cannot be satisfied.

****

EXTRA SUPPLEMENT FOR JULY, 1848.

THE GREAT PARTNERSHIP.

The word Society, in the languages from which it is derived, means the same thing as Partnership. And I really think that many misconceptions on the subject would be cleared away, if we could accustom ourselves to think of Society simply as the Great Partnership, either of one nation in itself, or of mankind at large, according as we look upon it from a special or a general point of view. One thing is clear, that the modern idea and word of "Socialism" could never have sprung up, but from the forgetfulness of this great fact of human partnership. Socialism is but the recoil of Individualism, of that splitting up of society under a thousand influences of sceptical and vicious selfishness in the last century, through which indeed nations seemed to have become mere aggregations of units, heaped together without cohesion, like the shingle on the sea-beach, instead of being built up into glorious palaces and temples of brotherhood and of worship. If men really felt themselves to be partners in the great business of life, they would not need to be reminded that they should be so. And thus the mere word of Socialism, — which means nothing of itself but the science of making men partners, the science of partnership, — conveys to us a great lesson and a great warning.

But the Socialists should not fancy, as they are too prone to do, that in the use of this word they are setting forth any new truth of their own discovery. That truth, such as it is, is a very old one; only it has lain slumbering more or less for centuries beneath the surface of our common speech. If they can show it to the world with more distinctness and energy than it has hitherto been exhibited, we at least shall be most grateful to them. We *do* need to be told anew, and unceasingly, that we are all partners; we *do* need to be made better partners than we are. Socialism as a science can but afford us the means of carrying out that partnership into new fields of material or intellectual exertion, of better husbanding the common stock, of more simply and successfully carrying on the common business, of assigning more judiciously to every partner such duties as he is best able to fulfil. But the germ of all these things lay in the simple word society, from the first hour when God put into some man's head to apply the same term to the common life of a whole nation, which had till then been confined to the fellowship of two or three traders. And from that hour to this, centuries and centuries before Robert Owen or Charles Fourier were born, all good men have been tending consciously or unconsciously, to the accoplishment of some or all of these ends, — to the making society a more thriving and a better partnership. True Socialism is thus not a new, but a very old thing, — and all the better for that.

A partnership always has an object in view; some benefit, to be common to all the members. That object, and not chance or fancy, is the sole foundation from which it springs; there can be no partners but for a purpose. And the purpose again can be but one of common benefit; — a benefit which can only be attained by joining the efforts of several in one. No man enters into a partnership, but for the sake of bettering himself, of adding in some shape or other to his wealth, or his influence, or his pleasure, or his sense of duty fulfilled; and no man remains in a partnership, but as a means of so bettering himself. And thus society must be felt to be a blessing, for men to enter into it, and for men to remain in it. It is not, as has been shown elsewhere in this paper, the giving up of a part of one's liberty as the price of certain advantges. For, indeed, Louis Blanc has added something to the truth of our conception of the word 'liberty,' when he has shown us that it includes the idea of power. It is increase of power to do that which man seeks to do, and to obtain that which he seeks to obtain; that is the real end of Society, as of every partnership. There may be fetters and burdens connected with the relation which were not felt before, and yet those fetters and burdens arise not out of the relation itself, but from a cause the very opposite to it, — from the spirit of individual selfishness jarring still against the higher spirit of fellowship and community of purpose. It is because the partners are not partners enough, — because they are not sufficiently impressed with the need of co-operation, not sufficiently willing to merge individual interests in the pursuit of the common object, that they quarrel and fall out with one another, and feel their union as a galling chain. The more harmoniously do they act together, the more will they feel their power, their true freedom increased and multiplied. Then, the confidence which they have in one another, allows each to devote himself the more entirely to his own branch of the business, to the purchaser or to the sales, to the books, or to the works.

And thus with society. So long as we look upon it only as a system of mutual checks and chains, hemming in on all sides I know not what so called natural rights (which if closely inquired into, would very likely be found nothing more than depraved and unatural rights,) still more when we openly rail at the tyranny of society, and speak of it as a mere mass of corruption and injustice, — we can never be really free within its bosom, we can never work successfully towards its ends. True, all the partners may not fill such places as they ought to fill, enjoy such share of the common profit as they ought to enjoy; the deed of settlement may contain useless and ill-devised clauses, which clog and hamper the partnership business instead of promoting its success. But still, it is a partnership; it is the union of men bent together for a common purpose, and whose true interest is not to quarrel and break up the concern, but to learn to manage it better, — nay to work each man the more wisely and zealously, the more the common business appears likely to lose by the folly or indolence of another partner, — though not without endeavouring by all possible means, by open reproof if necessary, to bring him round to a sense of his duty, nor without remembering that the party in fault may have to be turned out wholly, sooner than that the whole concern should go to ruin.

Let us all try to love the society in which we live, and we shall soon make it easy for us to live in. Let us learn to look not for difference, but for agreement, seeking to reconcile divisions and not to make them, and we shall at last understand and feel what a blessing and privilege it is to be members of the Great English Partnership, and we shall be able to exert the combined and harmonious efforts of that partnership to such great and good purposes as never nation achieved before.

* * * * * * * *

MORE LAST WORDS

Friends of all classes! Friends of the working class especially!

Before we part, there are one or two words which it is right, for our sakes and for yours, that we should speak.

Many people will say, 'These writers have failed because they set an unattainable object before them. They proposed to address the PEOPLE, and the people of England are split into classes and factions; to be heard by the one, you must slander the rest. They propose to write *Politics* for the People. Politics is the great subject of dissension among the people. What could they do? They were swimming against the tide; fighting, like Mrs. Partington with the Atlantic; of course they have been beaten.'

There are many who have strong interest in saying such words as these, and in believing them. It would be a comfort to party men, if they could persuade themselves that they were taking the only practical, rational course; a comfort to some whose consciences tell them they ought not to take that course, if they found themselves cut off by a stern necessity from any other. We also must be well disposed to acquiesce in this explanation of our disappointment. It would enable us to take our leave with an unblemished reputation. We did very well, were very clever, and so forth; the means were as good as possible, if the ends had been feasible.

But we cannot lay this flattering unction to our souls; or suffer any other persons to use it for theirs. It is not true that men must court parties if they wish to obtain a hearing. Parties are felt to be stale, obsolete, helpless; the men who belong to them are ashamed to confess it; those who have been the instruments of destroying them are denounced, but the denouncers cannot reconstruct them. It is not true that there is less hope of union upon the political ground than upon any other. The very word Polity implies union. It is felt to be contradictory when there is division. Recall men to the belief that they exist in a polity, and you make them, indeed, sensible of their strife. Accordingly, all the strongest impulses in our time are tending in this direction. The people's Charter is an assertion that Government cannot be carrried on for or by parties; all the various forms of Socialism declare that men, whatever ends they propose to themselves, must co-operate for these ends.

What we desired especially was, to meet these two great forms of thought as they are exhibited to us in our age; to investigate them; to study them in the light of history; to see what human sympathies are bound up with them; to consider what there is in them which makes them inconsistent and unreasonable; what there is in them which has a divine root and must live. Chartism and Socialism, we said to ourselves, may be as vulgar in their outward shapes as you please. But woe to our countrymen if they content themselves with laughing at their outward shapes, or with crushing them! The heart within must be studied; not merely anatomized, but seen living, beating, in its healthy and in its morbid conditions, else we shall not understand the real state of our own times, or be prepared for the future.

This task we have executed very imperfectly. We have grappled most with the first subject. Chartism has been considered under many of its aspects; considered from different points of view. For the more we reject party views, as such, the more we wish to profit by them. The Whig can tell us something which the Tory cannot tell; the Radical, things which are hidden from the Whig. Let each bring its own light to bear upon the great problem. Let them not think it a mean task to unfold the idea of Chartism, or in other words, to ask what is the root of *Government*; what principles must exist in it apart from what is accidental and artificial.

****

If we had really fulfilled our design, there would still have been enough mistakes in the way of handling our materials, arising from inexperience, to account for a more signal failure than ours, without resorting to any solution which would make the prospect hopeless for future adventurers. Still we should be merely affecting modesty and deceiving those adventurers if we did not tell them that when they have done their best — and that best infinitely better than ours — they must still arm themselves against an indifference and neglect which some earnest spirits find so much harder to bear than sharp persecutions. We are surely not sent into the world to get credit and reputation, but we speak such words as are given us to speak; to do such acts as are given us to do; not heeding much, nor expecting to know whether they have effected anything or nothing. Therefore, friends, be of good courage. Let not us have the burden of thinking that because we have been feebler than we ought, you have been dismayed. Whatever is true, must at last be mighty. The battle with principalities and powers is fought, for the most part by weak arms; which nevertheless, shall prevail. In that confidence, we wish you 'God speed.'

Chapter IV

The City: Prospects and Problems

Introduction

By mid-century England had become the most highly urbanized society in the world. The census of 1851 revealed that, for the first time, more people lived in cities and towns than in villages and the countryside. The urban experience, of course, was not new in the nineteenth century. London had for centuries been the cultural, commercial and political centre of English life and one of the world's largest cities. In the late eighteenth and early nineteenth centuries, however, there was enormous growth in London and a host of provincial towns as well. The population explosion and pressure from expanding industries contributed to the rapid development of new urban centres. In less than a generation some villages became great towns. Manchester, Leicester, Leeds and Birmingham are among the most notable examples of towns which quickly moved from provincial obscurity to rank among the largest cities in Europe.

Great hopes were initially entertained for the positive impact of the new urban culture. Advocates of commercial and industrial expansion, the sort of men to whom the free trade movement appealed, saw in the growing cities an emerging economic order that would benefit mankind. Dissenters and liberals who looked for social progress in an age of cities saw urbanization as a liberating force that would free Englishmen from the domineering squire and parson of the traditional countryside.

Accounts of urban poverty and the living conditions of the poor in cities had been published early in the century. From the early 1830s, such accounts appeared in increasing numbers in the reports of government inspectors, town missionaries, the statistical societies of London and Manchester, and in the novels, books and newspaper articles of social explorers. But these accounts drew little public outcry, and their impact on the social conscience is hard to measure.

Some ministers and some congregations developed admirable programs for social reclamation in the slums of Victorian cities. But for the most part the churches did not rise to the social challenge of the cities until late in the century. This apparent failure is partly due to the fact that many religious men, Churchmen and Nonconformists both, considered that the major problem of the poor in cities was their non-attendance at church or chapel. Perhaps more important was the view, remarkably widespread in the early and mid-Victorian periods, that the way to improve the condition of the poor was to teach the poor to improve themselves.

Guide to Further Reading

Still the best introduction to Victorian urban history, Asa Briggs, *Victorian Cities* (1964) includes excellent chapters on Birmingham and Manchester. *The Victorian City* (2 vols., 1973) is a massive collection of articles by forty contributors, edited by Michael Wolff and H.J. Dyos. *The Study of Urban History* (1968), edited by H.J. Dyos illustrates a variety of approaches to the history of towns and includes the well-known article by John Foster which prefigured his book, *Class Struggle and the Industrial Revolution: Early Industrial Capitalism in Three English Towns* (1974). A. Temple Patterson, *Radical Leicester* (1954) is a classic study of politics and society in which the important role of religion is given full treatment. P.T. Phillips, *The Sectarian Spirit* (1982) analyses the political and social roles of sectarian conflict in Victorian cotton towns. In *Engels, Manchester and the Working Class* (1974), Steven Marcus discusses contemporary observations of Manchester life in the two decades before the middle of the century. E.P. Hennock, in *Fit and Proper Persons* (1973), deals with Leeds and Birmingham, focussing on the civic renaissance in Birmingham in the sixties and seventies, and stressing the religious element in urban reform. The best modern discussions of the physical environment of the urban poor are "The Slums of Victorian London", *Victorian Studies* (1967), by H.J. Dyos, Anthony Wohl, *The Eternal Slum* (1977), and Anthony Wohl, *Endangered Lives: Public Health in Victorian Britain* (1983). R.J. Morris, *Cholera 1832* (1976) examines religious responses to the first great cholera epidemic of the nineteenth century.

Standish Meacham surveys urban religion in brief compass in "The Church in the Victorian City", *Victorian Studies* (1968). Hugh McLeod, *Class and Religion in the Late Victorian City* (1974), is a stimulating and meticulously researched investigation into the social aspects of religion in London at the turn of the century. For a fresh and critical discussion of the idea of secularization, see Jeffrey Cox, *The English Churches in a Secular Society: Lambeth, 1870-1930* (1982). *Religion and Voluntary Organizations in Crisis* (1976) by Stephen Yeo is an intellectually exciting exploration of how religion, organized recreation and industry fit into the autonomous culture of Victorian towns, and how that autonomous culture began to break up during the Edwardian period.

Three modern comments on the religious census of 1851 are K.S. Inglis "Patterns of Religious Worship in 1851", *Journal of Ecclesiastical History* (1960); W.S.F. Pickering, "The 1851 Religious Census: A Useless Experiment?", *British Journal of Sociology* (1967); and David M. Thompson, "The 1851 Religious Census: Problems and Possiblities", *Victorian Studies* (1968).

The Moral and Physical Condition of the Working Classes
Employed in the Cotton Manufacture in Manchester (1832), by
James Phillips Kay. Selections.

James Phillips Kay (1804-1877), who took the name Shuttleworth on
the occasion of his marriage in 1842, was a physician in Manchester
at the time of the cholera outbreak in 1832. *The Moral and Physical
Condition* ... is largely based on what he learned during that
epidemic. In the 1830s he strongly supported the parliamentary
reform campaign and the free trade movement.

The township of Manchester chiefly consists of dense masses of
houses, inhabited by the population engaged in the great
manufactories of the cotton trade. Some of the central divisions are
occupied by warehouses and shops and a few streets by the dwellings
of some of the more wealthy inhabitants; but the opulent merchants
chiefly reside in the country, and even the superior servants of their
establishments inhabit the suburban townships. Manchester, properly
so called, is chiefly inhabited by shopkeepers and the labouring classes.
Those districts where the poor dwell are of very recent origin. The
rapid growth of the cotton manufacture had attracted hither
operatives from every part of the kingdom, and Ireland has poured
forth the most destitute of her hordes to supply the constantly
increasing demand for labour. This immigration has been, in one
important respect, a serious evil. The Irish have taught the labouring
classes of this country a pernicious lesson. The system of cottier
farming, the demoralisation and barbarism of the people, and the
general use of the potato as the chief article of food, have encouraged
the growth of population in Ireland more rapidly than the *available*
means of subsistence have been increased. Debased alike by ignorance
and pauperism, they have discovered, with the savage, what is the
minimum of the means of life, upon which existence may be
prolonged. The paucity of the amount of means and comforts
necessary for the mere support of life, is not known by a more civilised
population, and this secret has been taught the labourers of this
country by the Irish. As competition and the restrictions and burdens
of trade diminished the profits of capital, and consequently reduced

the price of labour, the contagious example of ignorance and a barbarous disregard of forethought and economy, exhibited by the Irish, spread. The colonisation of savage tribes has ever been attended with effects on civilisation as fatal as those which have marked the progress of the sand flood over the fertile plains of Egypt. Instructed in the fatal secret of subsisting on what is barely necessary to life, — yielding partly to necessity, and partly to example, — the labouring classes have ceased to entertain a laudable pride in furnishing their houses, and in multiplying the decent comforts which minister to happiness. What is superfluous to the mere exigencies of nature is too often expended at the tavern; and for the provision of old age and infirmity, they too frequently trust either to charity, to the support of their children, or to the protection of the poor laws.

When this example is considered in connection with the unremitted labour of the whole population engaged in the various branches of the cotton manufacture, our wonder will be less excited by their fatal demoralisation. Prolonged and exhausting labour, continued from day to day, and from year to year, is not calculated to develop the intellectual or moral faculties of man. The dull routine of a ceaseless drudgery, in which the same mechanical process is incessantly repeated, resembles the torment of Sisyphus — the toil, like the rock, recoils perpetually on the wearied operative. The mind gathers neither stores nor strength from the constant extension and retraction of the same muscles. The intellect slumbers in supine inertness; but the grosser parts of our nature attain a rank development. To condemn man to such monotonous toil is, in some measure, to cultivate in him the habits of an animal. He becomes reckless. He disregards the distinguishing appetites and habits of his species. He neglects the comforts and delicacies of life. He lives in squalid wretchedness, on meagre food, and expends his superfluous gains in debauchery.

The population employed in the cotton factories rises at five o'clock in the morning, works in the mills from six till eight o'clock, and returns home for half an hour or forty minutes to breakfast. This meal generally consists of tea or coffee, with a little bread. Oatmeal porridge is sometimes, but of late rarely used, and chiefly by the men; but the stimulus of tea is preferred, and especially by the women.

The tea is almost always of a bad, and sometimes of deleterious quality; the infusion is weak, and little or no milk is added. The operatives return to the mills and workshops until twelve o'clock, when an hour is allowed for dinner. Amongst those who obtain the lower rates of wages this meal generally consists of boiled potatoes. The mess of potatoes is put into one large dish; melted lard and butter are poured upon them, and a few pieces of fried fat bacon are sometimes mingled with them, but seldom a little meat. Those who obtain better wages, or families whose aggregate income is larger, add a greater proportion of animal food to this meal, at least three times in the week; but the quantity consumed by the labouring population is not great. The family sits round the table, and each rapidly appropriates his portion on a plate, or they all plunge their spoons into the dish, and with an animal eagerness satisfy the cravings of their appetite. At the expiration of the hour, they are all again employed in the workshops or mills, where they continue until seven o'clock or a later hour, when they generally again indulge in the use of tea, often mingled with spirits accompanied by a little bread. Oatmeal or potatoes are however taken by some a second time in the evening.

The comparitively innutritious qualities of these articles of diet are most evident. We are, however, by no means prepared to say that an individual living in a healthy atmosphere, and engaged in active employment in the open air, would not be able to continue protracted and severe labour, without suffering, whilst nourished by this food. We should rather be disposed, on the contrary, to affirm, that any ill effects must necessarily be so much diminished, that, from the influence of habit, and the benefits derived from the constant inhalation of an uncontaminated atmosphere, during healthy exercise in agricultural pursuits, few if any evil results would ensue. But the population nourished on this aliment is crowded into one dense mass, in cottages separated by narrow, unpaved, and almost pestilential streets, in an atmosphere loaded with the smoke and exhalations of a large manufacturing city. The operatives are congregated in rooms and workshops during twelve hours in the day, in an enervating, heated atmosphere, which is frequently loaded with dust or filaments of cotton, or impure from constant respiration, or from other causes.

They are engaged in an employment which absorbs their attention, and unremittingly employs their physical energies. They are drudges who watch the movements, and assist the operations, of a mighty material force, which toils with an energy ever unconscious of fatigue. The persevering labour of the operative must rival the mathematical precision, the incessant motion, and the exhaustless power of the machine.

Hence, besides the negative results — the abstraction of moral and intellectual stimuli — the absence of variety — banishment from the grateful air and the cheering influences of light, the physical energies are impaired by toil, and imperfect nutrition. The artisan too seldom possesses sufficient moral dignity or intellectual or organic strength to resist the seductions of appetite. His wife and children, subjected to the same process, have little power to cheer his remaining moments of leisure. Domestic economy is neglected, domestic comforts are too frequently unknown. A meal of coarse food is hastily prepared, and devoured with precipitation. Home has little other relation to him than that of shelter — few pleasures are there — it chiefly presents to him a scene of physical exhaustion, from which he is glad to escape. His house is ill furnished, uncleanly, often ill ventilated — perhaps damp; his food, from want of forethought and domestic economy, is meagre and innutritious; he generally becomes debilitated and hypochondriacal, and, unless supported by principle, falls the victim of dissipation. In all these respects, it is grateful to add, that those among the operatives of the mills, who are employed *in the process of spinning*, and especially of fine spinning (who receive a high rate of wages and who are elevated on account of their skill), are more attentive to their domestic arrangements, have better furnished houses, are consequently more regular in their habits, and more observant of their duties than those engaged in other branches of the manufacture.

The other classes of artisans of whom we have spoken, are frequently subject to a disease, in which the sensibility of the stomach and bowels is morbidly excited; the alvine secretions are deranged, and the appetite impaired. Whilst this state continues, the patient loses flesh, his features are sharpened, the skin becomes sallow, or of the yellow hue which is observed in those who have suffered from the influence of tropical climates. The strength fails, the capacities of physical enjoyment are destroyed, and the paroxysms of corporeal suffering are aggravated by deep mental depression. We cannot wonder that the wretched victim of this disease, invited by those haunts of misery and crime the gin shop and the tavern, as he passes to his daily labour, should endeavour to cheat his suffering of a few moments, by the false excitement procured by ardent spirits; or that the exhausted artisan, driven by ennui and discomfort from his squalid home, should strive, in the delirious dreams of a continued debauch, to forget the remembrance of his reckless improvidence, of the destitution, hunger, and uninterrupted toil, which threaten to destroy the remaining energies of his enfeebled constitution.

The example which the Irish have exhibited of barbarous habits and savage want of economy, united with the necessarily debasing consequences of uninterrupted toil, have lowered the state of the people.

****

One other characteristic of the social body, in its present constitution, appears to us too remarkable and important to be entirely overlooked.

Religion is the most distinguished and ennobling feature of civil communities. Natural attributes of the human mind appear to ensure the culture of some form of worship; and as society rises through its successive stages, these forms are progressively developed, from the grossest observances of superstition, until the truths and dictates of revelation assert their rightful supremacy.

The absence of religious feeling, the neglect of all religious ordinances, afford substantive evidence of so great a moral degradation of the community, as to ensure a concomitant civic debasement. The social body cannot be constructed like a machine, on abstract principles which merely include physical motions, and their numerical results in the production of wealth. The mutual relation of men is not merely dynamical, nor can the composition of their forces be subjected to a purely mathematical calculation. Political economy, though its object be to ascertain the means of increasing the wealth of nations, cannot accomplish its design, without at the same time regarding their happiness, and as its largest ingredient the cultivation of religion and morality.

With unfeigned regret, we are therefore constrained to add, that the standard of morality is exceedingly debased, and that religious observances are neglected amongst the operative population of Manchester. The bonds of domestic sympathy are too generally relaxed; and as a consequence, the filial and paternal duties are uncultivated. The artisan has not time to cherish these feelings, by the familiar and grateful arts which are their constant food, and without which nourishment they perish. An apathy benumbs his spirit. Too frequently the father, enjoying perfect health and with ample opportunities of employment, is supported in idleness on the earnings of his oppressed children; and on the other hand, when age and decreptitude cripple the energies of the parents, their adult children abandon them to the scanty maintenance derived from parochial relief.

That religious observances are exceedingly neglected, we have had constant opportunities of ascertaining, in the performance of our duty as Physician to the Ardwick and Ancoats Dispensary, which frequently conducted us to the houses of the poor on Sunday. With rare exceptions, the adults of the vast population of 84,147 contained in Districts Nos. 1, 2, 3, 4, spend Sunday either in supine sloth, in sensuality, or in listless inactivity. A certain portion only of the labouring classes enjoys even healthful recreation on that day, and a very small number frequent the places of worship.

The fruits of external prosperity may speedily be blighted by the absence of internal virtue. With pure religion and undefiled, flourish frugality, forethought, and industry — the social charities which are the links of kindred, neighbours, and societies — and the amenities of life, which banish the jealous suspicion with which one order regards another. In vain may the intellect of man be tortured to devise expedients by which the supply of the necessaries of life may undergo an increase, equivalent to that of population, if the moral check be overthrown. Crime, diseases, pestilence, intestine discord, famine, or foreign war — those agencies which repress the rank overgrowth of a meagre and reckless race — will, by a natural law, desolate a people devoid of prudence and principle, whose numbers constantly press on the limits of the means of subsistence. We therefore regard with alarm the state of those vast masses of our operative population which are acted upon by all other incentives, rather than those of virtue; and are visited by the emissaries of every faction, rather than by the ministers of an enobling faith.

The present means or methods of religious instruction are, in the circumstances in which our large towns are placed, most evidently inadequate to their end.The labours of some few devoted men — of whom the world is not worthy — in the houses of the poor, are utterly insufficient to produce a deep and permanent moral impression on the people. Some of our laws, as now administered, encourage indigence and vice, and hence arises an increased necessity for the daily exertions of the teachers of religion, to stem that flood of prevailing immorality which threatens to overthrow the best means that political sagacity can divise for the elevation of the people.

The exertions of Dr. Tuckerman, of Boston, in establishing 'a ministry for the poor' have been, until very recently, rather the theme of general and deserved praise, than productive of laudable imitation. This ministration is effected, chiefly by a visitation of the houses of the poor, and he proposes as its objects, religious instruction, uninfluenced by sectarian spirit or opinions: — the relief of the most pressing necessities of the poor — first by a well-regulated charity, and secondarily, by instruction in domestic economy — exhortations to industry — admonition concerning the consequences of vice, and by obtaining work for the deserving and unemployed. The minister should also encourage the education of the children, should prove the friend of the poor in periods of perplexity, and, when the labourer is subdued by sickness, should breathe into his ear the maxims of virtue, and the truths of religion. He might also act as a medium of communication and a link of sympathy, between the higher and lower classes of society. He might become the almoner of the rich, and thus daily sow the seeds of a kindlier relationship than that which now subsists between the wealthy and the destitute. He might also serve as a faithful reporter of the secret miseries which are suffered in the abodes of poverty, unobserved by those to whom he may come to advocate the cause of the abandoned. The prevalence of the principles and the practice of the precepts of Christianity, we may hope, will thus ultimately be made to bind together the now incoherent elements of society.

The success of Dr. Tuckerman's labours in Boston had, before the commencement of a similar plan in Manchester, given rise to several societies for the Christian instruction of the people in the Metropolis, and in other parts of the kingdom. Six such societies are now in operation in Manchester and its out-townships — five amongst the Independent, and one amongst the Unitarian Dissenters. But we regret to add that their number is utterly insufficient to affect the habits of more than a small portion of the population. The vast portions of the town included in the Ancoats, Newtown, and Portland districts, are utterly unoccupied by this beneficent system; and, when it is further observed, that in those districts reside the most indigent and immoral of our poor, it will be at once apparent what need there is of the immediate extension of the same powerful agency to them.

The Age of Great Cities: Or, Modern Civilization viewed in its relation to Intelligence, Morals, and Religion (1843), by Robert Vaughan. Selections.

Robert Vaughan (1795-1868), was a Congregationalist minister, first professor of history at University College, London, president of the Lancashire Independent College from 1843, and editor of the *British Quarterly Review* from its beginning in 1845. A prolific writer on theology, history and ecclesiastical politics, he was a powerful figure within his denomination. His perspective on cities in general and Manchester in particular is very different from that of Kay-Shuttleworth, more abstract, less familiar with brute reality and probably more akin to that of the prosperous middle classes in their suburbs.

In the ancient republics, we find some of the greatest men no strangers to the handling of the plough. Even now, in the United States, the agriculturist is not inferior to the townsman in intelligence. But in both these cases, it is the citizen who has become the tiller of the ground, and he has not suffered the former character to become merged in the latter. In the old states of Europe, and in England among the rest, it is not so, and the ignorance and wretchedness characterizing the European peasantry are the consequence. They are no longer serfs, as regards their political condition, but hitherto their minds have shared little in the emancipation conferred upon their persons.

As men congregate in large numbers, it is inevitable that the strong should act as an impetus upon the weak. In other respects, also, the pressure of numbers is necessarily on the side of intelligence. It is a mistake to suppose that minds of the same class possess no more power collectively than they possess separately. Supposing the same degree of capability to belong to them all, its combinations will be more or less different in each, and the consequent modification of the view taken by each in relation to any given subject, must contribute to form an aggregate intelligence, which will be of much greater variety and compass than would have pertained to any separate mind. It is this which gives so much weight to public opinion. It is the opinion of persons who, taken separately, are all fallible, and who do not cease to be fallible by becoming united; but each has looked at the matter before him, not only in the exercise of the ability common to each, but also in a manner in some degree his own, and the opinion which comes forth the approved of all, may be said to be the result of what is common to all, and of what is peculiar to each. Will it now be said that inasmuch as each of these men is fallible they must all be fallible, and that, in consequence, by asking the opinion of any one of them we might have saved ourselves all trouble of going further? Such reasoning would not only repudiate all attempts to ascertain general sentiment, but would proscribe trial by jury as a piece of machinery made to be just eleven times more cumbrous than it need to have been!

Cities, then, are the natural centres of association. Of course the advantages derived from association are there realized in an eminent degree. Men live there in the nearest neighbourhood. Their faculties, in place of becoming dull from inaction, are constantly sharpened by collision. They have their prejudices, but all are liable to be assailed. Manufactures, commerce, politics, religion, all become subjects of discussion. All these are looked upon from more points, talked about more variously, and judged of more correctly, as being matters in which a great number of minds are interested, and on which those minds are not only accustomed to form conclusions, but to form them with a view to utterance and action. It may be the lot of very few to possess much vigour of thought, but each man stimulates his fellow, and the result is greater general intelligence. The shop, the factory, or the market-place; the local association, the news-room, or the religious meeting, all facilitate this invigorating contact of mind with mind. The more ignorant come into constant intercourse with the more knowing. Stationariness of thought is hardly possible, and if its movements are not always wise, the errors of to-day are as lessons of experience for tomorrow. Such, indeed, is often the astuteness acquired in the exercise of this greatest of free schools, that the smith of Sheffield, or the weaver of Manchester, would frequently prove, on any common ground, more than a match for many a college graduate. But does your man of technical education ever apprehend any such rencontre with the village ploughmen? Or has it ever occurred to him to reckon the ploughman's assistant as superior in shrewdness to the city apprentice? In short, nothing can be more plain, than that the unavoidable intercourse of townsmen must always involve a system of education; and that while instruction reaches, in such connexions, to a much lower level than elsewhere, minds of better capacity naturally make the common intelligence about them the starting-point in their own race of superiority.

It has been intimated that in towns there are greater facilities than in the country for conducting education in its more direct and technical form. These facilities are greater in towns, partly on account of their greater wealth, and their greater freedom from prejudice; and partly in consequence of their more general sympathy with popular improvement, and their comparative freedom from the discountenance or control of powerful individuals or classes. Towns are not like villages, subject, it may be, to the oversight and guidance of a single family, or of a single clergyman. They possess greater means and greater liberty, and, in general, a stronger disposition to use both in favour of education, even in behalf of the children of the poorest.

In towns also, where numbers may be more easily collected, masters find a better return for their toil, and the practice of teaching on a larger scale brings with it a greater proficiency in the art of teaching. In the one case, too, the public reap the benefit of competition; in the other it is hardly admissible. In the populous town, a field is open to different labourers. Every man has space in which to make trial of his favourite method. The observers are many, and the stimulus is proportionate. But in the rural district, it is probable that the schoolmaster will enter upon the duties of his office with no great aptness for the discharge of them; and when it is remembered that the number he will be required to teach will generally be small, that the instruction he will be expected to impart will be very limited, and that in imparting it he will know nothing of competition, and be subject in general to very imperfect oversight, it will be seen that the natural course of things, both as respects the character of the teacher and the result of his labours, in nearly all points the reverse of that which may be reasonably expected in a city population.

With regard to mechanics' institutes and literary institutions, it is obvious that the benefit to be derived from them must be restricted almost entirely to the people of towns and cities. In most of the towns of Great Britain such associations exist. In the larger cities they are numerous, and their advantages are made accessible to almost every grade of the community. Of course the knowledge communicated by such institutions must always be elementary and popular, rather than comprehensive or profound. But the natural effect of such associations is to strengthen the taste for improvement where it exists, and often to create it where it is not. They serve to bring something more of the intellectual into alliance with the commercial. By such means the mind is taken, in some degree, from the groove of its daily occupation, and glimpses are opened to it, showing the manner in which the closer exercises of thought have conduced to wealth, and power, and greatness. The library, the reading-room, the debating class, and the lecture theatre, all contribute to this result. Where this effect is produced, leisure ceases to be a burden. Much is done to redeem it from the bait of sensuality. The mental and moral habits of many thousands among our young men have been thus affected by such means. They have learnt to regard the desk of the lecturer as holding a relation to science and literature, similar to that of the pulpit with respect to religion. It is not expected that the former will suffice to make men great philosophers or scholars, any more than the latter will suffice to make them profound theologians. But the people among whom there is the most general feeling of sympathy with religion, are the people among whom we expect to find the greater number of sound divines; and, on the same ground, the connexion in which we find the most widely diffused sympathy with investigations relating to science and scholarship, is the connexion in which we may expect to find the greatest number of men distinguished by real science and real scholarship. In these things there is a constant action and reaction between the great attainments of the smaller number, and the smaller attainments of the greater. The great classical authors were, if we may so express it, a natural product from the general state of things which obtained in the cities with which their names are associated. In this manner, the excellence distinguishing the few, is seen to derive its nutriment and power from its relation to the average perception and feeling of the many.

Nor will it avail to object that religion is every man's business, and that the same is not true of science or literature. These subjects are alike the business of every man, in proportion to the capability and the time which every man may bring to them. If the trite saying — "a little learning is a dangerous thing," be true of any branch of knowledge, it is true of all branches — religious knowledge not excepted. Superficiality has its dangers everywhere, and especially in relation to those subjects which are in their own nature the most profound and mysterious. On this ground, the little knowledge possessed concerning religion, may be even more dangerous than the little possessed concerning any other topic. The little is liable to abuse, but not more than the great and not more in one thing than in another. The great in knowledge is no doubt preferable to the small; but a little knowledge is always better than none. If knowledge is to be counted a bad thing according to this law of mere quantity, we see not why all things liable to abuse should not be subject to the same law, and men be warned, in consequence, of the miserable fate awaiting them should it be their lot to become possessed of wealth, or power, or pleasure, only in small quantities! Be sure of it, the men who are upstarts in knowledge, are the men who would make a similar display of the character natural to them in the absence of knowledge. Keeping them in ignorance is not the way to cure them of their vanity, but rather the contrary.

In large towns, and in whole countries, where the civic feeling is allowed to predominate, the views expressed on this subject in the preceding pages generally prevail. In New England, a considerable course of religious and general instruction obtains, with which the mind of the young, without exception, is expected to become familiar. No youth is left in ignorance concerning the evidence or nature of the faith which he is expected to profess; nor concerning the history and constitution of the country in which he is soon to become possessed of franchise. What is said of New England, may be said of Connecticut, and Massachusets. Each of these states is in this manner a large school-house. It is rare to find a person in them imperfectly informed on the above topics, and a man in anything like ignorance respecting them would be regarded with astonishment.

Similar is the state of things in Switzerland. In the Protestant cantons of Switzerland we find the best-educated people in Europe.

Ignorance in the child is accounted a crime on the part of his parents, and the fine levied on such parental negligence is so heavy that it is very rarely incurred. In the schools, the rich and the poor, and, in some degree, the two sexes, mix together, without any of the evil consequences that may be thought to be natural to such associations. The apparent distance, indeed, between the rich and poor, and between the employer and the employed, is not so great in those cantons as among ourselves. But the mutual fidelity and esteem are much greater. More instructed than any other community in Europe, the Swiss are also more moral, and more constant in their observance of public worship. In many districts, the genius of Calvin is still seen to prevade the whole character of his disciples. This is observable in the secular in such places, no less than in the spiritual, — industry, and the love of order and liberty, all being raised to a place among the religious virtues.

It scarcely need be observed, that of such a state of society, especially as it exists across the Atlantic, the ancient world knew nothing. The ignorant and enslaved mass, which grew up around the small nucleus of enlightened and free citizens in all the ancient republics, is unknown to such communities: and instead of the costly library, which was counted among the luxuries of the opulent, we see that constant flow of cheaply printed knowledge which finds its way to the home of the humblest. Men, accordingly, who reason from the histories of Greece and Rome, to the history of such states, as though they were alike, may be wise in their own conceit, but their prophecies we may be well assured are little trustworthy. What New England possesses in common with Athens, or with republican Rome, is little, compared with what she possesses as strictly her own. But it is to be distinclty observed, that in both cases, the degree of popular intelligence existing is to be traced to the influence of civic institutions; and that the scattered cultivators of the soil become thus elevated, only as the industry which has given wealth and potency to towns, has served through their medium, to raise the country generally to the position of a large city.

* * * * * * * *

Every increase in wealth is so much increase on the side of indulgence — presenting, of necessity, so much temptation to the formation of habits which tend naturally to deterioration. It is thus with individuals in all such cases, and it is not less so with communities. The danger of our going wrong is always in proportion to the facilities and inducements which are held out on the side of doing so. As society advances, ruder modes of gratifying the appetites and passions are relinquished, but others, scarcely more favourable to morality, too often come into their place. Men become more capable of reflection, but the greater restraint which is laid upon irregular propensities by that means, is not necessarily so strong as the force which may act upon them in the form of new enticements. The consequences of this fact are momentous.

It is natural that the causes which give strength to an undue thirst after personal gratification, should give strength to all the selfish passions, and in the strength of those passions consists the essence of everything immoral — of everything opposed to individual happiness and to the stability of nations.

****

It will not be questioned, we presume, by persons who have bestowed any degree of reflection on the subject, that the standard of morality, so far as it respects some considerable portions of society, appears to reach its lowest point as you direct your attention from the smaller towns to the greater. It is no doubt true that there is both a kind and a degree of intelligence and virtue existing in large cities, which will not be found among any scattered and rural population; but is no less true, that we should fail of finding in any such population the same amount of the more deliberate and matured forms of depravity. In great cities men possess the power of becoming strong — eminently strong, for good or for evil. The more you crowd men together, the more you expose the pure to the hazard of infection, and the impure to the danger of waxing worse and worse. Human nature is too prone to imitate the evil rather than the good; and in great cities, the inducements to such a course occur with their greater frequency, and in their greater force. In such places, there are recesses in which every abomination may be practised, and no eye that might deter from the forbidden indulgence be the witness. Nowhere else, accordingly, does man acquire such expertness in iniquity, and nowhere else has evil so large a space over which to diffuse its pestilential influence. In the populous city, this poison may be said to insinuate itself almost as through every vein. The contact with it is close and perpetual. It has its incipient stages for all grades — for the needy apprentice, and for the young in the noblest families. It has its modes of displaying itself so as to make its conquests in the shop of the artisan and in the palaces of royalty. Nearness and constancy of association, necessarily sharpen the powers of the understanding; but in the history of minds so exercised, while shrewdness will generally come of itself, goodness will not, except as effort shall be made to realize it.

In great cities men may become offenders in almost every form with less probability of detection than elsewhere, and this fact has contributed powerfully to render such places the abodes of so much deliquency. In a neighbourhood where every man is known, where all his movements are liable to observation, and the slightest irregularity becomes a matter of local notoriety, a strong check is constantly laid upon the tendencies of the illdisposed. In such connexions it is felt that should the law fail to punish, society will not. In the populous city, restraint of this nature is of course much less felt. There, accordingly, the unprincipled are often tempted to act as basely as their nature may prompt, on the presumption that they may do so without penalty or inconvenience. Such scenes become a kind of centre, to which the most worthless in all the provinces around almost instinctively betake themselves. The crowded capital is to such men as some huge and intricate forest, into which they plunge, and find, for a season at least, the places of darkness and concealment convenient for them. If such men possess wealth, the facilities there afforded to every sort of gratification will be a powerful attraction; while the men who are both necessitous and depraved, cling to such associations with the same tenacity, as holding out to them the only prospect of enriching themselves at the cost of others.

****

Still, in forming our judgment with regard to the morality of great cities, both as compared with the population in each place, and as compared with the rural districts, great caution will be necessary if we would guard successfully against being misled. It is certain, that singularly exaggerated statements have been put forth on the subject, by well-meaning persons, who have been themselves deceived concerning it. When it is remembered that it has been well ascertained, that the women of known bad character in London do not exceed 7000, while even very recently they have been described in print as amounting to 60,000, and even to 80,000; when it is remembered, also, that the common thieves of the metropolis are known to be little more than 3000, and that these have been described, not long ago, as numbering 30,000, it will be obvious that it becomes us to look on all reports on such matters with much misgiving, except as they are furnished upon such authority as should entitle them to credit. This number of deliquents, it must be borne in mind, is found among a population of nearly two millions: and much as we may deplore this amount of the immoral, the wonder, all things considered, is, not that it is so great, but that it is no greater. Nor would it have been restrained within such limits, in such circumstances, had not our great city been made the centre of a great moral power, wisely adapted to counteract the natural outbreaks of depravity.

"Report on the Census of Religious Worship", Parliamentary Papers (1852-3, LXXXIX), by Horace Mann. Selections.

Horace Mann (1823-?), a barrister, on the strength of family connections was appointed by the Registrar General as an assistant commissioner to superintend the first (and only) religious census in 1851. His report on the results of that census, which consisted of statistics on attendance at church or chapel on Census Sunday (March 30th) 1851, shocked the public by its emphasis on the non-attendance of the urban working classes.

———————————

COMPARATIVE ACCOMMODATION FOR WORSHIP IN TOWN
AND COUNTRY DISTRICTS

As was to be expected, it is chiefly in the large and densely-peopled *towns* that a deficiency is felt; the rural districts are supplied in general with adequate, sometimes with superabundant, provision. It appears that the *urban* parts of England, containing an aggregate population of 8,294,240 persons, have accommodation for 3,814,215 or 46 per cent. of this number; while the rural parts, containing a population of 9,633,369 have provision for 6,398,348 or 66.5 per cent.

These "urban districts" here, however, include small country towns, which seem to be as well supplied as any other portion of the country. If we take the *large* towns only and include small country towns with the rural parts to which they virtually belong, the proportion per cent. in urban districts will be 37 as compared with 73 in rural districts. And the proportion is in inverse ratio to the size of the towns; so that while in towns containing between 10,000 and 20,000 inhabitants, the proportion is 66; in towns containing between 20,000 and 50,000 it is 60; in those containing between 50,000 and 100,000 it is 47, and in those containing upwards of 100,000 it is 34. This view suggests with singular force the mixture of sentiments which led to the erection of the greater portion of our sacred edifices. Piety and local attachments — benevolence and longing for perpetual remembrance — principally, doubtless, a sincere desire to honour God, and yet, with this, a natural desire to raise a lasting monument to themselves, — these were mingling motives to the influence of which may be attributed the existence of some thousands of our churches.

Hence, it was in the very spot where the founder had his dwelling that his church was built: no other neighbourhood possessed such a hold on his affections. Thus arose our village churches, and a multitude of structures in those ancient towns and cities where, in former times, the merchants were accustomed to reside. But our modern populous towns, — erected more for business than for residence — mere aggregates of offices and workshops and over-crowded dwellings of the subordinate agents of industry, — are inhabited by none whose means permit them to reside elsewhere. The wealthy representatives of those whose piety supplied our ancient towns with churches fly from the unwholesome atmosphere of our new cities, and dispense their charity in those suburban or more rural parishes in which their real homes are situated and their local sympathies are centred. The innumerable multitudes who do and must reside within the compass of the enormous hives in which their toil is daily carried on, are thus the objects of but little of that lively interest with which benevolent men regard the inhabitants of their immediate neighbourhood, and which produces, in our small-sized country parishes, so many institutions for their physical and moral benefit. The masses, therefore, of our large and growing towns — connected by no sympathetic tie with those by fortune placed above them — form a world apart, a nation by themselves; divided almost as effectually from the rest as if they spoke another language or inhabited another land. What Dr. Chalmers calls "the influence of locality," is powerless here: the area is too extensive and the multitude too vast. It is to be hoped that the influence of trade-connexion may ere long sufficiently accomplish what the influence of locality is now too feeble to secure; that heads of great industrial establishments, the growth of recent generations, may perform towards the myriads connected with them by community of occupation, those religious charities or duties which the principal proprietors in rural parishes perform towards those connected with them by vicinity of residence. Much, doubtless, has already been effected in this way; but the need for more is manifest and urgent.

* * * * * * * *

The absence of that local interest which leads to individual benevolence, and the evident inadequacy of all that can be reasonably expected from the great employers of industry, appear to call for the combined exertions either of the whole inhabitants of a particular neighbourhood, or of the Christian Church at large, as the only other method for relieving such deplorable deficiency. And this has been to some extent perceived and acted on. With reference to the Church of England, many churches have been raised by the united liberality of the inhabitants of populous town parishes, encouraged by assistance from the funds of central bodies, such as the Incorporated Church Building Society; and amogst the Dissenters many chapels have been reared in similar manner. But it cannot, it is feared, be said that these mere local efforts promise to diminish very sensibly the grievous lack of accommodation for the *masses* of our civic population. Hitherto the action of those central bodies which dispense the bounties of the general Christian public has been made dependent on the previous action of the local bodies in whose midst the additional church or chapel is to be erected; and unfortunately it but rarely happens that such local action is aroused, except to obtain accommodation for an increase of the middle classes, who already appreciate religious ordinances and are able and disposed to bear the pecuniary burden requisite in order to obtain them. The effect has been that the considerable addition made in recent years to the religious edifices of large towns has been in very near proportion to the rapid growth, in the same interval, of the prosperous middle classes; but the far more rapid increase in this period in the number of artizans and labourers has taken place without a corresponding increase of religious means *for them*. The only prominent example, within my knowledge, of a vigorous effort to relieve a local want without waiting for local demand, is the movement which, some years ago, the Bishop of London originated and successfully, beyond anticipation, prosecuted, for providing fifty new churches for the metropolitan parishes. And yet it really seems that, without some missionary enterprises similar to this, the mighty task of even mitigating spiritual destitution in our towns and cities hardly can be overcome.

Lord Ashley on the Public Health Bill. *Hansard's Parliamentary Debates,* 8 May 1848.

Lord Ashley (q.v.) contributed his time to innumerable philanthropic organisations and causes throughout his life. Along with the great sanitation reformer, Southwood Smith, he resolutely advanced the cause of public health. He was very active as chairman of the central board of health during the cholera epidemic of 1849. In Lord Ashley we have the preeminent example of the way in which philanthropic concerns for the physical environment of the urban poor was combined with evangelical concerns for the salvation of souls. Lord Ashley delivered the speech which appears below in the course of debate in the House of Commons on the Public Health Bill which created the central board of health. Local governments opposed this centralizing measure because it diminished their independence.

LORD ASHLEY was anxious to impress on the House the absolute and indispensable necessity of instituting some measure which might remove some portion at least of the grievances that pressed so severely on the working population. His hon. Friend near him said the other night that this was essentially a working man's question, and he had never in his life said a truer thing, for it affected the whole of the working man's life: it began at home; it affected his capacity to eat and sleep in comfort, to go abroad, and to gain a livelihood by which he might be enabled to rear his family in comfort and repectability. He knew that this question was well comprehended by the working classes, and was one of the questions they really had at heart. He had not attended a single meeting of working people in which this had not been a prominent feature; he had constant correspondence with them from all parts of the country, and in every part he found them alive to this question. He need only mention that the other day, when there was a meeting of trade delegates in the metropolis, amongst the grievances urged, and the first on which they came to a resolution, which they did him the honour to communicate to him, was the sanitary condition in which they and their families were left by the neglect of legislative enactments. He, therefore, assured the House that this was a most important question, not only with respect to the moral condition of the working classes, but also in reference to the amount of political content or discontent which

they would find existing amongst the masses. Nor was this a question
which touched persons of a higher class at second-hand only. They
knew the result of sanitary abuses by the large addition to the rates,
by the increased demands on private charity, by accessions to the
bills of mortality; and, more, they knew it in some cases by the results
on themselves. Fever might break out in some noxious and remote
district; but when at length it came to desolate some contiguous and
wealthier region, then they began to see the consequences of this
intolerable evil. He did not mean to conceal or deny that there were
great difficulties in legislating on this subject, and no doubt the
proposition of remedies was beset by every species of obstacle. A
great number of local interests were to be encountered, a great
number of local feelings to be provoked, and no doubt it required some
fortitude and perseverance to devise a legislative measure which
should apply a remedy to all these prodigious evils. But that could
be no argument whatever for stopping this measure on the very
threshold, for refusing to go into Committee, and there seeing
whether they could draw the teeth and pare the talons of this lion,
which had created so much terror. He gave the Government the
highest praise for the manner in which they had addressed themselves
to this question, and the boldness with which they had encountered
the opposition and braved the difficulties surrounding the question.
But he would fairly tell them, that he thought the measure was
susceptible of very great improvement in Committee; but whether
it was so or not, he implored the House to let the Government have
an opportunity of dealing with the measure in Committee; for it was
one, as he said before, which had taken such strong hold of the minds
of the people, that it was essentially necessary to prove to them, not
only by general argumentation, but in detail, what was feasible in
regard to the removal of the various abominations existing. He
confessed he was very much astonished when he heard it stated by
certain Members in that House, and out of it, that the law as it now
stood was adequate to the removal of those evils. If they looked at
the list of Acts on the Statute-book, they would find, no doubt, a great
number levelled at abuses of this nature, which might perhaps be
remedied if all those Acts were enforced; but to say that the Statute-
book was open to all, was like the well-known saying, that the London

Tavern was open to all: it was open, no doubt, provided you could pay for it. But this was a most perplexing and tedious process, which you could not call upon the working men, or any number of them, to put in operation. The old laws might be equal to the removal of abuses, but they were by no means equal to the institution of improvements: there was a law for removing masses of filth or noxious stenches, but there was none by which you could furnish to the working classes a pure, ample, and constant supply of water. The hon. Member for West Surrey (Mr. H. Drummond) had remarked that some persons had got up an agitation for the purpose of forcing this measure on the country. He (Lord Ashley) had been most deeply implicated in the movement, and was earnestly anxious to carry a legislative measure in furtherance of the object; he, therefore, took to himself all the blame of the hon. Member's reflection, and left him to prove what selfish interests he (Lord Ashley) had in the matter. He asked the hon. Gentleman whether it was not the case that in the opposition to this measure there was not full as much of selfish and pecuniary interest as in the advocacy of the great reform to which he looked? When the hon. Member treated this subject with such great jocosity, he (Lord Ashley) really thought the hon. Member must have forgotten, or perhaps never known, the very deep feeling entertained upon this question throughout the country, and could not have known that in almost every large town and populous locality boards had been formed for the purpose of making periodical reports, and exciting public interest on the subject, all beginning and ending with one and the same complaint, the utter inadequacy of the law for the removal of the great and pressing evils now endured. The city which he (Lord Ashley) represented, might almost be said to be in clover as regarded this question. Two petitions, very amply and respectfully signed by the inhabitants of Bath, had been presented to the House; one to the effect that, approving of many parts of the Bill, they thought that, on the whole, they could make out such a case for Bath that it ought to be exempted from the operation of the law; the other that, though many people took exceptions to parts of this Bill, yet upon the whole they thought it exceedingly good, and called for by the necessities of the country, and therefore requested their representatives not to give way to any local interests, but to suffer the general necessity to overrule them. He should, therefore, vote for going into Committee, with a view to the introduction of such amendments as might be found necessary. The hon. Member for West Surrey had asked, what possible connection there could be between typhus and crime? Could there be a doubt that the same condition of things and habits of life which gave rise to fever, also powerfully stimulated to the perpetration of crime. If the hon. Member would consider the modes of life too prevalent amongst some unfortunate classes, and the noxious influences by which they were surrounded, he would perceive with the slightest consideration that their operation on the physical state was such as made it impossible for them to practise many of the lessons of decency and virtue which they might have practised in their early life. The noble Lord then quoted, in illustration, the statements of Dr. Neil Arnot respecting the condition of Glasgow, and Mr. F. Cooper respecting that of Southampton: —

"In Glasgow, which I first vistited, it was found that the great mass of the fever cases occurred in the low wynds and dirty narrow streets and courts, in which, because lodging was there cheapest, the poorest and most destitute naturally had their abodes. From one such locality, between Argyle-street and the river, 754 of about 5,000 cases of fever which occurred in the previous year were carried to the hospitals. In a perambulation on the morning of September 24 with Mr. Chadwick, Dr. Alison, Dr. Cowan (since deceased, who had laboured so meritoriously to alleviate the misery of the poor in Glasgow), the police magistrate, and others, we examined these wynds, and to give an idea of the whole vicinity I may state as follows: — We entered a dirty low passage like a house door, which led from the street through the first house to a square court immediately behind, which court, with the exception of a narrow path round it, leading to another long passage through a second house, was occupied entirely as a dung receptacle of the most disgusting kind. Beyond this court the second passage led to a second square court, occupied in the same way by its dunghill; and from this court there was yet a third passage leading to a third court and third dungheap. There were no privies or drains there, and the dungheaps received all filth which the swarm of wretched inhabitants could give; and we learned that a considerable part of the rent of the houses was paid by the produce of the dungheaps. Thus worse off than wild animals, many of which withdraw to a distance and conceal their ordure, the dwellers in these courts converted their shame into a kind of money by which their lodging was to be paid! The interiors of these houses and their inmates correspond with the exteriors. We saw half-dressed wretches crowding together to be warm; and in one bed, although in the middle of the day, several women were imprisoned under a blanket, because many others who had on their backs all the articles of dress that belonged to the party were then out of doors in the streets. This picture is so shocking that without ocular proof, one would be disposed to doubt the possibility of the facts; and yet there is, perhaps, no old town in Europe that does not furnish parallel examples. London, before the great fire of 1666, had few drains, and had many such scenes, and the consequence was a pestilence occurring at intervals of about 12 years, each destroying at an average about a fourth of the inhabitants. Who can wonder that pestilential disease should originate and spread in such situations? And, as a contrast, it may be observed here, that when the kelp manufacture lately ceased on the western shores of Scotland, a vast population of the lowest class of people, who had been supported chiefly by the wages of kelp labour, remained in extreme want, with cold, hunger, and almost despair pressing them down — yet, as their habitations were scattered and in pure air, cases of fever did not arise among them."

With respect to Southampton, Mr. Francis Cooper, surgeon, stated.

"During the period of my parochial attendance on the poor, I have more than once been compelled, in the depth of winter, and at midnight, to stand in the street, and walk to and fro till my assistance has been required, not being able to breathe the air of the apartment in which the wretched sufferer lay. And very recently, on being sent for to a poor woman, I was obliged to absent myself till the very moment of parturition, the air being so bad, so offensive, that a sort of stupor and lassitude rendered me unable to remain. On visiting the patient the following morning, I was curious to ascertain the actual dimensions of the outlet at the back of the tenement, and found it six feet long by three feet wide, and at the end of the yard, so called, a privy was erected, only about three feet deep, and from which the urine and other liquid deposits were carried away by ground leakage, thus keeping up continual smells of a most noxious character, and acting as one of the most active agents of destruction to health. The rooms, too — only one above and below — were so low and small, so ill-contrived, as to be unfit for human residence; the structural arrangements so utterly bad as to be a reproach, not only to our civilisation, but to our very humanity. There was no water laid on, no convenience for stowage, the coals being under the stairs, and the pantry (I suppose I must call it so) being placed between the back door, opening on the yard and the sitting-room, into which every breeze from the west carried the effluvium from the spot at the back of the dwelling, and which, in warm weather, was continually breathed by the occupiers, whose powers of resistance to the deadly influence of such malaria could not possibly continue for any length of time. The tenements, several in number, were erected at the back of others of large dimensions, and on the side of undrained privies, without drainage, without water, with no positive useful structural arrangement of any kind — mere brick and mortar run up, as the technical expression is, no party-wall (the Act of Lord Normanby is constantly evaded), no basement elevation, no internal appliance for securing comfort or preserving health, and yet 3s. 6d. per week was paid for rent, 9£. 2s. a year, or 18 per cent, for what could not have amounted to more than 50£. or 60£., at the outside, as the original cost of erection. Who can wonder at the poverty and wretchedness of the poor? Who can be surprised that disease makes such havoc amongst the labouring population? Need we comment on the disastrous tendencies which such a state of things suggests?"

The unhappy beings who were compelled to live in scenes of such putridity and filth grew gradually debilitated and powerless. They became unable to do a day's work, and, sinking into the most abject condition of pauperism, were tempted to perpetrate deeds of violence, and to commit crimes of the foulest and most disgraceful description. There was no man whose evidence on matters affecting the poor was of higher authority than Dr. Southwood Smith; and in his examination before the Commissioners for Inquiring into the State of Large Towns and Populous Districts, he gives the following evidence: —

"Do you think that neglect of decency and comfort is likely to render those persons reckless of consequences, and inclined to a mode of getting their living dishonestly? — The neglect of the decencies of life must have a debasing effect on the human mind; and hopeless want naturally produces recklessness. There is a point of wretchedness which is incompatible with the existence of any respect for the peace or property of others; and to look in such a case of obedience to the laws when there is the slightest prospect of violating them with impunity, is to expect to reap where you have not sown.

I have myself seen a young man, 20 years of age, sleeping in the same bed with his sister, a young woman 16 or 17 years old. That incestuous intercourse takes place under these circumstances there is too much reason to believe; and that when unmarried young men and women sleep together in the same room, the women become common to the men, is stated in evidence as a positive fact; but I regard another inevitable effect of this state of things as no less pernicious; it is one of the influences which, for want of a better term, may be called unhumanising, because it tends to weaken and destroy the feelings and affections which are distinctive of the human being, and which raise him above the level of the brute. I have sometimes checked myself in the wish that men of high station and authority would visit these abodes of their less fortunate fellow-creatures, and witness with their own eyes the scenes presented there; for I have thought that the same end might be answered in a way less disagreeable to them. They have only to visit the Zoological Gardens, and to observe the state of society in that large room which is appropriated to a particular class of animals, where every want is relieved and every appetite and passion gratified in full view of the whole community. In the filthy and crowded streets in our large towns and cities you see human faces retrograding, sinking down to the level of these brute tribes, and you find manners appropriate to the degadation. Can any one wonder that there is among these classes of the people so little intelligence — so slight an approach to humanity — so total an absence of domestic affection, and of moral and religious feeling? The experiment has been long tried on a large scale with a dreadful success, affording the demonstration that if, from early infancy, you allow human beings to live like brutes, you can degrade them down to their level, leaving to them scarcely more intellect, and no feelings

and affections proper to human minds and hearts. Have you examined
frequently the houses of individuals among the poor in these neglected
districts? — Yes. Have you noticed particularly the state of the air in
their apartments? — I have; and it sometimes happens to me in my
visits to them, as physician to the Eastern Dispensary, that I am unable
to stay in the room even to write the prescription. I am obliged, after
staying the necessary time at the bedroom of the patient, to go into
the air, or to stand at the door, and write the prescription; for, such
is the offensive and unwholesome state of the air, that I cannot breathe
it even for that short a time. What must it be to live in such an
atmosphere, and go through the process of disease in it?"

There was another witness also, whose testimony on such questions
as those was of the very highest importance, the Rev. J. Clay, chaplain
of Preston gaol; and he too was most decidedly of opinion that the
physical condition of human beings exercised a most potent influence
over their moral condition: —

"It should be impressed upon every one desirous of the melioration
of his kind, that filthiness of person and sordidness of mind are usually
united; and if you would banish squalor and sickness from the labourers'
cottage, you must remove ignorance and corruption from his head and
heart. Amidst the dirt and disease of filthy back courts and alleys, and
yards, vices and crimes are lurking altogether unimagined by those
who have never visited such abodes."

Nothing could be more distinct than the rev. gentleman's statement
of the connexion between disease and crime, and between filth and
immorality. His own personal observation entirely corroborated the
testimony of Dr. Southwood Smith and Mr. Clay. From the
examinations he had himself made, as well as from the evidence he
had been able to collect, he had arrived at the conclusion that more
than one half of the habits of intoxication which disgraced large towns
and populous districts arose from the sanitary condition in which the
population were permitted to live. It was impossible to visit the squalid
localities in which the poor were huddled together in many of the towns
of England, and to view their pallid, sinking worn-out forms, and their
livid, hueless faces, without experiencing a feeling of compassion which
almost prompted one to justify the act of human beings, who to escape
from the contemplation of their unutterable anguish, and to prop a
sinking constitution, had recourse to ardent spirits, or other modes
of fictitious excitement. He had also discovered this terrible and
startling truth, that fever, which was the offspring of bad air and

defective drainage, fell, in the large proportion of cases, not on children, not on old people, but on adults in the very prime of life. It did not cut off those who, being very young, could not contribute to the general prosperity of the realm; nor those who, being very old, were a burden to it; but it hurried to the grave the heads of families, who left behind them a flock of children and a widow or widower, as the case might be, to be sustained out of the parish funds, or by the charity of private individuals. If the hon. Member for West Surrey, or any one else, doubted this statement, he would implore of him to perambulate the pauper districts of the metropolis, and judge for himself. He would then be able to know, by means of personal inquiries whether the poor people thus miserably circumstanced were or were not sensible of their condition, and did or did not desire to be relieved from it. He (Lord Ashley) had repeatedly heard, from the lips of the poor themselves, this sickening and awful complaint — the full force of which might be felt with peculiar emphasis, just at this moment when we were enjoying such delightful weather — that they looked with terror at the approach of fine weather. What was a blessing to others was to them a positive curse; for they assured him that when the sun shone forth in its full splendour, the "summer stinks" — that was their phrase — became altogether intolerable. Anything more pitiable, more touching, or more deplorable than that complaint, it was impossible to imagine. But the most cogent aspect in which this question could be viewed, was that which had reference to the influence of the physical condition of those poor people on their moral nature. Let them collect the evidence of all the clergymen of all religious denominations — let them collect the evidence of all the Scripture readers, district visitors, and city missionaries throughout the kingdom — and if, out of the entire body, ther could be found twenty to deny that there was an intimate connexion of misery with filth, and of crime with both — if there could be found twenty to deny that the connexion between the moral and physical condition of the poor was most intimate and inevitable, he (Lord Ashley) would not only oppose the present Bill, but would undertake to join any man or any number of men in an effort to resist any proposition that might at any future period be made to make this question the subject for a legislative enactment. His noble Friend the Member for Plymouth had been taunted for saying that all attempts to diffuse education amongst the poor were little better than vain and profitless, so long as they were permitted to continue in their present sanitary condition; but the noble Lord had said nothing more than had been already expressed on many occasions by others. He (Lord Ashley) concurred unreservedly in the statement, and was most distinctly of opinion that it was next to impossible that any genuine or lasting good should result from education so long as Parliament left the people in their present condition. His experience of the ragged schools confirmed him in the conviction, for he there saw the extreme difficulty, if not the absolute impossibility, of training children in the way they should go, who, after school hours, were permitted to return to the filthy purlieus from which they had issued in the morning, there to unlearn in one hour what their preceptors had spent a week in endeavouring to teach them. In a few isolated cases the power of education might prevail over all evil influences; but on the great mass of cases its beneficial effect would be wholly counteracted. He had to thank the House for the kindness with which they have heard him, and should apologise for having trespassed at such length on their attention. In conclusion, he would express an earnest hope that the House would permit the Bill to go into Committee, there to undergo such alterations and amendments as might be considered necessary. He trusted that they would concede thus much; and by so doing make one onward step to the recovery of those unhappy people, and to the recognition of their right to be placed on a level with sentient and immortal beings.

London Domestic Mission Society, 16th Report (1851). Report of
Mr. Vidler.

The London Domestic Mission Society, a Unitarian organization, was
founded in 1835 in an attempt to provide religious instruction for
London's poor. Like the nondenominational London City Mission,
established in the same year, the Domestic Mission played a
significant role in publicizing the conditions of life in the slums of
London.

MR. VIDLER'S REPORT.

It again becomes my duty to lay before the subscribers and friends
of the London domestic Mission, some account of my proceedings
during the past year — to call their attention to the state of the poor
in the district in which I labour — and to speak of the efforts which
have been made in connection with the Mission, for the mental, moral,
and religious improvement of the neighbourhood. While as years have
passed by, my own convictions of the necessity and importance of
the work in which I am engaged have become deepened and
strengthened — so amidst difficulties to overcome, and
disappointments to discourage, I have felt more and more certain,
that great good has been accomplished, and that the means which
we employ are mainly the right ones for the end which we seek. That
the familiar intercourse with the people at their own homes, the
education of the young in our schools, the assemblages for public
worship and Christian instruction, the social meetings, the visits of
consolation in seasons of afflicton, the regular lessons in knowledge
which have been given to the young men and women in our classes,
and other minor plans of usefulness, have all more or less been
accompanied with important results in the improvement of the habits,
characters, and dispositions of those who would otherwise have been
neglected. I say this with no disposition to boast of great things, for
I feel strongly, how much the good which I know has been done is
below what I could have desired — but at the same time, I feel that
we are working out no doubtful experiment.

The frequent and almost daily intercourse which the Minister to
the Poor has with them in their own homes, enables him not only
to become acquainted with their condition, to witness their struggles,

sorrows, and joys, but often at the right moment to give them unobtrusive advice. This is a valuable privilege, which can only be well employed when sympathy and confidence have been established. Much of my time is occupied in visiting in the district; and I have reason to think well employed, as I call to mind that many of these visits were paid to those who were suffering from sickness and bereavement; some of them in answer to direct calls for Christian prayer and consolation. Among many cases of illness, I will only here notice that of a girl, a Sunday scholar, whom I had known almost from her birth. The poor child was unable to lie down in her bed for nearly six weeks before her death, and sat night and day on a chair with her head resting on a pillow which was placed on the table. Though suffering much pain from disease of the lungs, she was very patient, often tried to comfort her mother, and spoke most sweetly, though with a childlike spirit, of the hope of a future life. I read the funeral service over her remains at Worship-street Chapel, and the young men who are our Sunday-school teachers made a small collection among themselves, amounting to eleven shillings and sixpence, for the assistance of the mother, who is a widow.

It is probable that the observations which I am about to make on the habits and condition of the people will apply to a great extent to most of the other poor districts in London. In my own district, as well as in others, there is a large substratum of crime and profligacy; an outcast class with whom I come but occasionally in contact. I fully sympathise with those who have been making efforts to reach these pariahs of our civilisation; but my own exertions have been mainly directed to those who, just above the danger, are in the peril of falling into the vortex. I speak then of those who are striving with more or less effort to obtain an honest living. In ordinary times, when regularly at work, the bulk of the people do not earn more than is fairly required for the payment of rent, and the food and clothing of their families. This is certainly the case with those who have large and growing families. The most prudent of them usually find that a lying-in, or the funeral of a child, will absorb any little savings they have made. They then only fairly live with the full exercise of all their powers; but from irregularity in their employment, many are subject to the occasional loss of two or three week's work. How keenly this

is felt! The children must still be fed — debts are incurred — the
pawnshop is visited — rent is unpaid — they get what is called
"behind;" and weeks, or even months, of regular work will hardly
put them straight. I could give many instances where circumstances
like these, have entirely broken up what I believe to have been well
meant and earnest efforts for moral improvement: of children who
have been withdrawn from our school, "no shoes" has been the true
reason: of men and women who have come to our Chapel until the
loss of clothes has kept them away, and the thread once severed, has
not been again re-united. Besides those who are in comparative
comfort when at work, there is a large class, happily less numerous
than theretofore, whose employment is precarious and wretchedly
underpaid. They generally follow sedentary occupations; and pale
faces and stunted forms — derangement of the general health —
weakness of mind and body — incapacity to mental exertion — and
a lower tone of moral feeling, are frequent results; this is the
dangerous class — dangerous from their ignorance and their
sufferings. Far worse off are they than the pitied agricultural
labourer. He, at any rate, has the stimulus of fresh air, the beauties
of God's earth about him, and perhaps his little plot of garden; but
the hundreds, nay thousands, who are pining in the closest courts
of the district, what stimulus have they, except the occasional glass
of gin? Look at their daily meal of weak tea and bread and butter,
seasoned occasionally by a herring or a slice of bacon — the close
room, which perhaps some of the family never leave from week's end
to week's end — the fetid atmosphere — the disorder and want of
cleanliness in which the children are nurtured — the ragged clothes
— and the apathy, listlessness, and even despair, which the parents
often exhibit. Some of the children may by great exertion be drafted
into our Sunday-schools, a few into our day-schools, a portion into
the ragged-schools, and for the rest there are the courts for play-
grounds, with their daily scenes of obscenity and vice. Let it be
recollected that these people are not the absolutely vicious and
dishonest class, they have no special acquaintance with the police
officer and the magistrate. I have known their very honesty and toil
mocked by those who fancied they had found an easier mode of getting
a livelihood. Some of them only want the helping hand and the word

of kindness to be roused to new and sustained effort.

About a year ago I met with a man who is a pocket-book maker: his earnings were then very precarious, eight, ten, or twelve shillings a week; to obtain which he told me that he frequently worked from five in the morning until twelve at night. His appearance was haggard and wretched; but he was evidently a man who had had an education beyond his class, and he spoke with much intelligence. He said that there was no hope for the working classes; that their condition was getting worse every year; that for his own part he had no love of life, it was almost unbearable to him; but that if he were removed there would be nothing but vice or the workhouse before his wife and family. I endeavoured to point out to him some of the recent improvements which have taken place in the condition of the people, and the reasonable hope, that there is of more. I gently told him that his mind had got into a diseased state; and as I went on and spoke to him of Christian duties, hopes, and responsibilities, his eyes glistened — he was evidently impressed. It was truly preaching the Gospel to the broken hearted. Since then I have had several conversations with the man. He and his wife have become usual attendants at our Chapel; and in spite of the drawback of an attack of fever, during which I visited him in the fever hospital, their circumstances have upon the whole improved. He has several times spoke of our first interview as having led him into a new train of thought, and given unto him fresh hopes and views of duty. It is only, however, here and there one of the struggling and suffering poor that I find susceptible to moral counsel and religious influence; the bulk of them are hardly touched by any power that I can exert; they do or our classes; the common plea is want of time or clothes, which is true to a great extent; but still more true is it that the want of education and habits of thought prevent their having any relish for instruction. With all the efforts which have been made of late years for the extension of education, it might be thought that nearly the whole of the population in our great city had had some advantages of school instruction; but this is very far from being the case. I should think that nearly one fourth of the people of the poorest class, above thirty or forty years of age, can neither read nor write; and more than half, especially females, cannot write at all Among the young men and women, say from seventeen to twenty-five years of age, who will in a few years be fathers and mothers, numbers will be found equally ignorant. Many who have come to our adult class have hardly known more than their letters; and with three-fourths of the young women we have to begin by teaching the first lesson in writing. Nor is the evil removed, though it may be lessened, in the case of those who are younger. Many great boys and girls who cannot read at all, pass through our Sunday-school. I say pass through, and this applies also to our adult classes, for the great majority of those who are thus ignorant, soon become weary of the necessary application, and give up the idea of learning in disgust. These facts seem to me to call for renewed and extended efforts in behalf of education. Though almost indispensable as means to the end, I am far from thinking that reading and writing are in themselves efficient safeguards, and will infallibly improve the moral habits of the people. The literature which is in circulation among the poor, seems to show this, and has not received that attention which I feel the importance of the subject deserves. When we think of the cheap periodicals of the day, we naturally call to mind "Chambers's Journal," "Household Words," "Half-hours with the best Authors," and "Family Herald," and other serials of the same class. We feel thankful that so much that is upon the whole good, is being read from week to week by large numbers of the people. Now, these are the very publications which are rarely found in the homes of the poor. their chief sale seems to be among the middle classes, and the most intelligent and skilled artizans; they are not stimulating enough for the bulk of the inhabitants of the courts and alleys. What then do they read? for two-thirds of these people can and do read a little now. The Christian Instruction Society and City Mission curculate large numbers of tracts, but the majority of these are never opened. The publications of the Christian Tract Society, which I have usually found more acceptable than the ordinary religious tracts, have been sometimes returned to me uncut. Many of the people will not read religous tracts. There are one or two publications so gross in their woodcuts and table of contents, that there is no occasion to examine them, to become acquainted with their contents — doubtless, the vicious of various classes buy them, but they are not the literature of the poor. The best class of publications is more frequent in their homes than the very worst. Some time ago a publisher of the name of Lloyd took the lead in bringing out novels in penny numbers; of these he published a great variety, and though full of wonders, murders, and mysteries, they were not, I believe, at all open to the charge of being licentious. They are still being published, but their sale must be greatly lessened by the popularity of translations of the French novels sold in penny numbers, and still more by some English imitations in which the worst features of the French novels are retained. These latter are much read by the young men and women among the poor, and are, I am sure, doing much mischief. Of one of them it is said that the sale is sixty thousand copies weekly. It is not only their impurity, which cannot but deprave the moral habits, that is objectionable, but the coarse declamation with which all but the lowest class are assailed, must generate a painful sense of discontent and oppression. The older men read newspapers and political pamphlets, some of which are violently written. The women who have advanced to middle life hardly read at all, being absorbed with the care of their families. Looking, then, at what forms the principal reading of the poor, we are warned not to trust too much to the power of mere elementary instruction, though good in itself: in order really to elevate and purify the character, it must be combined with sound moral discipline and Christian instruction.

In some parts of the metropolis, the streets on Sunday morning, just previous to the hour of Divine Service, present a quiet orderly appearance; numbers of well-dressed people may be seen going to the House of Prayer, and there are no signs of the business and struggle of every-day life. If we turn our steps into some of the poor neighbourhoods, the scene is changed: we find whole streets in which the shops are open, and crowds of people busily engaged, as if buying and selling were the whole objects of life. In my own district there is Upper Whitecross-street, the market of the neighbourhood, in which the Sunday morning traffic is larger than that of any other morning of the week. Nearly all the numerous buyers look slovenly and unwashed, while tradesmen and hawkers are shouting out the praises of their wares. I know that there are many valid objections against a legislative compulsion of Sunday observances, but I do not feel sure that they would apply to *all* interference with this Sunday trading, which is I think in many ways injurious to those for whose sakes it is professedly carried on. I have spoken to many shopkeepers who are engaged in it, and have heard a very general regret expressed by them, that they are compelled in self-defence to open their shops; they have said that three out of four did it unwillingly, and that they should be glad to close if their neighbours did the same, otherwise their doing so would involve a loss of their daily trade, as the people who go to a shop on the Sunday, are likely to go to the same in the course of the week. A butcher said to me, "If there were no Sunday trade we should take more money on Saturday, than we now do on the Saturday and Sunday put together; the public-houses would take less, for the people would not have so much time to stop in them, and would spend their money at once on the necessaries they required." A woman whom I knew often went to market on the Sunday morning, spoke to the same effect. She wished there were no Sunday trade, for then her husband would have to bring home his wages at once on the Saturday evening, instead of going to the public-house, and putting off the purchase of the Sunday dinner until the morning. This is just the truth. The Sunday marketing is for the convenience of the most idle, thoughtless, and dissipated. Most of the poor receive their wages, at the latest, by eight or nine o'clock on the Saturday evening, and the few who are without money until a later period, would have ample accommodation if the shops were open for but an hour, early on the Sunday morning. As it is, this large amount of Sunday trading leads to a very general lessening of the reverence for the uses of the day, and is felt by many who engage in it, to be a burden on their consciences.

It cannot, I think be denied, except from party and interested motives, that the changes of the last few years have effected most important improvements in the condition of the Poor. I can speak most confidently of the alterations which have gone on under my own observation, in the district in which I labour. Employment during the winter season, has been more uniformly steady for the last two or three years than it formerly was. As a rule it may be said that months of idleness have become shortened into weeks, and that the frightful cases of destitution once so common have become exceedingly rare. Though still it is often melancholy to meet with many who stand idle because no man hires them, and to know that their enforced idleness is causing suffering to their wives and children. This is especially the case in the winter, with bricklayers and house-painters. Numbers of the latter noted are uniformly out of work for the greater part of the winter.

Money-wages, it is true, are lower upon the average than they were ten or twelve years ago, but most working men can purchase much more food and clothing with a week's earnings than they could at that period. House-rent has been nearly stationary, but the rooms in which the poor live are more frequently repaired and cleansed than formerly. Most of the houses, especially in the City, have the advantage of good drainage, and the earthy foot-ways in the courts, which in wet weather became converted into mud, and were at all times covered with filth, have given way to hard, dry, and clean, stone flags. True, much remains to be done, especially in giving more light, air and water; but I have seen since I commenced my labours, changes going on, which have made the dwellings of the poor of Cripplegate as different in the year 1851, from what they were in 1834, as is now the neat house of the clerk, living on the borders of the town, from that of the skilled artizan. It is much more easy to speak satisfactorily of the physical improvement of the people, than of their moral progress. In the one case we can point to facts which hardly admit of contradiction; in the other — where so much is hidden which is only visible to the all-seeing eye — one man will hope while another despairs, and even the blessings which we enjoy will be spoken of as fruitful sources of evil. Thus it has been stated that since the return of "good times" — abundance of food and full employment — more money has been spent by the working classes in riot and drunkenness. It is likely that this is the case with a portion of them, but it is only a minority that thus abuse the increased means at their command. The bulk of our labouring population are not viciously disposed. They have a growing self-respect and love of order, combined with a strong desire for the comfort and instruction of their children, and I believe that the institutions which are maintained by the frugality of the people, such as savings-banks and building societies, are now flourishing to an unexampled degree. Bad times are the immoral ones — discontent in every home — the children in rags, and kept from school — the father sauntering in idleness, and easily tempted to vice. As far as my own district is concerned, I am firmly convinced that the moral habits of the people have improved. In fact, without a conviction of this kind, many of the duties of my office would become wearisome and lifeless. If I were asked what facts I could bring forward in support of this conclusion, apart from individual instances of moral improvement, I should say that there was less intemperance in the district than in former years. I make this remark more confidently from the recollection of the scenes which I have witnessed both publicly and privately — scenes which have latterly become rare. The most intemperate class in the district are the Irish labourers, who herd together in several of the courts in Golden-lane, and Milton-street. Fresh additions by immigration are continually being made to their numbers. And my whole experience has shown me, that little will be done for their moral improvement until their priests seriously take the matter in hand. To the advice or interference of a Protestant, they have an invincible objection. When his visits are tolerated, it is usually from a pecuniary expectation, and when his back is turned, he is probably spoken of contemptuously as a swadler, or in English a methodist. Again I should say, that we have more quiet and order in the streets than formerly — less fighting and tumult. I recollect a friend saying some years ago, that it was "like running the gauntlet," to pass down Milton-street, to our school on Sunday; such was the insult that might be encountered. Now I believe that there is not much fear of any molestation. The home habits of the people have also improved, there being I think a greater attention to neatness and cleanliness. In bringing about all this, many agencies have been at work — both public and private. From the number of persons who are living in the neighbourhood, who have been in some way connected with our Mission, I would venture to hope that our Institution has in no little way tended to their moral improvement, and still more, implanted within them some of the higher principles of the Christian religion.

I shall now briefly notice the operations of the Mission at Chapel-street, in all of which, with the exception of the day-schools, I more or less take a personal part.

I have now, for about a year and a half, given weekly instruction to a Bible-class, consisting of about thirty-six of the elder boys and girls of the day-schools, and have gone through with them the gospel of Matthew, and the greater part of the Acts of the Apostles. It has been my principal aim to impress upon the children the moral principles of the gospel, and to call forth their religious affections.

The Sunday-school is, I think, in a better condition than it has been at any former period. The children are clean and orderly, and with many there has been a marked improvement in their general habits. The average number on the books for the year ending March 31, 1851, has been, boys 166, girls 133, total 299. The average attendance of the children, during the same period, has been, in the morning 217, in the afternoon 240. The highest attendance during the year was in July 1850, for which month the average was, morning 249, afternoon 268. The lowest attendance was in March 1851; a season of much illness — when the average for the morning was 195, afternoon 212. To conduct the Sunday-school, which is under my own superintendence, there is at present thirty-three teachers, the whole of whom, with but few exceptions, attend both morning and afternoon. The large majority of these teachers, both young men and women, were formerly Sunday scholars — and are now engaged in repaying to others the benefits which they received themselves. With them I hold, in the course of the year, many delightful meetings for recreation and instruction — summer excursions and winter gatherings. They have my warm thanks, for their earnest, steady devotion to the instruction of the children under their charge. Connected with the Sunday-school, there are two auxiliary institutions, which should be mentioned here — the savings-bank for the children, long under the charge of Mr. Dobson, and the School Library. The number of depositors in the savings-bank for the past year has been 68, and the amount deposited about £29. For the use of the children's library, which contains about 400 volumes, the payment of one penny monthly is required. The number of subscribers is about 26. In June, nearly 340 of the children of the Sunday- and day-schools, had an excursion in ten vans to Epping Forest, and were accompanied by nearly 30 of the teachers. The day passed off most happily. At Christmas, there was a large and joyous gathering of the children, who were, after their tea, delighted with a "Christmas Tree." The main cost of this entertainment was defrayed by the contributions of several friends — and that of the summer party by the gentleman who has been so liberal in former years.

Reading-room and Library. — This branch of the Mission has gone on steadily increasing since its commencement — just ten additional members being added to it in each of the quarters of last year. — the number now subscribing being 78, of whom the majority pay quarterly. The terms are 1s. 6d. quarterly, or 2d. weekly — the average attendance each evening is about 20. There have been 1,505 volumes borrowed from the Library during the past year, besides the loan of separate numbers of the weekly serials, which are much read.

The Receipts during the year from subscriptions, profits, &c.,have amounted to £20. 14s. The expenditures during the same period, for Newspapers, Periodicals, Librarian's salary, &c., has been £13. 8s. and the balance has been laid out in the purchase of new books, binding, &c. The Library now contains nearly 1,500 volumes — more than 500 of which have been added to it, by gifts and purchases, during the two years and a half the reading-room has been projected.

The members feel greatly indebted to those kind friends who regularly send them the following papers: The Daily News, Athenaeum, Examiner, Inquirer, Atlas, London Labour, Working Man's Friend, and The Vegetarian Messenger The gentleman who gives the London Labour also kindly lends the members weekly, The Expositor, and The Leader, and Nation newspapers.

The members elect their own Committee, order periodicals, purchase books, and manage the affairs of the Room and Library, under the superintendence of a Secretary, appointed by the Domestic Mission Committee.

A Reading and Conversation Class is held every Friday night, and a Singing Class conducted by one of the members, every Wednesday night. The members have free access to the Evening classes, Lectures, &c., and of these privileges most of them avail themselves.

The Week Evening Classes are of two kinds — for children and adults. The children's classes meet on Tuesday and Thursday

evenings, and are composed of about seventy of the elder boys and
girls of the Sunday-school. The instruction is gratuitous, and consists
of Reading, Writing, Arithmetic, and familiar lessons in Geography.
The majority of the children so taught are employed in various ways,
and do not attend any day-school. The average attendance has been
boys 25, girls 28. In the adult classes, which meet on the same
evenings at a later hour, there are at present on the books, males
38, females 32. The attendance from a variety of causes is very
fluctuating, varying from 30 to even 70; about 45 is the average. The
subjects taught are, mainly, Reading, Writing, Arithmetic,
Geography, with occasional lessons on other branches of knowledge.
As valued coadjutors with myself in the instruction of all these classes,
I have again to notice the continued services of Mr. Wright and Mr.
Wade. On the Wednesday evening, a class of young men and women
are instructed in Singing by Mr. Snell, to whose persevering labours
in this department many are indebted for the power of joining
efficiently in the Psalmody which forms part of our public worship.
Besides the classes I have mentioned, there are two or three more
immediately connected with the members of the Reading-room — one
for Drawing, in which the system is almost one of mutual instruction,
and another for Conversation on some definite subject.

The Sunday Evening Congregation, though subject to fluctuations
from weather, illness of the members, and other causes, has been
mainly very steady, with an attendance ranging between 70 and 150.
On some evenings, we have had crowded attendances. It is not for
me to speak of the effect of these services. Judging from the uniform
thoughtful and serious attention of my hearers, it is apparent that
they come for prayer, guidance, and instruction.

The popular Week Evening Lectures, delivered on Mondays,
during the winter season, have not as a whole been so well attended
as in former years, though some of them have attracted large
audiences The following is a list of the Lectures: —

Volcanic Phenomena.
Notes on Western America, by Mr. Steadman.
Man, as he has been, as he is, and as he ought to be, by Mr. Wade.
Paris, by myself.
The Age of Reptiles, by Mr. Kearsley.
The Writings of Charles Dickens, by Mr. M. Wilks.

Vocal Music, by Mr. Snell.
Early English Poetry, two Lectures, by Mr. J.H. Dixon.
Paris, second Lecture, by myself.
Popular Music, by Mr. A. Jones.
The Recent Discoveries of Astronomy, by myself.

Social and Public Meetings. — Several interesting meetings of this kind have been held during the year; two of them, the half-yearly meetings of the Old Scholars' Society, in which we attempt to bring together the young men and women who have grown up and left our Sunday-school. These are I believe, very useful meetings. The largest meeting of the year was the Anniversary one, in celebration of the opening of our Chapel, held in June: several earnest addresses were delivered on subjects connected with Christian duty, and some singing was pleasantly introduced by the singing class. Smaller meetings in connection with the congregation and the reading-room have also been held — prefaced, as the others were, by social gatherings at the tea table.

I received during the year 1850, for my Poor's Purse, from several friends, £13. 10s., which I applied to the relief of severe cases of distress and the purchase of necessaries for the sick. I have also to return my thanks to several friends, for very useful parcels of clothing which have been forwarded to me.

I now conclude. The details I have given will, I hope, convey as correct an idea of the operations of the Mission, as the nature of the work admits.

Chapter V

Educating the People

Introduction

In the nineteenth century, most of the men and women who advocated popular education did so with two sorts of goals in mind. They wanted to teach the poor to read, and probably to write and do arithmetic as well, so that the working classes might function more effectively in their increasingly complex world. They also wanted to improve the poor in a more basic way, to help them develop better characters and lead more ethically disciplined lives. They hoped, through primary education, to make the poor more seriously pious as Christians, more industrious as workers, more thrifty as housewives and more peaceful and law abiding as citizens. In the first half of the century, when revolution seemed a possibility in England, popular education as a form of social control received a great deal of attention. As the likelihood of violent civil disorder receded after 1848, emphasis in popular education gradually shifted away from character formation to more strictly academic matters. Religion, of course, was generally considered fundamental to the character-building side of education.

The churches, furthermore, had traditionally considered education to be among the social duties that they alone were competent to discharge. The movement for developing a system of popular education got underway during the Napoleonic Wars; the majority of the new schools were organized either by the Nonconformist British and Foreign School Society (1814) or the strictly Anglican organization, the National Society (1811). Right through the century Dissenters and Churchmen remained acutely jealous of each other's educational activities, and their distrust and animosity made the development of a state supported national system of education politically very difficult. In 1839, a standing committee on education was established by the Privy Council, and that committee and its inspectors gradually evolved into the department of education. The Education Act of 1870 compelled areas not adequately provided for by the two education societies to set up school boards which would create nondenominational schools. By 1870, moreover, both Churchmen and Nonconformists were reconciled to having the state play an increasingly large role in popular education, for both groups recognized that only the state could find the large amounts of money which universal education required. This represented a major change of political strategy on the part of these Dissenters, like Edward Baines, who in mid century had argued against state financing on the grounds that it meant state control.

Pedagogical methods also changed considerably through the century. In the early days, when many educationists naively thought that children could be easily taught, the monitorial system had wide appeal because it was inexpensive to use older children as monitors to teach the younger ones. By the late 1850s, the budget of the education department had reached nearly one million pounds per year, and there were strong demands for economy. The Revised Code of 1862 established a new system for distributing grants to schools according to the success of their students in elementary examinations in the basic academic subjects. Officially, thereby, emphasis was shifted away from the early Victorian stress on character building and the maintenance of civil order, and basic training in reading, writing and arithmetic was given new importance. This marked the beginning of a trend that continued through the century.

Guide To Further Reading

The best general introduction to the complex issues involved in the history of the education of the poor in Victorian England is Gillian Sutherland's *Elementary Education in the Nineteenth Century* (1971). The best full account is Mary Sturt, *Education of the People: A History of Public Education in England and Wales in the Nineteenth Century* (1967). John Hurt, *Education in Evolution. Church, State, Society and Popular Education, 1800-1870* (1971) is a more analytical study, especially good on the critical period preceding the profoundly important Education Act of 1870.

The social aspects of education have recently attracted a lively and growing literature. Brian Simon's resolutely Marxist point of view leads him to stress social conflict and questions of social class in his *Studies in the History of Education 1780-1870* (1960). Richard Johnson argues forcefully that social control was the principal objective of the early advocates of public education in his influential article, "Educational Policy and Social Control in Early Victorian England", *Past and Present*, 49 (1970). Michael Sanderson discusses "Education and the Factory in Industrial Lancashire, 1780-1840", in *Economic History Review* (1967). J.M. Goldstrom bases his exceptionally interesting book, *The Social Content of English Education* (1975) on a systematic analysis of thousands of nineteenth-century school books. Philip McCann (ed) *Popular Education and Socialization in the Nineteenth Century* (1977) explores an important theme in a variety of situations many having to do with religion.

In his fine work on the growth of the central government in the 1830's and 1840's, *The Victorian Origins of the British Welfare State* (1960), David Roberts includes a perceptive discussion of the early school inspectors. Nancy Ball deals at greater length with the same men in *Her Majesty's Inspectorate* (1963). Frank Smith *The Life and Times of Sir James Kay-Shuttleworth* (1923) is, surprisingly, the only study of that interesting subject. The legislation of 1870 is summarized by Eric Rich in *The education Act, 1870* (1970), and studied from a number of viewpoints in the *British Journal of Education Studies* (1970). Geoffrey Best provides a framework for understanding the conflict between Church and Dissent in "The Religious Difficulties of National Education in England, 1800-1870", *Cambridge Historical Journal* (1956). There is a good chaper on Edward Baines, by Derek Fraser, in *Pressure from Without* (1974), edited by Patricia Hollis. The educational work of the Established Church up to 1870 is described by H.J. Burgess in *Enterprise in Education* (1958).

*The Teacher's Manual; or, Hints to a Teacher on Being Appointed
to The Charge of a Sunday School Class.* 4th ed. 1835. By W.F.
Lloyd. Selections.

William Forster Lloyd (1794-1852) was best known as a
mathematician. Educated in classics and mathematics, he held the
Drummond chair of poitical economy at Oxford from 1832 to 1837.
His most famous published works included treatises on population
and the poor laws. Though an ordained Anglican priest, he held no
clerical position in his lifetime.

Religious instruction is the great object of Sunday-Schools: it
constitutes their pre-eminent glory; and all their plans should be made
subservient to this their principal design. While all spiritual success
depends on the grace of God, he is pleased to direct the employment
of suitable means, and he has promised his blessing to accompany
them. We shall endeavour to suggest a few hints to you on this
infinitely important subject, the religious education of your scholars.

    1. Endeavour to give a spiritual direction to all the common means
of instruction. — When your scholars are reading, spelling, repeating,
or whatever be their employment, always keep in view the importance
of rendering these instructions conducive to their religious interests,
and especially to lead them to the cross of Christ. Let the souls of
your scholars be continually present to your mental eye: "He that
winneth souls is wise," Prov. xi. 30. When we have this one great
object continually before our minds, we shall find various means of
adapting our instructions to its promotion: and thus even the more
mechanical parts of our duties will be sanctified, and receive a spiritual
direction.

    2. Every Sabbath let some important evangelical lesson be taught
to your children. — I will here mention the plan which I have found
most useful for this purpose; and would call it Sentence-reciting. I
will suppose that I am surrounded by the Alphabet class. I then repeat
the following sentence:

                    "We are all poor sinners."

    This is said by each child, and sometimes repeated by them all
together. When *each* child can repeat the sentence in a very clear

and distinct manner, which will take up about two minutes, I proceed
to ask such questions as these: What are we? How many of us? What
sort of sinners? What you Thomas, and you James? What am I? Was
there ever any one who was not a sinner? What is it to be a sinner?
Should we be sorry or glad that we are all poor sinners?

In this way the proposition is thoroughly engrafted into the minds
of the children, and they are examined on it throughout and
reexamined the next Sunday. If any child is particularly dull, and lags
much beyond all the rest, I set one of the other children to teach him,
and to bring him up to me to be examined as soon as he is perfect.

I will just add three other specimens of the sort of sentences thus
proposed for the instruction of these young children:

"Christ died to save poor sinners."
"O Lord! save me, a poor sinner."
"O Lord! give me a new heart."

One such sentence, thoroughly understood by a child, every
Sunday, is likely to prove of inestimable value to these little ones.

With older scholars, I find connected sentences, constructed
somewhat in imitation of Hebrew poetry, to be very useful. The
following are specimens:

I. I am a poor sinner:
Jesus Christ is a great Saviour:
I must believe on him, love him, and obey him:
II. Jesus Christ loved little children on earth:
Jesus Christ loves those who believe on him now he is in heaven:
O Lord Jesus Christ! make me one of thy dear children.
III. Jesus Christ shed his blood on the cross to save sinners:
I confess that I am a sinner:
O Lord! take away all my sins:

In these longer sentences, each line is repeated all round the class:
then the whole sentence; and then the cross-examination takes place.
It will be observed that there is a prayer in two of these sentences:
these are frequently inserted, with a view of teaching the children
what to pray for. I hope that Teachers, from these hints, will be
enabled to draw up some sentence, containing an important spiritual
truth, for their scholars every week thus to learn and understand.
I will merely add, that texts of Scripture may be often introduced
to great advantage, as in the following sentence:

IV. O that I had a good heart!
I cannot make my own heart good:
Create in me a clean heart, O God!
and renew a right spirit within me.

I have found the classes much pleased with this plan; it keeps all the children occupied; and the rapid succession all round keeps up their attention.

3.Private conversation is a very important means of promoting the spiritual welfare of your scholars. — General observations applied to a class, or a whole school, may, through the sophistry of the human heart, receive no self-application; but an appeal made privately, and applied to an individual pointedly, cannot be thus easily evaded. Pride, too, will often resist the force of a public reproof, and produce gloomy stubbornness. Could we ascertain the secret thoughts of many a child, they would be thus expressed: "I can brave corporal punishment or public reproof for my pride will the sustain me; but the melting tenderness of a reproof from the affectionate heart of my teacher in private, that I cannot resist." Where there is opportunity for prayer with, or for a particular child, in addition to conversation, it is well adapted for usefulness.

4. Endeavour to guard your scholars against those particular temptations to which they are most exposed. — When you have ascertained the situations of your children at home, or in their daily employments, you will generally find some particular circumstances which will render your friendly cautions and advice exceedingly desirable. Perhaps some of your children have profane and immoral parents; perhaps they work with companions who will attempt to lead them astray; perhaps they are forming dangerous connexions: in all these cases, and many others, they will need the watchfulness and directions of a pious friend. Again, some of your scholars may possess strong passions, or be soon led astray, or be exposed to some easily besetting sin. How important is it to fortify the weakest part; to give them the most appropriate instructions, adapted to their peculiar cast of character; and to teach them the knowledge of themselves, of their own weakness, and exposure to temptation; and to lead them to Christ as the source of Divine strength and support!

5. Let your appeals to the hearts and consciences of your scholars be striking, close, and animated. — God has implanted feelings in the minds of men, and especially of the young, which respond to the instructions of his work: there, an exact adaptation is found to our

consciences, characters, and neccessities, which proves that He who created us, and who inspired the Scriptures, is the same Being: "All things are naked, and open unto the eyes of Him with whom we have to do," Heb. iv. 13. In availing ourselves of the Divine volume for the instruction of our scholars, we should keep this idea in view, and endeavour to bring its instructions home to the hearts of those whom we teach. "The sword of the Spirit, which is the word of God," is entrusted to us, who are "men of like passions" with those we teach, that while we personally feel its power, we may be enabled to wield it with energy, and, as it were, in close combat against sin. Religious instruction should not be communicated in a cold, abstract, generalizing style to children: it should be imparted in a feeling, lively, and pointed manner. Brevity, simplicity, and variety, must be kept continually in view, if we would interest and benefit the young. We should present religion to them in its most attractive form, as inviting the affections of the young: "Son, give me thine heart." Let the Saviour's love be the continual theme of your conversation and instructions; and let Calvary be the spot to which you are continually resorting: thus your mind will be enlivened, and thus a holy unction will be imparted to your instructions. Let your children take knowledge of you, that you have been with Jesus. Let them derive from you the impression, that "the ways of wisdom are ways of pleasantness, and all her paths, paths of peace." We fear that some pious teachers have produced an impression on the minds of the young, that religion was of a gloomy nature. While you are serious, let it be a cheerful seriousness. Let the light of your heavenly Father's reconciled countenance shed its lustre on you; let the beams of the Sun of righteousness irradiate your minds; and be not as though you were always involved in the mists which overhang the valley of the shadow of death. The early converts went on their way rejoicing. "There is joy among the angels of God over one sinner that repenteth." Let the joy of the Lord be your strength "and the peace of God, which passeth all understanding, shall keep you hearts and minds through Christ Jesus."

6. Study the manner in which Christ and his apostles communicated religious instruction. — Hereafter you will find this subject enlarged on; and, in reading the Acts and Epistles, it will be

easy for you to notice the manner in which the great truths of the gospel are illustrated and enforced; and you should carefully imitate these examples.

7. If you would succeed in imparting spiritual instruction to your children, be earnest in prayer for them. — You cannot have laboured long in a Sunday-School without feeling the inadequacy of mere human efforts. Paul may plant, and Apollos water; but God giveth the increase. In private, spread your class-book before the throne of grace, and supplicate for each one of your children those peculiar blessings which each individual needs. We know not the exact nature of the connexion between prayer and success, but yet we may be fully assured that He who has inspired the powerful desire, and prompted the earnest request, will not withhold his promised blessing. You will undoubtedly be heard and answered when, with faith and importunity, you implore the Divine benediction for yourselves and the children of your charge; that you may be enabled to teach, and that they may be induced to learn, the things which belong to their everlasting peace. May the time soon arrive when "all thy children shall be taught of the Lord, and great shall be the peace of thy children," Isaiah liv. 13. Meantime let us continue "praying always, with all prayer and supplication, in the Spirit, and watching thereunto with all perseverance," Eph. vi. 18.

8. Let the influence of a holy consistent example be constantly manifested. — The young are quick observers of the conduct of their teachers. Example speaks a universal language, which even a child can comprehend. Let us take care that our behaviour is always such as will bear a close inspection. Let no inconsistencies be manifested. In questionable things, as to propriety of which there are differences of opinion, let us always avoid those which might prove an injurious example to our scholars, or tempt them to approach the verge of danger. Labour to adorn the doctrine of God your Saviour in all things. Let your conduct be an embodying of the graces of the Spirit, a living exhibition of what christian excellence really is. There is an assimilating influence in a holy example, to the power of which children are particularly susceptible.

We shall conclude with two cautions: —

1. When any of the children appear to be seriously impressed,

be cautious as to the disclosure of our fond anticipations. — Should any child be induced, from our conduct, to suppose that we thought him truly pious, we fear this would lead him to think of himself more highly than he ought to think. There is much of the deceit of our fallen human nature discoverable in children. They are imitative beings, and often hypocrites. Undue praise and excitation will only tend to foster their corruptions. Let not our joy for promising appearances produce indiscreet confidence. Painful experience has led us to dictate caution on this subject: we have seen many a bud blighted, and many a blossom withered, when we were fondly anticipating the fruits of piety.

2. Let us not expect sudden success, but wait patiently, while we are diligently employing the most suitable means. — Some teachers give way to despondency, when they see no present apparent benefit from their labours. They are looking for the fruits of autumn in spring; they forget the progression: "first the blade, then the ear, after that the full corn in the ear," Mark iv. 28. God teaches us the gradual and imperceptible nature of his blessed influences: "My doctrine shall drop as the rain, my speech shall distil as the dew, as the small rain upon the tender herb, and as the showers upon the grass." Deut. xxxii. 2. "Precept must be upon precept, precept upon precept; line upon line, line upon line; here a little, and there a little," Isaiah xxviii. 10. The reiteration in this passage is peculiarly beautiful, and very instructive. Let it be sufficient for us to know that our work is approved of God, and that "a patient continuance in well-doing" will not fail of success.

Recent Measures for the Promotion of Education in England
(1839), by James Phillips Kay. Selections.

Sir James Kay-Shuttleworth (1804-1877) (*q.v.*), became increasingly
active in philanthropy after he published his account of the working
classes in Manchester in 1832. In 1835 he left Manchester to become
an assistant poor law commissioner, and in 1839 was appointed
secretary of the newly created education committee of the Privy
Council. While he held that position, until poor health forced his
resignation in 1849, he became the principal architect of the English
system of public, primary education.

———————

Our great commercial cities and manufacturing towns contain middle
classes whose wealth, enterprise, and intelligence have no successful
rivals in Europe; they have covered the seas with their ships,
exploring every inlet, estuary, or river which affords them a chance
of successful trade. They have colonised almost every accessible
region; and from all these sources, as well as from the nightly and
daily toil of our working classes in mines, in manufactories, and
workshops, in every form of hardy and continued exertion on the sea
and on the shore, wealth has been derived, which has supported
England in unexampled struggles; yet between the merchants and
manufacturers of this country and the poorer class there is little or
no alliance, excepting that of mutual interest. But the critical events
of this very hour are full of warning, that the ignorance — nay the
barbarism — of large portions of our fellow-countrymen, can no longer
be neglected, if we are not prepared to substitute a military tyranny
or anarchy for the moral subjection which has hitherto been the only
safeguard of England. At this hour military force alone retains in
subjection great masses of the operative population, beneath whose
outrages, if not thus restrained, the wealth and institutions of society
would fall. The manufacturers and merchants of England must know
what interest they have in the civilisation of the working population;
and ere this we trust they are conscious, not merely how deep is their
stake in the moral, intellectual, and religious advancement of the
labouring class, but how deep is their responsibility to employ for
this end the vast resources at their command.

* * * * * * * * *

Whenever the Government shall bend its efforts to combine, for the national advantage, all these great resources, we have no fears for our country. We perceive in it energies possessed by no other nation — partly attributable to the genius of our race; to a large extent derived from the spirit of our policy, which has admitted constant progression in our social institutions; in no small degree to our insular situation, which makes the sea at once the guardian of our liberties and the source of our wealth. But any further delay in the adoption of energetic measures for the elementary education of her working classes is fraught both with intestine and foreign danger — no one can stay the physical influences of wealth — some knowledge the people will acquire by the mere intercourse of society — many appetites are stimulated by a mere physical advancement. With increasing wants comes an increase of discontent, among a people who have only knowledge enough to make them eager for additional enjoyments, and have never yet been sufficiently educated to frame rational wishes and to pursue them by rational means. The mere physical influences of civilisation will not, we fear, make them more moral or religious, better subjects of the State, or better Christians, unless to these be superadded the benefits of an education calculated to develope the entire moral and intellectual capacity of the whole population.

A great change has taken place in the moral and intellectual state of the working classes during the last half century. Formerly, they considered their poverty and sufferings as inevitable, as far as they thought about their origin at all; now, rightly or wrongly, they think that by a change in political institutions their condition can be enormously ameliorated. The great Chartist petition, recently presented by Mr. Attwood, affords ample evidence of the prevalence of the restless desire for organic changes, and for violent political measures, which prevades the manufacturing districts, and which is every day increasing. This agitation is no recent matter; it has assumed various other forms in the last thirty years, in all of which the manufacturing population have shown how readily masses of ignorance, discontent, and suffering may be misled. At no period within our memory have the manufacturing districts been free from some form of agitation for unattainable objects referable to these causes. At one period, Luddism prevailed; at another, machine-breaking; at successive periods the Trades' Unions have endeavoured in strikes, by hired bands of ruffians, and by assassination, to sustain the rate of wages above that determined by the natural laws of trade; panics have been excited among the working classes, and severe runs upon the Savings' Banks effected from time to time. At one time they have been taught to believe that they could obtain the same wages if an eight hours' bill were passed as if the law permitted them to labour twelve hours in the day; and mills were actually worked on this principle for some weeks, to rivet the conviction in the minds of the working class. The agitation becomes constantly more systematic and better organised, because there is a greater demand for it among the masses, and it is more profitable to the leaders. It is vain to hope that this spirit will subside spontaneously, or that it can be suppressed by coercion. Chartism, an armed political monster, has at length sprung from the soil on which the struggle for the forcible repression of these evils has occured. It is as certain as any thing future is certain, that the anarchical spirit of the Chartist association will, if left to the operation of the causes now in activity, become every year more formidable. The Chartists think that it is in the power of Government to raise the rate of wages by interfering between the employer and the workman; they imagine that this can be accomplished by a maximum of prices and minimum of wages, or some similar contrivance; and a considerable portion of them believe that the burden of taxation and of all 'fixed charges' (to use Mr. Attwood's expression) ought to be reduced by issuing inconvertible paper, and thus depreciating the currency. They are confident that a Parliament chosen by universal suffrage would be so completely under the dominion of the working classes as to carry these measures into effect; and therefore they petition for universal suffrage, treating all truly remedial measures as unworthy of their notice, or as obstacles to the attainment of the only objects really important. Now the sole effective means of preventing the tremendous evils with which the anarchical spirit of the manufacturing population threatens the country is, by giving the working people a good secular education, to enable them to understand the true causes which determine their physical condition and regulate the distribution of wealth among the several classes of society. Sufficient intelligence and information to appreciate these causes might be diffused by an education which could easily be brought within the reach of the entire population, though it would necessarily comprehend more than the mere mechanical rudiments of knowledge.

We are far from being alarmists; we write neither under the influence of undue fear, nor with a wish to inspire undue fear into others. The opinions which we have expressed are founded on a careful observation of the proceedings and speeches of the Chartists, and of their predecessors in agitation in the manufacturing districts for many years, as reported in their newspaters; and have been as deliberately formed as they are deliberately expressed. We confess that we cannot contemplate with unconcern the vast physical force which is now moved by men so ignorant and so unprincipled as the Chartist leaders; and without expecting such internal convulsions as may deserve the name of *civil war*, we think it highly probable that persons and property will, in certain parts of the country, be so exposed to violence as materially of affect the prosperity of our manufactures and commerce, to shake the mutual confidence of mercantile men, and to diminish the stability of our political and social institutions. That the country will ultimately recover from these internal convulsions we think, judging from its past history, highly probable; but the recovery will be effected by the painful process of teaching the working classes, by actual experience, that the violent measures which they desire do not tend to improve their condition.

It is astonishing to us, that the party calling themselves Conservative should not lead the van in promoting the diffusion of that knowledge among the working classes which tends beyond any thing else to promote the security of property and the maintenance of public order. To restore the working classes to their former state of incurious and contented apathy is impossible, if it were desireable. If they are to have knowledge, surely it is the part of a wise and virtuous government to do all in its power to secure to them useful knowledge, and to guard them against pernicious opinions.

We have already said that all instruction should be hallowed by the influence of religion; but we hold it to be equally absurd and shortsighted to withhold secular instruction, on the ground that religion is alone sufficient.

We do not, however, advocate that form of religious instruction which merely loads the memory, without developing the understanding, or which fails to stir the sympathies of our nature to their inmost springs. There is a form of instruction in religion which leaves the recipient at the mercy of any religious or political fanatic who may dare to use the sacred pages as texts in support of imposture. We have seen that even a maniac may lead the people to worship him as the Messiah, whose second coming, spoken of in the pages of Holy Writ, was fulfilled. Many of the Chartists proclaim themselves Missionaries of Christianity. They know how to rouse the superstition of an ignorant population in favour of their doctrines, by employing passages of Scripture the true meaning of which the uninstructed mass do not reach. They continually set before them those verses which speak of the rich man as an oppressor — which show with how much difficulty the rich shall enter the kingdom of heaven. Poverty is the Lazarus whom they place in Abraham's bosom — wealth the Dives whom they doom to hell. They find passages in the writing of the Apostles speaking of a community of goods among the early Christians: on this they found the doctrines of the Socialists. Our Saviour, in the synagogue of Nazareth, opened the Scripture at the prophecy in which Isaiah describes His divine mission: 'The Spirit of the Lord is upon me, because he hath anointed me to preach the gospel to the poor, &c.' From these and similar passages, they gather the sanctions of their own Mission. Christianity in their hands becomes the most frantic democracy, and democracy is clothed with the sanctions of religion. Even the arming of the Chartist association is derived from our Saviour's injunction, 'he that hath no sword, let him sell his garment and buy one.' To such purposes may the Scriptures be wrested by unscrupulous men who have practised on the ignorance, discontent, and suffering of the mass.

Their power will continue as long as the people are without sufficient intelligence to discern in what the fearful error of such impiety consists. There are times in which it is necessary that every man should be prepared to give a reason for the faith that is in him. We loathe a merely speculative religion, which does not purify the motives, and which robs piety alike of humility and charity; but when the teachers of the great mass of the people unite the imposture of religious and political fanatics, preaching anti-social doctrines as though they were a gospel of truth, the knowledge of the people must be increased, and their intellectual powers strengthened, so as to enable them to grapple with the error and to overcome it.

Next to the prevalence of true religion, we most earnestly desire that the people should know how their interests are inseparable from those of the other orders of society; and we will not stop to demonstrate so obvious a truth as that secular knowledge, easily accessible, but most powerful in its influence, is necessary to this end.

Crosby Hall Lectures on Education (1848): "On the Progress and Efficiency of Voluntary Education in England", by Edward Baines. Selections.

Sir Edward Baines (1800-1890), was owner and editor of the *Leeds Mercury*, the leading provincial newspaper of the mid nineteenth century, an eminent Congregationalist layman, and an influential spokesman of liberal Dissent. He was M.P. for Leeds from 1859 to 1874, a dedicated supporter of free trade, and at mid century was deeply interested in the question of the role the state ought to play in providing education for the people. Baines was the foremost proponent of the voluntary principle in education.

Among the many controversies of the age, it is cheering to find some great truths which receive general assent. Few persons, for example, would question the proposition, that Religion, Knowledge, and Liberty conduce to the highest prosperity of nations. There would be great diversity of opinion as to the practical application of the truth, — as to the kind of religion, the method of promoting knowledge, and the best form of liberty. But it is an advantage, and one which England has not very long enjoyed, that the general principle is admitted. No English writer, now-a-days, commends Ignorance as the mother of devotion, or advocates the despotic in preference to the representative form of government.

Religion, knowledge, liberty, then, may be regarded as forming the golden tripod on which the genius of Britain sits, dispensing truth and happiness to the world. Each stem of the tripod should have the strength of the rock, and all should lean towards and support each other. The religion should be that divine principle which not merely restrains, but animates and ennobles, — which shuts out no ray of light, and sanctions no species of injustice. The knowledge should be pure truth, free from all superstition and servility, illustrating at once the claims of God and the rights of man among his fellow-men. The liberty should be according to knowledge, and consistent with the peace and order inculcated in the Gospel.

I shall not be understood by this figure to imply that I evaluate any right or interest of man into rivalry with the claims of his Maker. No. But I deem knowledge and liberty to be heaven-born, — to belong to religion itself, — to be embraced with it in the same radiant circle — even the girdle of righteousness and love with which the Almighty encompasses his decrees.

If this view be correct, it is the sacred duty of Englishmen to protect and advance religion, knowledge, and liberty, in their alliance with each other, and never to promote one at the expense of the rest. The facts to be brought out in this Lecture seem to me to illustrate the connection of which I have spoken, as natural and worthy of being perpetuated. Venerating religion and loving liberty, it will be my object to show that knowledge ought to be promoted among the youth of England with a due regard to both.

It is humbling but salutary to remember, that the influential classes of this country have not long admitted the duty, or even the safety, of encouraging the bulk of the people, that is, the labouring classes, to acquire knowledge. Popular education in England may be said to bear date from the commencement of the present century. Before that period, knowledge, like liberty, had been slowly though surely making way; but it very rarely extended beyond the upper and middle classes. It was thought unsuitable for the labouring class, or beyond their reach. The aristocracy, and even the clergy, regarded ignorance as the safeguard of order, and knowledge as incompatible with subordination.

In the middle of the nineteenth century, when education is more extended, and more rapidly extending and improving, than at any former period, our rulers have taken up the belief, that it is not safe to leave education to the people themselves, but that, in order to make it general and efficient, it must be aided and controlled by the Government. It is my firm and sorrowful conviction, that this is one of those aberrations in the progress of truth, of which history contains so many examples. How often have we seen error, when defeated on one side, unexpectedly making head on another, and threatening to recover all the ground it had lost! It has been so in the history of religion, of government, and in many of the departments of knowledge. Imperfect reformations, half conquests, and balanced advantages, characterize the march of truth through this erring world. The eagle gaze of Luther did not receive every ray of solar light. The Protestant Reformation of Germany, Switzerland, and

England did not quite destroy the shackles of prejudice. The almost blameless Revolution of America left the monster form of Slavery to rear itself beside the largest growth of Freedom. The great Reform of the English House of Commons was neither complete nor unblemished. In Germany and France we have seen philosophy debased by infidelity. The revival of spiritual religion in our own day is accompanied by revived superstition. And we have scarcely emancipated industry from Government control, under the name of "protection," when the same control, under nearly the same misnomer, lays its grasp on the more sacred interests of education.

It seems very remarkable that Government, which in all former ages held aloof from the education of the people, should now, for the first time, claim its superintendence as a right and duty, when the people have made such extraordinary advances in educating themselves. If it be indeed the duty of Government to promote the education of the people, it is a duty which has been so entirely neglected through all the periods of our history, that we could not safely rely upon the government for its discharge in future. Of this newly-claimed right and newly-discovered duty we may say, that no claim could be made with a worse grace, and that the duty is undertaken precisely when it is least needed.

It will hardly be denied, within the limits of England, that *the people* have a *right* to educate their own children, and that it is their *duty* to educate them; that this right and duty belong first, by the law of nature, to *parents*, and next, by the law of Christianity, to those whom Providence enables to assist their poorer neighbours.

I shall not further discuss this question, because it will be undertaken by an abler hand in a future Lecture. I will only remind you of the general rule, that the more responsibility is divided, the less efficiently is the duty performed.

Whilst I believe that education is the duty of the people themselves, I am equally persuaded that it does not come within the province of Government, according to just views of what that province is, under a system of political and civil liberty. But I am, if possible, still more strongly of opinion, that, wherever the duty lies, it is eminently the *interest* of the people to discharge it themselves; and for these, amongst other reasons: — 1st. That a duty is likely to be best discharged by the parties on whom it most directly rests, and who have the strongest motives for its performance. 2nd. That our duties are the discipline ordained by Heaven for our moral improvement, and that to relieve men of their duties is to deprive them of their virtues. 3rd. That the virtues especially cultivated by Voluntary education are those which most conduce to the interests of liberty and religion, namely, self-reliance, the great safeguard of freedom, — and active Christian benevolence, our only hope for the evangelization of the world. 4th That education conducted by a people themselves, is likely to have a more vigorous and healthful character, than it could have if the schoolmasters were continually looking with hope and fear to Government officers. 5th. That new and improved methods of instruction are more likely to be introduced under the free competition of a Voluntary system, than under the uniformity and *vis inertiae* which usually characterize a Government system. 6th. That with whatever zeal a Government agency might be worked at first, it would be likely to be perverted to purposes of Ministerial *patronage*. 7th. That though at present a wish is professed only to *aid* Voluntary effort, yet the natural tendency of the system is to deaden the Voluntary spirit, and to bring schools more and more into dependence upon the Government. 8th. That the question of education is implicated with that of *religion*, and therefore the serious objections which apply to Government interference with religion apply also to Government interference with education. 9th. That in the state of things which exists now, and is likely still to continue, a Government Education Board must be under the influence of the Church and the Aristocracy; and from this and other causes, the Church of England is sure to obtain the lion's share·of every education grant, — the only alternative being, the still worse evil of subsidizing the schools of all sects, which amounts to the subsidizing of all forms of religion.

I am aware that some of these reasons will not have their due weight with the friends of Church Establishments. It is evident that many have been prejudiced against the Voluntary system in education, by their rooted dislike to the Voluntary system in religion. Nor can I deny — on the contrary, I am fully convinced — that both rest substantially on the same principles, and must be opposed or defended by the same arguments. Whatever weakens the cause of

Voluntary education, weakens that of Voluntary religion; and whatever strengthens the one, strengthens the other.

Whilst I say this, I cannot but express a doubt, whether it was sound policy on the part of Churchmen to seek to extend the Establishment principle by obtaining a supplementary establishment for education, inasmuch as education had hitherto been free, and as the advantage they expect to gain will only aggravate the sense of injustice already felt by Nonconformists.

Two great and influential classes among our public men are jealous of the Voluntary Principle, — first, the partizans of the Church, because they regard that principle as hostile to the existing Establishment; and, secondly, the disciples of the Continental policy, of endowing all education and all religion, because, I believe, they really do not understand the Voluntary Principle, but connect it with over-earnestness, or fanaticism, in religion — an error with which they themselves are certainly not chargeable. Some object to the Voluntary Principle as *inefficient*. Most think it not trustworthy, on account of its alleged want of steadiness and uniformity: and, with all my admiration for the Voluntary Principle, I must admit that it has the same defects as — *Nature* and *Freedom*; — that it does not always move in straight lines, or array its forces in regimental order, or obey pedantic rules, or make the succeeding century a copy of the preceding, or flatter statesmen by limiting improvement within Acts of Parliament; but still I believe that, like Nature and Freedom, it has a magnificent rule and range — the rule of a living spirit, and the range of whatever achievement God has made possible to man.

I speak here of the Voluntary Principle in an enlarged sense, not confining myself to its operation in providing the means of religious instruction. Of course I do not ask for it, throughout the scope of my whole argument, that New Testament sanction and authority, which rests the support of religion on voluntary liberality, to the exclusion of the compulsory interference of the magistrate. We must, indeed, extend that New Testament principle to religious education; for, if we once receive public money for religious instruction in our schools, we should very soon receive it for religious instruction in our chapels. On that point there can be no dispute, except with men whose views are exceedingly confused; Nonconformists, giving religious education, are precluded by their religious principles from receiving Government money.

But I do not confine my views, in defending "Voluntary education," to merely religious education: I apply the terms to the cultivation of the human mind in all its extent — to literature, science, art, and politics — to colleges, newspapers, magazines, books, and literary and scientific institutions — to the life-long training of the adult, as well as the elementary instruction of the child. Concerning all these I am ready to declare my opinion, that the Voluntary Principle is adequate, is the most consistent with liberty, is conducive to the highest improvement; and, on the other hand, that these things do not come within the province of Government, whilst Governmental interference often retards advancement and shackles freedom. In support of my views, I appeal to the free press, the free literature, the free science, and the free education of England, in opposition to countries where all these things are taken under the care of Government.

If my argument should fail to vindicate the freedom of our schools, it must equally fail to protect the freedom of our periodical press and our general literature. The press is quite as important an educator as the school: the case for placing the former under Government help and superintendence, is a strong as for placing the latter, — nay, stronger, as any one will be convinced who reflects on the manifold defects and abuses of a free press, and on the unspeakable importance of that great engine, which so principally moulds the mind and will of England. Nearly all the Continental Governments which pay and direct the school, pay and direct also the pulpit and the press. They do it consistently. And our Government educationists at home would only be consistent, should they recommend Government grants and inspection to all our ministers, our editors, and our authors.

To prevent misconception, I may say, that I do not deny the power of an enlightened despot to erect a vast and complete machinery of education, and, by a large expenditure of his peoples's money on colleges, museums, galleries, and theatres, to force the growth of learning art, and taste among them, especially when they are precluded from the nobler duties and more practical enterprises of a free people. I look at the whole question, and at the whole man;

and, regarding man in all the capacity of his moral and intellectual
nature, and communities in all their interests, I reject the petty
advantages of despotism, and claim the more generous, though
perhaps looser, regimen of freedom.

It may be well also to explain, that the Voluntary Principle does
not exclude, or affect to be independent of, the aid which men of
wealth, power, and station can give to public objects. It even asks,
that "Kings should be nursing fathers and queens nursing mothers"
to religion. It invites the largest donations of princes and nobles
towards the erection of the temple, the college, or the school, when
"they offer *Willingly of their own proper goods*"— acknowledging
that "all things come of God, and that of his own they have given
him." It accords praise to our Alfred, our Henrys, and Edwards, and
to a long train of nobles, prelates, ladies, gentry, and merchants,
whose munificence founded, out of their own estates and incomes,
most of our ancient schools of learning. The only conditions of
accepting help which the Voluntary Principle requires are these —
first, that the gift be truly Voluntary, not the produce of exaction,
or the appropriation of what does not belong to the donor himself;
and secondly, that it in no way interferes with the absolute
self-government of the Church. Thus the Voluntary Principle is
independent, without pride, — willing to accept, without covetousness
or subserviency, — jealous for the purity of the Church and the
interests of liberty, — not anxious for endowments, because of their
liability to abuse, — more willing to give than to receive, — ever
appealing to, and thereby cultivating and strengthening, the highest
motives, love and duty to God, and love and duty to our fellow-men.

But we are told, by a thousand tongues and pens, — "The
Voluntary Principle is a failure; however plausible it may appear in
argument, experience proves its inefficiency."

I accept the appeal to experience; and boldly maintain that the
Voluntary Principle, so far from having failed, has triumphantly
succeeded.

                              * * * * * * * *

One of the grand arguments of our State Educationists is, that
the Voluntary Principle will not, and cannot, sustain the annual
expense of well-conducted schools. This argument is strongly pressed

both by Professor Hoppus and Dr. Vaughan; and my respected friend, the Professor, in a recent letter in the *Morning Chronicle*, after making a calculation of what he supposed would be the annual cost of public schools, appealed to me whether it was possible for the Voluntary Principle to sustain it. My reply is brief, but I think conclusive. First, That the Voluntary Principle, by its two modes of operation, namely, the payments of those who are benefited, and the contributions of the benevolent, can sustain, amply sustain, every needful cost, both of education and of religion. And secondly, That if the people cannot sustain it, the Government cannot; for the Government has neither strength nor money but what it derives from the people.

It may be responded — "We know that the people have the power, if they are disposed to use it, but they are not; and, therefore, it is necessary to compel them." Oh, then, it is not a pecuniary or a physical ability that is wanting, but a *moral* ability; and for *that* you leave the people and fly to the Government! — you abandon the Voluntary for the Compulsory Principle! For shame! — Where have you been living, that you know so little, and think so meanly, of the people of England? Have you been shut up within the walls of colleges, poring over German philosophy? Yet even those colleges should have spoken to you of the power of English liberality and public spirit; for every stone of them was laid by the Voluntary Principle. Have you never heard that the Nonconformists of England and Wales, who are the poorer sections of the community, have built about 13,000 places of worship, and are sustaining their own ministers and services; which, at an average of only 120l. a year for each place, implies an aggregate Voluntary expenditure of more than a million and a half yearly? Are you not aware that the Church of England have, within our own generation, built or rebuilt several thousands of churches, and that for most of them new funds have been provided? Do you forget the millions that must have been expended in building and supporting Sunday-schools and Day-schools; and the still more extraordinary fact of the moral and spiritual agency employed in the Sunday-schools? Do you not know that there are benevolent societies, having their centres in this metropolis, which collect from the people more than half a million sterling every year, by far the greater part both by Professor Hoppus and Dr. Vaughan; and my respected friend, the Professor, in a recent letter in the *Morning Chronicle*, after making a calculation of what he supposed would be the annual cost of public schools, appealed to me whether it was possible for the Voluntary Principle to sustain it. My reply is brief, but I think conclusive. First, That the Voluntary Principle, by its two modes of operation, namely, the payments of those who are benefited, and the contributions of the benevolent, can sustain, amply sustain, every needful cost, both of education and of religion. And secondly, That if the people cannot sustain it, the Government cannot; for the Government has neither strength nor money but what it derives from the people.

It may be responded — "We know that the people have the power, if they are disposed to use it, but they are not; and, therefore, it is necessary to compel them." Oh, then, it is not a pecuniary or a physical ability that is wanting, but a *moral* ability; and for *that* you leave the people and fly to the Government! — you abandon the Voluntary for the Compulsory Principle! For shame! — Where have you been living, that you know so little, and think so meanly, of the people of England? Have you been shut up within the walls of colleges, poring over German philosophy? Yet even those colleges should have spoken to you of the power of English liberality and public spirit; for every stone of them was laid by the Voluntary Principle. Have you never heard that the Nonconformists of England and Wales, who are the poorer sections of the community, have built about 13,000 places of worship, and are sustaining their own ministers and services; which, at an average of only 120l. a year for each place, implies an aggregate Voluntary expenditure of more than a million and a half yearly? Are you not aware that the Church of England have, within our own generation, built or rebuilt several thousands of churches, and that for most of them new funds have been provided? Do you forget the millions that must have been expended in building and supporting Sunday-schools and Day-schools; and the still more extraordinary fact of the moral and spiritual agency employed in the Sunday-schools? Do you not know that there are benevolent societies, having their centres in this metropolis, which collect from the people more than half a million sterling every year, by far the greater part resource is *functionarism*, — a policy which would impair the noble self-reliance of the people, and bring religion itself into bondage, — I call upon you to give it your utmost resistance, and to rally but the closer around that standard of *virtuous Willinghood*, which our fathers reared in worse times, which we will never desert, and which, I confidently believe, will wave over a regenerated world.

Minutes of the Committee of Council on Education, 1848-1849:
Report of the Rev. Henry Moseley. Selections.

Henry Moseley (1801-1872), Anglican clergyman and mathematician,
was a man of many talents. He is best remembered for his work in
marine architecture, and he wrote extensively on astronomy and
engineering. Before he became a school inspector in 1844, he had been
Professor of Natural and Experimental Philosophy at King's College,
University of London. His reports are among the most interesting
and clear-headed of the early school inspectors who were, on the
whole, an exceptionally able group of men. The following report by
Moseley is a cogently presented, pessimistic, view of public education
at mid-century. It stands in sharp contrast to the optimism of Edward
Baines and the high hopes of J.P. Kay Shuttleworth.

As a general result of my inspection, I may perhaps be permitted
to bear testimony to the great progress which the cause of elementary
education appears to be making in the public mind. It is obvious that
more interest is taken in the schools than heretofore, and that,
whether the educational movement is in alliance with your measures
or hostile to them, it is still a movement in advance.

When, on the other hand, I look at the result of this public
sympathy, and consider what is actually going on within the walls
of our school-rooms, and the chance there is of any given child
receiving a religious education (in any sense worthy so to be called),
or of its being instructed in such elements of human knowledge as,
when the child shall become a man, to make him a reasoning, an
understanding man, as to the state of life to which it has pleased God
to call him — and therefore, probably, a provident and industrious
man — the view I take of the present state of the educational question
is far less sanguine. I confess that I see nothing in what is now done
for the child which may reasonably be expected to produce these fruits
in the man. This impression would not moreover be shaken in my
mind if schools as good as we now have (I mean the majority) were
so multiplied that every child might attend them, and if the children
actually did all attend them as long as they now attend them.

I see no relation between the means and the end — the cause
and the effect it is supposed to be capable of producing. Education
must be something more than this, to effect the good we expect from

it; and I am contented to appeal, in evidence of this, to what has been done by it for the populations of many places where schools, amply sufficient in numbers, equal in efficiency to the great majority of present schools, and conducted on the same principles, have been in operation for the last 20 or 30 years — to the moral condition of these places, and to the number of persons educated in those schools, who are now regular communicants, or even attendants, at church.

We are too much accustomed to confound our notion of a religious education with that of religious instruction, and not to consider that a place should be sought for religion in the hearts and affections of children, as well as in their memories and their understandings. And, as to secular things, our idea of education almost always identifies itself with that which we ourselves have happened to receive. We can conceive differences in the degree, but not in the subjects of instruction, or in the manner of it. To all below us, we would give a greater or less fragment of the knowledge we ourselves possess, according to their standing; thus, reproducing ourselves, under different but inferior forms, in all the subordinate grades of society. It is thus that a very little learning, that dangerous thing, comes to be associated with our notion of the instruction which people in the lowest grades of society should receive. It would be one of the advantages of an education devised with a special reference to the pursuits of labouring people, that it would enable us to get rid of this thinness — this character of a *little learning* in popular education.

In respect to the objects which it contemplates, it might be a thorough and a complete education, and yet the higher classes of society might continue to be separated from the lower, as they now are, by higher forms of knowledge, education being still graduated according to men's social condition, but having an adaptation to each condition, and being good and complete with reference to that adaptation.

****

Considering what is the amount of education which a child under the age of 12 years could receive, under the most favourable circumstances, and how far the education which the children in the best schools are receiving falls short of that which, under more favourable circumstances, they might receive, and taking into my view that 95 per cent of them are actually under this age, I cannot disguise from myself that, notwithstanding all the zealous efforts and great personal sacrifices of their promoters, if all were equally good with these, and every locality were adequately provided with such schools, the impression made would be neither great nor permanent.

It is difficult by any stretch of imagination to conceive how that amount of learning shall be communicated to a child before he is 12 years of age which shall be too much learning for him to possess when he becomes a man; especially as he will have forgotten the greater portion of it in the interval. Certain I am that those persons who are beset by fears lest too much should be done for the education of those whose lot it is to earn their own bread in the sweat of their brow (and in the discharge of my official duties I have met with many such) may console themselves with this fact.

The early age at which the children are taken away from school is the *great* discouragement of the friends of education; it is the *hopeless* side of the question. No other obstacle appears to them altogether insurmountable but this.

True it is that the children remain longer in good schools than in bad ones; the parents thereby shewing that they are willing to make some sacrifice that their children may have the benefit of what they consider to be a good education; but they cannot make a *sufficient* sacrifice. The smallmess of the earnings of an agricultural labourer renders that sacrifice an impossibility to him. It is neccessary to the child's being fed and clothed that it should, itself, contribute to the cost of these wants from the earliest period when it is able to do so. To the sum (from 6s. to 10s. per week) otherwise applicable to the maintenance of the family, it is *neccessary* that the labourer should add the 1s.6d. or 2s. per week which his child can earn.

* * * * * * * * *

I have heard it alleged by parents as a reason for not sending their children to school, when they are of an age to be useful to them at home or to go to work, that they are fearful lest, having had too much learning, they should not take kindly to labour.

Some weight might be attached to this argument, if, in the kind of labour to which the child was first put, any consideration were had as to its influence on his future well being as a labourer. To those persons who deny that the growth of a man's understanding lends any aid to the development of his religious character, and who hold, that to make a labouring man sober, honest, industrious, and frugal, thews and sinews only are needed and not principles — a hardy constitution but not a sound mind — a body inured to labour but not an enterprising spirit, or a good understanding, or self-respect or forethought — it might seem a doubtful question, whether, in sacrificing the wages which the child would earn to send him to school, the labourer was in truth benefiting his child. If the child's pursuits when he left school were calculated to give him habits of industry and self-dependence, it might be considered better, by persons holding these opinions, that he should be taken as early as possible from school. The case is, however, far otherwise. There is no consideration had, of the influence of the sort of work to which he is first put, on the formation of the character of the good labourer in him. His usefulness, and not his welfare, is the thing considered; and a long and dreary interval is allowed to intervene, between the time he leaves school and that when his industrial education can, in any sense, be said to begin. He goes, it may be, into the fields at day-break, to drive away the birds from the growing crops, and continues there until sunset; or he is sent out to watch pigs or geese, or to keep cattle or sheep. Thus employed, he is conversant with the same horizon, contends with the same flock of sparrows, traverses the boundaries of the same field, leans daily against the same gate, or sits under the same hedge for months, and, perhaps, for years together. It is difficult to conceive what, under such circumstances, is the state of the mind of a poor child, stored with nothing to reflect upon, and unaccustomed to reflect; with nothing to undertake, and nothing to accomplish, beyond that one wearisome duty; passing months and years of the most characteristic portion of its life in a state approaching as nearly as may be to one of sterile indolence.

The intellectual stagnation of an existence like this eats into the soul of the child. I have often been told by those who have taken the pains to ascertain it, of the marvellous inroads it makes in his character; what a cloud it brings over his understanding, how in a few months scarce a trace remains of the knowledge he had acquired at school, except, perhaps, its most technical and mechanical elements; and how seldom his conduct gives any evidence of those religious influences to which it had been a principal object of the school to subject him. In truth, although his intellectual life has been stagnating, it has not been thus with the life of his senses. On the side of these lies all his danger. The school had established, indeed, some equipoise of the moral and intellectual elements of his being, and of the sensual; but the preponderance of the latter has begun; and the animal in him is destined to grow with his growth and strengthen with his strength, as the antagonist principle shrinks in its dimensions by disuse, until the one is wholly lost in the excess of the other.

It requires, moreover, but little knowledge of a labouring population to feel assured, that the persons with whom the boy associates in these idle hours may contribute, not less than his occupation, to form in him an indolent, a dishonest, and a profligate character. Nor is he likely to experience any useful moral supervision, or prudent guidance and support at the hands of his master, if the following character drawn of the relation of the agricultural labourer to his employer by an acute and impartial observer be true: —

"The farmer," says Mr. Dawes, "has no notion of worth in the labourer as a man or as a fellow-creature; but only values him as a machine or instrument by which a certain quantity of work is performed, and does not think that, although he professes to be a Christian, it is any part of his duty, as such, to endeavour to improve the moral condition of the labourers under him, by making them more intelligent."

Such being the industrial training of the agricultural labourer at that period of his life, the impression of which is the most durable, it is scarcely to be considered strange that in every parish there should be so large a portion of labourers trained up to be paupers — men without the intelligence or the energy, or the moral courage, or the spirit of independence necessary to pursue with success the humblest calling.

Having made many inquiries on this subject, I have learned with surprise how large a class, that is, of men who burden the rates, not by reason of inability to labour, or of profligacy, or dishonesty, but for the want of aptitude, a spirit of independence, thriftiness, and industry. It is difficult to explain this, except by supposing that at some early period of their lives indolence and apathy, and a sense of moral bondage, had been allowed to grow upon them.

As the demand for labour in the parish increases, these are the last men in respect to whom it is taken up; and when it diminishes, they are the first who are thrown out of employ, whilst the intelligent, enterprising, and industrious labourer, so long as he is in health, is rarely or ever unemployed.

The resources of education, taken in its widest sense as a religious, a moral, and an industrial education, must be strangely mismanaged if they do not diminish this great army of *able-bodied* paupers, which, considered with reference to its dependence upon the rates and to the recruits which it sends to the criminal population of the country, is among the greatest evils with which it is burdened.

In speaking of the unfavourable influence on the children of agricultural labourers, of the kind of work to which they are first put, when they leave school, I have referred only to the boys.

The case is, however, no better with the girls. It is true that they do not leave school so early as the boys, because work cannot be found for them so soon. Few of them remain, however, after the age of 12 or 13. When they have left, an interval is generally passed at home, occupied, perhaps, in assisting in household work or in nursing. Meanwhile a place is sought for them, to which they are considered eligible at 14. Their first service is commonly at the house of a little tradesman or small farmer; and but a small portion of them ever advance, I am informed, to any higher grade of service, the majority returning home, after a few years, to work in the fields.

The occupations of children of both sexes in town districts, and in rural districts which have some staple manufacture, are, of course, different, but in all I have found the opinion to prevail, that the period when they first leave school is fraught with danger; that the seeds of profligacy are then sown, and the foundations of pauperism laid; and that nothing is more to be desired than that some educational supervision should be exercised over them during the period which intervenes before they enter upon a life of active labour; associated with some well-considered course of industrial training.

Chapter VI

Converting The Working Classes

Introduction

Towards the middle of the nineteenth century, both Churchmen and Dissenters became anxiously aware that large numbers of working-class men and women, especially in large towns, were not associated with any church or chapel. The religious census of 1851 confirmed this worried impression, and during the second half of the century there were many attmepts to gain, or regain as they said at the time, the working class for Christ. In addition to the central evangelical impulse to save as many souls as possible from everlasting perdition, two more worldly motives lay behind the mid-century interest in converting the masses. Revolution still seemed possible in the years immediately after 1848, and men of property, of whatever denomination, tended to think that religion would preserve the social order by curbing the rebellious instincts of the poor. Churchmen and Conservatives had acted from this assumption throughout the first half of the century. In 1818 the Liverpool Administration allocated one million pounds to help build churches, and granted an additional five hundred thousand pounds in 1824. Peel's support for reforming the financial structure of the Church in the 1830s was informed by the same line of reasoning. Chartist activity encouraged Peel to try to adapt the rigid parish system to demographic change through the creation of quasi parochial districts in 1843, and also to authorize public funds for the payment of additional ministers. Another motive operated more among liberals and Nonconformists. For several generations before the 1840s, the evangelical Dissenting denominations had been rapidly increasing the numbers of their adherents. That growth slowed in the 40s, and some denominations began to worry about their own vigour. They saw in the working class a fresh supply of potential converts.

These two motives, often mixed together, encouraged much discussion of why the working classes were not in church, some of which is very intersting for what it reveals about inter class attitudes. But, with many exceptions, the churches remained basically insensitive to the social needs and political aspirations of the working classes until the 1880s. During the last twenty years of the century, middle class people became much more sharply aware of the conditions urban life imposed on the poor, and many churches made a great effort to meet the cultural and recreational as well as the spiritual needs of the working classes. The Salvation Army neatly reflects the changed emphasis, for it was created as a conversionist sect exclusively concerned with saving the souls of the poor. In the 1880s General Booth was converted to social work, and the social wing of the Army for a time rivalled the importance of the spiritual.

The success which evangelical Nonconformity enjoyed among the working classes in the late eighteenth and early nineteenth centuries was, however, not repeated in the later nineteenth century. Liberalism involved a continuation of the alliance of the middle and working classes similar to that which had passed for reform of the aristrocratic constitution before 1832, but Liberalism did not involve a similar cultural fusion. The Nonconformist denominations had become middle class in style.

Attendance at church or chapel was for many middle class Victorians a badge of social respectability. But the conventions of working class life were different, and organized religion remained on the fringe, or just beyond, of the working class culture that evolved in the commercial and industrial cities of nineteenth-century England.

Guide To Further Reading

Any explanation of the many attempts to extend religious influence among the lower social orders must begin with K.S. Inglis' excellent general study *Churches and the Working Classes in Victorian England* (1963) and Jennifer Hart's essay "Religion and Social Control in the Mid-Nineteenth Century" in *Social Control in Nineteenth Century Britain* (1977), edited by Tony Donajgrodzki. There are several good studies of religion and working class life in specific localities. E.R. Wickham's study of Sheffield, *Church and*

People in an Industrial City (1957) has become a minor classic. Ebenezer T. Davies has written an analytical account of *Religion in the Industrial Revolution in South Wales* (1965), and A. Allen MacLaren, *Religion and Social Class: The Disruptive Years in Aberdeen* (1974), distinguishes between the roles religion played in the lives of the middle and working classes. R.B.Walker's "Religious Change in Liverpool in the Nineteenth Century", *Journal of Ecclesiastical History* (1968) is a useful survey.

There are no first rate studies of religion and the labour movement. Although R.F. Wearmouth's works are more pietistic than scholarly, *Methodism and the Working Class Movements of England, 1800-1850* (1937) and *Methodism and the Struggle of the Working Classes 1850-1900* (1954) contain sufficient information to suggest that their subject might be very interesting. Harold U. Faulkner's work on *Chartism and the Churches* (1916) and Eric Hobsbawm's chapter on "The Labour Sects" in *Primitive Rebels* (1959) begin to explore the place of religion in the culture of working-class radicalism. *The Churches and the Labour Movement* (1967) by Stephen Mayor contains a useful discussion of the half-dozen newspapers upon which it is based.

Eileen Yeo's chapter, "Robert Owen and Radical Culture" in *Robert Owen: Prophet of the Poor* (1971), edited by Sidney Pollard and John Salt, provides a fascinating glimpse of the style of a quasi-Christian religion of social protest. John Kent deals with a more orthodox tradition in "Feelings and Festivals, an Interpretation of some Working Class Religious Attitudes", in *The Victorian City* (1973), edited by Michael Wolff and H.J. Dyos. Robert Sandall and Arch R. Wiggin have written the official *History of the Salvation Army* (5 vols., 1947-1968). General Booth's Army was probably the most successful religious organization among the urban working classes of Victorian England. Working with the new sociological approach developed by Bryan Wilson, Roland Robertson considers the Army as a conversionist sect in "The Salvation Army: The Persistence of Sectarianism", in *Patterns of Sectarianism* (1967), edited by Bryan Wilson.

Congregational Year Book (1848): "Thoughts on the Need for Increased Efforts to Promote the Religious Welfare of the Working Classes in England, by the Independent Churches and their Pastors", by Algernon Wells. Complete text.

Algernon Wells (1793-1850), a Congregationalist minister, left his provincial pastorate at Coggeshall in 1837 to become secretary of the recently formed Congragational Union, the central organization of the denomination. Passionately devoted to the denomination and extremely successful as its executive officer, his comments on social questions might fairly be judged as representative of the main body of opinion in the Union.

On examining the present social condition of England, no class of the people more fixes the attention, or awakens the anxiety, of a thoughtful observer, that that of the artizans: by which term it is intended to signify all who pursue skilled handcraft labour, whether they work singly with hand tools, or are grouped in numbers to conduct the operations of machinery. By this description it is meant to distinguish the class in question from all who carry on trade, employ capital, or belong to the mental and scientific professions, on the one hand; and, on the other, from all those whose toil is more rude and unskilled. Numbers alone render this class of great importance: and its numbers not only have rapidly increased, and do still rapidly increase in actual amount, but also in proportion to the entire community, and to the several other classes it includes. The artizans are a vastly more numerous and important branch of English society than they were half a century ago, and half a century hence they will be vastly more so than now, unless some great and unforeseen change in all present tendencies should take place. The moral and religious condition of such a portion of our people deserves and demands the best consideration of every patriotic mind. These numerous artizans add unspeakably to the commerce, physical resources, and wealth of our country — do they, in any equal degree, contribute their quota to its virtue and religion, and therefore to its soundness and security, as one of the chief communities now flourishing in the earth? Would that the answer to this question involved no more pain and fear, than it does doubt or difficulty.

Artizans in general cannot be wanting in quickness, shrewdness, and intelligence. They are selected when boys for occupations requiring these qualities, because they are seen to possess them. Their education for their craft, and practice in it, further develops and sharpens intellect. Their association with each other, and the instructions often given by their employers for difficult operations, have the same effect. Then they read, discuss, and attend lectures. Without much depth, they thus acquire considerable surface knowledge, and the lower power of knowing becomes far more developed in them than the higher faculty of thinking. They become conscious of their mental advancement, and presume upon it, quite unconscious even of the existence of wide fields of truth they have never explored. They compare themselves advantageously with mere uninstructed labourers, but seldom learn humility by placing their own acquirements in contrast with those of men possessed of far more enlarged knowledge than their own. Moreover, they feel themselves to be a class with interests and sympathies peculiarly their own, which they naturally conclude that they ought to vindicate and promote by their combined efforts. Nor are they well-satisfied with their position, either political or social; they think that capital absorbs too large a portion of the profits of their labour, and that the middle and upper classes monopolize political power, to their exclusion from their just share. To a great extent, they are not religious in either their sentiments or habits. A serious belief in revelation is not their general characteristic, neither is the observance of the Sabbath, or attendance on public worship, their prevailing custom. their domestic life need not be painted in dark colours, but it wants improvement and elevation. They do not attach themselves to their employers, or confide in the classes higher than themselves in the social scale.

It can hardly be necessary to add, that the connection of this great artizan class with the religion of their country, in any of its various forms, is very slight. They resort to the Established Church for the rites of marriage, and they bury their dead in its parochial graveyards, with the prescribed ceremonial — and they may also generally present their children for its baptismal service. A portion, indeed — would that it were multiplied tenfold! — of this class of our countrymen is found attached by conviction and choice to each of the several Evangelical communities, and add their full share to the honour and strength of those churches. But the great religious movement of the age seems to pass by the artizans of England, leaving them untouched and unstirred. The superstitions of Puseyism have not attracted them — Evangelical ministrations seem to have no charms or power for them. Our great enterprises of religious benevolence have not won their approval or attention. They look on, quite unconcerned spectators of our struggles for religious liberty, advocates as they are for freedom in all its other applications. They are not converted by Romish zeal, or any longer gathered by Wesleyan energy, or drawn by the more intellectual discourses of Independent and Baptist preachers. All this is sorrowful. It is, moreover, dangerous. It must work to disastrous issues, if not soon remedied. The continent of Europe multiplies on us its examples and its warnings. Every body of Christians should inquire how, and why is this? What are the causes, and what the remedies of so great a peril?

We enjoy ourselves this morning in conference on a topic of deepest interest to ourselves and to our country. We are not able in this matter to plead any favourable distinction of our denomination above others. We are not more successful with the artizans of our country, or in more favourable estimation with them, than are other religious bodies. The fact is plain. The reasons should be sought. If discovered, they may admit of remedy. Why is it that the preaching of our ministers, except in very rare instances, is not attractive to them? Why have they no sympathy for our testimony, or our struggles for religious liberty? Why do our new-built chapels gather congregations of tradesmen, but never of artificers? Taking their relative proportions in general society, those of the latter class should form the majority of worshippers. Why do not our schools either win the parents or retain the children to our chapels? Why has our literture no charms for them? They are readers, but we do not seem to write for their taste. Why do not our domiciliary visits succeed in establishing friendly relations and sympathies between our religion and their affections?

The writer of this paper will leave it to his colleagues in the present service to assign such causes as may be supposed to operate in the minds of the artizans themselves, for producing the alienation inquired into — be they political, social, infidel, or all three combined — his purpose being rather to inquire what obstacles on our own part operate to repel the approach of our artizan countrymen to fellowship in our religion and our worship — what in our preaching, service, discipline, spirit and opinions may give them an aspect or a savour unattractive to the shrewd and hard minds of the mechanics of our time and country. As it is admitted that our own sentiments and practices are not more uncongenial to the working classes than those of other classes of Christians — as they seem alienated and hostile from all alike — the obvious and natural inference might be, that the causes are more with them — that modes of thought and habits of life, unfavourable to religion altogether, prevail to draw them far aloof from all Christian churches and worship. Careful inquiry will probably show that the main causes of this lamented severance of the working classes from the religion of their country, in all its forms, do lie with them; and the other papers to be this morning presented, will probably place this fact in a clear light. But the entire object of the present inquiry is to make, if possible, some breach in this wall of separation, and to open some way by which we may commence, at least, an approach to this large class of our countrymen, so as to gain their attention and win their more friendly regard. For this end it is necessary to seek for, in order to remove, even minor and circumstantial hindrances — to ascertain whether, though we cannot alter our religion that it may be made pleasing to any, we ought not to modify some of our modes of advocating its claims, so as to render them attractive instead of repulsive to those who we would gain, herein imitating the example of Paul in a like case. This inquiry is the more necessary for us, because, in looking at the sentiments, constitution, and practices of Congregational churches, we find much that might be supposed likely to meet the tastes of the class, concerning whose alienation inquiry is now made. Our appeal to the understanding, our struggles for liberty, our doctrines of equality, and our rejection of pomp, might all seem congenial to the known sentiments of the working classes on other related interests, and in other analogous instances. And if this is found out to be the case in fact — if we no more than other Christian churches, holding views on such points obviously repulsive to the artizan class, succeed in gaining their sympathies — then we naturally ask, what is there in our modes that counteracts the known tendencies of our principles? What do we connect with our principles which nullifies and neutralizes their proper effect? Is it any thing that can be discovered, or that, being discovered, can be removed and corrected?

No doubt some things with us which are our glory and strength, and which for no conceivable reason or object ought ever to change, operate repulsively on the working classes, and indeed on all classes around us. Our evangelic doctrine, our spiritual religion, our watchful discipline, and our strict Sabbath observance, are all repugnant to the carnal mind generically, and in every class and station; yet, by these alone, when blessed of God, can we, or any other people, convert enemies to friends, and gather souls to Christ.

Subordinate to these our cardinal religious glories, there are with us modes of thought and action — good, sound, and not to be changed — which are probably repulsive to the working classes: such as our firm faith in the Scriptures, our high veneration for them, and our constant appeal to them; the relative provinces we assign to reason and scripture in religion. Alas! the working classes have been but too successfully plied with the shallow and frivolous objections of infidelity against the inspired Word, till with them the entire presentiment is adverse to the Bible, not in its favour.

Also our firm attachment to points of objective truth — our witness for them — the stress we lay on them in reference to their place both in the system of truth and in the formation of character — our conscience respecting such points — our separation from other Christians on their account and for their sake. All this is unpleasing to the freethinking habits of the working classes. They think themselves superior to it, and more free and impartial in their judgments. They condemn us as sectarian and narrow in such convictions. They have caught this supercilious superiority to any serious judgment of the excellence and importance of some doctrines over others from the tone of speakers in Parliament, and writers on politics, as well as from mere avowed unbelievers. A taste has been thus formed in them, to which our zeal for opinions is most repulsive. No less is our exclusively religious character repugnant to them. In our public services, in our church proceedings, and in our general activities, we still cleave to a strictly spiritual dispensation. If we discourse or act at all on any political subject, we do it religiously, and regard the matter only as it touches religion. If we mingle in any literary or scientific associations, the same view to religion is apparent — when we handle such topics, or unite in such institutes, it is seen that we cannot put out of view our highest and special object. We must at least tinge every thing we touch with this mixture. No less is this peculiarity apparent in our movements for education and general charity. We cannot establish a daily school, or join a sick or clothing society, but we must turn the opportunity to religious account. This is plainly discerned by the working clases, but it is not justly appreciated. It is not attributed to honest and loving fervour. It is ascribed to sectarianism, not to benevolence. We are thought to be at work for our party, not for their souls. They think we would get them to chapel, not that we would conduct them to heaven. Our good is evil thought of. What ought to attract, in fact, repels.

Rather — the working of our church system casts itself too much into an aristocratic mould to present a pleasing aspect to the working classes. The constitution of our churches is as truly as it is avowedly democratic; but the action of a sound democracy will always work to produce a necessary and useful aristocracy. The unbiassed suffrages of an enlightened constituency secure of its privileges, and using them only for the common good will uniformly place the best qualified men in office and authority. Thus it is in our churches. Social position is one qualification for office in every society. This is the dictate of common sense, and the lesson of all experience. Possessions must always form an element of confidence, and therefore of influence. Thus it comes to pass among us. Brethren who add to those qualifications for usefulness which are of a mental and religious nature, such also as arise from position and substance, are preferred for office in our churches. This is so general a practice, that exceptions do but prove it the rule. Nor is management either employed, or necessary, to secure this really desirable result. It arises from the common and prevailing sentiment of all classes among us. Unusual merit in humble life is not excluded by it from honourable service with us, but other things being equal, station determines the preference. Now this is very distasteful to a class fretting against exclusions, jealous of all the advantages ceded to the possessors of property, and anxious to remove all social distinctions not based on personal pretensions. They turn from the world to the church, and think they see operating, in sacred relations, the same inequalities they deem so unjust in the structure of general society.

And, lastly, it is probable, that so far as the action of our system as carried on in our church meetings, wherein their business is transacted, comes to their knowledge, it also displeases the working classes. The procedures are too tranquil and devout. The eldership is too active, and the members too quiescent. Promiscuous speeches and resolutions — spontaneous movements originated by individuals — discussions on topics, rarely or never introduced — would be far more in accordance with the prevailing tastes of active-minded artizans. This is not meant of such as, being converted, enter our churches as spiritual and humble disciples of Christ, but of the on-looking and unfavourably impressed multitude of alienated workmen around us — not of those who do come among us, but of those who are prevented from so doing by the notions they form of what we are, and of what we do. Doubtless, it is a nice point in theory — and more difficult to define abstractly than to attain in practice — what degree of freedom in speech and proposals should be sanctioned among the members of churches constituted as ours are. Probably no rules on the subject would admit of indiscriminate application to all churches. The greater strictness of some, the greater liberty of others, in this particular, may be most salutary where adopted; but, to transpose these wholesome adjustments, might be most fatal to peace and order. But, as all the great purposes for which church proceedings are conducted, bear a decidedly spiritual character, they can never be properly ordered, where they cease to harmonize with the grave, subdued, and heavenly spirit, which is alone appropriate for the business as well as for the devotions of Christ's churches. It may be hoped that we have attained considerable success in so ordering our affairs; and it may be feared that, in proportion as we have done this, our practices will appear uninviting to a class, whose conceptions, on such matters, are derived from a vehement spirit, exciting associations, and clamorous meetings.

Now, all these points of supposed repulsion in our religious order, operating to sever the working classes from us, are such as we deem our excellencies — things that we must not alter, even did we know that the effect would be to gather to us great numbers of the artizan population. For in that case it would really be that we joined them, not they us. It is not believed that policy so fatal to our purity would augment our numbers; but were it so, to change a great and consistent religious denomination into an eager and tumultuous party, in which the political should predominate over the spiritual, would be indeed a folly and a ruin.

Two considerations, however, remain to be mentioned, in which, probably, may be seen peculiarities attaching to the independent denomination unfavourable to its influence on the working classes, which, if neither positively blamable, nor entirely removable, should be counteracted and corrected as far as possible: for it is not easy to mention a matter, at this moment, of greater religious and national importance than that of bringing multitudes of our artizans under the power of the Gospel.

The first of these two considerations is the essentially middle-class character of our congregationalism, and of our churches — and, therefore, of everything about them — preaching, buildings, ministers, manners, notions, and practices — all have on them the air and impress of English middle-class life. Our churches have more and more worked themselves into this mould, as time and change have proceeded. They are at this time for more exclusively of that class than was the case a century ago. The higher orders, then not sparingly sprinkled among them, have now left them almost to a man: though it must, however, be acknowledged, that probably a larger proportion of poor may be now found among them than at the beginning of this century: but their access, as yet, has had little influence in changing that paramount impress of the middle class, so obvious on our denomination. The effect of this is that persons of that station in life find themselves most at home in our fellowship. All things among us are adapted to their tastes and habits. We equally eschew the refined, imaginative, and hierarchic forms so congenial to the higher ranks on the one hand, and on the other, the rough simplicity that might attract keen but impolished artificers. Undoubtedly this circumstance presents us in a very unfavourable point of view to the artizans, whose great quarrel with English society altogether turns on its class structure, who complain incessantly of class interests and class legislation, and who are ever at war with the class spirit. It may be that these complainants are as deeply imbued with an exclusive class sentiment as any other portion of the whole community; but this does not alter the fact of their strong dislike of that in others with which they themselves are no less thoroughly imbued. Also, it is obvious that of all the classes prevailing in England, the artificers most dislike the middle class. This antipathy is as apparent as it is strong. It prevented them from rendering any assistance in the great anti-corn law struggle, and severs them widely from their natural allies in all political interests and elections.

Now, if we cannot — and it is believed that we cannot — alter much this class character of our churches, ought we not to discern that it does constitute a strong impediment to our success among the working people, and try to mitigate its intensity in any way within our power? Wherever possible, we should sympathize and act with the mechanics in any movement to promote their intelligence, privileges, and welfare. In our religious proceedings and order, we should meet their tastes as far as practicable. We should remove whatever barriers to association and sympathy between us and them, in the religious life, admit of correction. Especially, our ministers should aim to understand this class, and to remove, both from their public services and pastoral deportment, whatever may possibly render them unacceptable to so numerous and important a section of the English people.

The second consideration worthy of notice in this inquiry, as both tending to alienate the working classes from us, and also capable of some remedy, is our essentially antagonistic position. This we cannot avoid or alter. We may pronounce it a woe; but it remains no less on that account a fact, that we are born unto strife, as a religious community — hallowed strife, we believe — strife only for truth against error — no other strife than that essential to those who will stand faithful to their convictions, and to their Master. But such is the antagonism of our position — in doctrine, in worship, in polity, we are witnesses against what we deem most injurious errors. As such we are separated and marked. All eyes are on us, and all unfriendly. Our testimony troubles the land. We disturb the indolence, the security, and the interests of powerful bodies. We are greatly disliked and resisted. We are as much misunderstood and misrepresented. Such being our position and our repuute, we can expect the adhesion of none but those powerfully convinced, and thoroughly decided. There is nothing to attract to us the timid, the careless, and the self-interested. Still it is not for the sake of this objective view of our position that the circumstance of its polemic character has been adduced, but rather to offer a remark or two on its subjective influence on ourselves, and how it renders our churches abodes as unattractive as garrison towns. It tends to make our preaching technical, narrow, and hard. Some abstract topics are too frequently discussed — some simple, generous themes are almost altogether excluded — we move in a doctrinal orbit, remote from the common sympathies of men — whatever be our theme, we are prone to reason and dispute, rather than to melt and glow. Moreover, it is not impossible that antagonism has driven us too far in rejecting indiscriminately whatever has been adopted by others, who have doubtless associated much good with their evil; and whose ill use or association of anything true and good, ought not to have driven us to its rejection. Also our energies have been so much directed to testify against evil, that the strength and energy have been thus absorbed which ought to have been employed rather in spreading truth, and strengthening by increasing our own body. We have seemed more intent on removing unsound systems than on establishing others truly scriptural. No doubt a further evil has accrued to us from our essential antagonism in its effect upon spirit, which has been far more perceptible to others than to ourselves. The devout, gentle, and calm temper, so gracefully accordant with our holy religion, has with us suffered damage from our controversial calling. It were well if, as a religious class in this country, at the present juncture, we could see ourselves as others see us. If we could quite correctly ascertain how our buildings and devotions, our churches and discourses look in the public view. How far they excite reverence, attract regard, command respect, or kindle hope in our onlooking countrymen. In particular, whether we are the people towards whom by preference and sympathy the working classes would be chiefly drawn, were their present antipathy to all religion removed — and, if not, what in us admits of such change and improvement as might tend to win the hearts, as well as to convince the judgments of those that have been so long without. Most probably to the working classes we seem to stand in competition for their adherence with the other religious bodies of the country. As yet, they have rejected all alike. Nothing, however, has indicated that they have turned from us less resolutely, or more reluctantly, than from others. Are we, indeed, as repulsive as would seem, and can we neither discern nor remove the causes?

The imperfection of these remarks in strongly felt — their freedom is intended to be quite free from offence — their design is to move and help discussion. The subject to which they refer is confessedly most important. The facts they state or imply will hardly admit of question. A meeting of the Congregational Union cannot be more legitimately and usefully employed than in attempts to ascertain the exact character and position of the Independent churches at this time. To exercise the honesty and courage by which alone faults can be discovered, acknowledged, and corrected, is a most wholesome virtue. To think more highly of ourselves than we ought to think, is a corporate, quite as much as a personal fault — perhaps more so. Yet we ought not so to depreciate ourselves as may exceed truth, or damp zeal and spirit, If we are not, indeed, a body adapted to act powerfully on the working classes, that may not be our calling of the Lord. It may be enough that we bear witness, maintain our truth, and carry on our struggles through all disadvantages — and having done this, the Great Master may say — "Well done! good and faithful servants!"

Working Men and Religious Institutions. Report of the Speeches at the Conference, at the London Coffee House, Ludgate Hill, Monday, January 21, 1867 (1867). Selections.

The conference included prominent Churchmen and Dissenters as well as working men. It was organized and financed by politically oriented dissenters, and Edward Miall took the chair. Because the *Report* of the conference provides a spectrum of working-class opinion on organized religion, it is a valuable historical source.

———————————

Mr. BATES (engineer) said: The working men had been asked why they did not attend places of worship. There were many reasons why they did not. Some men worked too many hours, and when Sunday came they were glad to get into the country or into the parks for fresh air, believing they stood more in need of that than of what they got when they went to church or chapel. Others had an objection to going to churches and chapels because they believed the ministers did not preach or teach Christianity, and they absented themselves for the same reason that they kept away from the shopkeeper who gave short weight and measure and adulterated his things. ("Hear, hear," and laughter.) If he spoke at all he must speak what he thought. (Hear, hear.) He told them candidly he was one of those who believed that they did give short measure. He believed, too, that priests and parsons had from time immemorial given short weight and short measure and an adulteration of Christianity, or whatever they dealt in, to the working classes. (Hear, hear.) They, therefore, did not want it. Working men had been called all sorts of hard names because they said these things: sometimes they were called atheists, sometimes infidels, sometimes trade union demagogues, and so on. They were not atheists — they believed in pure practical Christianity, and if the ministers of religion would teach them a pure, practical and useful Christianity they would come amongst them and help them with all their might. If, however, it was to be merely a matter of feeling and a matter of believing, they could not see much use in it. They certainly brought up a good set of Sunday-school teachers who were doing a useful service, but with regard to their feelings, their dogmas, and their denunciations, working men saw no good that came from them. If they were to believe in God (as he believed most working men did), they must believe in their own way. They believed God was good, not bad; that He was the highest conception which men could have of goodness and truth and wisdom. If God was that, He could not be the opposite; if IIe was wise, He could not be foolish; if He was true, He could not be false; if He was what His name implied, He could not be a devil, and that was what many religionists made Him. They attributed to Him all the bad faults they found in themselves, and all the evil passions of human nature; because they could not reach to God's purity they dragged him down to a level with themselves. Working men did not want such stuff. They would have no more of it. Christianity, in his opinion was the work of God; Jesus Christ was the Son of God. God was His Father, as He was our Father, and Jesus Christ must be like His Father. He wished to know what society was based upon at the present time. Was there any unity of interest between the different classes, or even any unity of feeling? Society was based upon selfishness and greediness with which the prevailing forms of Christianity did not interfere. He was an Odd Fellow, and one of the fundamental principles of that society was, "You shall neither wrong a brother, nor see him wronged." Ought not Christianity to go higher than Odd Fellowship? Were they prepared to go into the practical part of the matter, and to dig down to the foundation of society and see upon what it rested, and if it was wrong to alter it? Were they prepared to use their education and influence to being about a unity of interest between class and class; to alter the relations between capital and labour, and to enable the working man to rise to his legitimate position? Why should not the working man have time to be educated? He would be educated if the Mammon spirit of the age did not prevent it. Because he was not educated, he was called all manner of hard names — brutish, drunken, vile, venal, and so on. Would they try to alter that, and bring about a system of co-operation in which the interest of one man should be the interest of all? Christianity was wide enough for all this, and more, and if the clergymen would only be honest enough to help to bring about this state of things, they would not have to ask the working men why they did not go to their churches and chapels. (Applause.)

The Rev. NEWMAN HALL spoke as follows: This of course, is not an occasion for making a speech, but only for a spontaneous utterance of one's thoughts. Let me say, as having been connected with my friend Mr. White from the commencement of the preparations for this Conference, that, though the scheme is strictly his, our desires are already accomplished in the outspoken utterances of our friends who have given us their opinions. The earnest desire of all connected with the Conference is to have a most frank and full expression of thought by our brethren of the working classes, as to their reasons for non-attendance at our churches and chapels. We honestly wish to do them good, to show them that we are their brethren, to get them to love us as brethren; and we are honestly grieved if we see any class of the community holding aloof from what we feel would be an infinite benefit to them. Though we may think that some of their objections may be untrue, we want to know what those objections are; and I trust that as the result of this Conference we may be able to amend some of our ways, and that our brethren of the working classes may be led to modify some of their opinions. I have been thrown among working men during the whole of my public life, and I have long lamented that so many of them are outside the organisations of Christianity. By no means would I say that they repudiate Christianity itself. I have met with many working men who do not attend churches and chapels, but who have a reverence for God and for Christianity, and I am more and more persuaded that there must be something wrong in our methods which keeps so many away from us. It is not Christianity itself. When it is remembered that the Founder of our religion was a working man; that He wrought with His own hands with adze or hammer and nail; that He honoured labour in His own practice; that He always advocated the cause of the poor; that He denounced the scribes and pharises, hypocrites and tyrants; and all His teaching was based on the great principles of unity and love; and when we see the tendency of this religion to elevate every one who embraces it, to give wisdom to the foolish, comfort to the afflicted, and nobleness even to the slave, it seems utterly impossible that any working man can examine it without feeling that if it is a religion for the rich and great it is eminently a religion for the working classes and the poor. (Hear, hear.) Some of the objections that we hear are of a political nature. It is said that religion is too much mixed up with politics. One might expect that those of our brethren who objected to the union of Church and State would flock to the places where the union is protested against; but that is not the fact; therefore that objection does not keep them away. Then with regard to seats in church: I know some churches which are occupied on some occasions by those who are said to be the proprietors of the pews, but which are perfectly free on other occasions; yet working men do not avail themselves of the opportunity. I know one case in which a church was established by working men, who came to a unanimous vote that half the church be appropriated and let out, because they liked to have their own individual seats. Then we sometimes hear the objections that ministers are paid. I have a long letter in my pocket in which the writer says that all parsons are hirelings because they are paid. I wrote in reply, "You are a working man, and I suppose receive wages; are you a hireling?" People must live. I know many who devote themselves to the ministry, who, if they were seeking money, might make ten or twenty times as much as their salaries in other occupations. I know many, too, who devote half their time to work for which they do not receive an additional penny. I do not find working men who work over time without over pay. (Hear, hear.) Now what are the real objections? I think they are of a very practical kind. I think that often the self-indulgence of the working classes themselves keeps them away from places of worship. I am thankful that our brethren have told us our faults; let me frankly tell them theirs. (Hear, hear.) The working classes of this country spend fifty millions a year in strong drink. If they object to pay 3d. a week for seat rent, they do not object to spend 6d. a day for drink. That is one great reason that keeps people from the house of God. One cure for that is by ministers plunging into the great vortex, and endeavouring to stop the evil by their own example of self-denial and earnestness. It seems as if everything was done to make the working man degraded. At every corner at every street these places are put up, with all that can make them attractive, leading men body and soul to ruin. Another great evil that keeps men from houses of worship is the degrading amusements in which they indulge. The Christian Church is doing very little in the way of amusing people, only occupying their attention one day in the week; while those whose only object is gain pander to the lowest tastes of the people to make their occupation the more profitable. We all want to play as well as work, and if the only play provided for the working classes is that which is calculated to lower their morals and their intellect, we are not so much surprised that they have not a taste for religious organisations. Then many feel very strange in places of worship, thinking that they are not welcome. Complaints are made that they go to the parks. I say, Let religious men go after them, and preach to them. (Hear, hear.) I should never desire a more attentive congregation. If anybody the worse for liquor should interrupt, the working people themselves would stand by the preacher who is trying to do them good. (Hear, hear.)

* * * * * * * * *

Mr. GREEN (tailor) said it must be admitted that the working classes desired to be honest as far as they could in their dealings and opinions. He thought the key-note of the indifference, or the alleged ·indifference, of the working classes to religious teaching was struck by the Rev. Newman Hall when he said that Christianity ennobled the slave. The teaching of Christianity was that a slave and it could not exist together. That was precisely one of the points on which religious teaching had failed. He did not say it was wrong to teach a man patience under adversity, but Christianity, or rather the Christianity that was taught, taught a man to be perfectly satisfied with the condition in which he was placed, and to be patient under it, whilst at the same time it taught him it was his duty and his privilege to rise to something better. He could conceive that there was extreme difficulty felt by gentlemen of high education in intimately associating with those who had little or no education, who could not talk to them in a familiar manner upon common topics. That placed a barrier betwen the clergyman and the working man. How was that barrier to be removed? If a clergyman was sent as a missionary among savages, what did he do? Why, he worked along with the people whom he was sent to convert; he cast aside entirely all his gentility, and became along with them a practical working man. Now they had in this country a highly-trained class of gentlemen who made religion a profession. That was at the bottom of the whole evil. (Hear, hear.) He did not say that because the working men were not in attendance upon Christian churches that they were not Christians;

but it was one of the principal reasons why the clergy did not obtain hearers that they were not familiar enough with those whom they wished to listen to them, and they were divided amongst themselves into sects and classes. There were numbers of gentlemen of one religious persuasion who would not associate with those of another, and there were very few professors of religion who in any way attempted to carry their teaching into practice.

****

Mr. WYNN (plasterer), said there were deeper causes than those which had been mentioned for the disaffection among the working classses with regard to the Churches. The sinners who had really given offence were in the room. Science and religion had for a great number of years been considered to be at variance. When he looked at a number of gentlemen around him who had, to a certain extent, dissented from the established religion of the day, who had advanced in their opinions with regard to geology and other sciences, he did not wonder that working men, who had, to a certain extent, intellectually examined the subject, felt a good deal dissatisfied with the Churches already existing. The distinction of classes was another great bar. This was more particularly manifest in country churches. If a working man was invited into one of those churches, he felt there was an intolerable gulf between the classes, and that it was a mere matter of condescension to recognise him as one of God's people outside the Church. Working men had most sympathy with Dissenting chapels, for there was something like equality there. But then they did not know which they were to believe. He had heard Mr. Macgregor speaking against Catholicism, whilst the Catholics would defend their own system. Working men say, "Why, whom are we to believe? which of these two principles are we to endorse?" He had heard that stated many, many times. And then when he found a minister in the Church stating that the Mosaic cosmogony was necessarily true, and that Professor Huxley was a heretic, or something worse than a heretic; and on the other hand, heard the Professor or Mr. Ramsay, or some competent searcher of geology or ethnology, dispute the statements made in the Church, and saying that the old cosmogony was not to be believed, there was a great source of infidelity. He would frankly state to them that working men had examined these questions extensively.

****

The Rev. Dr. MILLER: Some allusion had been made to politics. It was generally thought, though it did not happen to be his lot, that all the Church of England parsons were Tories. He was not, and never was, though he did not know if that was at all to his credit. They said, "If you would join with us and seek to get us our political rights, we should love you better, and we would go to your churches." Did a working man consider what would be the effect of a clergyman in a parish becoming a political partisan? It must be remembered that if on the one hand there were a great many Liberals in his parish, there were also a great many on the other side, and he would ask any sensible working man in the room whether it was the business of a clergyman so to identify himself with political parties in the State as not only to lose his influence with half his people, but probably to excite the most bitter feelings against himself. He did not part with his rights as an Englishman because he was a clergyman, but was content to hold everything in abeyance rather than peril his spiritual influence with his people.

****

Mr. GLAZIER (joiner) said it appeared to him, having been present during the whole of the Conference, that it was quite time they came to some practical conclusion with reference to this matter. They had heard a number of reasons assigned for the abstraction of his own class from places of religious worship, and some of them had been advanced again and again. He had come prepared to advance some reasons of his own, but thought, after what had transpired that it would probably be as well to offer a few practical suggestions or remedies for a state of things that they must all deplore. He should like to name one reason which had not been adverted to that afternoon, but which he had often heard mentioned, and that was that too many of the ministers of the Gospel took too gloomy a view of the aspect of human nature, and of the aspect of society. They told them that this world was a vale of tears, and were continually preaching that to them. He did think that ministers of the Gospel ought to take a more happy and bright view of human society than they seemed to know. This world was a beautiful and glorious world, and he believed they were sent here for enjoyment — (Hear, hear) — and that whatever suffering they endured was not sent as a punishment exactly, but to show there was a wrong existing somewhere. Reference had been made to the lack of sympathy that existed between the ministers of the Gospel and the people. He believed the ministers had sympathy with them and endeavoured to manifest it; but the sympathy that was too often shown was a sort of pauperising sympathy. He was well aware of the charity that had been given, but there was a higher charity than the mere giving out of the pocket. The truest charity was to teach men how to help themselves, and this was what, to a very considerable extent, the ministers of the Gospel failed to do. Nay, more; they sometimes opposed the men in their organisations. There was one way in which they could show their practical sympathy towards the working man. Something had been said about trade unions. Never mind whether they were right or wrong, they would exist. Now, it was in the power of the ministers to relieve them of one evil in connection of the holding of their trade unions. They were absolutely compelled to hold them at public-houses. Why not open the vestries attached to the churches, and say to the working man, "Here is a place where you can meet and transact your business; do what you like, and say what you like, so long as you conform to the decencies of society, away from the public-house"? He had formed his ideal of what a church should be, and of what an individual should be who took an active part in the promulgation of Christianity amongst the working classes. Looking around and seeing what had been done, he believed the man who most nearly approached what might be considered a working man's minister was Mr. Murphy. Why did he conform to his ideal? Becasue he had a practical sympathy with all popular aspirations after that which was good and right. No social movement could be named but it had his sympathies, and he would not only give the hand of fellowship, but also his practical aid. This was what ministers of the Gospel ought to do, but instead of that they too often got the cold shoulder. All their social organisations ought to centre in the Church, and ought to be supported by the clergy; and when the clergy showed this practical sympathy in their aspirations after social progress, and without pauperising the working men, gave the right hand of fellowship, saying, "We do not want to interfere with or control your organisations, but we will gladly give what help we can," then the working classes of this country would take a greater interest in the cause which ministers upheld.

****

EDMUND BEALES, Esq: A very serious question had been raised by Dr. Miller as to politics connected with the clergy. No doubt many of the working classes were alienated in great measure from the Church by the consideration that too many of the clergy were linked up with the ruling powers in the State against them. Dr. Miller repudiated it with regard to himself, and he (Mr. Beales) would accept that repudiation with all his heart; but there was no question that too many of the clergy were keen political partisans, and filled a duty which was wholly inconsistent with their position as clergymen, namely, that of magistrates, compelled, and frequently too willingly, to give judgments utterly at variance with their character and position as ministers of the Gospel. Other things of the kind might be mentioned, but on the other hand, let working men remember that there were hundreds and thousands of those clergy whose life was spent in doing good, and contributing not only to the spiritual happiness of the poor, but to their temporal happiness in every way. There were also thousands of men and women, gentlemen and ladies, in the character of district visitors, missionaries, and others, whose whole life was employed for the same purpose. From all he could gather, the main difficulty was was that the working classes had not sufficient satisfactory means to themselves of attending religious ordinances; that their churches and chapels were of such a nature as to have the effect more or less of excluding the working classes from them — that in fact there was a too great class distinction. There was the fact. It had been repeated several times that night, and he knew from experience, that one of the great reasons for the artisans of this great country not attending their churches and chapels as they otherwise would do, was that they did not feel themselves at ease and in comfort. How was that to be met? Probably many were aware of the movement going on in the Church of England for the express purpose of having free churches, and doing away with pews altogether. That was almost the only practical method of meeting the difficulty. It was not that the working men were opposed to the Gospel of Christ. That Gospel was received with such delight by the common people when the apostles were preaching, it would be received with equal delight by the common people now, if they could get at it in the way in which it was got at then. It must be so.

* * * * * * * * *

Mr. MCSWEENEY (licensed hawker) said this, in his opinion, was a great night and a great day for England — the priests and the people coming together in conference. He should like to know if any rev. gentleman present had ever known such an occurrence taking place before. The lion had lain down with the lamb. (Laughter, and cries of "Which is the lion?") The people had made the priests what they were and the priests had made the people what they were. England had opened a grave for all the superstitions of the past. The Druids died and were buried in England. (Laughter.) The Roman heathendom was buried in England, and so was heathen Saxonism. Roman Catholicism had taken a fit that she had never got over, and Colenso and the "Essays and Reviews" had trodden upon the old lady's corns. The reason the working classes did not go to church was that while they were taught there and in the national schools, over which the clergy had the control, the Mosaic cosmogony, the geologists told us that the earth could not have been made in so short a time as that specified, but was a thing of gradual development. Astronomers, anatomists, and chemists too, told us a different story from that taught in the churches, and the working class had come to the conclusion that the priests must be very lazy, or very ignorant, or very unwilling to come over to the side of science and truth and knowledge. He had no doubt that a mixed meeting such as the present would be held at the West-end of London next, to know why the aristocracy and the rich merchants of England alienated themselves from the Churches; and he supposed that a coroneted peer's soul, or a rich merchant's soul, was equally as precious as the soul of a licensed hawker such as himself, and he did not know why working men should be singled out. For the first time it was now established in England as a great fact that the difference which had separated the priests from the people existed no longer. The priests of Europe would be told that they had neglected their duty, and that if they did not do their duty to the people, the people would do it for themselves. Why should there exist any difference between the teacher and the taught? He knew many of the working classes who did not go to a public-house and get drunk, but who had money and books and instructed themselves. He imagined the time when the priest would, however, have the confidence of the people and lead them, and be a protection to them against the inroads of the man with the sword.

* * * * * * * *

HENRY LEE, Esq., said he did not know that he had any right to be present at the Conference, except that which the committee gave him by inviting him to come up from Manchester, and sending him a card of membership. The discussion during the afternoon and evening seemed to have been between the ministers and the working men. Now, he supposed, he might say that he stood somewhat midway between these two classes of persons. A remark was made by the second speaker in the afternoon to the effect that he saw no good that had been done by ministers, but he did see that Sunday-school teachers had done some little good amongst the working classes. Now he happened to have been a Sunday-school teacher for seven-and-thirty years, and for thirty years of that time it had been his lot to teach a class of married men: he might therefore claim to have had some opportunity of knowing what working men were, because his present class consisted of butchers, and bakers, and mechanics, and brewers, and engineers, and two or three other trades. He told his class that he was about to come to London for the purpose of attending this Conference, and invited them the last Sunday but one to spend the afternoon in telling him something about the condition of their own class of society, and what they knew by inquiry were the objections which the working classes had to going to a place of worship. He thought they could not better spend a Sabbath afternoon than by going into a question of that kind. Now, the first objection which seemed to strike the members of his class most arose from the habits of the working classes. These habits were inconsistent with attendance at a place of worship, because in the minds of the working class there was this feeling, at least so far as he had ascertained it in the North, that a man who attended a place of worship thereby made a profession of religion; and if a man was known by his fellow-workmen to attend a place of worship, and he got drunk or something else, he was immediately taunted by his companions, who would say to him, "Ah, thou art a fine fellow to be going to a place of worship! Look how drunk thou wert last saturday night!" He had striven to tell them in many cases that by coming to a place of worship they made no profession at all, but simply came there as they might go to a teetotal meeting, to hear what was said about the Gospel. He had said to them, "You only make a profession of Christianity, when, before the world, you confess that you are the disciples of Jesus Christ, but until you do that you are hearers of the Gospel, and therefore you are not to be rated by your fellow-men as inconsistent because you enter into a place of worship." But he could well understand that a man who frequented the betting-ring, and betted on racehorses, was not to be found in a place of worship, and there was a great deal of this among the working classes. He appealed to those present to say if this was not so. Being himself one of a firm employing 1,500 people, he knew something of it. And why was not the man who frequented the betting circle to be found in the place of worship? Because the practice of his life was so inconsistent with the truths which he would hear of in the latter place. He would go further and say that a man who habitually spent his time in a public-house was not a man who would be found in a place of worship. The associations of the public-house, the songs that were sung there under the influence of drink, the people with whom the man must necessarily be a companion when he went there, were inconsistent altogether with attendance at a place of worship, and the man who went to a place of worship after having had a Bacchanalian spree at a public-house on a Saturday night would feel very uncomfortable. Then another thing was the habit of pleasure-seeking on the Sunday. Now he (Mr. Lee) was not one of those strict Sabbatarians, but he must say to every working man, "If you value your own comfort, apart altogether from the question of conversion, you will frequent a place of worship, because of the regular habits of life in which it gets you, and for the sake of the influence which it exerts upon your children." This brought him to one very important point. The speakers at the present Conference had been talking all day about working men: what about the women? He would say, and say it deliberately, that the weak point of all our Christian organisations was not the working man, but the working women. When did they come to a place of worship? He wanted to know what opportunity they had for going? And which parent was it that formed the mind of the child? It was the mother. He had seen many a man get up in meeting after meeting, and when asked the question, "To whom do you ascribe the influences which led you to better your condition and appear as you are now?" they had each said, "I ascribe the influence exerted on my mind by my mother." Therefore, if we wanted the next generation of children to grow up in the habits of regularity, habits of prudence, habits of industry, habits of virtue, we must get at the women, and he felt certain, from what he had seen, having had a good deal of experience, that this was one of the weak points that we had to get at. The working man wanted a comfortable home. He (Mr. Lee) walked up to his mill the other day, and had to pass by a great many rows of cottages. The snow was upon the ground, and he saw many a clean doorstep with sand sprinkled over it, and all nice and inviting, but they were all public-houses. That indicated to him at once that the publican knew, at any rate, what would attract the working man — it was a nice doorstep and a cheerful fireside. He thought the views of working men with respect of conversion were exceedingly cloudy, and they had become so from this fact: they asked themselves the question, "Who are the parties to whom we are to look for the Gospel of Jesus Christ?" Very naturally, they said to themselves, "We must look to converted men." But were all the men who preached the Gospel of Jesus Christ converted men? Unhappily many a man went into the ministry not from love of the truth, or from love of setting forth the truth, but for a piece of bread, and this did produce, and would produce until it was changed, in the minds of working men, a prejudice against all forms of religious organisations, whether connected with the Establishment or with Dissent. Then another objection which he had himself heard urged, urged in his own class, and urged against himself, was this. One of his workmen, a very intelligent man, and a Christian man, said to him, "You are one of the inconsistent." He asked "Why?" "Because," said the man, "You don't come out publicly to advocate the political enfranchisement of your fellow-countrymen." "Well," he replied, "I have considered the matter, and I thought I had other work to do." "Well," said the man, "one of the reasons which keep us as a class from taking part with you in public worship, is that we believe your class does not care whether we get the franchise or not." He (Mr, Lee) then said he had privately done what he could for the cause of reform, but he felt that if he were to go upon a platform he would be doing another kind of work for which he was not so well adapted as that which he was already doing, and as he could not do both, he considered he ought, as every man ought, to do that for which he was most capable. Still he was a manhood-suffrage man as well as anybody, and he had said as much. He had met a great many working men amongst his own workpeople, and he must say he found in them a deep sense of justice, and he, for one, was not afraid to trust himself with any body of working men. He had felt, and he believed it was the opinion of many, we had to trust our property entirely in their hands, and he asked no questions about it. He believed the worst thing that any employer of labour could do was to harbour in his breast a suspicion of the honesty of those who were about him. There was no necessity for it, because there was in the minds of the working men of this country a deep sense of justice, and if you only appealed to that in the right way, they would never be found wanting. (Cheers.)

Moody and Sankey at Manchester: *The Christian,* 24 December 1874.

Dwight Lyman Moody (1837-1899), was a noted American evangelist. Resigning from a successful career in business in 1860, Moody became an independent city missionary in Chicago. In the eighteen-sixties he gained fame for his various philanthropic and educational activities including the Presidency of the Chicago Y.M.C.A. Moody visited England a number of times in this period in order to study similar work in that country. In the summer of 1873 he was invited to conduct evangelistic meetings and together with the musician Ira D. Sankey, Moody began his tour at York. Within five months news of the success of his North of England services was known throughout Britain. He was invited to both Scotland and Ireland where he was again successful. The culmination of the tour, however, was the four month London mission in 1874. It is said that over two and one half million were present at the meetings in various parts of the metropolis. Moody returned to Britain for more evangelistic forays from 1881 to 1884 and again in 1891-92. Moody made similar tours in North America — chiefly in Chicago and other major cities. *The Christian* was a newspaper that specialized in news of evangelism. The following account first appeared in the *Daily News,* a major London paper.

———— •• ————

To the majority of people the fact that between four and five thousand men and women assembled in a public hall at eight o'clock on a frosty morning in December will be *primâ facie* evidence that they were very much in earnest about the business they had in hand. There were nearly five thousand persons in the Free Trade Hall here this (Sunday) morning, to hear the "American evangelists," Messrs. Moody and Sankey. I arrived at a quarter to eight, under the impression that I was rather early than otherwise. But I hear that at seven o'clock the approaches to the still closed doors of the hall were thronged, and the people waiting patiently under the bleak sky, through which the morning light was struggling. I know that I had to stand during the whole of the service, being one of a crowd wedged in the passages between the closely-packed benches. Every available seat was long ago occupied. The galleries were thronged, and even the balconies at the rear of the hall were full to overflowing. The audience were, I should say, pretty equally divided in the matter of sex, and were apparently of the class of small tradesmen, clerks, and well-to-do mechanics; that was the general class of the morning congregation. But it must not, therefore, be understood that the upper class in Manchester stand aloof from the special services of the American gentlemen. In the afternoon meeting elegantly attired ladies and gentlemen, wearing spotless kid gloves, and coats of irreproachable cut, struggled for a place in the mighty throng that streamed into the hall when the doors were thrown open.

Punctually at eight o'clock the meeting was opened by one of the local clergymen, who prayed for a blessing on the day and the work, declaring, amid subdued but triumphant cries from portions of the congregation, that "The Lord has risen indeed! Now is the stone rolled away from the sepulchre, and the kingdom of God is at hand." Mr. Moody, who sat at a small desk in front of the platform, then advanced and gave out the hymn, "Guide us, O thou Great Jehovah," the singing of which Mr. Sankey, sitting before a small harmonium, led and accompanied, the vast congregation joining with great heartiness. "Mr. Sankey will now sing a hymn by himself," said Mr. Moody; and Mr. Sankey broke in with the first line of the hymn, "What are you going to do, brother?" After this solo he began to play a tune well known at these meetings into which the congregation struck with one mighty voice. The hymn would probably excite the unfavourable criticism of Dr. Eadie, if it were proposed to insert it in the Hymnal of the Scotch Kirk, being amenable to some of the objections recently quoted in the *Daily News* as having been urged before the Glasgow Presbytery by the reverend Doctor. The words have a martial, inspiriting sound, and as the verse rolled forth, filling the great hall with a mighty and musical noise, one could see the eyes of strong men fill with tears.

> Ho, my comrades! see the signal
>   Waving in the sky!
> Reinforcements now appearing,
>   Victory is nigh!
> "Hold the fort, for I am coming,"
>   Jesus signals still,
> Wave the answer back to heaven,
>   "By thy grace we will."

The subject of Mr. Moody's address was "Daniel." One might converse for an hour with Mr. Moody without discovering from his accent that he was from the United States. But it is unmistakable when he preaches, and especially in the colloquies supposed to have taken place between characters in the Bible and elsewhere. He began his discourse this morning without other preface than a half apology for selecting a subject which, it might be supposed, everybody knew everything about. But for his part, he liked to take out and look upon the photographs of old friends when they were far away, and he hoped that his hearers would not think it waste of time to take another look at the picture of Daniel. There was one peculiarity about Daniel, and that was that there was nothing against his character to be found all through the Bible. Now-a-days, when men write biographies they throw what they call the veil of charity over the dark spots in a career. But when God writes a man's life He puts it all in. So it happened that we find very few, even of the best men in the Bible, without their times of sin. But Daniel came out spotless, and the preacher attributed his exceptionally bright life to the power of saying "No."

After this exordium Mr. Moody proceeded to tell in his own words the story of the life of Daniel. Listening to him it was not difficult to comprehend the secret of his great power over the masses. Like Bunyan, he has the great gift of being able to realize things unseen, and to describe his vision in familiar language to those whom he addresses. I am afraid his notion of "Babylon, that great city," would barely stand the test of historic research. But that there really was in far-off days a great city called Babylon, in which men bustled about, ate and drank, schemed and plotted, and were finally overruled by the visible hand of God, he made as clear to the listening congregation as if he were talking about Chicago. He filled the lay figures with life, clothed them with garments, and them made them talk to each other in the English language as it is to-day accented in some of the American States.

The story of Daniel is one peculiarly susceptible of Mr. Moody's unusual method of treatment, and for three quarters of an hour he kept the congregation enthralled whilst he told how Daniel's simple faith triumphed over the machinations of the unbeliever. Mr. Moody's style is unlike that of most religious revivalists. He neither shouts nor gesticulates, and mentioned "hell" only once, and that was in connection with the life the drunkard makes for himself. His manner is reflected by the congregation, in respect of abstention from working themselves up into "a state." But this makes all the more impressive the signs of genuine emotion which follow and accompany the preacher's utterance. When he was picturing the scene of Daniel translating the King's dream, rapidly repeating Daniel's account of the dream, and Nebuchadnezzar's quick and delighted ejaculation, "That's so!" "That's it!" as he recognized the incidents, I fancy it was not without difficulty some of the people, bending forward and listening with glistening eye and heightened colour, refrained from clapping their hands for glee that the faithful Daniel, the unyielding servant of God, had triumphed over tribulation, and had walked out of prison to take his place on the right hand of the king. There was not much exhortation throughout the discourse, and not the slightest reference to any disputed point of doctrine. The discourse was nothing more than a re-telling of the story of Daniel. But whilst Nebuchadnezzar, Daniel, Shadrach, Meshach, Abednego,Darius, and even the 120 princes, became for the congregation living and moving beings, all the ends of the narrative were, with probably unconscious, certainly unbetrayed, art, gathered together to lead up to the one lesson, that compromise, where truth and religion are concerned, is never worthy of those who profess to believe God's word.

"I am sick of the shams of the present day," said Mr.Moody, bringing his discourse to a sudden close, "I am tired of the way men parley with the world whilst they are holding out their hands to be lifted into heaven. If we are going to be good Christians and God's people, let us be so out-and-out." Last night I heard him deliver an address in one of the densely-populated districts of Salford. Admission to the chapel in which the service was held was exclusively confined to women, and, notwithstanding that it was Saturday night, there were at least a thousand sober looking and respectably-dressed women present. The subject of the discussion was Christ's conversation with Nicodemus — whose social position Mr. Moody incidentally made recognisable by the congregation by observing that "if he had lived in these days he would have been a doctor of divinity, Nicodemus, D.D., or perhaps LL.D." His purpose was to make it clear that men were saved, not by any action of their own, but simply by faith. This he illustrated, among other ways, by introducing a domestic scene from the life of the children of Israel in the wilderness at the time the brazen serpent was lifted up. The dramatis personae were a young convert, a sceptic, and the sceptic's mother. The convert, who has been bitten by the serpent, and, having followed Moses' injunction, is cured, "comes along," and finds the sceptic lying down "badly bitten." He entreats him to look upon the brazen serpent which Moses has lifted up, but the sceptic has no faith in the alleged cure, and refuses. "Do you think," he says, "I'm going to be saved by looking at a brass serpent away off on a pole? No, no." "Well, I don't know," says the young convert, "but I was saved that way myself. Don't you think you'd better try it?" The sceptic refuses, and his mother "comes along," and observes, "Hadn't you better look at it, my boy?" "Well, mother, the fact is, that if I could understand the philosophy of it I would look up right off; but I don't see how a brass serpent away off on a pole can cure me." And so he dies in his unbelief.

It seemed odd to hear this conversation from the wilderness recited, word for word, in the American vernacular, and with a local colouring that suggested that both the sceptic and the young convert wore tail coats, and that the mother had to "come along" in a stuff dress. But when the preacher turned, aside, and in a very few words spoke of sons who would not hear the counsel of Christian mothers, and refused to " look up and live," the silent tears that coursed down many a face in the congregation showed that his homely picture had been clear to the eyes before which it was held up.

Hymns of the Revival

Ira David Sankey (1840-1908), was the best known of the revivalist musicians. An American, trained as a bank clerk, Sankey had from childhood a passion for sacred music. He met Moody at a Y.M.C.A. gathering in Indianapolis in 1870, and soon joined him as a partner on the revival circuit. Sankey's singing voice was not trained, and it was of limited range, but his gifts as a popular entertainer overcame these technical difficulties and helped put him in emotional touch with his audiences. The following three hymns were all favorites of Sankey. They illustrate well the simple evangelical theology of the revival, and they reflect the popular culture of those who enjoyed revival meetings.

Almost Persuaded
by Philip P. Bliss

"Almost persuaded" Now to believe;
"Almost persuaded" Christ to receive;
Seems now some soul to say,
"Go, Spirit, go Thy way,
Some more convenient day
On Thee I'll call."

"Almost persuaded" Come, come to-day;
"Almost persuaded" Turn not away;
Jesus invites you here,
Angels are lingering near,
Prayers rise from hearts so dear:
O wanderer, come.

"Almost persuaded," Harvest is past!
"Almost persuaded," Doom comes at last!
"Almost" can not avail;
"Almost" is but to fail!
Sad, sad, that bitter wail —
"Almost — *but lost!*"

Rescue the Perishing.
by Fanny J. Crosby

Rescue the perishing,
Care for the dying,
Snatch them in pity from sin and the grave;
Weep o'er the erring one,
Lift up the fallen,
Tell them of Jesus the mighty to save.

Chorus
Rescue the perishing,
Care for the dying;
Jesus is merciful,
Jesus will save.

Tho' they are slighting Him,
Still He is waiting,
Waiting the penitent child to receive.
Plead with them earnestly,
Plead with them gently:
He will forgive if they only believe.
Chorus

Down in the human heart,
Crushed by the tempter,
Feelings lie buried that grace can restore:
Touched by a loving heart,
Wakened by kindness,
Chords that were broken will vibrate once more.

Chorus

Rescue the perishing,
Duty demands it;
Strength for they labor the Lord will provide:
Back to the narrow way
Patiently win them;
Tell the poor wanderer a Saviour has died.

Chorus

The Ninety and Nine
by Elizabeth C. Clephane

There were ninety and nine that safely lay
In the shelter of the fold.
But one was out on the hills away,
Far off from the gates of gold —
Away on the mountains wild and bare,
Away from the tender Shepherds care.

"Lord, Thou hast here Thy ninety and nine;
Are they not enough for Thee?"
But the Shepherd made answer: "This of mine
Has wandered away from me,
And although the road be rough and steep
I go to the desert to find my sheep."

But none of the ransomed ever knew
How deep were the waters crossed;
Nor how dark was the night that the Lord passed
through
Ere He found His sheep that was lost.
Out in the desert He heard its cry —
Sick and helpless, and ready to die.

"Lord, whence are those blood-drops all the way
That mark out the mountain's track?"
"They were shed for one who had gone astray
Ere the Shepherd could bring him back."
"Lord whence are Thy hands so rent and torn?"
"They are pierced to-night by many a thorn."

But all thro' the mountain, thunder-riven,
And up from the rocky steep,
There arose a glad cry to the gate of heaven.
"Rejoice! I have found my sheep!"
And the angels echoed around the throne.
"Rejoice, for the Lord brings back His own!"

The Salvation Army: Three Accounts from *The Times* (1883 and 1884).

The Salvation Army was formed in 1878 under the leadership of "General" William Booth, a former renegade Methodist preacher and ex-Chartist. The movement began in the form of a number of Christian missions mainly in the poorer areas of London in the 1860s and 70s. Initially concerned with the moral degradation of the working classes, Booth, eventually was led to emphasize the physical hardships of the poor and engaged the Army in its famous social welfare activities. His book *In Darkest England and the Way Out* (1890) outlined his program for the social rejuvenation of the nation. It was, however, principally through its popular evangelizing, which stressed spiritual revival and the importance of being born again, that the Army made its impact in the nineteenth century. With street corner missions, revivalistic preaching, brass bands, and attention grabbing techniques borrowed from the popular music halls, the Army organized its assault on the poor in cultural terms they could easily understand. While they understood the message of the Army, the poor did not by any means give it universal approval. From the beginning, the Army supported the temperance movement and identified drink with the devil. Termperance, particularly, among the various righteous causes of the Salvationists, encouraged enemies of the Army, possibly supported by the drink trade, to resist what seemed to them an attack on their way of life. The riots involving the Salvation Army and the opposing "skeleton armies" in the 1880s attest to the success of the Salvationists in making their voice heard in the slums.

The Times 7 February 1883

THE SALVATION AND SKELETON ARMIES. — The riotous and disorderly scenes which have recently occurred outside the Salvation Army Hotel, formerly the Eagle Tavern, City-road, yesterday formed the subject of a long discussion on the part of the St. Luke's Vestry. Mr. J.W. Gabriel proposed a resolution denunciatory of the riotous proceedings of the Skeleton Army, especially on Sunday, and requiring the Vestry, in view of the alleged fact that this army was instigated and supported by the publicans of the metropolis, to petition Parliament for the closing of all publichouses throughout Sunday. Last Sunday, he said, owing to the conduct of the roughs who composed the Skeleton Army, it was impossible for any respectable citizen to pass along in or near the City-road without danger of molestation, and two inoffensive female salvationists were savagely assaulted by the mob. He was convinced the publicans were at the bottom of the mischief, and moved his resolution accordingly. Mr. A. Memory, in seconding the resolution, remarked that some of the proceedings of the Salvation Army were little better than those of their antagonists and promoted disturbances. Mr. J. Hurran, a licensed victualler, denied that the actions of the Skeleton Army were instigated by the publicans. Mr. J.S. Lucraft advised the Salvationists to remain within doors and not to march out in procession if they wished to live in peace. The question of closing publichouses on Sunday was irrelevant to that under consideration, which was simply one of police. Mr. J. Daniels believed that if the Salvationists themselves behaved in a more orderly and peaceable manner they would not encounter the opposition they did. What with Salvation, Skeleton, and Blue Ribbon Army processions and meetings the general public seemed to be in danger of losing the free user of the public highways. Mr. E.R. Allen proposed, and Mr. E. Howes seconded, the following amendment, which was passed all but unanimously: — "That a memorial be presented to the Home Secretary requesting his immediate attention to the tumultuous assembly of large mobs in the City-road contiguous to as well as in front of the Eagle Tavern, mobs so numerous and ill-conducted that the roads are impassable by the respectable inhabitants, whose persons and property are rendered most insecure and are very frequently greatly injured."

****

The Times 7 May 1883

THE SALVATION ARMY. — What was called a "Free and Easy" was held on Saturday afternoon at Exeter-hall by the members of the Salvation Army. The large hall was crowded. "General" Booth presided, and was supported by Mrs. Booth, Miss Booth, Mr. and Mrs. Armitage, and others. The band of the army and representatives from all parts of the country were present. At the beginning of the meeting Big Ben, the champion light-weight of Yorkshire, lately converted, sang a hallelujah medley beginning "The devil and me we can't agree." "General" Booth, who did not arrive till late, in the course of his address apologized for being behind time, and explained that an unpleasant circumstance had kept him away. He had been obliged, unfortunately, to attend in a law court a case connected with the army. Strange to say the case had gone against them. This he considered a most unusual thing, as they had generally come off victorious on such occasions. He thought, however, they should not despair, for the Lord would surely bring them safely through all their trials. (Cries of "Hallelujah!" and "Glory!") He was sure that some day they would get a settlement according to law and justice. Though he had lost that afternoon in Westminster he meant to enjoy himself at Exeter-hall. He intended being free and easy. To be easy one ought to be free. He was sure all present who had got salvation were both free and easy, and he earnestly hoped they might always continue so. (Cheers and cries of "Hallelujah!") Later on in the meeting, between the verses of a song from Big Ben, "General" Booth said the gathering did not seem like a Salvation Army meeting at all. One would think that all present, like him, had lost a lawsuit. He suggested that everybody should shake hands with everybody else, whereupon all present did so, amid laughter and shouts. At the end of Big Ben's song a volley was fired, which was done by waving handkerchiefs and shouting. "Major" Smith, of the London division, stated that the work of the army was going on well in London, and that since they had entered Stratford something like 120 persons per week had been saved. Mr. Armitage, after several other songs, and after members of the army had stated in rather loud voices that they were saved and felt happy, said the worst of the Salvation Army was the noise. ("Oh, oh.") He was sure some of those present would agree with him when he said the noise they made sometimes was too great. He was certain the "General" would not be angry with him if he gave him a word of warning. At some of their meetings they had very loud prayers. Some people, he was sure, were literaly frightened away on account of the noise. He thought they ought to be wise, and take not consideration the nerves of people who were not quite as young, and had nto quite such strong lungs as some of the members of the army. (Shouts.) The object of the army was to save souls. He believed they could do that quite as well in a quiet voice as by making such a noise. "General" Booth replied, and cited several instances of how, through the noise, as it was called, of the army, several persons had been converted. A second "Free and Easy" was held in the evening between 7 and 9 o'clock. It was even better attended than that of the morning meeting. The "General," in the course of the proceedings, made it known that in addition to 455 different stations where meetings were held services also took place in 142 villages. Since the meetings which were convened at Exeter-hall three weeks ago 7,650 services had taken place. — *Observer*.

****

The Times 16 May 1884

THE SALVATION ARMY. — Last night, at Exeter-hall what was termed a "great demonstration of saved drunkards," was held under the presidency of General Booth. There was a very full audience. Hymns were sung to the accompaniement of various instruments and General Booth delivered an address. Amid "Hallelujahs," and other exclamations, the speaker urged the goodness of "aggressive Christianity," as he termed the work of the "Army." He touched upon the question of a collection, and said that he wanted   10,000 before they slept that night. Then was sung a hymn to a popular tune, and "Boss Phillips" was introduced to give his experiences. He stated that he was formerly "a black one of Camberwell," who had committed every crime but murder, and nearly committed that crime twice. He declared that he was converted by following the band of the Army in the streets, and going, when drunk, into the meeting. Then followed a Devonshire girl, now a lieutenant, and she recited a somewhat similar story, as did a man, an old soldier, known as "Old Whisky." A reclaimed thief from Kent-street, Mint, Southwark, amid exclamations of rejoicing, described his conversion, and was followed by one who was described as a "little cockney Brandy Drinker," but who proved to be a Yorkshire man. A man who had been a sailor, and "Black Bishop," a negro, next described their conversions. A converted washerwoman entered upon what might have been a long story, but was interrupted by the band and the singers. The "Drunken Tramp," who was described as a "sort of poet" next took possession of the platform, and proceeded to sing a speech, the band and singers joining in with a chorus. Then followed brief speeches from many others, who declared themselves "saved" from drunkenness and sin by the Army. Their declarations were received with cries of "Hallelujah" and "Amen." They all described themselves as formerly drunkards, liars, thieves, and wife-beaters, or, in the case of women, as neglecting their families. Brevity of speech was enforced by the General's whistle. General Booth again addressed the meeting, and said that it was intended to start a "Salvation Navy," and one yacht would soon start to bombard the sailors on the sea. The subscription list was then read. It included three sums of £1,000, one of £500, two of £250, one of £200, one of £150, three of £100, several of £50, and a great number of smaller sums. The larger sums General Booth called "good kegs of powder." The total reached at that stage was £6,000 and General Booth said they would have to make it to £10,00 before they had their suppers. Mrs. Booth afterwards delivered an address, in the course of which she expressed her gratitude for the help given to the Army in its emergency. Other collections were make, and the Army left the hall in procession.

Life and Labour of the People in London. Third series: Religious Influences, **Vol. VII** (1902), by Charles Booth. Selections.

Charles Booth (1840-1916) was both an active businessman and a famous writer on social questions. In 1862 he was made a partner in his brother's steamship firm eventually becoming chairman of his own company. His managerial position, however, did not dull his interest in the working classes. Early in his life he was very supportive of the trade union movement. By the eighteen-eighties he became intensely interested in the welfare of the working classes and began to gather statistics on their social conditions. Booth was much more systematic in his methods of collection and presentation of evidence than previous investigators such as Henry Mayhew. Over a sixteen year period he wrote the various volumes of *The Life and Labour Of the People in London.* The earliest material was published in the *Tower Hamlets Magazine* in 1887. Subsequently various parts appeared in print from 1889 to 1903 including four volumes on poverty, five on industry, seven on religious influences and a final volume. In his treatment of social conditions Booth related the level of wages to the standard of living enjoyed by the masses — thereby developing the concept of a "poverty line."

Religion And Class

No class has a monopoly of religious-minded persons. If only those are to be counted as religious whose whole souls are filled with the faith they profess, then each class yeilds its proportion of the few who are chosen out of the many that are called. Or if we take the broadest view, and accept as religious all those whose nature is open to good influences and who, thus helped and fostered, grow straight and true, like the trees, towards heaven, again we find no class advantage. But as regards certain religious developments, class conditions seem paramount, alike with those whose religion absorbs their entire spiritual life, whose sole anchorage it then becomes; and those who merely find in it a useful framework upon which to rest sympathies of which the roots are widely spread; and most of all with those for whom religious observances are only matters of taste and habit and who hardly have a spiritual life at all.

There are some amongst the oldest of English families whose

traditions hold them faithful to the Church of Rome, but with these and a few other exceptions of less importance, the great bulk of those of rank and station amongst our people belong to the Church of England, and their relations with the Church are easy and confident. They are not only steady supporters, but for the most part, truly and warmy attached members. For them the union of Church and State is more than a phrase. Both in town and country they and their families attend the services of the Church; many of their women devote their lives to Church work, while from their men have come large numbers of clergy and some of the greatest of religious philanthropists. Their devotional expression is, as a rule, cold and unemotional, but with no class is religion more completely identified with duty. They belong to all branches of the Church: High or Low, or what may perhaps be called 'Central,' and ask as a rule, no further licence. Doctrinal difficulties do not trouble them much; their balance is not easily upset. The same mental as well as social position is occupied, and the same course pursued from generation to generation, handed down from father to son, and from mother to daughter. All their traditions are conservative. The part played by religion in their lives is as a rule by no means large but it is constant.

Those who come next in the social scale, who fill the principal places in the Civil Service, officer the Army and Navy, and plead in our courts of law, are also mostly members of the Church of England, and supply the Church with many of her clergy. Amongst this class religious observance is usual, but the attitude towards religion is perhaps less calm than that described above, it may be because less simply connected with duty. With these people religious feeling when it arises is very likely to take the shape of reaction and revolt from the stress of worldly existence, which is otherwise apt to be the law of their being, and then they, and especially the women, fling themselves into good works, or rush into extremes of religious doctrines and practices. There are among them many restless minds and lives with no safe anchorage; and it is the troubled condition of such souls, more than anything else, that has given rise to the wild hopes of Rome for the conversion of England, and to the dreams of others who live in expectation of a new spiritual dispensation, accompanied by strange credulities and dabblings in mediaeval magic.

shared to the full in the stress of wordly life, and in the characteristics it produces both with men and women. If belonging previously to some religious denomination outside the Establishment, they have usually left it behind them and joined the Church of England; but it is much to be wished that with the general rise in social stature of the Nonconformist bodies, this unsatisfactory form of conventional development may come to an end; and of this change there are now some hopeful signs.

With the next social layer, consisting of legal and other professional men, some civil servants, men of business, wholesale traders and large retailers, the Nonconformist bodies — Presbyterians, Congregationalists and Wesleyans, with Unitarians and the Society of Friends, and a few of the Baptists — take the lead of the Church of England. Class position amongst the Nonconformists goes very much by congregations, the worshippers sorting themselves in this way much more than do those who attend the parish churches. Amongst these people those of highest social grade share in the worldly striving and push of the class above, but their religious anchorage, with the Nonconformists at least, is likely to be more secure. The place of religion in their lives is fully recognised. If they succeed they give thanks to God, it is 'the Lord who prospers them.' The language they use often savours of cant, and there may be sheer hypocrisy sometimes, but in general their religion is to them a daily reality, and they are content in it and untroubled by doubt. If their souls are shaken it is by the personal sense of sin and of the need for salvation, not by revolt against the weariness of life and the hollowness of religious professions, nor by any doubts as to the foundations upon which the whole structure of organized religion is reared.

Those of this social grade who belong to the Church of England, make less display of religion than their Nonconformist brethren, and except in the extreme Low Church section, are not so prone to invoke the sense of sin. They take religion more easily, but in a very simple, unquestioning, wholesome spirit.

A little lower in the social scale, among those of inferior rank in the same professions, men of business in both wholesale and retail trade, with 'lower division' civil servants and an enormous variety of salaried people, we have a heterogeneous group of whom it is even more difficult to speak as one class.

The oratorical division of our population into 'masses' and 'classes' entirely omits this great section, and yet it is, perhaps, mainly of its members that most large general audiences gathered in any part of London are constituted.the word 'popular' is invariably used to describe these audiences, to bespeak their presence,and to characterize the entertainment offered, as well as the prices which, it is inferred, will be readily paid. Whether for theatre, concert, or exhibition, these people can afford to pay their way, and they form the bulk of most large religious assemblages. I have elsewhere spoken of them as the new middle class, and though in strict arithmetical sense somewhat above the middle line, the social position which they hold between the masses and the classes is truly a central one.

But the limits are not well defined. The ranks of this body are constantly recruited from below; and while some may fall back, others pass on, from them or through them, to the ranks above. This gives elasticity and the range is wide. The characteristics vary greatly. If I think of these people as young and aspiring and full of energy in all kinds of directions, my mind turns also to the failures, worn out and broken down, and to the 'pathos of pinched lives.' If I think of them as achieving solid comfort regardless of show, I remember that it is not always so; for many, going on too fast, or attempting too much, have tied round their necks a burthen of debt. Moreover there are decreasing as well as increasing incomes. Thus some lag behind, sick or sorry, but on the whole it is an advancing crowd filled with confidence and energy; and to this crowd, as we have repeatedly seen, all the religious bodies appeal with some measure of success, each after its own particular fashion, and able each to find sympathizers who may become adherents, and finally active members, of some particular church.

It is impossible to estimate with any exactness or certainty the proportion of this large and much mixed section of the people, that may be regarded as religious; but many of the Nonconformist churches are entirely filled from it, as are most of the great preaching mission services, while many scattered members attend the Church of England. They value greatly and therefore seek the social side of religion, but furnish devoted workers and hold their religious opinions firmly. These opinions they have generally inherited, and, on the whole, rarely change. Among the great variety of doctrine and practice offered in any neighbourhood in London, the various members of this class can usually find some church or chapel that will suit them.

I have made no attempt to classify those whose rank is the stamp of Education or the seal of Art. On them, whatever their social grade, organised religion has less than average hold. They too, each in their own way, are teachers and preachers.

No class lines in England are strictly maintained; everywhere there is some interchange between class and class, but the uncertainty of the division between lower middle and upper working class is quite special in character, and may perhaps point to a coming change of great importance, if it should indicate a diversity of status amongst the working classes that is likely to break up their solidarity of sentiment. In this direction several causes are now operating.

The great section of the population, which passes by the name of the working classes, lying socially between the lower middle class and the 'poor,' remains, as a whole, outside of all the religious bodies, whether organized as churches or as missions; and as those of them who do join any church become almost indistinguishable from the class with which they then mix, the change that has really come about is not so much *of* as *out of* the class to which they have belonged. Other causes operate in the same direction. The organization of modern industry finds room for much cheap clerk work for which the elementary schools ensure a copious supply, and requires also, on the practical side of the work, men of skill and character, who earn higher wages then these clerks. Thus the financial distinction between clerk and working man tends to break down, and when for any purpose they consort together, or make common cause, the social distinction is apt to break down too. Moreover, many of the children of working men become clerks. So that finally where working men are dwelling in the same streets, and under the same conditions, with well paid clerks and others of like station, the two classes approximate in their lives and habits, Socially it depends on the individual character of the man or of his wife, and financially, on the way in which their money is spent, whether a first-class workman and his family remain in, or, in effect, step out of the class to which they have hitherto belonged. At the same time the cleavage between the upper and lower grades of manual labour has become more marked industrially.

On industrial questions it may be that high and low class labour may continue to coalesce, as has hitherto been the case, in spite, frequently, of sectionally divergent interests; and cheap clerks, even though of working class parentage, may follow in the wake of those of higher grade; but away from workshop and office and as regards other than trade questions, social influences will prevail. To trace all the possibilities of this movement would take me too far; but the point I desire to make is that in this way a road has been opened between the religious bodies and the working classes, by which, though it can hardly be said that these classes are reached, an increasing proportion do pass under the influence of organized religion and recognise its claims. But meanwhile the bulk of the regular wage-earning class still remain untouched, except that their children attend Sunday school.

Of this class many — it may be because of illness or extravagance or bad management, a large family or low pay — belong to those we call 'the poor.' So far as they remain independent they are to be counted with the rest of the class. But great efforts are made to reach them; and their needs open the door to attempts which lie in the middle ground between religious and charitable care. These attempts, mingled inextricably with those made to help people who can no longer pretend to independence, are the mainstay of missionary activity in London, and have been sufficiently described. They are summed up in the pregnant phrase, 'practical Christianity.' By it almost all are touched, but while the good done on the material side to these pauperized people is questionable and undermined by many inherent drawbacks, the profit to them on the religious side is still more doubtful.

As regards religious influence the Roman Catholic poor stand out as an exception. They constitute a class apart, being as a rule devout and willing to contribute something from their earnings towards the support of their schools and the maintenance of their religion; but at the same time they are great beggars, as well as heavy drinkers, and there is no sign that the form which practical Christianity takes in their case helps to make them in these respects either more self-reliant or more self-restrained.

****

The Attitude Of The People To Religion

It may be said of the inhabitants of London, as of the people of England, that they would all (except the Jews) repudiate the imputation of belonging to any other of the great religions of the world. Which of them would not laugh in the face of an inquirer who gravely demanded of him whether he were Mahommedan, Buddhist, Brahmanist, Zoroastrian, or Christian? To such a question there can be no doubt as to the reply. Furthermore, it may be said that though the mass of the people may not understand the exact force and bearing of various doctrines of which the Christian system is built up, they are acquainted with them in a general way. The doctrines of the Incarnation, the Atonement, the Resurrection, are fairly well known to them, and though many would say they did not well understand them, there would be no general disposition to question their truth. It would be mainly among the very intelligent, educated members of the more highly paid working class that formal disagreement would find expression.

But something more is demanded than a mere acquiescence which is often felt to amount to little more than 'not being prepared not to believe' and such sentences as 'It is heathen London still;' 'It is heathen London with which we have to deal;' 'The rich have purses but no souls;' 'You may write indifference across it all;' are familiar in the mouths of the ministers of religion.

There is, however, another point of view. According to many, including not a few of the clergy themselves, everything that is beneficial may be brought under the aegis of religion. 'Only that which is harmful is irreligious,' says one, while some go so far as to 'recognise no distinction between the sacred and the secular,' in which case all moral life could be accepted as religious, and of moral conscientious life in London there is much.

If, however, religion is not simply a moral mode of life, neither is it merely a devotional expression; religion is also an impulse and a persistent attitude, an intimate possession of the soul, perhaps not understood even by the individual, and very difficult of interpretation by others. But if we consider the recognition of the divine and the spiritual in life to be the distinctive characteristic of religion, judgment is still obscured. In this sense men are often more religious than is known. The most religious may be those whose professions are fewest; who may give no sign to the world of their inner spiritual life. The form of reserve that hates to display feeling is a national quality.

Although it is thus difficult to form any definite judgment as to the religious character of London, the fact must be admitted that the great masses of the people remain apart from all forms of religious communion, apparently untouched by the Gospel that, with various differences of interpretation and application, is preached from every pulpit.

Of the effect of age, sex and class on this aloofness much has been said. Children cannot be regarded as having any attitude of their own in this matter, save that of willing acceptance of anything pleasant that may come within their reach. It is not doctrine or ritual, but the measure of kindly welcome and the rewards, that determine the direction of their feet. And taking London as a whole, it is the young children alone who in the mass are responsive. Though easily won they are held with difficulty, and there is little continuity in their religious training. The habit of the home is stronger than the precepts of the school, or the influence of the churches. Girls are more amenable than boys, and throughout London the female sex forms the mainstay of every religious assembly of whatever class. Otherwise the palpable distinctions are those of means.

* * * * * * * * *

Among the working classes there is less hostility to, and perhaps even less criticism of the Churches than in the past. The Secularist propaganda, though not suspended, is not a very powerful influence. Pronounced atheism is rare. There is evidence that a wave of such feeling did pass over London nearly a generation ago, but the last twenty years have witnessed a notable change in this respect. The success at the polls, whether for Boards of Guardians, Borough Councils, or the School Board, of men and women who in the name of religion are giving their lives to the service of the people, is one of the noteworthy facts in democratic rule. The sub-warden of a

Congregational mission sits as Mayor of Southwark today.

While there has been this change of attitude towards the Churches, they also have been changing alike in the breadth of their sympathies and the scope of their work. Direct response was doubtless looked for and might have been expected, but there is little sign of it in the sense of an increased acceptance of the particular teaching of the Churches, and at this disappointment is felt.The humanitarianism of the clergy and others is approved of, but their doctrinal teaching carries no weight. The fact that working men are more friendly, more tolerant perhaps of clerical pretensions and in a sense more sympathetic, makes them no more religious in anything approaching to the accepted meaning of the word. And to this we must add that a liberalised form of Christianity, as preached by some, makes no better headway; the fact, indeed, remains that in those chapels and missions in which the greatest proportion of really attached working men are found, the teaching is strictly and even narrowly orthodox.

What then is happening? If the working classes are not becoming more religious, what direction does development take? It is claimed that changes making for improvement are in progress among them, that habits are becoming softened, that the influence of education is making itself felt, that intelligence is spreading, that the range of interests is widening: are, then, their interests becoming more political, or more social, more intellectual or more material? No conclusive answer can be given. We only know that such interests as trade unions and friendly societies, co-operative effort, temperance propaganda and politics (including Socialism) with newspapers and even books, are filling, in the mental life of the average working man, a larger space than in the past, and with some may be taking a place which might have been otherwise been occupied by religious interests; but this usurpation and engrossment of the mind may probably be asserted much more confidently of pleasure, amusement, hospitality and sport. In these matters a measure of the demand is found in the facility of the supply, and for all the last-named facilities readily keep pace.

For most wage earners the claims of the working day are not so exacting as in the past. The great mass of men have more leisure, but the time freed goes in some of these other directions; religion hardly gains. One who fought hard for the Saturday half-holiday, hoping that Sunday would then be given to God, sadly admits his mistake. The maw of pleasure is not easy to fill. The appetite grows. Sunday is increasingly regarded as a day of mere recreation. Nationally we have yet to learn how to use this day. The old 'dulness' which one witness regarded as 'our salvation, physically as well as spiritually,' has been rejected; but the full force and the best form of alternative interests and attractions are not yet realized.

Apart from the Sunday question, the other interests mentioned are, however, not in themselves absolutely incompatible with the maintenance of active religious connexions. In practice the associations of the public-house, the music-hall or the race-course conflict with those of church and chapel, but there is nothing inherently or theoretically inconsistent between the two sets of interests. There is nothing that is found so in Roman Catholic countries, nor among ourselves, by many middle-class families who are able to enjoy the theatre on Saturday and yet join in active Christian communion on the following day. The conflict arises from the character which these amusements have acquired, and the spirit in which they are sought, both of which religion, if accepted, might successfully modify. We therefore turn rather to the special obstacles which in the case of the working classes prevent church going. These have been largely studied in the preceding volumes, and may be taken as constituting the attitude of these classes to religion.

The churches have come to be regarded as the resorts of the well-to-do, and of those who are willing to accept the charity and patronage of people better off than themselves. It is felt that the tone of the services, especially in the Church of England, is opposed to the idea of advancement; inculcating rather contentment with, and the necessity for the doing of duty in, that station of life to which it has pleased God to call a man. The spirit of self-sacrifice, inculcated in theory, is not observed among, or believed to be practised by, the members of these churches in any particular degree, and this inconsistency is very critically and severely judged. Phrasing it somewhat differently, the working man would doubtless heartily endorse the opinion of the clergy themselves, that 'what we want for the recovery of the lapsed masses is not more but better Christians.'

There is also an incompatibility of moral temper. The average working man of to-day thinks more of his rights or of his wrongs than of his duties and his failures to perform them. Humility and the consciousness of sin; and the attitude of worship, are perhaps not natural to him. He is not helped by calling himself a miserable sinner and would probably feel the abasement somewhat exaggerated, and, in the same way, perhaps, triumphant praise strikes in him no sympathetic note.

'The dawn of hope for the working man, who has begun to realize that he has ample opportunities to improve his position,' was regarded by one of our witnesses, himself a clergyman of the Church of England, as 'the main factor in the improved moral tone of the present day,' due otherwise to a combination of causes — religious, educational, and administrative. But how does the ordinary religious service fit in with this ideal? Neither the Prayer Book nor the New Testament itself give any prominence to the idea of progress, either for the community or for the individual, except in so far as it is involved in the ideas of moral and spiritual regeneration. It may, indeed, be urged, that with these all true progress will be ensured, and without them none, but it is difficult for those below to regard the matter in this light.

As to religious truth, among many teachers, the inquirer in the end is thrown back upon himself to form conclusions as best he may, and, in most instances, finding no satisfactory solution he puts the issue by. Amongst all the reasons for abstaining from public worship, genuine, conscientious, reasoned unbelief takes a very small place.

The clergy and ministers have no authority that is recognised, but their professional character remains, and owing to it they perhaps lose influence. It is accounted their business to preach, they being paid to do it; and their manner, though accepted as a pose necessary to the part they play, is somewhat resented. No prestige covers them — 'they are no better than other men.' In the case of the Roman Catholic priesthood alone do we find the desired combination of professionalism and authority, safeguarded because accepted, and resting not on the individual but on the Church he serves; and where most nearly approached, it is by the saintly lives of some of the High Church clergy. To live a life of voluntary poverty seems to be the only road to the confidence of the people in this matter.

To the reasons adduced to account for the abstention of the working classes may be added the habit of detachment itself, bringing a feeling of discomfort in unaccustomed surroundings if this habit be at any time broken through; and answering to this we have the recognition that it is to warmth of welcome that success is mostly to be attributed when success is secured at all.

Finally, it may be said that London surroundings bring little or no pressure to bear in the direction of conventional church-going. Even men who have been churchwardens in the country feel, we are told, no obligation to attend church here, and the ordinary resident knows that, in this respect, his conduct, so far as non-attendance goes, is for the most part free from observation, and, if observed, from comment. Among the working classes the pressure exerted is apt to be on the opposite side, such as in the 'ragging' of the workshop, or the sneers of neighbours who connect religious observance with cupboard love. But in a general way, London life secures for all men the maximum freedom of conduct. Even criminals find it their best hiding-place. To ask no questions is commonly regarded as the highest form of neighbourliness.

Chapter VII

Politics and Sectarian Conflict

Introduction

An important feature of Victorian society and politics was the great divide between Churchmen and Nonconformists. Nonconformists for generations had resented the stamp of social inferiority placed on them by Churchmen who dominated national life. When parliamentary and, more important in the short run, municipal reform created opportunities for political influence for Dissenters whose economic position had been recently enhanced, the scene was set for a struggle between Church and Dissent that remained a significant factor in English politics until the coming of the First World War.

In the 1830s and 1840s Nonconformists tended to concentrate their political activity on gaining power over Tory oligarchies in town councils. Indeed, throughout the century Nonconformists were able to mobilize their political power much more effectively at the local than at the national level. Their time of greatest national effectiveness was probably the period from 1867 to 1885 when they were able to control many local Liberal associations and thereby influence the parliamentary party.

Compulsory church rates which were levied at the parish level on Anglicans and non-Anglicans alike for the upkeep of the parish church, constituted the most persistent Dissenting grievance until they were abolished in 1868. Control over primary education was a politically explosive issue throughout the century. The law relating to burials in the public cemeteries that were created in 1855 was a contentious issue for a quarter century. Oxford and Cambridge were not fully open to Dissenters even after 1871. The list of Nonconformist complaints was a long one, and, in a pattern familiar to those acquainted with civil rights movements, each step forward brought new difficulties to overcome. First, the struggle for liberty from vexatious legal disabilities; then the demand for equality.

Equality was the goal of those Dissenters who organized the movement for disestablishment and disendowment of the Church of England. They wished to place that privileged body on an equal footing with the other denominations. Organized by Edward Miall and the Liberation Society, the campaign for disestablishment in England reached its height in the 1870s when the ties between Dissent and the Liberal Party were strongest. But even at the peak of his career, it was difficult for Miall to find parliamentary support for such a drastic proposal. The Dissenters were always more successful in fighting for relief from specific grievances.

To some extent, the struggle between Church and Dissent reflected tensions between economic and social interest groups. Dissenting strength lay mainly in the industrial towns of the Midlands and the North, while the strength of the Church lay in the countryside of the counties. Dissenters tended strongly to be Liberal; Churchmen less strongly to be Conservative. Dissenters tended to welcome democracy, Churchmen inclined towards postponement. But the division between Church and Dissent also cut across class lines, dividing regions and neighbourhoods and occupational groups, introducing another element to the complex web of interests, ideas and traditions that underpinned Victorian politics.

By the eighteen-forties English Roman Catholics deserved better clerical administration than its mission territory status under the Sacred Congregation of Propaganda. The increasing number of Catholics (mostly Irish immigrants) as well as the prestige of the clergy demanded it. Various proposals were raised until the Pope replaced the system of vicars apostolic with an episcopacy in September 1850. The sees were given titles which were different from the existing Anglican ones in accordance with provisions of the Catholic Emancipation Act of 1829. This, however, was not sufficient to prevent an outburst of anti-Catholic feeling throughout the country. Anti-Catholicism had long been a feature of English life, and remained such through the nineteenth century.

Guide to Further Reading

There is no satisfactory general study of the very large role played by religion in Victorian politics. A useful introduction to the subject is contained in the long chapter on "Political Attitudes of the Victorian Church" in E.R. Norman, *Church and Society in England 1770-1970: A Historical Study* (1976), in G.I.T. Machin, *Politics and the Churches in Great Britain, 1832 to 1968* (1977), and in P.T. Marsh, ed. *The Conscience of the Victorian State* (1979). H.J. Hanham, *Elections and Party Management: Politics in the Age of Disraeli and Gladstone* (1958) indicates how important religious issues were in elections between the second and third Reform Acts, while Peter Marsh's study of A.C. Tait as Archbishop of Canterbury, *The Victorian Church in Decline* (1969), concentrates on religious issues at the parliamentary level in the 1870s.

There is no study of the link between the Conservative Party and the Church of England, an association of political interests that can be traced at least as far back as the first Reform Bill, and probably to the Whig support of Nonconformist aspirations in the later eighteenth century. Perhaps because historians, like Victorians themselves, have been slow to recognize that the Church by the beginning of the Victoria's reign was behaving more like a denomination than either a department of state or the English expression of the Church universal, there is no overall study of the politics of the Church of England.

The connection between Liberalism and Nonconformity, and the politics of Nonconformity in general, have been more thoroughly explored. In his pamphlet on *Dissenters and Public Affairs in Mid Victorian England* (1967) Frank Salter surveys the political aspirations of Nonconformity. J.R. Vincent discusses the multitude of intricate ties between Dissent and Liberalism in his important work on *The Formation of the Liberal Party, 1857-1868* (1966) and D.W. Bebbington, *The Nonconformist Conscience* (1982) surveys the period from 1870 to 1914. John F. Glaser considers "English Nonconformity and the Decline of Liberalism", in the *American Historical Review* (1958). Stephen Koss, beginning with the 1890s, surveys *Nonconformity in Modern British Politics* (1975). David Thompson describes the Liberation Society in the 50s and 60s in *Pressure From*

Without (1974), edited by Patricia Hollis. S.M. Ingham discusses "The Disestablishment Movement in England, 1868-74", in the *Journal of Religious History* (1964).

The political aspects of anti-Catholicism are best described by E.R. Norman, *Anti-Catholicism in Victorian England* (1968). Anti-ritualism in politics has recently been discussed by James Bentley, *Ritualism and Politics in Victorian Britain* (1978) and G.I.T. Machin, "The Last Victorian Anti-Ritualist Campaign, 1895-1906", *Victorian Studies* (1982).

The Social Influences of the State-Church (1867), by Edward Miall.
Selections.

Edward Miall (1809-1881) [*q.v.*], militant Dissenting politician and
journalist, was the leading proponent of disestablishment from mid-
century until his death. He founded the Anti-State Church Association
in 1844, called the Liberation Society after 1853, an important
political pressure group with close links to the Liberal Party in the
60s and 70s. He continued to edit the *Nonconformist*, the principal
newspaper of militant nonconformity, until his death. From 1823 to
1857 he sat as M.P. for Rochdale; from 1869 to 1874 he sat for
Bradford.

A BIRD'S EYE VIEW OF THE TOPIC

The social organisation of the inhabitants of this country is extremely
complex, and it is indispensable to a fair estimate of the effect upon
it of any given class of influences that this complexity be taken into
account. English society consists of many grades, the relative position
of which towards each other is usually determined by more than one
cause — often, by several causes in combination. Rank, for instance
prescribes one set of limitations to freedom of intercourse, customary
co-operation, and social responsibilities, wealth another, education
another, moral character, trade occupations, nature of employment,
and so on, each of them another. But the circles formed by these
several agencies are not kept wholly separate. They intersect one
another more or less according to the circumstances, the opinion, or
the fashion of the times; and, although the larger groups into which
they arrange themselves are very distinct one from another, there
is a link of connection between them, narrow as it often is, which
serves to constitute of the whole a single community.

One might conceive the possibility of mapping out English society,
with at least an approximation to accuracy, upon a sheet of paper.
Each of the causes in operation by which social division is effected
might be represented by a belt of a different colour running across
the sheet from right to left, the topmost standing for rank, the
lowermost for pauperism, and every intermediate grade in its
supposed relative position to the others, the extent to which it
intermingles with others being displayed by the blending of the
distinctive colours. At any rate, we may ask our readers to imagine

the gradations of society mapped out in some way. In order to get a broad conception of the dislocation resulting from the State-Church, let the map be vertically cut in two, and one side of it pushed up an inch or two above the side with which it previously matched. The effect would be that every belt on one side would be severed by that interval from its corresponding belt on the other, and on passing the finger along it from right to left, it would, in each case, reach a line where it must abruptly drop in order to continue passing over the same colour. All the gradations on one side would be lower down than those of the same kind on the opposite side. In fact, out of one community you would make two, separated by no natural differences, but merely in consequence of an arbitrary misplacement of one half above the other.

Now, speaking generally, and with due allowance for variations of detail, this shadows forth the sort of division which the Chruch Establishment in this country superadds to all those which arise out of other causes. It dissevers one half of society from the other, and permanently alters the relation of the several grades of the one moiety to those of the other. It may help us therefore, to a fuller understanding of our subject, to examine into the precise character of the disturbing force which produces this effect, and into the general mode of its operation.

The first phenomenon presented by an analysis of that mental state which, through all the various classes of society, attributes social inferiority to such as are outside the pale of the Establishment, is that it is almost entirely independent of religious considerations. It is true that the difference between the Churchmen and Dissenters arises out of circumstances connected with religion. It is in this region that the rift occurs. But the active force which produces it is not a religious force. There are theological differences between the outside denominations quite as great as any which sever them from the State-Church, but they do little or nothing to alter the relative positions of the classes comprised in each. There are also similar divisions *in* the Church of England, but they do not in the least degree disturb the social standing of those who take part in them. Doubtless, the feuds of the several schools more or less affect social intercourse even within the precincts of the Establishment, but they do not touch any man's class position in society. A Church of England linendraper may be High Church or Low Church, ritualistic or sceptical, without prejudice to his social whereabouts — but should he become a Dissenting linendraper, although all the articles of his theological faith should remain unchanged, he would instantly drop out of the status which had been previously accorded him, and would descend several degees in the estimate of his neighbours. We must therefore look in some other quarter for the causes which may explain the phenomenon above alluded to.

The first, and perhaps the most potential of them, is the association of religious profession with the sanction or discountenance of the law of the land. A reverence for public law, as such, happily pervades the whole community. Nourished by what influences it has grown into its present strength, it is hardly necessary to our immediate purpose to inquire. It may not be irrelevant, however, to state that, in common with the most zealous supporter of the State-Church, we account this habitual deference of the English people to legal authority as an inestimable blessing, and we heartily thank God for it. But it is obvious, that when the law sets the seal of its sanction to any particular religious system, it is possible that conscience may prescribe a course of action which clashes with this sentiment of loyalty, and, on that supposition, the highest motives of religion may enjoin us to do what the law of the land views with systematic disfavour. A man may be sometimes called upon to choose between what God expects from him as a Christian and what his country expects from him as a citizen, and it is by his conduct in the latter case that the greater part of society will be apt to judge him. As a matter of fact, this is so. A Dissenter is regarded as a *quasi* rebel. He might hold views as to truth which the majority might pronounce erroneous without forfeiting his social position — but he cannot, with similar impunity, set at nought the embodied authority of the State without derogating from his character and claims as a citizen. He does that which it is assumed and implied by the law of the land he should not do. He is not a criminal — no; he is not in a political sense guilty of rebellion; but there is a department of thought and action, and a very wide one, in which he withholds allegiance to national authority, and sinks into the position of what the Constitution regards as a wilful anarchist.

We have to remember, moreover, that the stigma which society inflicts on Dissent does not owe its existence to modern reason. It is merely the attenuated form of a traditional sentence much more pronounced in its character. Time *has been* when Dissent was criminal — when the law of the land visited it with penalties severer than those awarded to theft or homicide — when non-compliance with what the law enjoined in relation to the National Church entailed the disgrace as well as the punishments measured out to felony. The Toleration Act rescued us from the latter, but there was always a considerable proportion of the clergy who took care that we should not escape the former. They classed us with Republicans, levellers, Jacobins, infidels. They denounced us as saturated with the spirit of sedition. They preached against us as wilfully disobedient to "the powers that be." They persuaded the Legislature to exclude us from all offices of trust. They stirred up the rabble to hunt us down, and pelt, and maltreat us, as if we were vermin not to be tolerated in decent society. Some of them, *even now*, do their little best to cast scorn upon us as a lawless faction, and disfigure the clerical press with epithets that can have no intelligible meaning but this — Dissenters are enemies of their country. The atmosphere of society is laden with the offensive odours which the rampant demon of persecution left behind it; and it is difficult even for educated men to get quite clear of the impression that social degradation is justly due to those who are outside the pale of the Endowed Church.

To the influence of law we must add that of fashion. The Sovereign is placed by the Constitution at the head of the Established Church, and must, of course, be a professing member of it. The Court naturally reflects the lustre it borrows from the Crown. The great territorial nobles follow suit. The upper ten thousand, with a very few exceptions, regard connection with the authorized ecclesiastical institution of the kingdom as inseparable from their elevated position. Until comparatively recent times, both Houses of Parliament were closed against Nonconformists. To this day, the great national universities are governed with a view to interests of the State-Church. Is it surprising that, under such conditions, the higher professions gravitate towards it? To belong to the Church is to side with respectability; to dissent from it is to cast in your lot with the vulgar. Accordingly, Dissenters, simply as such, are esteemed inferior. They are, at any rate, usually treated as if they were, and certainly much has been wilfully and deliberately done to make and keep it so.

The consequence is, that English society is divided into two castes — an upper and a lower one — of the first of which the spirit of ecclesiastical ascendancy is a dominant characteristic, and for the last of which scant courtesy is considered not inappropriate. We have put the fact broadly. It is, of course, susceptible of many minor modifications. But such as we have stated is the general social effect of the law-established Church. It has split society into two parts, and pushed one of them relatively higher than the other. We shall see, in future papers, how this central fact operates in disturbing social organization and development.

"NOT KNOWN IN THIS NEIGHBOURHOOD."

Thus superscribed, letters are often returned by the district postmaster to the head office. Giving an old sense to the word "known," namely, "recognized," or "acknowledged," the sentence pretty fairly describes that half of society in England which declines the religious teaching of the Established Church. They are not known by the other half. "The Jews have no dealings with the Samaritans."

Now, we have no wish to exaggerate. Separation is not carried to such lengths, socially we mean, between the members of the National Church and of the Free Churches, as it was between the orthodox and the heterodox of the children of Israel in our Lord's time. Some two centuries ago it used to be, but since then the temper of the times has become much milder. Still, although the letter of the text finds only a partial application in our day, the spirit of it is pretty generally exemplified. There are, of course, numerous instances in which Churchmen meet Dissenters on a social footing, undisturbed by their politico-ecclesiastical difference, and there are some places where the chasm which divides them is bridged over by mutual respect, neighbourly feeling, and true Christian charity. They are exceptional, however, as may be proved by the pleased surprise which they awaken wherever they become known. As a rule, and in respect of free social intercourse, the two parties do not mingle. There may be little bitterness of feeling between them — though, unhappily, so much cannot be said in reference to many parishes — but they are interlaced by no friendly ties, they have very little in common, they are ignorant of each other's affairs, and don't care to be enlightened — and, like oil and water, although they may touch each other, they do not coalesce.

There are, as we have said, exceptions, the most conspicuous of which, we are bound to add, occur in towns where the Church is not only numerically but socially weak. Where the lines of division are so rubbed down as to remain scarcely visible, it will generally be found that the obliterating process has been mostly originated and kept up from the side of Dissent. On the other hand, where the State-Church is all-powerful, it is usually, in its social influences, most exclusive. The main ingredient of repulsion, not on the side of Dissent, but of the Church is the clerical element. If this element be in considerable force, whether in urban or in rural districts, division is not only marked, but, if we may so say, it is designedly aggressive. It is to the clergy of the Establishment, and to their professional narrowness of sympathy, and sensitiveness of jealousy, that the disseverance of which we speak is chiefly due. If that element were eliminated, social unity would be easy enough. The traditional feeling of many successive generations would, no doubt, require time before it would altogether disappear — but disappear it would, rapidly, too, if it were not perpetually urged into active exercise by the clergy.

To come back, however, to the line of observation on which we set out, we hardly know whether it will be necessary to expatiate on the evil arising out of this non-recognition of each other by the two great sections of society. If they lived wholly apart — if a range of mountains or an ocean intervened between them — although, ten chances to one, they would in that case be much more fully acquainted with each other's characteristic habits and ways of life, there would be less reason to deplore their want of knowledge one of another. But it is not so; the individual men and women of whom such sections consist live intermingled over the whole surface of the country. They speak the same language — they are subjects of the same Sovereign — they have the same ultimate standard of religious truth and duty — they jostle one another along the great thoroughfare of life — they meet and transact business in marts and on 'change — they frequent the same places of amusement — entertain or instruct themselves chiefly from the same books — but socially ignore one another; know as little of one another's homes, families, domestic joys and cares, types of thought and shades of feeling, as if they were of different race, spake different tongues, and dwelt in different lands. It will be seen at a glance how sensibly this state of things must detract from the advantages of neighbourhood; how it checks the growth of natural companionships; how it narrows the play of kindly sympathies; how it impoverishes the resources of a community in regard to many of its purest pleasures and its best benefits.

This, however, is only the negative side of the evil. It has a positive one. Unhappily, where knowledge is absent, prejudice is usually but too forward to fill up the vacancy. The uncultivated land is soon covered with weeds. Absurd and unjust surmises, the seeds of which are dropped into the mind as if by the birds of the air, quicken, spread their fibres, and get a permanent hold upon the soil. Want of understanding easily becomes misunderstanding, and positive distaste and dislike not uncommonly has its origin in the self-imposed restraint put upon the sympathies, State ecclesiasticism has brought about in England an antipathy analogous to that which is produced in America by the colour of the skin. There are myriads of intelligent people in this country, some of whom have received the highest culture, in whose view Non-conformity is a taint that spoils all the virtues — who if they find themselves casually in close social proximity to a Dissenter are conscious of an undefinable revulsion of feeling, and who, if they succeed in wholly suppressing it, and in bearing themselves towards him with courtesy, take credit to themselves for having done a magnanimous thing, as a man might who had sat down to meat with a leper. Gentlemen, and we regret to say with increased emphasis, ladies, shall be thrown together by chance in a railway-train or on a steamboat — at the seaside or during a trip to the Continent, and become mutually charmed with one another's society, and desire, on their return home, to keep up the intercourse which has auspiciously commenced; but if it turn out that the difference between Church and Dissent lies between them, the discovery goes very far to cancel all that has passed. One meets with the traces of this social antipathy in almost all the grades of life. They are so customary that they scarcely excite surprise, or provoke censure. The feeling which they indicate appears to rise up with such spontaneity, and so much as a matter of course, that no one thinks of pausing to examine it, or ask whence it comes, or what it means.

But what a reflection it is upon English society that it can harbour such an unmitigated barbarism? And what a mischiefmaker the State-Church must be to sanction and encourage it! It is the one trait of social life in this country which our colonists look back upon with wonder and contempt, and which, whenever they revisit their native land, greatly abates their pride in it. And well it may! For consider what it indicates. Could this forced ignorance of certain classes of Englishmen dwelling side by side, hold its ground among Churchmen in the face of any independent exercise of their own reason on the matter? Would any civilized man, left free to yield to the impulses of his nature, deliberately exclude from among his acknowledged neighbours and his possible friends a large section of the community, separated from that to which he himself belongs, only by their convictions as to the mode in which the Christian Church should be supported, and the ultimate authority by which it should be governed? Can any better reason be assigned for ignoring the social claims of ecclesiastical negroes in this country than are put forward in America for despising people of African descent? To say nothing of the wretched insularity of mind and manners it betokens, does it not point to something even more humiliating — the prostration of the highest rights and attributes of man as a social being, at the behests of professional jealousy and ecclesiastical assumption? But we are getting indignant. Let us shut up for the week, or the illustrations we have yet to exhibit will be apt to overpower our self-mastery.

****

DOUBLE STANDARD OF MORALITY.

We are not aware that anthropological research has discovered any structural difference between the two categories of Englishmen into which the Established Church throws the inhabitants of England. It has been very successful, we are given to understand, in showing the essential inferiority of the negro type, and has thereby greatly relieved the consciences of that rather numerous class of white men who claim the prerogative of treating dark-skinned humanity as devoid of rights. Looking at the occurrences which agitated society in Jamaica about twelve months ago, and at the sympathetic feelings which they stirred in this country, one is perplexed how to determine the precise extent within the limits of which the maxims of Christian morality are to be considered applicable. Is it true of the negro that he is "a man and a brother?" As between a white man and a black, is there any obligatory force in the precept — "Whatsoever ye would that men should do unto you, do ye even so likewise unto them?" We are aware that "circumstances alter cases," and that "one man may steal a horse, while another may not look over a hedge." But we should like to ascertain for certain, whether the double standard of morality which, in special instances, society finds it convenient to adopt, receives the sanction of the Supreme authority. If it does not, we can undertake to point out a sphere in which obligation and practice are sadly at variance, without going to the Antilles for our illustrations.

One of the social effects of our State-Church is to reconcile not only to the feelings, but apparently to the consciences, of not a few of its members the customary application, in regard to the two great ecclesiastical divisions which, for convenience, we shall designate the "ins" and the "outs," of a different code of right and wrong-doing. Many things which, when done in reference to the "ins" and their interests, would lay a man open to self-rebuke, and bring him under the censure of his circle of friends, when done in reference to the "outs," are regarded as perfectly legitimate. No doubt there are ways of interpreting the prescriptions of honour and duty in each of these cases, which, to the consciousness of the doers, presents no visible distinction between the rules accepted as equally binding in both. The human mind, especially when assisted by professional astuteness, is infinitely ingenious in devising theoretical justifications of practical anomalies. But it is with facts, not motives, that we are just now concerned. What we wish to bring under the cognizance of the reader is the fact that, in the judgment of the self-same individual, rightness in the "ins," is not necessarily rightness in the "outs," and that much that would be condemned as wrong in the "outs," is looked upon as praiseworthy in the "ins." Of course, there are "excellent good

reasons" for this variation of the compass — reasons that any
clergyman could give extempore — but these, although they may put
a different gloss on the fact, hardly touch even the surface of it. The
rights, the duties, the morality, and, we may add, the Christian
graces, of the section favoured by law, are not always rights, duties,
the morality, not Christian grace, in the section unrecognized by law.
The standard regulating the one is not in every instance, or in nearly
every instance, the standard regulating the other. What it allows to
this it often forbids in that. What in the first it pronounces consistent
with the most delicate honour, it denounces in the last as a breach
of moral obligation. Let us give an illustration or two of what we
mean.

Apart from all ecclesiastical controversies, it is usually regarded
as unjust and oppressive to make men contribute to a common object,
and then exclude them from the benefits it was intended to secure.
Well, now, turn to our parochial burying grounds. They are the
property of the parishioners. They are kept in decent order by funds
supplied *pro rata* by all the parishioners — and all have a common-
law right to interment therein. Suppose, now, that in any parish in
which the "outs" are a majority they were to say to the "ins" — "You
are welcome to your rood of earth in the freehold held in trust for
you, as for us, for the burial of your dead — but you will not henceforth
be suffered to have your customary burial-service read by your own
religious pastor over the grave. *We* have ordered the rites, and
appointed the officer, that we consider best suited to the decent
observance of that ceremonial, and we prohibit the use of any other."
What would the minority of "ins" think of that arrangement? But,
on the hypothesis that they were a vast majority, and by a tradition
or twist of the law were still ousted from the share of the common
inheritance, by what term of vituperation would they be sure to
characterize it? Everyone will see at a glance that the disabled party
is most unfairly, most dishonestly treated. But when the same thing
is done by the "ins" every day, and in thousands of parishes, not only
is it considered perfectly equitable, but every attempt of the "outs"
to obtain an equality of rights is loudly denounced as an impudent
disregard of the tenderest sentiments and most sacred feelings of
their fellow-parishioners. The thing which would be intolerable if

Dissenters were actors instead of sufferers, is natural, comely, and just, when the case is reversed.

This is only one illustration of many. We have gone into it rather more fully than either our own space or the patience of our readers will admit of with regard to others. Our columns, week after week, exhibit startling varieties in the application of this double standard of right and wrong. If a charity founded by Dissenters on a catholic basis, is converted by the Charity Commissioners into a Church of England institution, from the government and conduct of which Dissent is rigidly excluded, the transaction, of course, is honourable, and the motives which have prompted to the transference are highly commendable, but if Churchmen were the founders, though the foundation were equally unsectarian, the claim of Nonconformists to, not an exclusive, but to a proportionate share, in the management of the charity, is scouted as an almost incredible example of the "*alicni appetens.*" Where the "outs" are in a small minority, they are deemed presumptuous in expecting that in the distribution of public aid for educational purposes, their consciences should be protected from coercion, but where, as in Wales, the "ins" chance to be a mere insignificant fraction of the community, it is not protection, but *ex-officio* presidency, that is proposed on their behalf. Intemperate language squeezed out of an opponent of Church-rates in the course of a hot contest, is deplored as a lamentable breach of the kindly spirit of the Gospel, but to come down to the poll for the purpose of taxing a neighbour for your own Church accommodation, or to send the constable into his house to seize his bed and sell it to the highest bidder, is what a clergyman of the State Church can do on the Saturday, and on the Sunday preach that "love is the fulfilling of the law." A man who will not take off his hat to a bishop is a bear — a clergyman who ostentatiously walks out of the room when at a public festival, "the ministers of other denominations" are linked in the same toast with "the bishops and the clergy," is a gentleman. What would ecclesiastical niggers have? Can they imagine that the same rules of conduct are applicable in their case as in the case even of "mean whites."?

That, to whatever extent this propensity to use measuring rods of different lengths to different parties may prevail, it is socially a mischief as well as a grievance, hardly requires to be insisted upon. Nothing is more indispensable to the growth of a nation in its moral capacity, to its emergence from the slough of animalism, and its development of the higher and grander features of character, than an assiduous cultivation of a delicate sense of justice. When public sentiment, and public law as the expression of it, recognize no distinction between citizen and citizen, save that which may be tested by the same moral standard, namely the standard of doing as we would be done unto, the govening power may put aside the coarser instruments with which it enforces its will in the last resort, and mainly trust to the irresistible potency of its influence. Reverence for right as right is the most conservative of all human motives, and, when fairly appealed to, the best and most precious interests of society may be unhesitatingly committed to it. Any public institution which, in its own provisions, or by its social influence, appraises right and wrong, generosity and meanness, honour and infamy, by systems of valuation arbitrarily changed in obedience to the dictates of ecclesiastical prejudice, must tend more or less to throw the community back upon the force of passion and the predominance of mere physical might, for the adjustment of its internal dissensions. And in doing so, it exaggerates and exasperates what would otherwise be harmless disagreements, and spoils men whom it should mould into nobleness. This the State-Church does in England, and it is the highest prized of all our institutions!

The Liberator, (1861; 1865; 1874). Selections.

The Liberator, begun in 1855, was the monthly journal of the Liberation Society. It circulated principally among subscribers to the Society, and it served as a clearing house and newsletter for information on specific cases of discrimination against Dissenters. From 1855 until 1877 it was edited by J. Carvell Williams, the influential secretary of the Society. The Liberation Society was the principal organization of politically aggressive nonconformity.

STATE-CHURCHISM AND MUNICIPAL CORPORATIONS:
1 December, 1861

At Windsor, it is stated that Mr. R. Harris has been this year excluded from the mayoralty because of his unwillingness to attend the Established Church in his official capacity. On the occasion of the election, that gentleman said "it was no use contesting the fact — and he spoke as a gentleman and a man of honour — he had received ample proofs that he was passed over because he refused to accept the office excepting in the way provided by the laws and constitution of his country. He had been consulted by one and the other, but he was happy to state that the laws of England did not recognise the conditions with which the office had been in an indirect manner, offered to him. Had he acceded to such terms, the chain of office would be a badge of servility, degradation, and slavery. Standing on his constitutional right, he certainly would not take office on any conditions excepting those recognised by law. He was anxious to know whether every gentleman who assisted in public affairs, although his religious opinions might not concur with those of the majority of the council, was to expect similar treatment? Was it to be understood that any gentleman who refused to adopt a certain dress, and attend a certain place of worship, was to be deemed disqualified for that reason? If such were to be the case, the ground of objection, as he had observed, was not recognised by the law of England; it was not acknowledged by the Constitution, but was a condition imposed by a portion of the corporation of Windsor. He did not express his own opinions as a Nonconformist, but he knew that there were in the town numerous Churchmen, who, if asked whether such a ground could be fairly or justly acted upon, would unhesitatingly say, "No."

At Leeds, also, the re-election of Mr. Kitson, was objected to by some members of the Town Council, because he will not go with mace and gold chair, to the parish church. Mr. K. is a Unitarian, and finding that the law will not let him take the insignia of office to his own place of worship, he very properly refuses to take them to church, when he goes there, as he has done once or twice, officially.

At Kingston-on-Thames, the corporation attended church the first Sunday after the election, and the vicar took advantage of the opportunity to read the new mayor a lecture on the duty he owed to the Church, and to preach a sermon on the necessity for upholding the union of Church and State.

At Tynemouth there has been a novelty. Mr. Spencer, the Quaker mayor, accompanied by the corporation, went to the parish church, when after divine service a collection was taken for the dispensary. In the afternoon the corporation accompanied the mayor to the Friends' Meeting, where another collection was taken for the dispensary.

RIOTOUS MEETING AT MACCLESFIELD: 1 January 1865

Macclesfield is a town in which the friends of the Society have not hitherto been very demonstrative; but the shutting out from the Mayoralty of a Nonconformist — after he had been invited to fill the office — who refused to worship at the altar of the State-Church, on the Sunday after the election, has thoroughly aroused them. Determining to have a meeting of the Liberation Society, they secured a deputation — Mr. Carvell Williams, of London, and the Rev. P.W. Clayden, of London — and also secured the Town Hall, after pledging themselves to the Mayor that free discussion should be allowed. Thereupon the Rev. C.A.J. Smith, one of the established clergy, remonstrated with the Mayor for allowing a "Government office" (!) to be "open to attacks on the Government;" but the Mayor stood firm. What followed will be learned from a few extracts from the local papers: —

"The admission was free to all, but there were a few reserved seats to which access was had on payment of sixpence. The assembly-room was filled to overflowing. A very respectable assembly occupied the front seats, and conducted themselves as became respectable people throughout the evening. In the back seats, and in the standing space also, there were many tradesmen and working men whose quiet demeanour was equally creditable; but at the extreme end of the room there were a number of individuals whose behaviour from first to last was certainly not that of civilised Englishmen. Before the promoters of the meeting made their appearance on the platform, all kinds of noises were raised by these people, who appeared to have been well primed with 'barley bree;' and it was evident that they were bent upon preventing, if possible, the meeting being held. The appearance on the platform of the intended speakers was the signal for a clamorous opposition, all kinds of noises and catcalls being raised. One individual, a member of our town council too, was seen blowing a penny whistle in imitation of a railway-whistle, and he was accompanied by the performances of other gentlemen on the bones, rattles, halfpenny-trumpets, crying dolls, and squeaking toy-cats. Simultaneously with the discordant sounds were whistling, stamping of feet, rattling of sticks on the wainscot, barking, and other cries, the purpose of which it was impossible to catch owing to the general hubbub."

The Chairman (Alderman Jesper), and Mr. Greg, a magistrate, vainly tried to obtain a hearing, and, after several scuffles, some of the ringleaders were expelled; though they were afterwards re-admitted at the instance of one of the magistrates of the town.

After a while the *Rev. P.W. Clayden* contrived to utter a few sentences, which, however, had more reference to what was going on in the hall than to the society and its principles. He reminded the meeting that it was sought to put down the Anti-Corn Law League in the same way, but in vain. He also said that the very fact of that disturbance showed that there was something wrong in the religious condition of English society. As he was speaking, songs were sung, and one of the Society's friends was much knocked about in trying to quell the disorder. This fearful din continued till nearly ten o'clock, when

Mr. Carvell Williams asked for silence for a few minutes, and for a minute or two obtained it, but afterwards fared much as his predecessors had done. He assured the meeting that he had never felt so satisfied of the progress which this cause was making, as it was evident that the supporters of State-Churchism in Macclesfield, afraid to let the voice of truth be heard, had called in the ruffianism of the town to silence by clamour those whom they could not otherwise reply to. He proposed that the meeting be dissolved, which was carried; though many of the rioters kept possession of the room a considerable time afterwards.

These proceedings have occasioned "tremendous excitement" in Macclesfield. "I have seen," says an informant, "many a sensation here, but this beats all." At the close of the usual business on 15th ult., the borough magistrates discussed the subject. Mr. Greg complained that, after the superintendent of police had removed some of the disturbers, another magistrate urged their re-admission. "Are we," he asked, "to live here under the protection of the laws, or are we to be obliged to ask a certain party in the town for permission to hold a public meeting before we can hold it? As it is, we are held up in disgrace to the world." In reply, it was contended that there had been no breach of the peace, and that people had a right to express their feelings at a public meeting. Mr. Greg said that he should communicate with the Home Secretaty on the subject.

The Episcopalians of Macclesfield have not thought it right to repudiate the proceedings of those who did their work on this occasion. The *Macclesfield Courier's* correspondents write to the Liberation Society in the usual truculent strain, while the Rev. C.A.J. Smith, who objected to the use of the Town Hall for the meeting, commences a letter with — "I know scarcely a more melancholy exhibition of human nature than that made in the person of the 'political Dissenter.' " Without making any reference to the disgraceful occurrences of two days before, he calmly proceeds to quote Baxter, Doddridge, and Owen, for the benefit of the "misguided men who are not contending merely against us, but against everything that is greatest and most venerable in the annals of Nonconformity itself."

The speeches intended to have been delivered by Messrs. Williams and Clayden are now published, and will, no doubt, be widely read in the district.

THE RESULTS OF THE GENERAL ELECTION: 2 March 1874

The appeal to the constituencies has been made, and the result has been the conversion of a Liberal majority of 68 into a Conservative majority of about 50; and the substitution of a Conservative Government, headed by Mr. Disraeli, for the greatest Liberal administration and the most popular Prime Minister of modern times.

The causes of this startling and unlooked-for change are admitted to be various. The "interests" which, in the interest of the nation, Mr. Gladstone's Government has successfully attacked during the last five years, were longing for revenge, and they have now had it.

That has been notably the case with the "drink interest"; so that, as the *Guardian* admits, the new Parliament has "a decidedly beery smell," and as another Church journal says, will be known as the "publican's Parliament." Then, it must be acknowledged, that the majority of the population desire rest before undertaking more great organic reforms. Conservatism, also, has become a fashion, rather than a political creed, and the fashion has grown with the growth of the wealthy classes.

These things are quite sufficient to account for what has happened; but the severity of the Liberal defeat is, in part, explained by another circumstance, and that is, that the Government dissolved Parliament without having made peace with its Nonconformist allies. The result of this was, not antagonism, but the absence of that enthusiasm which helped to secure the great Liberal triumph of 1868. Even the *Daily Telegraph* admitted that the Liberation Society might "comfort itself with the thought that it has done the bidding of common-sense, and that it has ever followed the wisest of the Puritan counsels," but its supporters had the heart taken out of them by the silence, or the ambiguity, of Mr. Gladstone's Address, and, in regard to "the 25th clause" had, in some cases, to insist, and to negociate, when, to ensure Liberal success, they should have been energetically at work.

We regret the necessity for such a course of action, but not the action itself — first, because it proved that those who threatened had the firmness to execute their threats; next, because the policy succeeded, by compelling Mr. Gladstone and all the ministerial leaders, except Mr. Forster, to virtually abandon the 25th clause; and, lastly, because a re-formation of the Liberal party will be impossible without a new educational platform. The course pursued by the friends of religious equality, in regard to both this question and that of Disestablishment, has, we believe, been characterized by discretion and moderation. Had they done less than they have done, they would have lost the respect of their allies, and self-respect also. They were prepared for the consequences of their acts, and they can now bear them with perfect equanimity.

The Politics of Nonconformity (1871), by R.W. Dale. Selections.
R.W. Dale (1820-1895), Congregationalist minister at Carr's Lane,
Birmingham, was an influential theologian who played a significant
role in softening the mental rigidities and broadening the intellectual
outlook of orthodox Dissenters and evangelically-minded Churchmen.
He was also eminent in public affairs, especially so in Birmingham
where he was closely associated with Joseph Chamberlain in
promoting nonsectarian public education and a broadly conceived
policy for improving municipal life. Until Gladstone's decision to
support Home Rule for Ireland in 1885, Dale was active in organizing
support for the Liberal Party. In the following lecture delivered in
the Free Trade Hall, Manchester, Dale refers to nonconformist
disappointment with the Liberal education act of 1870, and reflects
the increased militancy in the movement for disestablishment.

————————————

Three years ago, when we were just emerging from the excitement
of that great contest which determined the fate of the ecclesiastical
Establishment in Ireland, there were many Nonconformists who, in
the enthusiasm of their delight, supposed that the protracted struggle
for perfect religious equality in this empire was near its final triumph.
There was a presumptuous hope that the principles of justice which
the Liberal party was pledged to apply to the Established Church
in Ireland, would before very long determine its policy in relation
to the Established Churches of England and Scotland. Even those
of us who were less sanguine, believed that we might rely on Mr.
Gladstone and Mr. Gladstone's Government not to augment the
disadvantages under which English nonconformists were already
suffering, and not to create new difficulties to impede the gradual
development of the principle of religious liberty. At the close of the
last general election, Mr. Gladstone was regarded by Nonconformists
with passionate admiration, and with unmeasured confidence.
Speaking for myself, I must declare that my admiration for the genius
of the leader of the Liberal party is undiminished, and that my
confidence in his integrity is unshaken. (Hear, hear.)

But the relations of the Nonconformists to Mr. Gladstone's
Government have undergone a great and startling change. Confidence
has given place to distrust, and enthusiasm to resentment. The
Ministry in which we so perfectly confided has already, in the

judgment of many of us, inflicted upon Nonconformity a great wrong. Its future policy is regarded with apprehension. During the last few months, announcement after announcement has appeared in the columns of the newspapers of the formation of Nonconformist committees in one great town after another, from Newcastle to Plymouth, to resist what are alleged to be the offences already committed by Mr. Gladstone's Government against the principles of religious equality, and to avert offences graver still which seem likely to be committed before many months are over. Conferences are being called together in the North and in the South, in the East and in the West, to deliberate on the policy which Nonconformists should follow, and to concentrate and organise their power for a conflict which seems inevitable. There is universal alarm; and the alarm is greatest in those parts of the country where three years ago the confidence in Mr. Gladstone's Government was most hearty. The zeal, the energy, and the self-sacrifice of the Nonconformists contributed very much to the winning of the magnificent triumph of the Liberal party at the last election — (cheers); — and now those who are watching most carefully the movement of the public mind are predicting that the Liberal party is in danger of being broken to pieces by Nonconformist discontent.

The causes of this singular change are not far to seek. It appears that justice was to be done in Ireland because injustice had made the government of Ireland by peaceful and constitutional means impossible. But justice is still to be delayed in England, because those who suffer wrong in this country are men capable of an almost inexhaustible endurance; and it is their settled habit and their immovable purpose to secure the redress of their grievances, not by disturbing the public peace, but by endeavouring to convince the judgment and awaken the conscience of the nation. (Cheers.) To this work the Nonconformists in every part of the kingdom are addressing themselves; and I heartily congratulate the nonconformists of this great city, which has borne so illustrious a part in the political history of the empire, that they are taking their place in the van of the movement. The old energy which wrestled successfully 30 years ago with the most powerful and compact of all the political interests of this country — the courage which no difficulties could daunt — the high spirit which no temporary disappointments could subdue — the resolute persistency, unexhausted by the tremendous and protracted strain upon your resources — the unfaltering faith in the certain victory of the principles which it was then your distinction to defend — all the elements of intellectual and moral force, which secured for you the triumph of which this hall is the visible and permanent memorial — will, I trust, be revealed once more in the struggle to which you are now committed, and will achieve a not less glorious success.

If I understand the present temper and disposition of Nonconformists, they are rapidly coming to the determination not to be satisfied with the defence and illustration of their principles in public lectures and public meetings, and by all those means through which the opinion of the country is gradually influenced; but to adopt a definite line of political action. We have hitherto been content to accept a subordinate place in the Liberal party. We have very seldom taken a separate and independent position at elections. Our political leaders have never been asked to pledge themselves to our abstract principles. We have, it is true, won a long succession of victories, and these victories have resulted partly from the spirit of justice with which we think that Nonconformity has gradually inspired large masses of the English people. But the principles for which we are contending have never been accepted by any organised political party. Catholic emancipation was not a frank homage to the principles of religious equality; it was a political necessity. The abolition of church rates was carried by the Liberal party, not because the Liberal party was convinced of the injustice of compelling Nonconformists to contribute to the maintenance of a form of worship which they disapproved, but because church-rate contests were an intolerable scandal, and because the Liberal leaders, like the unjust judge in the Gospels, were wearied out by our incessant appeals for relief. (Laughter and cheers.) The abolition of the Irish Church was determined upon because Irish discontent had become formidable to the empire. Even the abolition of University Tests was not achieved by Nonconformist agitation; it was not the expression of a cordial acquiescence in the doctrine that the Episcopal Church has no right to the exclusive enjoyment of national wealth and national distinctions; it was largely the result of a conviction which had been growing for years in the minds of Churchmen themselves, that the tests were injurious to public morality.

It is now proposed that Nonconformist electors in every constituency in the country should insist on the acceptance of their abstract principles by every candidate for their suffrages. No such dictatorial spirit, so far as I know, has ever yet been manifested even by those whose indignation at the recent policy of the Government is most vehement. We do not claim to represent the majority of the Liberal party throughout the kingdom. Most of us, I think, are prepared to say that we intend to follow the example of our ecclesiastical ancestors, who, when suffering oppression from which we are happily free, were always prepared in critical moments of our national history to suppress their own complaints, to be silent about their own wrongs, and to give their hearty support to the political leaders whose power appeared to be necessary to avert the immediate perils of the State. But in many constituencies we constitute such an overwhelming majority of the Liberal electors, that we think we have a right to claim that Liberal candidates shall accept our principles in all their breadth, and be prepared to carry them to their ultimate issue as the condition of our support. (Cheers.) In other constituencies we are so necessary to the Liberal party, that we think we have a right to demand that Liberal candidates shall at least pledge themselves to resist any new violations of those principles of religious equality which we regard as a sacred trust, and which we are under the most solemn obligations to defend. For the sake of the nation, to turn aside any great danger which menaced national safety, to secure the success of any great measure urgently neccessary to the national well-being, we should be prepared to waive our claims; but we are not prepared to waive them for the sake of the Liberal party. We are told of what the Liberal party has done for us in past times; we have done as much for the Liberal party as the Liberal party has done for us. (Cheers.) If there is any unsettled balance in this old account, the balance is not against the Nonconformists. (Laughter and cheers.)

In determining to carry the controversy out of the region of abstract discussion into the region of practical politics, we must be willing to incur the charge of being political Dissenters. There are many excellent people, both among Churchmen and Nonconformists, who seem to think it a crime for religious men to interfere in political struggles. How it should be possible for Nonconformists to regard the neglect of political duty as a virtue, I have very great difficulty in understanding; but for Churchmen to tell us that our religious faith should lead us to abstain from political life is, if possible, more unreasonable still; for let me ask those Churchmen who are accustomed to charge us with the offence of being political Dissenters — What would happen if religious men ceased to be political? Your bishops, and your deans, and your canons are appointed by the Prime Minister — do you think it desirable that such appointments should be made by men who have no religious faith, and are indifferent to the religious life of the nation? How are you to have a Prime Minister with the religious discernment and the religious earnestness necessary for the the wise administration of such patronage as this, if religious men are not to touch politics? The House of Commons is the supreme legislative court of the Episcopal Church. The Prayer Book is a mere schedule to an act of Parliament. If you want to make a change in the order in which the Holy Scriptures are to be read in your public services, the change cannot be made unless Parliament consents. I have an act at home, passed only last session, determining what chapters of the Bible may be read in future in the public services of your churches. There is hardly a session in which some bill is not introduced, either into the Lords or the Commons, affecting your ecclesiastical organisation. I hear of a bill which is to provide for the establishment of parochial councils, and of a bill which is to enable Nonconformist ministers to preach in your churches, and to give the Bishop of Manchester liberty, if he wishes to do it, to ask my friend Mr. M'Laren to preach in the Cathedral. (Loud cheers and laughter.) Unless you believe that an assembly of atheists and of profligates will be likely to give the Church better laws than an assembly of religious men, and that a statesman who regards the Christian faith as an obsolete superstition will select better bishops than a devout and earnest Christian, you ought to be eager to fill the benches of the House of Commons with the best representatives you can find of the religious life of the country. But if religious men should transact the political business of the nation in the House of Commons, why should religious men abstain from the political action in the country by which the members of that House are returned?

If you think that Dissenters, when they are religious men, ought to leave politics alone, how is it that you do not try to teach this singular faith to the members of your own Church? (Hear.) Is our religion so much less secular and so much more spiritual than yours — (laughter), — that while you are astonished that a devout Nonconformist should engage in political contest, a Churchman may be political without inconsistency? There is a saying which you and we regard with equal reverence, about the man who wants to take a mote out of the eye of his brother, when there is a beam in his own eye. I never heard that there was any difficulty in inducing Churchmen to become Lords of the Admiralty, Home Secretaries, Chancellors of the Exchequer, or Prime Ministers; I never heard that it was hard to persuade country rectors to vote for the Conservative candidates for the county — (laughter); — and what is most surprising, I have never seen leading articles in Church newspapers in which Churchmen were condemned for accepting high political office, or in which they were told that they ought never to be seen at the hustings or at a polling booth. The *Standard* and the *Record* are filled with great horror when Nonconformists meddle with politics; but they appear to believe that for a Churchman to be political is no crime at all.

Why are Nonconformists to incur odium if they attempt to discharge their political duties? Why is it insinuated that we, and we alone, cease to be religious when we presume to touch the affairs of the country? We, too, are affected in our personal rights, in our property, and in all the interests which human law can touch, by the acts of the Imperial Legislature and by the general policy of the Government. The great traditions of England, and its greater hopes, are ours as well as yours. We too are Englishmen, and our religious faith does not disqualify us for rendering service to the State. (Cheers.) If the charge that we are political Dissenters means anything, it means that all political power in this country should be vested in the hands of Churchmen; that we should receive from them the laws by which we are to be governed, and that to Churchmen should be entrusted the administration of those laws; that we should submit without complaint to whatever disabilities may be the penalty of Nonconformity; that in separating ourselves from the communion of the national Church we should renounce all claim to the rights of citizenship, and live as aliens in the country which gave us birth. We refuse to submit to this insulting degradation. (Cheers.) We decline to be excluded from the political life of the State.

* * * * * * * * *

The immediate necessity which is laid upon us for organising our political power, and detemining on a definite line of political action, has been created by the recent policy of the Government. But, year by year, the ultimate question involved in the history and position of the Nonconformists is assuming more definite outlines and attracting larger public attention. Before long this question will divide the great political parties in the State, and the discussions in which we are now engaged are preparing the mind of the country for that supreme struggle. I frankly confess that I never appear on a public platform to discuss the relations between the Church of England and the State but with reluctance and pain. I am far more vividly conscious of the religious sympathies which unite the majority of Nonconformists with vast numbers of the clergy and laity of the Established Church than of the theological, ecclesiastical, and political differences which separate us. To be regarded as an enemy by men for whom I have the deepest affection and admiration, to be charged by such men with pursuing a policy which in relation to the Church is a policy of confiscation and sacrilege, and in relation to the State a policy of Atheism, is to me a source of keen distress. But we have no choice.

We believe that the separation of the ecclesiastical and civil powers would be an act of homage to the principles of political justice, and would contribute to the strength and stability of our national institutions. We believe that it would diminish sectarian bitterness, increase Christian charity, and greatly promote the energy and purity of the religious life of the country. Should we be successful, the Church would sustain no harm. The only property it would lose is property which it should not desire to keep — property which belongs not to itself, but to the whole nation. After disestablishment the Church will still retain its great traditions. The magnificent succession of theologians, scholars, and saints who have illustrated its history will still be its glory and its strength. Its ancient creeds, its stately liturgy, the devotion of ten thousand clergy, the simple reverence and trust of thousands of the poor, the hearty confidence of the vast majority of the gentry and aristocracy of the country — these will still remain. Its prayers will still find access to God. Its devout ministers will still be moved by the Holy Ghost. The presence of Christ will still be granted to its congregations when gathered together in His name; and it will rejoice in the consciousness of a vigour and courage which are inseparable from freedom.

The State will receive no harm. For generations the Nonconformists, notwithstanding their disabilities, have been loyal to the throne, and the loyalty of the members of the Church of England will not be impaired by the loss of their political privileges and supremacy. The religious faith of the nation, — the strongest support of private virtue, the noblest inspiration of patriotism, the surest defence of the august authority of law — will not perish with the disappearance of the Establishment. The vices of the rich and the vices of the poor will still be denounced and restrained by the eloquence of the Christian pulpit; and through the gentle ministry of innumerable men and women inspired with the spirit of Christian charity, poverty and wretchedness will still receive consolation. Our political differences will no longer be embittered by theological and ecclesiastical animosities, and Christian men of every Church — their strength no longer consumed in sectarian conflicts, no longer divided by sectarian jealousies — will unite to promote the religion, the virtue, the happiness, and the freedom of all classes of the State.

We utterly reject the dogma that a nation ceases to be a Christian nation when it ceases to assert the Christian faith by the authority of public law and to maintian its ministers from the national resources. Its Christianity depends upon the intensity and purity of the Christian life which dwells in the hearts of its people. If a man is a Christian he will carry with him the whole energy of his faith in Christ and of his reverence for the law of Christ into every province of his activity. The Christian life will reveal itself in the courage with which the elector votes for the man in whose political principles he believes; and the very spirit which has made the memory of martyrs immortal on earth, and has crowned them with a brighter glory in heaven, has been expressed at the polling-booth by men who, rather than be false to their political convictions, have risked the loss of their farms and the destruction of their trade. The Christian life will reveal itself in the chivalrous honour with which landlords and employers of labour abstain from exerting an illegitimate influence over electors whose fortunes happen to be in their power; and in the determination of working people to protect from insult and injury the men who may conscientiously reject the political creed of their shopmates and neighbours. The Christian life will reveal itself in the honesty with which candidates for seats in the House of Commons will declare their opinions before their election, and the fidelity with which they will keep their pledges after they have been elected. It will control the debates of Parliament; it will neutralise the acrimony of party spirit; it will subdue the personal ambition of statesmen; it will make a nation sensible that the true prosperity of States does not lie in mere material wealth, but in the fidelity of its people and its rulers to the laws of eternal righteousness, which are the strong foundations of the very throne of God. It will render impossible the selfishness and the baseness which have too often disgraced our foreign policy — the domineering and insulting tone which we have assumed to weak States and the cowardly subserviency of which we have been guilty to successful and powerful wickedness; it will inspire all our transactions with other nations with courageous justice, with frankness and generosity. It will bind together in mutual respect and confidence all ranks and conditions of men.

This is our ideal of national life. We believe it is to be fulfilled — not by conferring on the ministers of a single church or the ministers of all churches, social dignity, political authority, national wealth, but by the devout and earnest work of all who are inspired with the true spirit of patriotism and a hearty loyalty to Christ.

For the perfect triumph of its spiritual power, the Church must be free from the restraints and trammels of that political bondage which is inseparable from political privileges. We are Nonconformists — we are political Nonconformists — not because we wish to make the political life of England less religious, but because we wish to make it more religious; and we intend, God helping us — unmoved by the storm of hostility, of misrepresentation, and of slander which our great enterprise may provoke — to pursue it until the time shall come — it is not far distant — when the principles of which it is our glory to be the representatives and the guardians shall control the legislation and the policy of our country.

Mr. Dale, after speaking for upwards of two hours, resumed his seat amid loud and prolonged cheering, the audience rising and waving their hats.

"Why Should I Join the Church Defence Institution?" (circa 1872).
Complete text of the tract.

The Church Defence Institution, founded as the Church Institution
in 1859, was revitalized and renamed in 1871 in response to increased
activity on the part of Edward Miall and the Liberation Society. The
Church Defence Institution was closely linked with the Conservative
Party. It set out to attract working men newly enfranchised by the
Reform Act of 1867, but did not succeed. In the 1880s its activity
declined as the threat from the Liberation Society diminished.

A FEW PLAIN WORDS IN ANSWER TO THIS QUESTION.

A society, now called the "Liberation Society," was formed some
years ago, with the express object of bringing about the
Disestablishment and Disendowment of the Church of England. This
Society has spent thousands of pounds in its efforts to get the people
of England to destroy the union of Church and State. But for a long
while — except in a few cases — the Members of the Church of
England took no steps to counteract these efforts. When, however,
in the Parliament of 1871, Mr. Miall brought forward a motion, the
avowed object of which was to disestablish and disendow the Church
of England, and succeeded in getting nearly 100 Members of
Parliament to vote in its favour, — it seemed right that measures
of defence against such an aggression should be at once taken. The
"Church Institution," originally established in 1859, was
reconstituted, and its name changed to that of "The Church Defence
Institution," for the purpose of uniting Churchmen and lovers of real
religious liberty, in the *defence* of what the Liberation Society and
Mr. Miall have so wantonly attacked. Branches of The Church
Defence Institution are now established in various parts of the
Country.

The Liberation Society expends thousands of pounds yearly in
spreading what are really either falsehoods or fallacies, against our
Church, its Ministers, and its revenues. When the Church's foes are
thus conspiring to destroy and to despoil, surely you will not — if
you are a real friend of the Church — refuse to join us, who are now
combining to defend and preserve. We are not a political society. Our
Members are, some Conservative, some Liberal, but all desirous of

upholding the union of Church and State.

You are asked to join us, not only by being a consistent member of the Church in your daily life, but by enrolling your name on our list of Members.

Let me just briefly give you one or two reasons why you should do so.

1. To disestablish the Church would be to give up as a nation, all recognition of religion. If the Church is disestablished now, it would not be as it was when Oliver Cromwell — more than 200 years ago — disestablished it to establish Independentism in its stead. No, the avowed object now is, *to have no national profession of religion* at all. Thus, as a nation, we should be *ungodly*.

2. To Disendow the Church would be to rob her of all her property and possessions, which have been hers — some for hundreds of years, and some for but a few years. The tithes and other possessions then taken would not be allowed to go to any religious object.

3. By the present union of Church and State, every Parish has its separate Minister and Church, a Minister whose *duty* it is to perform all religious and ministerial offices, private and public, in that Parish and for *all* the parishioners. The poorest person has a *claim* on the Parish Clergyman for his religious services. All this would cease if the Liberation Society succeeds in its object — that is, it would cease on the death of the present Incumbent of the Parish.

4. "Tithes" are altogether distinct from "taxes." Taxes are imposed by Parliament year by year, and may be repealed at any Session. Parliament has nothing more to do with tithes than with any endowment of Nonconformist Chapels, or of Hospitals.

Tithes are no burden upon any single individual. Hundreds of years ago, tithes — the tenth part of the produce of land — were voluntarily given by owners, for the support of the Church and its Ministers. The present owners of the lands never were owners of these tithes. The present tenants never were owners, surely, of these tithes. Even the State itself has not a *tittle* of claim to the ownership of these tithes. The only owner is the Established Church. When Independentism was established by Oliver Cromwell, tithes were paid to, and received by, "Independent" Ministers. It is now proposed by the Liberation Society to rob the Church of tithes, and devote the money to some secular and non-religious purpose.

5. Under God's direct government of the Jews, Church and State were united. The Jewish Church was an Established Church — its Priests and Levites received tithes and had endowments. There were constant abuses with their Established Church, as with ours. But to *reform* the Church from its abuses is a good work, distinct from *disestablishing* it. The Church Defence Institution is also a Church *Reform* Institution. And surely, because you have a carbuncle on your neck, you will not cut off your head. By all means, reform the abuses. Call in the aid of the State for the purpose. But ask not the State to shew its *reforming* power by exercising its power for *destruction* and *annihilation*.

6. The Church of England combines all the advantages of Religious Endowments and the Voluntary System, and, as *established*, is free from *some* of the disadvantages, confessedly attending each of these religious Systems.

7. The question is not simply, is Establishment or mere Voluntaryism preferable? But, shall we now *disestablish* the Church which *has been Established* for *centuries*? Similarly, as to Republicanism, the question is not simply, is Republicanism or Monarchy preferable? But, shall we now *disestablish* the Monarchy, which *has been Established* for centuries? N.B. The disestablishment of Monarchy would almost certainly follow close upon the disestablishment of the Church. The Throne and the Church were once disestablished together. They were *re*-established together. If one of the two should ever be disestablished, the other will not be very secure.

8. In former days, religious Dissenters strongly advocated a continuance of the Union of Church and State. As to the founder of the Wesleyan body, John Wesley — he was a Churchman all his life, and exhorted his followers *never to leave the Church*. There is no reason why Wesleyans, and the pious and patriotic members of all Nonconformist bodies, should not repudiate all connection with the Liberation Society.

9. The calling the Clergy "State paid," the Tithes "Taxes," the Church "the favoured Sect," — all this is false and fallacious. The State does *not* pay the Clergy. The Tithes are *not* Taxes. The Church

remains *the* Church of England, though scores of "Sects" may vex and annoy her.

10. Say not, "there is no real danger." If the danger is averted, it will be because of the counter-action of the efforts of the Liberation Society by the work of these Church Defence Institutions. *I do not believe the Church of England will be disestablished and disendowed.* But *it may be so, if Churchmen refuse to unite in its defence.*

11. "Union is strength." And Union itself, besides all ulterior advantages, is a good thing. In all worldly matters, as every day testifies, union and co-operation give strength and stability, and, also, inpart much pleasure. Let us unite — for God — for our Church — for our Nation — because it is good for ourselves to be thus united — let us unite in one glorious

CHURCH DEFENCE INSTITUTION!

12. "Disestablishment" would be a National breach of the 1st Commandment of the Decalogue.

"Disendowment" would be a National breach of the 8th Commandment of the Decalogue.

Do not aid in abolishing, so far as our National Statute Book is concerned, those two Commandments of God, but *do* aid in keeping England back from such National sinfulness. And give a practical proof of your wish thus to serve God and your country, by becoming a Member of The Church Defence Institution.   A.J.P.

Ritualism: *Hansard's Parliamentary Debates.* Selections from the debate in the House of Commons on the Public Worship Regulation Bill. Mr. Gladstone spoke 9 July 1874. Disraeli spoke 15 July 1874.

It is difficult to imagine how ritualism in the Church of England could have been so bitter an issue in the latter half of the nineteenth century. The elaborate ritual and vestments adopted in some anglo catholic or high church parishes were associated with Rome and regarded by some as an insult to the Protestantism of the nation. The controversy within the established church between high churchmen and low churchmen eventually reached the point where it could not be ignored by politicians. Mr. Gladstone, himself a high churchman, was strongly opposed to legislative interference in this matter. Though privately concerned about the wisdom of the action, Disraeli was pushed into support for legislation by Archbishop A.C. Tait and by public pressure. There had been a massive demonstration against ritualism a year earlier at Lambeth. The legislation embodied the erastian claim of Parliament to regulate in spiritual matters.

MR. GLADSTONE: Perhaps it may seem somewhat strange that I should desire to interpose thus early in the debate, and I can assure the House that I do not do so because of the avidity to take part in ecclesiastical discussions on which the right hon. Gentleman opposite (M. Disraeli) rallied me very good humouredly the other night. If this were a proper occasion I think I could show that, considering the length of time I have sat in this House, and the number of hours it has been my unhappy fate — or the unhappy fate of the House — to have occupied their attention, if a percentage were taken, the percentage of my ecclesiastical speeches would be extremely small. But I have been dragged from what I should wish at the present moment to be retirement by the urgent call of duty to take part in the discussion of a subject which I feel to be of the greatest difficulty and importance. I have, indeed never, for more than 40 years approached the discussion of a public question with a greater sense of embarrassment or perplexity.

* * * * * * * * *

I have never known a more extraordinary case of ignorance on the part of the public and on the part of the partizans on the one side and on the other than appears to prevail in reference to this Bill. I have received — and I suppose many other hon. Members have received — most impassioned appeals to support or oppose the Bill, as the case might be. But all those appeals convey to me the impression that, from whatever quarter they come, they are written for the most part in profound ignorance of what the operation of the Bill would be and of the dangers which its provisions are calculated to cause. Nor is this strange.

* * * * * * * *

Under the circumstances, the country seems to have fallen back on the safe and unfailing remedy of general assumption. At the commencement of the controversy we were told that Ritualism was a great evil, and that we must have a Bill to put it down, while at the same time there was no definition of what Ritualism was. I have lived a public life for 40 years, and during every one of those years Ritualism has borne a different meaning. What was Ritualism 40 years ago was not Ritualism 20 years after, and what is Ritualism now was not Ritualism 20 years ago; so that it is a term which requires to be defined.

* * * * * * * *

I take my stand upon the broad ground that a certain degree of liberty has been permitted in the congregations of the Church of England; that great diversity exists in different parts of the country and in different congregations; that various customs have grown up in accordance with the feelings and usages of the people; and, whether the practices that have so grown up are or are not in accordance with the law, I say they ought not to be rashly and rudely rooted out.

* * * * * * * *

I speak with all due deference to lawyers in the House when I express my opinion that one of the propositions of this Bill is that in some parishes the rubrics of the Church of England shall in all respects, both as to additions and omissions be invariably, strictly, and absolutely obeyed. That is exactly the thing that ought not to be done. Law is quite exceptional in its nature. The business of law is to prohibit and to punish crime. Directory law is comparatively rare. Directory statute, entering into a countless multitude of minutae, and telling 20,000 clergymen what they are to do every day of their lives — how they are to turn, and stand, and speak, and how every congregation is to behave — this is exceptional law; and even if it were a new law, every rational man would say that it is not literal uniformity, but honest and general obedience that is desirable. If that were true of a rubric cut down and considered in order to meet the newest fashion, much more is it necessary for a rubric framed in 1661.

* * * * * * * * *

I wish every man in this House was as old as I am. ["No, no!"] If my young Friends had allowed me to finish the sentence, I should have said that I wish every man in the House was as old as I am for the purpose of knowing what was the condition of the Church of England 40 or 50 years ago. At that time it was the scandal of Christendom. Its congregations were the most cold, dead, and irreverent; its music was offensive to anyone with a respect for the House of God; its clergy, with exceptions somewhat numerous, chiefly, though not exclusively, belonging to what was then called the Evangelical school, and was then prosecuted as such, but not to the extent of being driven out by Act of Parliament — its clergy with that exception were, in numbers I should not like to mention, worldly-minded men, not conforming by their practice to the standard of their high office, seeking to accumulate preferments with a reckless indifference, and careless of the cure of the souls of the people committed to their charge, and, upon the whole, continually declining in moral influence. This is the state of things from which we have escaped; and when I hear complaints as to the state of things in the present day, I cannot forget the good which has been achieved by the astonishing transformation that has come over the character of the clergymen of the Church of England. That change makes it now almost a moral certainty that whenever you go into a parish you will find the clergyman a man who, to the best of his ability and with little sparing of his health and strength, is spending morning, noon, and night, upon the work of his calling; teaching the young, visiting the sick, preaching the Word, and conforming as far as he can to the model his master left for him to follow. Is it not well, then, to have a little pause and deliberate carefully before rushing too wildly into a course which may break up a state of things in which so much good has been done?

* * * * * * * * *

My contention is broad, clear, and plain. I say it is not a good object, with respect to a law more than 200 years old, and in carrying out which there is a variety of practice, to rush in with a high-handed Act of Parliament and cast aside all regard to what has prevailed through many generations in order to substitute an uniform rule of observance in cases where the proper limits were in the first place fairly fixed.

****

Well, then, the House may say fairly — "Do not you think something ought to be done?" and I think the idea that something ought to be done is what weighs upon the minds of most men. I will tell you what I think ought to be done in principle. The House can do nothing without acknowledging how much we owe to the great mass of the clergy of the Church of England for their zeal and devotion. For 18 years I was a servant of a very large body of them. My place is now most worthily occupied by another; but I have not forgotten, and never can forget, the many sacrifices that they were always ready to make and the real liberality of mind which upon a thousand occasions they have shown. But even that is a thing totally insignificant in comparison with the work which they are doing. You talk of the observance of the law. Why, Sir, every day and night the clergyman of the Church of England, by the spirit he diffuses around him, by the lessons he imparts, lays the nation under a load of obligation to him. The eccentricities of a handful of men, therefore, can never make me forget the illustrious merit of the services done by the mass of the clergy in an age which is beyond all others luxurious, and, I fear, selfish and worldly. These are the men who hold up to us a banner on which is written the motto of Eternal Life, and of the care for things unseen which must remain the chief hope of man through all the vicissitudes of his mortal life.

****

I do not hesitate to say that legality in some cases is an evil — that is to say, that in cases, innocent in themselves, where the habits of congregations are fixed, and where there have been omissions under the ancient rubrics, it would be utter folly to tell every clergyman of every parish, without consulting the wishes of his parishioners and the members of his congregation, to make everything exactly square with this ancient law. Why, most of the excitement which has existed in this country during the last 40 years has arisen from the endeavours of clergymen hastily and precipitately to revert to the practices prescribed by the ancient law of the Church. Take the old controversy about the surplice in the pulpit. The surplice is, no doubt, the legal vestment; but it convulsed the city of Exeter, and might even have led to bloodshed. I would not be responsible for reviving what is now in many instances the dead corpse of legality itself as against expediency and long usage. Apart, therefore, from provisions of legality, I should like to see provisions against all precipitate and sudden change which might be introduced on the sole will of the clergyman against the general feeling of the people. These are, in my opinion, rational subjects of legislation.

* * * * * * * * *

MR. DISRAELI: Sir, the Bill that is now before the House has received very different descriptions in the course of this debate. It has been described as a very small measure, merely a measure of procedure, by one hon. Gentleman; while on the other hand, the right hon. Gentleman opposite, the Member for Bradford (Mr. Forster), who spoke early in to-day's debate, said it was by far the most important measure that has been before Parliament for years.

* * * * * * * * *

What, however, is the object of the Bill which we are now considering? I will at first say what I consider is not the object of it. It is not the object of the Bill to attack any of the legitimate parties in the Church. Were it so, I certainly should not have facilitated the discussion of its merits in this House. I look upon the existence of parties in the Church as a necessary and beneficial consequence. They have always existed, even from Apostolic times; they are a natural development of the religious sentiment in man; and they represent fairly the different conclusions at which, upon subjects that are the most precious to him, the mind of man arrives. Ceremony, enthusiasm, and free speculation are the characteristics of the three great parties in the Church, some of which have now modern names, and which the world is too apt to imagine are in their character original. The truth is, that they have always existed in different forms or under different titles. Whether they are called High Church, or

Low Church, or Broad Church, they bear witness, in their legitimate bounds, to the activity of the religious mind of the nation, and in the course of our history this country is deeply indebted to the exertions and the energy of all those parties. The High Church party, totally irrespective of its religious sentiment, fills a noble page in the history of England, for it has vindicated the liberties of this country in a memorable manner; no language of mine can describe the benefits which this country has experienced from the exertions of the Evangelical school at the commencement of this century; and in the case of the Broad Church, it is well that a learned and highly disciplined section of the clergy should show at the present day that they are not afraid of speculative thought, or are appalled by the discoveries of science. I hold that all these schools of religious feeling can pursue their instincts consistently with a faithful adherence to the principles and practices of the Reformation as exhibited and represented in its fairest and most complete form — the Church of England. I must ask myself what then, Sir, is the real object of the Bill, and I will not attempt to conceal my impressions upon it, for I do not think that our ability to arrive at a wise decision to-day will be at all assisted by a mystical dissertation on the subject-matter of it. I take the primary object of this Bill, whose powers, if it be enacted, will be applied and extended impartially to all subjects of Her Majesty, to be this — to put down Ritualism. The right hon. Gentleman the Member for Greenwich says he does not know what Ritualism is, but there I think the right hon. Gentleman is in an isolated position. That ignorance is not shared by the House of Commons or by the country. What the House and the country understand by Ritualism is, practices by a portion of the clergy avowedly symbolic of doctrines which the same clergy are bound in the most solemn manner to refute and repudiate. Therefore, I think, there can be no mistake among practical men as to what is meant when we say that it is our desire to discourage Ritualism.

* * * * * * * *

I can say most sincerely that I have never addressed any body of my countrymen for the last three years without having taken the opportunity of intimating to them that a great change was occurring in the politics of the world, that it would be well for them to prepare for that change, and that it was impossible to conceal from ourselves that the great struggle between the Temporal and Spiritual power which had stamped such indelible features upon the history of the past was reviving in our own time. I never spoke upon these subjects with passion, nor did I seek in any way at any time to excite such feelings in the minds of those I addressed. I spoke upon a matter which it was difficult for the million immediately to apprehend, and therefore it was not a topic introduced in order to create political excitement. I spoke from strong conviction and from a sense of duty when I wished to direct the public mind as far as I could to the consideration of circumstances in which it was so deeply interested, and which could not fail to influence the history of the country. I said then, that it appeared to me to be of the very utmost importance — and I am speaking now of the time when I addressed a large body of my countrymen as lately as autumn last — I said then, as I say now, looking to what is occurring in Europe, looking at the great struggle between the Temporal and Spiritual power which has been precipitated by those changes, of which many in the House are so proud, and of which, while they may triumph in their accomplishment, they ought not to shut their eyes to the inevitable consequences, — I said then, and say now, that in the disasters, or rather in the disturbance and possible disasters which must affect Europe, and which must to a certain degree sympathetically affect England, that it would be wise for us to rally on the broad platform of the Reformation. Believing as I do that those principles were never so completely and so powerfully represented as by the Church of England; believing that without the learning, the authority, the wealth, and the independence of the Church of England, the various sects of the Reformation would by this time have dwindled into nothing. I called the attention of the country, so far as I could, to the importance of rallying around the institution of the Church of England, based upon those principles of the Reformation which that Church was called into being to represent.

* * * * * * * * *

I wish, I may add, most sincerely, and in the strongest manner, that all should understand that if I make the slightest allusion to the dogmas and ceremonies which are promulgated by the English

Ritualists, I am anxious not to make a single observation which could offend the convictions of any hon. Gentleman in this House.

* * * * * * * * *

What I do object to is Mass in masquerade. To the solemn ceremonies of our Roman Catholic friends, I am prepared to extend that reverence which my mind and conscience always give to religious ceremonies sincerely believed in; but the false position in which we have been placed by, I believe, a small, but a powerful and well-organized body of those who call themselves English clergymen, in copying those ceremonies, is one which the country thinks intolerable, and of which we ought to rid ourselves. The proposition before us is a moderate and temperate one. No one can deny it is but a measure of procedure, and I am prepared to look upon it as a Bill simple in its character, and professing nothing more than that which may be found in its clauses.

Papal Aggression: 1850. Selected documents.

On 29 September 1850 the Pope, Pius IX, regularized the organization of the Roman Catholic Church in England by establishing thirteen sees with English territorial names. For the first time since the Reformation there were to be Roman Catholic bishops with English territorial names. Nicholas Wiseman was named Archbishop of Westminster and made a cardinal. The restoration of the Catholic hierarchy in England, received there as an act of Papal aggression, was met with an outburst of anti-Catholicism at all social levels. This anti-Catholic fervour was in part a reaction against the drift towards Romanism in the Anglican Church which was encouraged by the Oxford movement. It was also associated with concern about Roman Catholic Ireland and the increasing number of Irish immigrants in England. Anti-Catholicism, moreover, had been an important element in English nationalism since the Reformation, and protestantism continued to be associated with patriotism throughout the nineteenth century. The reaction to the Papal aggression in 1850 illustrates the strength of anti-Catholic sentiment in Victorian England. The character of that sentiment is reflected in the following four documents.

1. *The Times*, 7 November 1850. Published letter from Lord John Russell (the prime minister) to the Anglican Bishop of Durham. Complete text.

Downing Street, 4 November, 1850.

MY DEAR LORD, — I agree with you in considering 'the late aggression of the Pope upon our Protestantism' as 'insolent and insidious', and I therefore feel as indignant as you can do upon the subject.

I not only promoted to the utmost of my power the claims of the Roman Catholics to all civil rights, but I thought it right and even desirable that the ecclesiastical system of the Roman Catholics should be the means of giving instruction to the numerous Irish immigrants in London and elsewhere, who without such help would have been left in heathen ignorance.

This might have been done, however, without any such innovation as that which we have now seen.

It is impossible to confound the recent measures of the Pope with the division of Scotland into dioceses by the Episcopal Church, or the arrangement of districts in England by the Wesleyan Conference.

There is an assumption of power in all the documents which have come from Rome; a pretension of supremacy over the realm of England, and a claim to sole and undivided sway, which is inconsistent with the Queen's supremacy, with the rights of our bishops and clergy, and with the spiritual independence of the nation, as asserted even in Roman Catholic times.

I confess, however, that my alarm is not equal to my indignation.

Even if it shall appear that the ministers and servants of the Pope in this country have not transgressd the law, I feel persuaded that we are strong enough to repel any outward attacks. The liberty of Protestantism has been enjoyed too long in England to allow of any successful attempt to impose a foreign yoke upon our minds and consciences. No foreign prince or potentate will be at liberty to fasten his fetters upon a nation which has so long and so nobly vindicated its right to freedom of opinion, civil, political, and religious.

Upon this subject, then, I will only say that the present state of the law shall be carefully examined, and the propriety of adopting any proceedings with reference to the recent assumption of power, deliberately considered.

There is a danger, however, which alarms me much more than any aggression of a foreign sovereign.

Clergymen of our own Church, who have subscribed the Thirty Nine Articles and acknowledged in explicit terms the Queen's supremacy, have been most forward in leading their flocks 'step by step to the very verge of the precipice'. The honour paid to saints, the claim of infallibility for the Church, the superstitious use of the sign of the cross, the muttering of the liturgy so as to disguise the language in which it is written, the recommendation of auricular confession, and the administration of penance and absolution, all these things are pointed out by clergymen of the Church of England as worthy of adoption, and are now openly reprehended by the Bishop of London in his charge to the clergy of his diocese.

I have little hope that the propounders and framers of these innovations will desist from their insidious course. But I rely with confidence on the people of England; and I will not bate a jot of heart or hope, so long as the glorious principles and the immortal martyrs

of the Reformation shall be held in reverence by the great mass of
a nation which looks with contempt on the mummeries of superstition,
and with scorn at the laborious endeavours which are now making
to confine the intellect and enslave the soul. — I remain, with great
respect, &c.

J. Russell

If you think it will be of any use, you have my full permission
to publish this letter.

2. A petition from Southampton on the occasion of the re-introduction
of the Roman Catholic hierarchy into England. November 1850.

To the Queens most Excellent Majesty.

MOST GRACIOUS SOVEREIGN,

WE, your Majesty's faithful subjects of the Town and County
of the Town of Southampton, beg leave to approach your Majesty
with assurances of our devoted loyalty to your Majesty's person and
crown.

Firmly attached to Protestant principles which placed your
Majesty's illustrious house on the throne of these realms, and
ascribing the commercial greatness, social freedom, internal peace,
and extensive empire with which God has blessed our beloved
Country, to the maintenance of Scriptural Truth as freed from Papal
corruptions at the Reformation, and to the protest against the
superstitions and usurpations of the Church and See of Rome then
stamped on our Constitution, and interwoven with our Laws, we
regard it as a most sacred national obligation to *resist* everything
calculated to impair the distinctiveness and strength of that protest.

We venture, therefore, to lay at your Majesty's feet this
expression of our earnest remonstrance against the attempt now
being made to create Episcopal and Arch-Episcopal Sees in England,
subject to the jurisdiction of the Pope, or Bishop of Rome, by virtue,
as alleged, of certain Papal Letters, Briefs, or Bulls; and against the
appointment, by virtue thereof, of persons within this realm, owing
allegiance to your Majesty, to such pretended Sees, and the
assumption by such persons of Episcopal titles and functions, as an
act of aggression on the part of a foreign potentate, and as contrary
to the Protestant Institutions of this country.

We therefore humbly pray that your Majesty will cause such steps to be taken as your Majesty, with the advice of your Councillors shall see fit, for the retraction of all claims, or pretensions, by the Bishop of Rome, to any ecclesiastical or spiritual jurisdiction in this realm, and the prevention of the promulgation of Papal Letters, Briefs, or Bulls, or the assumption or exercise of ecclesiastical functions or powers within your Majesty's dominions by any persons, by virtue of any pretended authority of the See of Rome — together with such other measures for securing the supremacy of the Crown, and freedom form Foreign ecclesiastical interference as to your Majesty shall seem meet.

3. A poster advertising anti-Catholic lectures. November 1850.

On the Downfall of the Church of Rome
A COURSE OF FOUR
LECTURES

Will be delivered (D.V.) by the SLAVONIAN MISSIONARY, the
Rev. JOHN TEODOR, D.D.
FORMERLY A ROMISH ARCHDEACON,
ON MONDAY EVENING, NOVEMBER 4th, 1850
AT THE MOUNT ZION CHAPEL,
LYE, STOURBRIDGE.

On Tuesday, Nov. 5, a Tea Meeting will be held in the above Chapel,
In the evening at Five o'Clock. After which, Dr. Teodor will deliver ANOTHER LECTURE.
On Wednesday November the 6th, at Rev. J. Richard's Chapel, Stourbridge.
On Thursday, Nov. 7, at the Rev. J. Hossack's Baptist Chapel, Stourbridge.
EACH LECTURE WILL COMMENCE AT SEVEN O'CLOCK.

NO DISCUSSION WILL BE ALLOWED IN THESE PLACES OF WORSHIP;
But DR. TEODOR will be happy to meet elsewhere any Jesuits, from the Pope
down to any slavish Priest, to contend with him by the force of truth.

NO COLLECTION WILL BE MADE;
But the following Anti-Popish Publications may be had at the Doors, or the
Vestry of the Chapel, at the close of each Lecture.
1. — "Demonstrations of Catholicism, with new facts never before published."
— 10th Edition, 1s. 6d.
2. — "Eliza Barry, Child of a Cloister, who endeavoured to gain back Dr. Teodor
to Popery, but was finally convinced by him of Popish Errors, &c." Dedicated to
the Pope. — Sixpence.

3. — "Popery in Poland; or, Conversion of Dr. Teodor from Popery, and his Escape from Siberia." — *22nd Thousand, price Sixpence.*
4. — "Catholic Worship of Lifeless Objects and Ideal Saints." — *Price Eightpence.*

On Lord's Day, November 3rd, Dr. TEODOR will preach in Mount Zion Chapel, Lye, Stourbridge, commencing at a Quarter to Three o'Clock

PRINTED BY JOHN W. SHOWELL, TEMPLE STREET, BIRMINGHAM.

4. A handbill reporting the foundation of The Protestant Alliance. June 1851.

THE PROTESTANT ALLIANCE.

On Wednesday, June 25, 1851, a Meeting was held at the FREEMASON'S TAVERN, Great Queen Street, London, of those persons whose signatures had been attached to a series of Resolutions agreed to on April the 4th, at a Conference held at the CALEDONIAN HOTEL. The EARL OF SHAFTESBURY having been called to the Chair, and the Meeting having commenced with prayer by the Rev. EDWARD AURIOL, — the Honorary Secretary read the Report of the Committee appointed at the former Meeting, in which it was stated that the names of more than one thousand influential persons of the various Protestant denominations had been appended to the document cirulated by the Committee.

The Hon. and Rev. H.M. VILLIERS then moved the following Resolution, which was seconded by the Rev. Dr. STEANE, and carried unanimously: —

I. That it appears desirable to form an Association which shall combine all classes of Protestants, whose object is, not merely to oppose the recent aggression of the Pope as a violation of national independence; but to maintain and defend, against all the encroachments of Popery, the Scriptural doctrines of the Reformation, and the principles of religious liberty, as the best security under God for the temporal and spiritual welfare and prosperity of this Kingdom.

The Second Resolution was moved by the Rev. W. CHALMERS,

seconded by JOSIAH CONDER, Esq., and carried unanimously.

II. That such an Association may promote this most important object by the following among other methods: —

By awakening British Christians of various classes, and of different opinions on politics and church government, to such a sense of Christian patriotism as shall lead them, in the exercise of their constitutional privileges, to regard the interests of Protestantism as the paramount object of their concern, keeping minor and merely political differences in subordination to this great end.

By uniting the Protestants of the Empire in a firm and persevering demand, that the national support and encouragement given to Popery of late years shall be discontinued. In this demand would be included all endowments of Popery, in every form and of every kind, drawn from the public revenues, — the concession of rank and precedence to Romish ecclesiastics, — and the allowance of conventual establishments not subject to the inspection and control of the law.

By extending, as far as may be practicable, the sympathy and support of British Christians to those in froeign countries who may be suffering oppression for the cause of the Gospel. By seeking to call forth the influence of the British Government to obtain for Protestants, when residing in Roman Catholic countries, religious liberty equal to that which is granted to Roman Catholics in Great Britain, especially the liberty of public worship, and of burying their dead according to their own rites, — and, above all, freedom in the use and circulation of the Word of God.

J. HEALD, Esq., M.P., moved the Third Resolution, which was seconded by J. CARTER WOOD, Esq., and carried unanimously.

III. That in now forming such Association, the Members present, considering that they have to contend with an adversary at once crafty and bold, and whom all European history shews to be the most formidable the Church of Christ has ever encountered, express strongly and devoutly their sense of dependence upon the grace of God to prosper the efforts thus recommended, and attach supreme importance, under His blessing, not to legislation or political measures of any kind, however valuable and necessary in their place they may be, — but to the circulation of the Bible, the revival of pure Protestant

Christianity, the faithful and zealous preaching of the Gospel, and, in a word, to the use of those "weapons which are not carnal, but mighty, through God, to the pulling down of strongholds."

The Rev. J. HATCHARD moved the Fourth Resolution, which was seconded by C. CAWLEY, Esq., supported by T. FARMER, Esq., and carried unanimously.

IV. That the name of this Association be the PROTESTANT ALLIANCE. That the conduct of the Association, and the prosecution of these objects, be confided to a General Committee, selected in such a manner as to furnish the fullest representation of the Protestantism of the nation. And of this Committee twenty-four shall be appointed the Managing Committee, with power to fill up Vacancies from the General Committee, to appoint the necessary Officers of the Association, and to make Regulations for the due management of its business. These Committees are to be appointed, and annually renewed, by a General Meeting of the Members. Lay Members of the Association to contribute an Annual Subscription of at least Ten Shillings; Clerical Members, of at least Five Shillings. A donation of Five Pounds to constitute a Life Member.

Chapter VIII

Improving the People

Introduction

Informing the majority of early and mid-Victorian efforts to improve the condition of the people was the idea that self-help was the only firm foundation of social progress. The multitude of private philanthropies that flourished in Victorian cities, culminating in the Charity Organization Society which was founded in 1869, worked towards training the poor as individuals to help themselves. The thrust of the most important legislation relating to poverty was the same. The new poor law of 1834 embodied policy that was not abandoned until the beginning of the century. This view of social improvement assumed that the basic structure of society would not change, but that an increasing number of individuals could learn to cope successfully with the existing social system. With its stress on individual responsibility, this outlook on society harmonized well with the evangelical emphasis on the role each individual must play in determining his eternal destiny.

Towards the beginning of the century, this individualistic view of society tended to be associated with political radicalism because it set a high value on individual independence and was antagonistic to the aristocratic social order which had at its theoretical centre the paternalistic landlord and his loyal dependents. But even in the early nineteenth century the political ambiguity of the philosophy of self-help was apparent, for there were many Conservative philanthropists and the Wesleyan Methodists tended to support the Tory party until the middle of the century. As the century moved on, self-help became an increasingly conservative idea.

Perhaps the most important and well organized Victorian attempt at social reform through the reformation of individual character was the temperance movement. Drunkenness was a serious problem among the working classes throughout the century, and it seemed to many philanthropists the greatest single obstacle to general social advance, especially in large towns. In its early years, in the 1830s and 1840s when it was closely associated with free trade, the temperance movement was politically radical and involved both middle class and working class leaders. It became increasingly conservative as time went by, and increasingly controlled by middle class leaders. At first the movement was overwhelmingly dominated by Nonconformists. As it became more conservative, after the middle of the century, Churchmen began to play a larger part.

Teaching the poor to help themselves meant teaching them to be thrifty, to be clean, to be punctual, to work hard and to concentrate on the tasks at hand as well as to be sober. Victorian philanthropists all preached similar lessons from a similar canon of values. It seems clear that they were attempting to impose their middle-class cultural priorities upon the working classes who had different living styles. But it is also clear that many among the working classes valued the possibility of individual social mobility and general social improvement, and working class culture generated no alternative vision of progress in which drunkenness or dirtiness were prized.

A large proportion of Victorian philanthropists acted from what they considered religious motivation, and some Victorian schemes for personal and social improvement took on many of the characteristics of a religious denomination. The temperance movement is a case in point. One explanation for the tendency of so many nineteenth-century men and women to interweave programs for spiritual and social salvation lies in their commitment to the idea of self help. Most Victorians who hoped to improve society through reforming individuals assumed that some degree of moral reformation was involved. Sobriety, cleanliness and thrift were taught as moral conditions, good in themselves as well as useful to the respectably ambitious. Because morality and religion were considered inseparable by conventional Victorians, the idea that cleanliness was next to godliness carried significant meaning for many contemporary philanthropists.

Guide to further reading

In his solid book, *English Philanthropy 1660-1960* (1964), David Owen provides a good general picture of the wider variety of philanthropic activity in nineteenth-century England. His work is the only serious, wide-ranging survey. The close association between evangelicalism and philanthropy is examined by Ford K. Brown in *Fathers of the Victorians* (1961). Hostile to the evangelicals, Brown argues that their philanthropy was an attempt to make the working classes conveniently docile. Kathleen Heasman's pietistic *Evangelicals in Action* (1962) is useful for its documentation of the extent to which evangelicalism permeated Victorian charitable activity. In his chapter on Spurgeon in P.T. Phillips, ed., *The View from the Pulpit* (1978), R.J. Helmstadter suggests that evangelicalism and the mid-Victorian philanthropic style declined together after 1880.

The most accessible introduction to Samuel Smiles, with whom the doctrine of self help is associated, is the chapter on "Samuel Smiles and the Gospel of Work" in *Victorian People* (1954) by Asa Briggs. The place of self help in the culture of the working classes is discussed by Trygve R. Tholfsen in his important book on *Working Class Radicalism in Mid-Victorian England* (1976). Tholfsen also explores the question of middle class cultural aggression.

In *Religion and Respectability: Sunday Schools and Working Class Culture 1780-1850* (1976), a stimulating work with wide ranging implications, Thomas W. Laqueur argues that Sunday schools were genuinely working class institutions, not agencies of social control, and that the cultural divide between the middle classes and the working classes was not very great. John F.C. Harrison, in his first rate work on *Learning and Living 1790-1960: A Study in the History of the English Adult Education Movement* (1961), explores what he calls "the minority tradition" of self help among working men. P.H.J.H. Gosden, *The Friendly Societies in England 1815-1875* (1961) is the authoritative history of those undeniably working-class associations for mutual protection and improvement. The temperance movement was among the most important Victorian efforts at social reform, and perhaps more than any other it became, along with drink, a significant feature of working class culture. Brian Harrison gives the temperance movement magisterial treatment in his splendid social history, *Drink and the Victorians* (1971). The temperance story is completed by A.E. Dingle in *The Campaign for Prohibition in Victorian England* (1980).

The Charities of London (1850), by Sampson Low. Chapter IV.

Sampson Low, junior (1822-1871) was the eldest son of a well known London publisher, and he passed his career working with his father in the family firm. The father was an ardent and very active philanthropist, and both father and son were among the founders of the Royal Society for the Protection of Life from Fire. Low's comprehensive guide to *The Charities of London* appeared first in 1850, and more than any other document it illustrates the range and rich variety of philanthropic activity in Victorian London. Much of the philanthropic work illustrated by Low was religiously inspired as is evident in the descriptions that follow. Evangelical churchmen were particularly active in philanthropy. Kathleen Heasman, *Evangelicals in Action* (pp. 13-14), concludes, after studying their officers and directors, that as many as three quarters of the organizations listed by Low were Evangelical in character or control. The first edition of Low's work contains descriptions of nearly 500 charitable organizations. A representative chapter from the first edition appears below.

————◆————

FOR THE PRESERVATION OF HUMAN LIFE, HEALTH, AND PUBLIC MORALS.

The Humane Societies. — Sanitary Improvement Measures. — Model Buildings for Poor. — Establishments for Baths and Washhouses. — Eary Closing. — Temperance Societies. — Prevention of Vice.

The Institutions comprehended in this chapter are, for the most part, of a preventive character, and follow here, from a consideration of the *causes* of a vast deal of the suffering and disease designed to be relieved by the charities already described. Very many of the ills of human life, no one can deny, are incident to want of care and common precautionary measures. That such is pretty well recognized, may be inferred from the following institutions having been called into esistence by practical experience of their need. That much may be done, under the blessing of God, for the saving of human life from the casualties of domestic and every-day life, is abundantly evidenced by the details of such as have had years to test their usefulness; and that much will be effected, both for the safety and comfort of the lower classes especially, there is great reason to hope. Very cheering and animating is the announcement of one or two of these contemplated new institutions, and satisfactory the progress of those already formed in the cause of public health and morals: it shows, at the least, that public attention is *energetically* directed to the subject, if not, as yet, thoroughly and systematically; and there cannot be a doubt but that such efforts will exercise a powerful influence and effect a great social improvement throughout the metropolis, to the benefit of our crowded localities of courts and alleys clustering with human beings.

It may occur to the reader, that some of the institutions detailed in this and the following chapters, appear, at first sight, rather strangely diverse in design and operation, and embrace more of social than charitable details; but, upon a closer consideration, it will be seen there is a link running through all — illustrative of an anxious desire to render subservient to general humanity the benefit of every fresh suggestion for the common weal, immediately upon a need or necessity manifesting itself — and the *endeavour* to supply it upon benevolent and liberal principles.

The institutions here treated of may thus be classed: — Preservation of Human Life, 3; Prevention of Cruelty, 1; Improvement of Dwellings, 1; Promoting Cleanliness, Comfort, etc., 3; Limiting Hours of Business, 1; Promoting Temperance, 2; Suppression of Immoral Books, 1; Total, 12.

Although reckoned as but twelve institutions, it must be borne in mind that each has its local operations; and in some cases, such as Baths, etc., they result in separate establishments.

With one exception, these are all the product of the present century; and those in full operation are conducted at an annual expense of £11,503.

To defray which, the voluntary contributions amount to £8,730.

This is exclusive of those now self-supporting, or nearly so, but founded originally at a first cost, raised by voluntary contributions, of £72,000.

THE ROYAL HUMANE SOCIETY, 3, Trafalgar-square, Charing-cross. Instituted 1774. For collecting and circulating the most approved and effectual methods for recovering persons apparently drowned or dead; and for suggesting and providing suitable apparatus for, and bestowing rewards on, those who assist in the preservation and restoration of life.

Since the establishment of this society, many hundreds of individuals have been rescued by its direct agency, in the neighbourhood of the metropolis alone, from premature death. The following summary of operations during the past year, may be considered as a fair average of what is effected by the direct exertions of its own officers: fourteen persons were prevented from effecting suicide; twenty rescued, whilst in danger of drowning, from cramp or getting beyond their depth whilst swimming; and, during the ice season, thirty-four rescued from various degrees of danger whilst skating. The number of rewards voted in cases of meritorious exertion or prompt remedial measures, extending over the world: one gold, sixteen silver, and twenty-one bronze medallions; and pecuniary amounts to 125 individuals. The principal receiving house of the society is on the north bank of the Serpentine in Hyde-park. The methods of treatment under emergent circumstances, published by this society, are very excellent, and may be obtained gratuitously on application. The annual amount spent for rewards, salaries, wages, adverisements, etc., is £1,620, and for receiving house and marquees, £200. This is defrayed by an income of £1,800, arising from voluntary contributions and dividends. The items are not more minutely specified in cash statement.

A subscription of one guinea annually constitutes a Governor; 2 guineas annually, a Director; 10 guineas, a Life Governor; 20 guineas, a Life Director. Persons claiming rewards, must produce testimonials within one month to the Secretary, signed by three housekeepers acquainted with the particulars.

President, The Duke of Norfolk. — Treasurer, Benjamin Hawes, Esq. — Secretary, Mr. Joseph Charlier, at the Society's office, 3, Trafalgar-square. — Collector, Mr. Abbot, 2, Agar-street, Strand.

THE ROYAL SOCIETY FOR THE PROTECTION of Life from Fire, 169, Fleet-street. Re-established 1843. The principal object endeavoured to be attained by the Society is the establishment of Fire Escape Stations, half-a-mile distant from each other throughout the metropolis, and maintaining a body of Conductors, well instructed in the use of the "Escapes," one at each station throughout the night. It also seeks to stimulate to intrepid exertions, in the preservation of human life at fires, by presentation of silver medals and pecuniary rewards. The Society's honorary silver medallion can only be obtained by such as have personally rescued human life from the flames.

The number of Fire Escape Stations at present maintained by the Society is twentyseven. The average annual cost of each is £80, and first expenses, for "Escape," etc., £70. It is the duty of every conductor to attend the fires in his district at the very first alarm, whether actually required or not; and the promptitude with which they attend is always to be remarked, generally arriving before fire engines. The gradually decreasing number of fatal fires in London, clearly demonstrates the benefit of such an institution.

The following extract from the present annual report, shows at one view what has been effected by the Society during five years and three months, the time the present Committee have had the management of its affairs.

The expenses of maintaining the conductors and stations, with inspectors, amount to £1,900 per annum, and the management expenses only £180; the whole defrayed by voluntary subscriptions, of from 5s. to 2 guineas annually, assisted by about £400 or £500 a-year, voted by the vestries of some 80 parishes.

Patron, The Queen. — Treasurer, John Dean Paul, Esq., 217, Strand. — Secretary, Mr. Sampson Low, Jun., 14, Great James-street, Bedford-row. — Bankers, messrs. Strahn, Pauls, and Bates. — Inspectors of Stations: East District, Mr. William Baddeley, 29, Alfred-street, Islington; West District, Mr. Spencer, 7, Great Portland-street.

Royal National Institution, for the Preservation of Life from Shipwreck, 20, Austin Friars. Founded 1824. For the establishment of life-boats, and other apparatus, in the most eliglble situations of the British Isles, and rewarding persons who may have assisted in saving lives from shipwreck. For carrying these good intentions into effect, local associations have been formed in various parts of the united kingdom, by the instrumentality of which many hundreds of persons have been saved from shipwreck. The cash statement presents an account of about £700 per annum, arising, half from dividends, and half from voluntary contributions; £400 spent for the objects of the institution, and £350 for expenses of management: but no report has been issued by the Society, we are informed, since 1842.

Ten guineas at one time, or one guinea annually, constitutes a governor, with one vote at all general meetings.

Treasurer, Richard Percival, Jun., Esq. — Trustees: Thomas Wilson, Esq.; John Cazenove, Esq.; John Clark Powell, Esq. — Auditors: Timothy A. Curtis, Esq.; Mr. Ald. Thompson, M.P.

ROYAL SOCIETY FOR THE PREVENTION OF Cruelty to Animals; office, 12, Pall Mall. Established 1824. The object of this Society is to prevent the cruel and improper treatment of animals. Much of the cuelty committed by coachmen, carters, drovers, and others, might be prevented by the mild and kind interference of humane individuals, by the police, and by the parochial authorities, whom the committee solicit to unite with them in the above object. Amongst the results of the Society's operations, may be summed up — "the prosecution to conviction of more than 3,000 cases of aggravated cruelty; the obtaining, in 1835, an amendment of Mr. Martin's Act, whereby more extensive legislative powers were granted; in 1839, the insertion of a clause in the New Police Act, prohibiting the use of dogs in carts and trucks; in 1844, an amendment of the law relative to knackers' yards; and, in 1849, a new and much improved act for the more effectual prevention of cruelty to animals." The annual average of cases proceeded against appears to be 150, either by the direct or indirect operations of the Society. The disbursements consist of office expenses, salaries, prosecution, and incidental, to the amount of £900 annually. The income is derived, from voluntary sources, £820, and from dividends, £200; and the cash statement for 1849 presents the finances in a most satisfactory position.

Ten guineas donation, or one guinea annual, constitutes a Governor. The Committee meet at the office every second monday in the month; and the Secretary attends daily, between eleven and four.

President, vacant. — Treasurer, Samuel Gurney, Esq. — Sub-Treasurer, Lewis Pocock, Esq. — Secretary, Mr. Henry Thomas. — Collector, Mr. George Middleton.

LABOURERS' FRIEND SOCIETY, for improving the condition

of the Labouring Classes; Office, 21 Exeter Hall. Established 1831. Is actively engaged in endeavouring to ameliorate the condition of the working classes, in the three important points of dwellings, land, and money. It has built a range of dwellings for the industrious classes, on sanitary principles, at Bagnigge-wells, Gray's-inn-lane. Here 23 families and 30 single women are accommodated. Also, in George-street, St. Giles's, a model lodging-house for working men, where 104 persons of this class find a comfortable habitation. It has repaired and rendered fit for healthy occupation four houses in King-street and Charles-street, Drury-lane, wherein 108 working men are accommodated, for fourpence per night. Also, at No. 76, Hatton-garden, a house for the accommodation of 58 females of the working classes.

It is now building, in Streatham-street, Bloomsbury, a range of dwellings for mechanics and their families, wherein about 48 such families will find good and healthy habitations. At Tunbridge-wells it is aiding to raise a series of cottages for agricultural labourers, of which six, and a lodging-house for single men, are already completed and occupied. It is also in constant correspondence with a great number of benevolent persons in all parts of the kingdom, who apply for its aid in the building or improvement of cottages, or the setting out of cottage allotments. In these various works it has expended, or now is expending, more than £23,000.

The income of the Society wholly depends on the contributions of the benevolent; and the extent of its operations is entirely contingent upon the amount entrusted to it. Thus, by a simultaneous movement amongst the metropolitan clergy at the last general "Thanksgiving," a very large collection was placed at the disposal of the Committee — nearly £4,000. This, with additional donations, enabled them forthwith to develope corresponding efforts to establish upon a large scale a fresh "model building," for the improvement of the lodgings of the labouring classes generally. For the purpose of increasing the comfort and promoting the health of the poor, the benevolently inclined will find no better opportunity for exertion than that afforded by this institution, or fairer probability of the same being attended with success.

An annual subscription of one guinea, or more, constitutes a member of the Society, and donors of £10 and upwards are Governors for life. Donations of £50 and upwards may be paid immediately, or by four yearly payments.

President, Prince Albert. — Chairman of Committee, Lord Ashley. — Treasurer, John Labouchere, Esq. — Secretary, John Wood, Esq. — Collector, Mr. W.B. Emmery. — Agent, Mr. Henry Martin.

METROPOLITAN ASSOCIATION, for improving the Dwellings of the Industrious Classes, 19, Coleman-street, City. Incorporated 1845. The object of this association is to enable the labouring classes to procure a comfortable, cleanly, and healthy habitation, at a less expense than is at present paid for very inferior and unhealthy accommodation, arising from want of ventilation, bad drainage, and the crowded state of the apartments.

Their operations during the past four years have resulted in the erection of a commodious pile of buildings in the Pancras-raod, at a total cost of about £17,000, affording accommodation for 110 families, in sets of two or three rooms each, with a separate scullery, water-closet, ample supply of water, and other conveniences, at rents far below the amounts usually paid in unhealthy and inconvenient abodes. A piece of land has likewise been recently purchased by the association, in Spicer-street, Brick-lane, for the establishment of a model lodging-house for single men: both establishments, it is computed, will be self-supporting and remunerative as soon as in full action.

The funds have been raised in shares of £25, and liabilities of joint-stock avoided, by obtaining letters patent under the 1st Victoria, c. 73, secs. 2 and 4, which limits the responsibility of shareholders; £5 per share is required to be paid into the bankers' hands. Communications and applications for shares to be addressed to Mr. C. Gatliff, Honorary Secretary, 19, Coleman-street.

Chairman, Sir Ralph Howard. — Auditors: John Finlaison, Esq.; Edward Hurry, Esq. — Bankers, Messrs. Barclay, Bevan, Tritton, and Co. — Architect, William Beck, Esq. — Honorary Secretary, Charles Gatliff, Esq., 19, Coleman-street.

THE METROPOLITAN SANITARY ASSOCIATION, 12, St. James's-square, is now forming under the presidency of the Bishop of London, with the exertions of several influential friends to the cause of the labouring poor; at its foundation meeting recently held (February 6, 1850,) the advantages of efficiently conducted sanitary measures were fully and powerfully urged by Lord Ashley, Mr. Dickens, and other gentlemen. Their arguments were to the effect, that the imperative necessity of health measures, adequate to the wants of the 2,000,000 inhabiting this great metropolis, has been incontrovertibly established by the disclosures made during the late epidemic, and the appalling sacrifice of life, amounting in all to a loss of 18,423 lives, demonstrate that a time has arrived when the people are entitled urgently to demand from the legislature efficient and comprehensive enactments, in order to prevent recurrent ravages of pestilence and attendant misery. The clergy of the metropolis were particularly called upon to assist the association to the utmost of their power by the formation of branch associations in every district and parish. With these the parent association, it was stated, will gladly cooperate.

The zealous support of all classes may, in short, be solicited in this work or prevention, the benefits of which must extend to all, though they will be most apparent in the improved state of the dwellings of the poor and of the labouring classes, and in the elevated social condition of the people, in greatly reduced local burdens, and in the diminished amount of widowhood and orphanage.

An annual subscription of 1 guinea, and a donation of five guineas, constitutes a member.

Messrs. Glyn and Co.; Messrs. Barclay, Bevan, and Co.; Messrs. Williams, Deacon, and Co.; and the London and Westminster Bank, receive contributions. — Honorary Secretaries: M.W. Lusignan, M.A.; Hector Gavin, M.D.; Adolphus Barnett, M.B., 12, St. James's-square, and Crosby Hall, Bishopsgate.

BATHS AND WASH-HOUSES for the Labouring Classes, in the North-West District of the Metropolis, George-street, Euston-square. Established 1846. The first establishment *practically* tried in the metropolis. It was founded by voluntary contributions, at a total cost of about £6,000; but is now, with continuation of slight assistance, self-supporting, and will doubtless be soon entirely so. The benefits conferred on the surrounding districts have been substantial, and are increasingly displayed.

Thus, in 1847, 110,940 persons bathed, and 137,672 individuals had their clothes washed, dried, &c.; while, during 1848, notwithstanding the unusually cold and wet season, 111,788 bathed, and 246,760 were washed for: besides this, 1,433 rooms, closets, areas, &c., have been cleansed and purified.

President, Lord Southampton. — Bankers, Sir Claude Scott and Co. — Honorary Secretary, T.H. Smith, Esq. — Secretary, Mr. John Bell.

COMMITTEE for Promoting the Establishment of Baths and Wash-Houses for the Labouring Classes, 5, Exeter Hall, and Goulston-square, Whitechapel, London.

The first operations to promote this purpose were in 1844, but various difficulties, occupying much time and considerably greater expense than was calculated upon, retarded the object, and it was not until July 1847, that the first half of the baths and wash-houses, at the model establishment, were opened. The total cost, under the peculiar expenses, of experiments, &c., swelled the amount to £26,000; but the purpose served both to afford to a wretchedly poor district the benefits of cheap cleanliness, and at the same time presented data to ground application for legislative measures, authorizing such establishments in every parish, and offer a model for future operations.

At the present establishment 20,000 people can bathe weekly, and accommodation be afforded for 42 women to wash at one time, with tubs, drying closets, and every requisite.

There are 96 baths and 84 pairs of tubs; and the committee are of opinion that similar extensive establishments may now be completed, after the model, for about £12,000: also that this, as well as others, when in full operation, will not only be self-supporting, but remunerative; thus, it is computed, £2,000 a-year will be the continued receipts, at the present charges of 1d. for cold baths, and 2d., or 6d., for warm baths; and £400 a-year from the washers at 1d. per hour: whilst the continued working expenses cannot exceed £1,400 annually.

President, The Lord Bishop of London. — Chairman, Rev. Sir Henry R. Dukinfield, Bart. — Deputy Chairman, William Hawes, Esq.

— Trustees: Samuel Jones Loyd, Esq.; Sir William Magnay, Bart.; Sir A. De Rothschild, Bart.; Abel Smith, Esq. — Honorary Secretaries: James Farish, Esq.; John Bullar, Esq. — Assistant Secretary, Mr. George Woolcott.

St. Martin in the Fields Establishment has now 72 baths open, and during the past nine months upwards of 150,000 bathers have availed themselves of the benefit, paying from 1d. to 3d. for cold baths, and 3d. or 6d. for warm baths: this is the first establishment opened under Sir Henry Dukinfield's "Public Bath and Wash-House Act".

The following parishes have likewise adopted, or are about doing so, the provisions of the same act: —

St. Marylebone establishment, in the New-road, opposite Lisson-grove. Superintendent, Mr. James Crafter.

St. Giles and St. George, Bloomsbury.

St. James's, Piccadilly: site secured near Messrs. Broadwood's Brewery.

St. Margaret and St. John, Westminster, and

Lambeth;

And the cities and boroughs of Hull, Liverpool, Bristol, Plymouth, Preston, Worcester, Birmingham, &c.

THE METROPOLITAN EARLY CLOSING ASSOCIATION, 32 Ludgate-hill. Established 1842. Its object is, by means of argument and persuasion, with employers, and public co-operation, so to abridge the hours of business as to extend to assistants opportunity for recreation, and for physical, intellectual, and moral improvement.

As some of the earliest results of this society in the advancement of these latter objects, may be instanced, the establishment of "The Church of England's Young Men Society," "The Young Men's Christian Association," and others, each full of promise for the spread of Christian principles, and all more or less promoted by the pioneering operations and earnest exertions of the promoters of this society.

President, Sir James Emerson Tennent. — Trustees: George Hitchcock, Esq.; Ambrose Moore, Esq.; T. Winkworth, Esq. — Treasurer, W.D. Owen, Esq. — Collectors: Mr. Butts; Mr. J. Hankes. — Secretary, Mr. John Lilwall, 32, Ludgate-hill.

NATIONAL TEMPERANCE SOCIETY, 11, Tokenhouse-yard. Established 1842. For the purpose of assisting efforts for the cause of temperance in every part of the country, by encouraging and assisting the formation of county and other district associations, ascertaining the character and qualifications of advocates, recommending agents, and assisting in their exchange from one association to another; by collecting and diffusing statistical and other valuable information bearing on the subject of intemperance, and by watching the proceedings of Parliament in questions connected with intemperance, and taking every suitable opportunity of bringing the subject under the notice of the legislature.

Connected with, and promoted by this society, was the great "World's Temperance Convention," held in London, August 4, 1846, and following days, brought together from all parts of the world: the society consists of annual subscribers of 1 guinea and upwards, and of donors of not less than 10 guineas, who have signed a declaration involving total abstinence from intoxicating liquors.

The cash statement appended to last report shows an income of about £1,000 annually, with the exception of about £50 supplied by voluntary contributions, and expended chiefly in printing pamphlets, expenses of meetings, travelling, lecturing, &ct.

Tresurer, G.E. Alexander, Esq., 40, Lombard-street. — Secretary, Mr. Isaac Doxsey. — Missionaries, Mr. James Balfour; Mr. Richard Hodgson.

British & FOREIGN TEMPERANCE SOCIETY, Aldine Chambers, Paternoster-row. Established 1830. Consists of such persons as subscribe to the following declaration: — "We agree to abstain from distilled spirits, except for medicinal purposes, and to discountenance the causes and practice of intemperance." The members promote the circulation of publications which have received the sanction of the committee. The society recognizes as members those who adopt its general declaration; while those who show their good will, by contributing to the funds of the society, without adopting the declaration, are considered as honorary members.

The last report of the institution represents a continued increase of drunkenness; also an increasing consumption of spirits throughout the British empire, and presents altogether anything but a gratifying account of the society's influence.

There are some very good tracts and other papers published by the society, which are worthy an extended circulation; but the present funds at its disposal appear totally inadequate to carry out efficiently the great object it attempts to effect, the whole amount being under £250 per annum.

President, the Bishop of London. — Honorary Secretary, Rev. H. Hughes, A.M. — Secretary, Rev. Owen Clarke, 6, Northampton-square. — Bankers, Messrs. Barclay, Bevan, and Co. — Collector, Mr. Shrewsbury, 3, King's-row, Walworth. — Agent, Mr. James Simpson.

SOCIETY FOR THE SUPPRESSION OF VICE, 57, Lincoln's-inn-fields. Established 1802. Established chiefly at the instance and by the exertions, of the late William Wilberforce, Esq. About four or five years back its operations were obliged to be suspended, from increasing debts and generally disarranged funds. Latterly, however, by a successful appeal to the public, it has been enabled to resume active measures against the promoters of infidelity and vice; and the last report represents an extent of considerable usefulness achieved by it in two years, chiefly consisting in the suppression of infidel lectures and discussions, and the destruction of immoral books, and punishment by law of their vendors. It is the axiom of daily experience that a bad man's influence can, in some measure, be traced and counteracted; but that that of a bad book can never be known, and is incalcuable; with this conviction it is that we hail, with pleasure, the information afforded by the committee of the very large number of villanous publications annually destroyed by their means, which would otherwise have been spreading their poisoning influence over the country, corrupting the minds of the young, and disturbing peace and order wherever introduced.

The object and operations of this society, demand for it the support and cooperation of every advocate for extending the influence of moral and religious principles; its funds appear to require increasing, and its general management stregthening.

Treasurer, Charles Hoare, Esq., Fleet-street. — Secretary, Mr. Henry Prichard, 57, Lincoln's-inn-fields.

Ipswich Temperance Tracts, No. 212: "Drinking and Lawlessness"(n.d. circa 1850), by Jabez Burns. Selections.

The *Ipswich Temperance Tracts* were compiled by Richard Dykes Alexander, the chief supporter of the Ipswich Temperance Society and publisher of the *Temperance Recorder* from 1840. The Tracts were often reprinted. Jabez Burns, (1805-1876) a well-known evangelical Nonconformist was raised a Methodist, and became pastor of a Baptist chapel in London. He was an early member of the Evangelical Alliance, formed in 1845 to strengthen ties between orthodox Nonconformists and Evangelicals in the Church of England. Burns frequently spoke for the temperance movement, and is thought to be the first minister to preach teetotalism from the pulpit.

DRINKING AND LAWLESSNESS
A SERMON.

"Lest they drink and forget the Law." — Prov. xxxi, 5

OUR text is the fragment of a paragraph found among the words of heavenly wisdom. Though only part of a sentence, it contains a complete sense, and suggests matter for very grave and momentous consideration.

The thoughts which the text breathes were of Divine inspiration, and they were addressed by a holy mother to her son. They obviously refer to the pernicious influence of wine and strong drink on the minds and consciences of men, and therefore an entire abstinence from their use is urged, that the evils specially stated may be avoided. The admonitory caution, you will observe, is not addressed to the illiterate and debased of the people, but the lofty and the great. "It is not for kings to drink wine, nor for princes strong drink ," and for this most important reason: "Lest they drink and forget the Law." But if kings, and rulers, and law-makers should abstain from the use of wine and strong drink, so also should those who are responsible to the law, who should be its ornaments and supporters. In one word, the great doctrine of the text is, the necessary connection between drinking wine and strong drink and lawlessness. We may appeal, therefore, to monarchs, and judges, and senators, and magistrates, and also to every class of the people, and say: Abstain entirely from wine and strong drinks, lest you forget the law. It should be remembered, too, that the caution as to wine relates of necessity to the wines then used, most of which possessed only a small share of the intoxicating spirit compared with the wines of our day, as the text was uttered more than two thousand years before the production of alcohol by distillation, which forms so large a per centage of the wines now in use — so that in every view the text is most appropriate both the the age and country in which we live, and especially as presenting a motto for the grand occasion which has brought us together.

In further discussing the subject we notice —

I.—THAT THE DRINKING OF INTOXICATING LIQUORS TENDS TO LAWLESSNESS

In the words of the text, by drinking wine and strong drink men forget the law. They forget,

1st. The law of self-respect and self-cultivation.

Much of our character is left to our own formation. Our mental and moral education is mainly in our own hands. A high regard to our own true dignity is one of the most powerful springs to proper emulation. Thus, self-respect is one of the chief bonds of society, and is a leading incentive to virtuous exertion and noble enterprise. Weaken this and man sinks; destroy it entirely, and he becomes reckless as it regards himself, and valueless as it regards others. This element of our being is constantly addressed in the Divine Word. It is said, "a good name is rather to be chosen than great riches."

We are to seek to have the approval, no only of God, but of wise and good men. Now nothing so entirely enfeebles this in man as strong drink, and no one so fully makes utter shipwreck of it as the drunkard. Of all men he most glories in his shame. He is obtuse to all delicate emotions; he utterly disregards the opinion of others, and wallows in the mire of self-prostrated degradation. With this, too, there will be utter indifference to self cultivation. To the improvement of the mind there must be wisely applied leisure; but the drinker's spare hours are devoted to the tavern or the beer-shop. To self-cultivation there must be the right and cool adjustment of the mental faculties; but the drunkard lives in a region of excitement and sensual passion. To the pursuit of knowledge there must be reading and reflection, and persevering study, and investigation; but the craving for intoxicating liquors produces a state of heart and life at utter variance with these, and hence mental deterioration and intellectual sterility are the usual results of a drinking life. Who can tell the number of blighted minds and stunted intellects which are produced by drinking habits among the youth of our land? Such forget,

2ndly. *The law of love towards their fellow-men.*

Man was designed by his Creator to love himself, to seek his own mental and moral exaltation and well-being, and then he is required to love his neighbour as himself. In this love of our kind there are the outgoing emotions of warm and unselfish affection which bind the husband and wife,and parents and offspring together. There is the soft and genial attachment of brothers and sisters, of friends and kindred; and then in the more outward circles there is the esteem and love of neighbouring residents, or persons of our class and order, or our trade and profession, or of our religion and social circle. There is the general affection of goodness towards all men — of pity and compassion towards the suffering, and of commiseration for the unfortunate or self-ruined of our species. But drinking wine and strong drink produces a gradual obliteration of this law of Love, from the heart and the mind. It makes its victims selfish as well as sensual; it hardens the heart; dries up the sympathies of our gentler and kindlier emotions. It produces alienation between the dearest friends, and separation between the closest kindred. It withers conjugal love, and annihilates parental or filial affection. It converts man both into the brute and the demon, so that the father cares not for his offspring, and the mother forgets her sucking child. It rends asunder all relative bonds, and makes home and its associations the horrid scene of strifes, contentions and disorders, and cruelties, too appalling for description or illustration. It sets the tongue on fire of hell, and it ossifies the heart, so that the common benignities of social life have neither a habitation nor a home.

3rdly. *By drinking wine and strong drink, men forget the law of reverence and love and obedience to God.*

A disbelief of Divine things, and a rejection of Divine claims, usually proceed from the heart. A sensual state of mind has no relish for the spiritual and the holy. Nothing tends more to the rejection of Divine beliefs than a state of moral degradation, which unfits us for both. Hence the habit of drinking disqualifies for calm and serious reflection, and utterly unfits for all devotion and real worship. This state of mind will be succeeded by a disrelish for all religious services and pursuits, and then God and His claims will be rejected — His name blasphemed — His authority utterly despised. Can reverence for God and a love of artificial excitement dwell in the same mind? Can love of the sensuous enjoyment of wine harmonise with the pure love of God's holy spirit? Can the devotee of carnal passion be obedient to the moral law? Can any man serve the two masters of pleasure and God? — worship with real profit both in the barroom and the sanctuary — in the boisterous profane tavern and in the secrecy of the closet, or at the family altar? No; let man yield himself up to intoxicating drinks, and the Word of God will lose its savor, the sanctuary its social attractions, the closet its sublime associations, and the domestic altar its holy, its sweet, and genial influences.

By drinking wine and strong drink men forget,

4thly. The civil laws by which society is governed.

There are certain great boundary lines within which men must be kept, or society and nations would run into confusion and mutual destruction. The liberties of men, their property, and the security of their lives and homes, must be preserved. But drinking carries the conscience not only into open rebellion against the laws of God, but also to an utter disregard of the civil statutes of society. Drinking engenders idleness and dissipation. These lead to improvidence and recklessness. These will be followed by craft and cunning, by evil associates, and leagueship with the viscious and dangerous orders of society. Debts will be contracted — the industrious and orderly tradesman will be plundered. Then thefts, processes of swindling, and other crimes against property will follow. Dishonesty and utter disregard of other men's rights, drinking speedily produces. Men often first plunder their own homes, and then the habitations of others. The man who will rob his wife of her raiment, and his children of their food, for drink, is not likely to stop even in that degraded and inhuman position. Hence nine-tenths of all our criminals are made, and trained, and sustained, and perfected in their lawlessness in the tavern, beer-shop and the gin palace. The pickpocket, the burglar, the murderer, are alike dependent for their demoniacal daring on the intoxicating medium. And from the extravagant self-ruined bankrupt to the vilest and deepest blood-stained criminal, there is scarcely an instance where drink has not been the main incentive in the business of desolation and horror. How clear, then, that drinking and lawlessness are almost inseparably allied; and this connection is not only between ignorant and illiterate drinkers, but we see it in the self-ruined condition of men of education and intellectual attainments. This is the natural order of things, whether the person be young or old; whether among the lofty or the low; whether found among the irreligious, or the professed moral and Christian population. Men, by drinking, have forgotten every law divine and human, who have had every advantage of birth, of education, of station in life. Men have been thus ruined who have swayed sceptres, commanded armies and navies, who have occupied the bench of the judge, the chair of the philosopher, and the desk of the minister. Men of fortune, of fame, of literary pre-eminence, of moral distinction, have fallen in multitudes — men in every profession and class of life, both in the world and in the church, so that we may well say: it is not for kings nor princes, nor senators, nor magistrates, nor men of science, nor for moral teachers, nor Christian professors, to drink wine nor strong drink. Lest they forget the law. If evidence were wanting to establish this, I need not descend to the lowest haunts of the degraded and wretched, often the unfortunate members of society; but I would appeal to the testimony of men like Samuel Johnson, the Leviathan of British literature, and to the experience of Addison and Steele, to Pitt and Fox, to Sheridan, to Burns, to Hartley Coleridge, and to a host of the greatest and most renowned in our country's history, whose moral weaknesses, and in many instances early deaths, would give both fearful scope and terrible intensity to the text: That it is not for any order or class of men to drink wine or strong drink, lest they forget the law. We notice

—

II.–THAT THE TRAFFIC IN INTOXICATING DRINKS IS NECESSARILY ON THE SIDE OF THIS LAWLESSNESS.

1.st. It is based on a violation of the laws of reason and gratitude, in the perversion of the bounties of Divine Providence.

If the intoxicating medium existed in Nature (which it does not), the question would then properly arise: Shall we not confine the use of it to disease, and place it by the side of hemlock and henbane, and opium? But that which is the foul curse of the civilised world is not a natural production, but is the result of scientific discovery, a thing made by man's device. It must, in every instance, be manufactured by man , and is therefore altogether an artificial and and non-natural production. And we ask: What is requisite to produce it? Not merely human cunning and skill, but the perversion of that which is the very staff of life — the bread corn of mankind, sent by the benignant and kind presiding Parent of our race. This, the children's bread, is thus worse than wasted or cast to the dogs; it is perverted into poison. It is robbed extensively of its nutritious properties, and it becomes not the staff of life, but the fluid of woe, desolation, and death. I cannot perceive of any argument, either philosophical or moral, by which this perversion can be vindicated. It would be deemed unnatural to throw the wheat and barley thus prostituted to the dunghill; it would excite general indignation to heap together the untold myriads of bushels of golden grain and burn it; but either of these courses would be acts of mercy to mankind, if by this way the supply of the distillery and the brewery could be stopped. To employ it in the production of intoxicating drinks is a sin against reason, against humanity, against God — so that the very traffic is based on iniquity. Every creature of God is to be used, not perverted, not wasted, not transformed into a deadly evil. The manufacture of idols from the metals of iron, and silver, and gold, is not a more wicked and senseless line of action than the taking God's precious bounties, and rendering them, by man's device, the agent of misery and ruin to mankind.

2ndly. It provides and offers to men the agent of demoralisation and crime.

How few would be at the pains privately, and for their own personal use, to make barley into malt, and then to distil alcohol from it. The trouble and inconvenience would go far to prevent men from attempting the labour necessary to produce it. But by the traffic how extensively it is made and sold as one of the needful ordinary things of every day life. It is put before the public in every conceivable form for sale, and at every turn it meets you; it has its market during the whole week; it is associated with every device likely to render it attractive; its praises are spread forth in every form of poesy and prose; it is held up as the invigorator of the laborer, the cheerer of the lonely, the solace of the afflicted, and a cordial for all. It might be more necessary than bread, or more essential than the vital air. Water, the gift of God, and one of the real essentials of our physical existence and health is condemned in most reproachful terms if mentioned in comparison with alcoholic drinks. This fluid is presented in every variety of colour, and flavour, and degrees of strength. It is said to be needful for all classes, and ages, and conditions of life. In one form it is classified with bread and beef, and thus it is offered to the working masses, and they are so befooled as to drink it by millions of barrels in a year. In another form it is placed in the sparkling decanter, and it is to be in attendance at the social board of the rich and the literary and the great, and without it hospitality, it is said, would wither and die. It is then respectably conducted into the house of God, and the votaries of piety are taught that not only does it give vigour to the preacher, but it is the best symbol of the precious blood of our redemption. Thus at home and abroad, in the city tavern and in the floating steam-ship, in the hotel and in the sanctuary, is this wicked and accursed thing paraded, praised, almost worshipped. Indeed, if the preference of the heart constitutes mainly the sin of idolatry, then Britain has her monster national idol, and that idol is unquestionably strong drink, for whose degrading worship our land is crowded with thousands of polluted altars and temples. Having this public and prominent position, is it to be marvelled that the traffic should be the main agent in the demoralisation and crime of the land?

3rdly. It breaks down the barriers to lawfulness both in the trafficker in drinks and those who use them.

Men who make and sell these drinks first persuade themselves that it is right to do so. They believe and teach that to produce and sell these drinks is lawful in the most comprehensive sense of the term. Those who use these drinks have similar articles of belief; therefore the way is open for both to proceed, the one in dealing them out, and the other in using them with impunity — no barrier is therefore raised to the wide and dreary scene which drinking necessarily involves. It is thought as righteous, and as safe, and as good, to make beer as to make bread — to sell intoxicating drinks as any of the ordinary necessaries of life. If the dealer does not poison over again that which is in itself a poison, and if the drunkard does not take it in doses so large that he falls its destroyed victim at once it is all supposed to be right, and respectable, and good. Thus men are most deplorably deceived, and surround this real upas tree as though health and longevity, and not disease and death, would be inhaled from it. Thus men go and walk blindfolded in the midst of the most deadly pitfalls, and snares, and precipices of moral ruin, all the while exulting in the supposed absolute safety by which they are surrounded. And what is the result? Both the dealers and users, in fearful numbers perish. The withering mists of perdition could not be more adverse to moral purity or happiness than the atmosphere of drinking establishments is to those who keep them. The owners and their children live in a region of fearful moral corruption and death. The servants and waiters, as a rule, sink early by the ruin which they are hired to dole out, as a matter of trade, to others; and as is the morally hardened state of those who minister in these temples of desolation, so is the undone condition of a great proportion of the deluded worshippers. In every sense these places, however externally decorated, are wide openings by which the unwary and dissipated descend with fearful rapidity into the gloomy regions of crime, misery, and death.

Ipswich Temperance Tracts, No. 228: "Dirt: and a Word about Washing" (n.d. circa 1850), compiled from writings by W.C. Clayton, Joseph Livesey and others. Selections.

William Clayton (1799-1892), was a successful barrister. He wrote a little on technical legal matters. Joseph Livesey (1794-1884), a successful cheese monger in Preston, became famous as the leader of the early teetotal movement in the 1830s. He is best known as a temperance advocate, but was also active in other radical and Nonconformist causes.

———————

DIRT:
An extract from a Lecture delivered before the Harrow Young Men's Society, February 24th, 1852.
"DIRT! JACOB, WHAT IS DIRT?" — Southey.

THE *Dictionary tells us that dirt is "whatever, adhering to anything, renders it foul or unclean."* Our eyes tell us that it takes away the beauty of whatever it touches. Our noses tell us that it is extremely disgusting. And our feelings tell us that it is repugnant to health and comfort, and purity, and social enjoyment.

Dirt is not part of our nature: it is a parasite, thriving on our heart's blood, like a vampire. They say the vampire sucks away the life without the poor patient's knowing anything about it. It is just the same with dirt. Four-fifths of mankind live in dirt, and lose a large part of their health and comfort in consequence. What is it that robs the working classes, in many of our large towns, of nearly half their natural term of life? Dirt — dirt on the person, in the houses, in the streets, and in the air. What is it that makes the children fretful, impatient and bad tempered? DIRT again. What is it that keeps rich people from associating with the poor, from sitting by them at meetings, or letting them come to their houses? Often not so much pride as DIRT. What is it that destroys self-respect, makes men careless and degraded, and weakens the natural restraints of modesty? DIRT, again. What is it that makes the prettiest face ugly, the finest clothes tawdry, the cleverest man disagreeable, and the most splendid house uninhabitable? DIRT, again.

AWAY THEN WITH DIRT

Welcome Water and Air, Sand and Soap, even Besoms and Scrubbing Brushes! The child who fetches a pail of water into the house is an angel of mercy; while the man that brings in a jug of ale is beginning the work of a demon. The man who takes the nourishing food that God sends for our support, turns it into poisonous spirit, and (after mixing it with corrupted water) offers it to his brother to drink, gives pleasure to friends. But the poor mechanic who takes the pitiful tallow and dirty ashes, and changes them into dirt-destroying soap, is doing a noble work. It is like what the Divine Being does in nature. HE takes the filthy particles that nauseate us, and the bad air that robs us of our health, and with this he nourishes the plants, and forms a new store of food to support, and of herbage and flowers to delight us.

LOATHE DIRT

You cannot help it at work: but when work is over taste no food till you have cleansed yourself. Wash your whole body over every morning; and put on clean clothes as often as you can. You could soon afford plenty of clean shirts and sheets, if the publican gave you back your money, and you gave him back his ale. *Don't take those dirty drinks:* cool yourself with the fresh clear water that Nature filters so beautifully for you in the bowels of the earth. White-wash your cottage, and open your windows. Don't grudge either time or money that is spent in cleanliness: and try to live where your neighbours are clean also, lest you suffer from their dirt. For,

DIRT IS POISON

It gets into the body through the pores of the skin; and the dirty gases enter with the air into the lungs. It mixes with the blood, and makes it corrupt; and often fevers, cholera, consumption, and other fatal diseases are the result. All slops, middens, and undrained places help to poison the air; and we should wash them away as fast as ever we can. There ought to be a drain and water-closet in every house; a sewer in every street; and, above all, a plentiful supply of water to flush the dirt away. The places where many of the poor reside are only fit for drunkards; they are too bad for beasts. If working men spent part of their drinking money in house-rent, such places would be deserted and soon pulled down.

A clean man respects himself, and educates his eyes and nose to the observance of decency. He is not afraid of going anywhere, or ashamed of being in the company of any one. The dirty man cares for nobody, and yet slinks away from respectable people.

CLEANLINESS IS NEXT TO GODLINESS.

An habitual dirty man can hardly be religious. He is breaking one of the first of Nature's laws. Cleanliness in person prepares for purity of heart, and for a reception of the life-giving principles of the Gospel.

FRESH AIR, PURE WATER, AND GOOD SOAP FOR EVER!

DOWN WITH DIRT.

READER! If you have not done so already, go and wash yourself NOW. *Throw the tobacco box into the fire: leave intoxicating drinks at the public-house, and NEVER GO THERE; and become a clean, a sober, and a religious man.*

A WORD ABOUT WASHING.

NOW is the time for timid people who dreaded to start in cold weather the new-fangled but most important operation of washing the whole skin daily. I say, *now is the time* to begin in good earnest. Don't be content with an occasional bathing when you happen to be conveniently situated for taking the bath, but begin the practice of a complete ablution all over every morning. Those whom I have persuaded to do so, without an exception, speak well of it, and regret they had not commenced long before. It is astonishing that we should be so over-attentive to some of the wants of nature, and so utterly neglective of others. We never forget to supply the wants of the stomach, and generally we over-supply them; we seldom omit to provide covering for the body, and in most cases those that can afford it carry this provision to excess. The same may be said of sleep. But the removal from the skin of all the excreted effete matter, and the supplying it with water and fresh air, are systematically neglected by most people, except merely the face and hands. We breathe through the skin as well as through the lungs; but while this is closely wrapped up in flannel, and the pores corked fast with dirt, how is it possible that this breathing can be performed freely? Blotched skins, head-aches, and lung complaints are frequently the effects of obstructions of the skin. How fresh and revived a dirty person feels by merely changing his linen, and, were such to wash all over, they would be surprised to find the delightful feelings which could be the result. How pleasing it is to begin every day with a clean skin; and how disgusting to wrap up inside of your flannel or your linen one week's and one month's dirt upon another! I often feel sickened to be obliged to come in contact with persons of this description; and wherever they go, I am sure their absence will be more welcome than their company. A good wash in a morning is a great inducement to take exercise, while dirt is the certain cause of laziness and inactivity. Only get the water on to you the moment you get out of bed, and the effect is such, after a good rubbing, that you cannot be slow. You will dress in one-third the time that the non-washers usually take. I wash, rub, and dress in eight minutes. I noticed the other morning how long a friend of mine took, belonging to the dirt and flannel school; he was just half an hour and five minutes. See the difference! There is nothing puts the body into such good order for walking, working, thinking, as a good splash in cold water the first thing in a morning. A man really feels so light, so active and vigorous, that on the score of fitness for exertion only, the washing system is invaluable.

I commenced in March, either eight or nine years ago, and have never missed since, excepting one morning, and during the whole of that day I felt quite uncomfortable. About three days after commencing, I threw away my flannels, although I had worn them by the doctor's orders for five-and-twenty years, extended to the wrists of my hands and the wrists of my feet. I felt a little bare for a week or two, but it soon wore off, and now I could not endure flannel next to the skin. In cold winter weather, when extra covering is required, I have my clothes lined with flannel, but never next to the skin. Too much clothing and too much bedding is an error which we ought to avoid. In this respect poverty has often the advantage over wealth. As to the mode of washing, if you have a plunge-bath convenient you cannot do better than to use it. But as not one in twenty can have this convenience, you may wash either in your own bed-room, or in one adjoining, minding this, to let as little time elapse as possible between getting out of bed and getting the water on to you. We should never bathe when the body is cold, and, though it may astonish some, it is a fact, that the hotter the skin when the cold water is applied, the more striking is the benefit experienced. No one need fear applying cold water, even when in a state of perspiration (provided that the body has not been fatigued or exhausted by previous exercise. When in a state of exhaustion, the reactive powers of the system are at so low an ebb as to render cold baths exceedingly dangerous. The occasional instances of sudden death recorded in the papers from the use of cold water, both externally and internally, have doubtless resulted from this cause). When at the Hydropathic Institution, I have been taken out of the "pack" in a state of perspiration, and plunged suddenly over head in cold water with the best effect. In ordinary cases, then, all you have to do is to fill your wash-basin with water the night before, containing a towel or large sponge, ready for morning. You then junp out of bed, throw off you night-dress, squeeze the towel on your head, and then rub it over each part of the body. This is done in half a minute. Have two coarse towels ready (not little, soft, mangled things,) about 4ft. by 2ft.; with these you give yourself a good rubbing for about three minutes, just as if you were rubbing a horse. You then put on your clothes in a crack, drink a tumbler of water, and go to work, or if you are not of the working class, take a brisk walk. This is worth more than all the doctor's physic in Great Britain. If the mistress complains about your "slopping" the floor, get a square yard of thin oil-cloth, and whip a cord round under the edge, which will keep the water off the floor. Never be afraid of a little water on the bed-room floor or anywhere else; it is one of our best friends. You see, then, that this washing is very little trouble, and as to time, it is so decided a saving, that the poor man, tied to the factory bell can have no more excuse than the rich. When I began washings I was regularly "done up," and did not expect to be of any more use to myself or to the world; this water has been my constant stay ever since. Before this I took, to use a common saying, "loads of medicine." Since, I have not taken a shilling's worth, and it is now so long since I took any, even as an aperient, that I do not remember the time. I never had a strong constitution; I have injured it much with over mental exertion; I have even done so since my health was improved by the use of water, and am now experiencing the consequences; but I find no relief but from the water application; it is my best friend. The use of water at the Hydropathic Establishments is constantly doing wonders; and if people really knew the benefits to be derived from this treatment, they would, as I have done, abandon the drug system to the dogs. I write this from Windermere, where an establishment has recently been opened, with decided results; and if it had not been for the reviving and inspiring effect of the element which gushes so plentifully through the rocks in this enchanting district, most certainly the August number of the *Progressionist* would have been wanting in any articles bearing my signature.

J. LIVESEY.

WASHING IN WINTER.

And now for a few words with those who may incline to discontinue their cold water washing during the winter months.

In the first place, then, it may be observed that there are three benefits to be derived from such ablutions. First, the very important one of a clean skin. Secondly, the bracing and invigorating effects on the system generally. And thirdly, the increased circulation of the blood in the external parts of the body, by rubbing with the towel, etc. Now, it is manifestly most unwise to lose the first-named and most important benefit of a clean skin, simply because we may not be able to have also with it the full measure of benefit, resulting from the increased coldness of the water. If we really cannot bear the water at its winter temperature, let us at any rate have it at its summer or autumn temperature. Have water, at any rate, and at as low temperature as you can bear it. There is no reason whatever why, under ordinary circumstances, every man, woman and child in the British dominions, should not be washed all over with water every morning of their lives. The unpleasant feelings which some experience after washing are entirely owing to not beginning their exercise (either in-door or out) the moment they put their clothes on; leaving shaving and all minor matters of the toilette till the circulation has been well set going by sufficient exercise. If you cannot manage to get a little warm water early in the morning, take up a pitcher-full into you bedroom over night, covering it over to prevent the escape of the steam.

The towel is recommended as being in most repects better than a sponge. By using a large or a small quantity of water you may greatly vary the effects. A large, broad towel, well saturated with water, and thrown over the whole of the back part of the body at once, and pulled together in front, will produce a considerable momentary shock, and is very near aproach to immersion in water.

And now a word at parting, with those who, notwithstanding the daily use of water, taking exercise in the open air, and adopting other means to promote health, are still at times tried with feelings of lowness and depression, which is to some extent the lot of all who are not in robust health.

Avoid, as you would, over-exertion of body or mind. The excessive expenditure of nervous power is a most prolific source of indisposition in various ways. Take especial care also that while doing your best to have all the benefit you can from fresh air by day, you have a good supply of it during the night, by properly ventilating your bed-rooms. In nothing are people more thoughtless and inconsistent than in this; they will take great pains, and often spend much money to have the benefit of fresh air by day, whilst by night they shut themselves up in close rooms, and inhale a poisonous atmosphere for eight hours together.

Religious Tract Society, No. 661: "Waste" (n.d. circa 1860). Complete Text of the tract.

The Religious Tract Society (1799 —) was a non sectarian evangelical organization founded to publish and distribute literature that would lead to spiritual salvation. During the course of the nineteenth century it began to publish, as well, tracts encouraging general moral and social improvement and a broad range of popular literature aimed at the working classes and designed more to instruct than entertain. The annual circulation of tracts alone reached more than ten million in 1850, and more than 22 million by 1875.

While many persons are suffering great distress from want of the needful supports of life, there are also many who wastefully consume the bounties of Providence. There is a common and just saying, "Wilful waste makes woeful want." Want, though not always, is often the consequence of waste. Waste deprives many of the ability to help their fellow-creatures; and the distresses of the poor are often greatly increased by their wasteful habits.

The object of this tract is to call attention to the duty of care, and the sin of waste; more particularly in reference to the daily use of common provisions.

By waste, is meant needless expense, or useless consumption. Much property is wasted upon luxury and display. Some persons gratify every whim, without regard to cost, and without considering whether it will do them any real good; perhaps, even priding themselves on having costly dainties which others cannot afford, and indulging freely in what they like, though they know it does them harm. This folly is not so common as it was formerly. Many rich people keep a moderate table, and take only simple food, as a matter of preference as well as of conscience; even when they have company they do not think it necessary to prove their friendship by a costly entertainment.

But there is still room for improvement. Some housekeepers might, without any want of comfort or charge of meanness, adopt a plainer mode of daily living; and when preparing for the company of friends, spare one or two of the most costly dishes, at no small saving of time and expense, while real enjoyment would not be lessened.

During the pressure of general distress, some persons have, from a sense of duty, given up certain articles of luxury, and devoted the saving to the relief of the suffering poor. The blessing of many who were ready to perish has come upon them, and their own health and enjoyment have been improved rather than injured by the exercise of self-denial. The first chapter of the book of Daniel affords a fine example of the advantages of self-control in matters of appetite, as promoting true greatness of character. It may also suggest that one important way of extending the ability to do good is by adopting personal habits of moderation. But in costly self-indulgence there is great waste.

That is especially wasted which is *consumed in sin*. Oh, what a wasteful man is the drunkard! Such a one will frequently, in one evening, spend as much on intoxicating liquors as would supply his whole family with bread for a day, or perhaps for a week; and if they have no other source of supply to depend on than his earnings, to what wretchedness are they exposed by his wicked self-indulgence! Charitable persons who willingly deny themselves lawful indulgences that they may relieve the distresses of the poor, often meet with cases of extreme distress in families, occasioned by this very sort of misconduct; and it is next to impossible to afford such families any effectual relief, unless the guilty cause of the suffering be turned from the error of his way. Apart from the positive sinfulness of intemperance, as a mere matter of waste its effects are frightful. Look into yonder house; the walls are nearly bare, there is scarcely any furniture, little or no fire: there are perhaps a number of children, scantily fed and almost destitute of clothing; and the mother, a living picture of want and woe. Time was when that dwelling was well furnished with articles for use and convenience; and the appearance of the inhabitants was that of health, comfort, and content. What has wrought this change? the husband and father, who was then sober, has become a drunkard. He earns less than he did formerly; what he earns is wasted in base intoxication; and his family are barely kept from stavation by parting with one after another of the little comforts and decencies by which they were formerly surrounded.

Mark that other dwelling. A few years since it presented a desolate and poverty-stricken appearance. But now how different!

Observe the neat furniture, the comfortable bedding, the sufficient provision of food, the decent clothing of the family. What has caused this change for the better? How are these people so enriched? The man, who was intemperate, has abandoned his vicious habits. He is sober and industrious; and the money that used to be squandered in wilful waste, is now prudently applied to its proper uses, and has furnished the family with these various comforts. Never let it be forgotten, then that imtemperance is wasteful as well as wicked; and that, according to the homely saying, "It takes more to maintain one vice than to feed two children." "The drunkard and the glutton shall come to poverty." Prov. xxiii. 21.

That is wasted which is *used in excess*. Many persons regularly eat and drink a little more than nature requires; and indulge still a little further if they have something before them that is nice and tempting. What is thus taken affords no nourishment — does no good whatsoever; but hurts the constitution, and makes way for disease. At all events, it is taken in waste.

That is wasted which is suffered to perish through *neglect*. It is grievous to think how much waste of this kind there is in some families. If the mistress does not "look well to the ways of her household," or if, in case of her illness or absence, the management of affairs should be left to an untrusty or careless servant, in her kitchen and pantry might be seen a large fire burning in waste; two or three candles where one would serve, and very likely flaring away by being placed within the draught of a door; meat spoiled for want of being hung up, or put in salt as soon as brought into the house; broth, gravy, and milk left to become sour; pieces of bread, pudding, and vegetables mouldy; meat dressed two or three days ago going to decay, while what has been dressed since, has been freely consumed. Now, all these provisions have cost money, and ought to have been taken care of, and made use of, while they were good; perhaps they ought to have made a meal, or part of a meal, for the family, either cold or re-warmed. If not, they ought to have been given to some poor neighbour. Now they are spoiled and worthless, and are injuring other things by being suffered to remain near them; but they have not come to this state without sinful waste, for which somebody is answerable. To say that a shilling or two is daily wasted in this manner in many families, would be far below the mark.

There is much wasted by being actually thrown away. Liquor in which meat has been boiled; bones from which the meat has been used; bits of bread; cold vegetables; grotts or barley from which gruel has been made: these and many other things are, in some families, habitually thrown away as worthless; while, in other families, they are properly turned to account, and made the best of either for home consumption or for charitable purposes. Every young servant, and young mistress too, should make it a point never to throw away anything without having considered whether it might not be put to some use; an apt notion of turning little things to best account, surprisingly lessens the expenses, and increases the comforts of families.

Instances might be multiplied, to show how property to a large amount, though made up from a number of trifles, is in some families consumed or destroyed in sinful waste; the same amount in other families being carefully preserved, and properly employed. But if those already mentioned should draw the reader's attention to the subject, personal observation will furnish many proofs of the evils of profusion and waste, and the importance of prudence and economy.

There are some classes on whom the subject especially presses:—

1. Female heads of families. Let not any one whose specific charge is to guide the house, deem any duty that comes within that province, too mean or too trivial to deserve her attention. The character of other members of her household will, in a great degree, be formed by her example. Let her instructions and injunctions and habits all tell in favour of order, moderation, and economy; and those around her can scarcely fail to be convinced that these are even favourable to real enjoyment.

Let her make it a part of her daily business, to look round and direct the purchases and consumption of domestic provisions; let her train her servants to habits of frugality and care; and let her firmly discountenance waste in any form. While she desires to act uprightly and kindly, she need not be afraid of the charge of meanness, which servants whose conduct will not bear looking into may be disposed to cast on her. She will not long lie under so undeserved a charge. Many occasions will arise to prove that liberality and economy are not at variance with each other; that on proper occasions, the frugal, and they only, can afford to be really generous.

Servants who are conscientiously frugal, deserve encouragement; and the liberality of a judicious mistress will be well bestowed in giving it. A careful servant will save her employers many pounds in the course of a year, which might be almost imperceptibly wasted by one of an opposite character. To reward such care tends to encourage and confirm the deserving individual, and to produce a good impression on others.

The influence of a female head of a family materially affects the formaion of character in her children. Many children are injured in their health, and yet more in their character, by false indulgence. Luxurious tastes and wasteful habits are formed in the nursery, and many seeming trifles go to form them. Children should not be encouraged in daintiness or greediness by allowing them to have everything they fancy, or to eat more than is proper for them, of what they esteem a delicacy; or to leave one thing for the sake of getting something they like better; or to waste their food in any way. In all these, and many such matters, a judicious mother will keep in view, not merely avoiding unnecessary present expense, but also the more important object of training her children to habits of propriety and moderation.

The care exercised by the good mother in training her children to habits of frugality, will not be limited to matters of appetite. She will teach them care in everything they have to do with; for instance, in regard to their clothes, to avoid making them unnecessarily dirty, by spilling grease, or walking through mud, or wantonly tearing and destroying them by mischievous tricks. Without being at all kept uncomfortably restrained, children may, and ought to be, trained to habits of care of clothes, furniture, books, playthings, and pocket-money. They should be taught to know the value of things, and the uses to which they may be applied. It should be impressed upon them that what is done in one form, may be useful in another; that what is no longer wanted by them may be acceptable to others; and that nothing must on any account be wasted. Children may thus be taught at a very early age; and so long as utility and benevolence are kept in view, this training will not promote a spirit of selfish hoarding.

The wife of a working man has especial reason for training her children to habits of frugality and care. Most likely it is necessary to their living in comfort; and it will tell in their favour, if, at a future time, they should go into service, as well as be highly valuable to them when they come altogether to depend on their own earnings and their own management. And yet, some poor women sadly fail in this branch of duty to their children, both indulging them in luxuries even when they are ill provided with necessaries, and in suffering them to waste and destroy what ought to be made use of.

2. Domestic servants, and all who have the property of others passing through their hands in the form of daily provisions, are called upon to exercise moderation and care, as a matter of fidelity to their employers. A wasteful servant is dishonest, because, though the agreement between master and servant engages for wages and food, it makes no provision for extravagance and waste. Some servants are more than twice the expense of others: not that they actually eat and drink more but they hanker after costly dainties, they are always getting some little nicety for themselves; and whatever they can get at they consume lavishly, without regard to the intentions or interests of their employers. This is a great failure in the duty of doing as they would be done by, and is likely — indeed certain — to be as injurious to the person who practises it, as the the person whose property is thus squandered. If the misconduct be detected, the servant probably loses her place and her character; or, if not so, forms habits that, sooner or later, lead to poverty and want, perhaps to a course of sin.

Religious servants are especially called upon to maintain and manifest "all good fidelity, that they may adorn the doctrine of God their Savious in all things," Tit. ii. 10. Remember, Christian servants, the honour of Christ is concerned in the propriety of your conduct in little things. Be not satisfied with merely abstaining from stealing, lying, and drunkenness; but be, in everything, conscientious and trustworthy. Act upon principle, and avoid the very appearance of evil. Think of the claims of religion, as extending to your smallest actions, even to the burning of a candle or a shovel of coals, the cutting of a piece of meat, or the using a piece of soap or sugar. If you act differently when out of sight of your employers from the way in which you would do when in their presence, or differently from what you could reasonably wish them act towards you, if you were in their place, you do not live up to your profession; you do injury by your example; and you probably harden some who wish to excuse themselves in their neglect of religion.

In conclusion: Every person should avoid waste, because waste is a sin against God. Nothing was made to be wasted.It is everyone's duty to employ whatever the providence of God puts within his power, in such a way as will bear looking back upon and giving account of.

Avoid waste if you are your own provider, because it cripples the means of doing good.

Avoid waste if you are dependent on others, because it is a robbery on those who provide for you.

If you have plenty at command, avoid waste, because it is possible you may not always have plenty; — you and yours may come to want; wasteful habits naturally lead to poverty; they make want the harder if it comes, and add to it the sorrow of bitter reflections.

The Lord Jesus Christ, when by his Divine power he had afforded a plentiful repast to many thousand persons, directed his disciples to "gather up the fragments that remained, that nothing might be lost," John vi. 12. Thus he put an honour on frugality as connected with liberality, and taught his followers to practise it as a Christian duty.

Should this tract be read by some frugal, careful person, who is proud of being free from the faults here pointed out, let such a person take care to avoid the opposite extreme — a selfish, grudging disposition; a love or hoarding for its own sake. This is not less criminal than wilful squandering. All prudent care of property should be directed to a good and benevolent end. Ask not only, How can I save? but, What good can I do with it? "If the clouds be full of rain, they empty themselves upon the earth," Eccles. xi. 3. The water is treasured up in them on purpose that they may shed plenty. Hence we are taught that God bestows gifts on men not merely for their own sakes, but that they may do good; nor can their possessions profit them if they do not benefit others.

Let the mere selfish hoarder tremble at this solemn appeal, "Whoso hath this world's good, and seeth his brother have need, and shutteth up his bowels of compassion from him, how dwelleth the love of God in him?' " 1 John iii. 17.

But suppose you are both careful and liberal, take heed that you be not worldly-minded, content with earning and saving, and enjoying and imparting the good things of this world as if you were to live here always, and unconcerned about a portion above the skies. Remember the world passeth away; even its lawful possessions, and its virtuous pleasures will not long endure. Time, with you, will soon be no longer; and what will be your portion in eternity? Rest not satisfied without having your heart and your treasure in heaven.

However proper your conduct and feelings may be in the matters above referred to, or in any others, do not imagine that they will do to rely on for salvation. These things are good and profitable to men; good for those who practise them; and laying claim to the gratitude and respect of others. But they cannot atone for sin; they cannot afford a plea to present before God; they cannot give a right to heaven. No; these blessings can be attained by the most exemplary and amiable of the human race, only on the same ground as they are free to the chief of sinners, by "the kindness and love of God our Saviour towards man," manifested in the atonement of the Lord Jesus, and received by faith in him. "Not by works of righteousness which we have done, but according to his mercy he saved us, by the washing of regeneration, and renewing of the Holy Ghost; which he shed on us abundantly through Jesus Christ our Saviour; that being justified by his grace, we should be made heirs according to the hope of eternal life," Titus iii. 4—7.

John Ploughman's Talk (1869) and *John Ploughman's Pictures* (1880), by C.H. Spurgeon. Selections.

Charles Haddon Spurgeon (1834-1892), was a Baptist minister in London and the most popular preacher in England. His published sermons and his works on personal improvement, *John Ploughman's Talk* (1869) and *John Ploughman's Pictures* (1880) achieved wide circulation.

HOME.

THAT word *home* always sounds like poetry to me. It rings like a peal of bells at a wedding, only more soft and sweet, and it chimes deeper into the ears of my heart. It does not matter whether it means thatched cottage or manor house, home is home, be it ever so homely, and there's no place on earth like it. Green grow the houseleek on the roof for ever, and let the moss flourish on the thatch. Sweetly the sparrows chirrup and the swallows twitter around the chosen spot which is my joy and rest. Every bird loves its own nest; the owls think the old ruins the fairest spot under the moon, and the fox is of the opinion that his hole in the hill is remarkably cosy. When my master's nag knows that his head is towards home he wants no whip, but thinks it best to put on all steam; and I am always of the same mind, for the way home, to me, is the best bit of road in the country. I like to see the smoke out of my own chimney better than the fire on another man's hearth; there's something so beautiful in the way in which it curls up among the trees. Cold potatoes on my own table taste better than roast meat at my neighbour's, and the honeysuckle at my own door is the sweetest I ever smell. When you are out, friends do their best, but still it is not home. "Make yourself at home," they say, because everybody knows that to feel at home is to feel at ease.

> "East and west.
> Home is best."

Why, at home you are at home, and what more do you want? Nobody grudges you, whatever your appetite may be; and you don't get put into a damp bed. Safe in his own castle, like a king in his palace, a man feels himself somebody, and is not afraid of being thought proud for thinking so. Every cock may crow on his own dunghill; and a dog is a lion when he is at home. A sweep is master inside his own door.

No need to guard every word because some enemy is on the watch, no keeping the heart under lock and key; but as soon as the door is shut, it is liberty hall, and none to peep and pry. There is a glorious view from the top of Leith Hill, in our dear old Surrey, and Hindhead and Martha's Chapel, and Boxhill, are not to be sneezed at, but I could show you something which to my mind beats them all to nothing for real beauty: I mean John Ploughman's cottage, with the kettle boiling on the hob, singing like an unfallen black angel, while the cat is lying asleep in front of the fire, and the wife in her chair mending stockings, and the children cutting about the room, as full of fun as young lambs. It is a singular fact, and perhaps some of you will doubt it, but that is your unbelieving nature, our little ones are real beauties, always a pound or two plumper than others of their age, and yet it don't tire you half so much to nurse them as it does other people's babies. Why, bless you, my wife would knock up in half the time, if her neighbour had asked her to see to a strange youngster, but her own children don't seem to tire her at all; now my belief is that it all comes of their having been born at home. Just so is it with everything else: our lane is the most beautiful for twenty miles round, because our home is in it; and my garden is a perfect paradise, for no other particular than this very good one, that it belongs to the old house at home.

I cannot make out why so many working men spend their evenings at the public house, when their own firesides would be so much better and cheaper too. There they sit, hour after hour, boozing and talking nonsense, and forgetting the dear good souls at home who are half starved and weary with waiting for them. Their money goes into the publican's till when it ought to make their wives and children comfortable; as for the beer they get, it is just so much fools' milk to drown their wits in. Such fellows ought to be horsewhipped, and those who encourage them and live on their spendings deserve to feel the butt end of the whip. Those beershops are the curse of this country — no good ever can come of them, and the evil they do no tongue can tell; the publics were bad enough, but the beershops are a pest; I wish the man who made the law to open them had to keep all the families that they have brought to ruin. Beershops are the enemies of the home, and therefore the sooner their licences are taken away the better: poor men don't need such places, nor rich men either, they are all worse and no better, like Tom Norton's wife. Anything that hurts the home is a curse, and ought to be hunted down as gamekeepers do the vermin in the copses.

Husbands should try to make home happy and holy. It is an ill bird that fouls its own nest, a bad man who makes his home wretched. Our house ought to be a little church, with holiness to the Lord over the door, but it ought never to be a prison where there is plenty of rule and order, but little love and no pleasure. Married life is not all sugar, but grace in the heart will keep away most of the sours. Godliness and love can make a man like a bird in a hedge, sing among thorns and briers, and set others a singing too. It should be the husband's pleasure to please his wife, and the wife's care to care for her husband. He is kind to himself who is kind to his wife. I am afraid some men live by the rule of self, and when that is the case home happiness is a mere sham. When husbands and wives are well yoked, how light their load becomes! It is not every couple that is a pair, and the more's the pity. In a true home all the strife is which can do the most to make the family happy. A home should be a Bethel, not a Babel. The husband should be the houseband, binding all together like a cornerstone, but not crushing everything like a mill-stone. Unkind and domineeering husbands ought not to pretend to be Christians, for they act clean contrary to Christ's commands. Yet a home must be well ordered, or it will become a Bedlam, and be a scandal to the parish. If the father drops the reins, the family coach will soon be in the ditch. A wise mixture of love and firmness will do it; but neither harshness nor softness alone will keep home in happy order. Home is no home where the children are not in obedience, it is rather a pain than a pleasure to be in it. Happy is he who is happy in his children, and happy are the children who are happy in their father. All fathers are not wise. Some are like Eli, and spoil their children. Not to cross our children is the way to make a cross of them. Those who never give their children the rod, must not wonder if their childen become a rod to them. Solomon says, "Correct thy son, and he shall give thee rest; yea, he shall give delight to thy soul." I am not clear that anybody wiser than Solomon lives in our time, though some think they are. Young colts must be broken in or they will make wild horses. Some fathers are all fire and fury, filled with passion at the smallest fault: this is worse than the other, and makes home a little hell instead of a heaven. No wind makes the miller idle, but too much upsets the mill altogether. Men who strike in their anger generally miss their mark. When God helps us to hold the reins firmly, but not to hurt the horse's mouths, all goes well. When home is ruled according to God's word, angels might be asked to stay a night with us, and they would not find themselves out of their element.

Wives should feel that home is their place and their kingdom, the happiness of which depends mostly upon them. She is a wicked wife who drives her husband away by her long tongue. A man said to his wife the other day, "Double up your whip;" he meant, keep your tongue quiet: it is a wretched living with such a whip always lashing you. When God gave to men ten measures of speech, they say the women ran away with nine, and in some cases I am afraid the saying is true. A dirty, slatternly, gossiping wife is enough to drive her husband mad; and if he goes to the public house of an evening, she is the cause of it. It is doleful living where the wife, instead of reverencing her husband, is always wrangling and railing at him. It must be a good thing when such women are hoarse, and it is a pity that they have not as many blisters in their tongues as they have teeth in their jaws. God save us all from wives who are angels in the street, saints in the church, and devils at home. I have never tasted of such bitter herbs, but I pity from my very heart those who have this diet every day of their lives.

Show me a loving husband, a worthy wife, and good children, and no pair of horses that ever flew along the road could take me in a year where I saw a more pleasing sight. Home is the grandest of all institutions. Talk about parliament, give me a quiet little parlour. Boast about voting and the reform bill if you like, but I go in for weeding the little garden, and teaching the children their hymns. Franchise may be a very fine thing, but I should a good deal sooner get the freehold of my cottage, if I could find the money to buy it. Magna Charta I don't know much about, but if it means a quiet home for everybody, three cheers for it.

I wish our governors would not break up so many poor men's homes by that abominably heartless poor law. It is far more fit for

a set of Red Indians than Englishmen. A Hampshire carter told me
the other day that his wife and children were all in the union, and
his home broken up, because of the cruel working of the poor law.
He had eight little ones and his wife to keep on nine shillings a week,
with rent to pay out of it; on this he could not keep body and soul
together; now, if the parish had allowed him a mere trifle, a loaf or
two and a couple of shillings a week, he would have jogged on, but
no, not a penny out of the house; they might all die of starvation unless
they would all go into the workhouse. So, with many bitter tears and
heartaches, the poor soul had to sell his few little bits of furniture,
and he is now a houseless man, and yet he is a good hard-working
fellow, and served one master for nearly twenty years. Such things
are very common, but they ought not to be. Why cannot the really
deserving poor have a little help given them? Why must they be forced
into the union house? Home is the pillar of the British Empire, and
ought not to be knocked to pieces by these unchristian laws. I wish
I was an orator and could talk politics, I would not care a rush for
Whigs or Tories, but I would stand up like a lion for the poor man's
home, which, let me tell the lords and commons, is as dear to him
as their great palaces are to them, and sometimes dearer.

If I had no home the world would be a big prison to me. England
for me a country, Surrey for a county, and for a village give me
————— no, I shan't tell you, or you will be hunting John Ploughman
up. Many of my friends have emigrated, and are breaking up fresh
soil in Australia and America. Though their stone has rolled, I hope
they may gather moss, for when they were at home they were like
the sitting hen, which gets no barley. Really these hard times make
a man think of his wings, but I am tied by the leg to my own home,
and, please God, I hope to live and die among my own people. they
may do things better in France and Germany, but old England for
me, after all.

STICK TO IT AND DO IT.

SET a stout heart to a stiff hill, and the waggon will get to the
top of it. There's nothing so hard but a harder thing will get
through it; a strong job can be managed by a strong resolution. Have
at it and have it. Stick to it and succeed. Till a thing is done men
wonder that you think it can be done, and when you have done it they

wonder it was never done before.

In my picture the waggon is drawn by two horses; but I would have every man who wants to make his way in life pull as if all depended on himself. Very little is done right when it is left to other people. The more hands to do the work the less there is done. One man will carry two pails of water for himself; two men will only carry one pail between them, and three will come home with never a drop at all. A child with several mothers will die before it runs alone. Know your business and give you mind to it, and you will find a buttered loaf where a sluggard loses his last crust.

In these times it's no use being a farmer if you don't mean work. The days are gone by for gentlemen to make a fortune off a farm by going out and shooting half their time. If foreign wheats keep on coming in, farmers will soon learn that —

> "He who by the plough would thrive,
> Himself must either hold or drive."

Going to Australia is of no use to a man if he carries a set of lazy bones with him. There's a living to be got in England at almost any trade if a fellow will give his mind to it. A man who works hard and has his health is a great deal happier than my lord Tom Noddy, who does nothing and is always ailing. Do you know the old song of "The Nobleman's generous kindness"? You should hear our Will sing it. I recollect some of the verses. The first one gives a picture of the hard-working labourer with a large family —

> "Thus careful and constant, each morning he went,
> Unto his day labour with joy and content;
> So jocular and jolly he'd whistle and sing,
> As blithe and as brisk as the birds in the spring."

The other lines are the ploughman's own story of how he spent his life, and I wish that all countrymen could say the same.

> "I reap and I mow, I harrow and I sow,
> Sometimes a hedging and ditching I go;
> No work comes amiss, for I thrash and plough,
> Thus my bread I do earn by the sweat of my brow.

> "My wife she is willing to pull in a yoke,
> We live like two lambs, nor each other provoke;
> We both of us strive, like the labouring ant,
> And do our endeavours to keep us from want.

"And when I come home from my labour at night,
To my wife and my children in whom I delight,
I see them come round me with prattling noise.
Now these are the riches a poor man enjoys.

"Though I am as weary as weary may be,
The youngest I commonly dance on my knee;
I find in content a continual feast,
And never repine at my lot in the least."

So, you see, the poor labourer may work hard and be happy all the same; and surely those who are in higher stations may do the like if they like.

He is a sorry dog who wants game and will not hunt for it: let us never lie down in idle despair, but follow on till we succeed.

Rome was not built in a day, nor much else, unless it be a dog-kennel. Things which cost no pains are slender gains. Where there has been little sweat there will be little sweet. Jonah's gourd came up in a night, but then it perished in a night. Light come, light go: that which flies in at one window will be likely to fly out at another. It's a very lean hare that hounds catch without running for it, and a sheep that is no trouble to shear has very little wool. For this reason a man who cannot push on against wind and weather stands a poor chance in this world.

Perseverance is the main thing in life. To hold on, and hold out to the end, is the chief matter. If the race could be won by a spurt, thousands would wear the blue ribbon; but they are short-winded, and pull up after the first gallop. They begin with flying, and end in crawling backwards. When it comes to collar work, many horses turn to jibbing. If the apples do not fall at the first shake of the tree your hasty folks are too lazy to fetch a ladder, and in too much of a hurry to wait till the fruit is ripe enough to fall of itself. The hasty man is as hot as fire at the outset, and a cold as ice at the end. He is like the Irishman's saucepan, which had many good points about it, but it had no bottom. He who cannot bear the burden and heat of the day is not worth his salt, much less his potatoes.

Before you begin a thing, make sure it is the right thing to do: ask Mr. Conscience about it. Do not try to do what is impossible: ask Common Sense. It is of no use to blow against a hurricane, or to fish for whales in a washing tub. Better give up a foolish plan than go on and burn your fingers with it: better bend your neck that knock your forehead. But when you have once made up your mind to go a certain road, don't let every molehill turn you out of the path. One stroke fells not an oak. Chop away, axe, you'll down with the tree at last! A bit of iron does not soften the moment you put it in the fire. Blow, smith! Put on more coals! Get it red hot and hit hard with the hammer, and you will make a ploughshare yet. Steady does it. Hold on and you have it. Brag is a fine fellow at crying "Tally-ho!" but Perseverance brings home the brush.

We ought not to be put out of heart by difficulties: they are sent on purpose to try the stuff we are made of; and depend on it they do us a world of good. There's a sound reason why there are bones in our meat and stones in our land. A world where everything was easy would be a nursery for babies, but not at all a fit place for men. Celery is not sweet till it has felt a frost, and men don't come to their perfection till disappointment has dropped a half-hundred weight or two on their toes. Who would know good horses if there were no heavy loads? If the clay was not stiff, my old Dapper and Violet would be thought no more of than Tomkins' donkey. Besides, to work hard for success makes us fit to bear it: we enjoy the bacon all the more because we have got an appetite by earning it. When prosperity pounces on a man like an eagle, it often throws him down. If we overtake the cart, it is a fine thing to get up and ride; but when it comes behind us at a tearing rate, it is very apt to knock us down and run over us, and when we are lifted into it we find our leg is broken, or our arm is out of joint, and we cannot enjoy the ride. Work is always healthier for us than idleness; it is always better to wear out shoes than sheets. I sometimes think, when I put on my considering cap, that success in life is something like getting married: there's a very great deal of pleasure in the courting, and it is not a bad thing when it is a moderate time on the road. Therefore, young man, learn to wait, and work on. Don't throw away your rod, the fish will bite some time or other. The cat watches long at the hole, but catches the mouse at last. The spider mends her borken web, and the flies are taken before long. Stick to your calling, plod on, and be content; for, make sure, if you can *undergo* you shall *overcome*.

> If bad be your prospects, don't sit still and cry,
> But jump up, and say to yourself, "I WILL TRY."

Miracles will never cease! My neighbour, Simon Gripper, was taken generous about three months ago. The story is well worth telling. He saw a poor blind man, led by a little girl, playing on a fiddle. His heart was touched, for a wonder. He said to me, "Ploughman, lend me a penny, there's a good fellow.' I fumbled in my pocket, and found two halfpence, and handed them to him. More fool I, for he will never pay me again. He gave the blind fiddler one of those halfpence, and kept the other, and I have not seen either Gripper or my penny since, nor shall I get the money back till the gate-post outside my garden grows Ribstone pippins. There's generosity for you! The old saying which is put at the top of this bit of my talk brought him into my mind, for he *sticks to it* most certainly: he lives as badly as a church mouse, and works as hard as if he was paid by the piece, and had twenty children to keep; but I would no more hold him up for an example than I would show a toad as a specimen of a pretty bird. While I talk to you young people about getting on, I don't want you to think that hoarding up money is real success; nor do I wish you to rise an inch above an honest ploughman's lot, if it cannot be done without being mean or wicked. The workhouse, prison as it is, is a world better than a mansion built by roguery and greed. If you cannot get on honestly, be satisfied not to get on. The blessing of God is riches enough for a wise man, and all the world is not enough for a fool. Old Gripper's notion of how to prosper has, I dare say, a good deal of truth in it, and the more's the pity. The Lord deliver us from such a prospering, I say. That old sinner has often hummed these lines into my ears when we have got into an argument, and very pretty lines they are *not*, certainly:—

> "To win the prize in the world's great race
> A man should have a brazen face;
> An iron arm to give a stroke,
> And a heart as sturdy as an oak;
> Eyes like a cat, good in the dark,
> And teeth as piercing as a shark;
> Ears to hear the gentlest sound,
> Like moles that burrow in the ground;
> A mouth as close as patent locks,
> And stomach stronger than an ox;
> His tongue should be a razor-blade,
> His conscience india-rubber made;
> His blood as cold as polar ice,
> His hand as grasping as a vice.

His shoulders should be adequate
To bear a couple thousand weight;
His legs, like pillars, firm and strong,
To move the great machine along;
With supple knees to cringe and crawl,
And cloven feet placed under all."

It amounts to this: to be a devil in order to be happy. Sell yourself to the old dragon, and he will give you the world and the glory thereof. But remember the question of the Old Book, "What shall it profit a man, if he gain the whole world, and lose his own soul?" There is another road to success besides this crooked, dirty, cut-throat lane. It is the King's highway, of which the same Book says: "Seek ye first the kingdom of God, and his righteousness; and all these things shall be added unto you." John Ploughman prays that all his readers may choose this way, and keep to it; yet even in that way we must use dilligence, "for the kingdom of heaven suffereth violence, and the violent take it by force."

Chapter IX

The Impact of Science

Introduction

That science and religion were at war in the Victorian period is a widely accepted exaggeration that tends to cloud the nature of their complex relationship. But the idea that science and religion were enemies was widely believed during the second half of the nineteenth century, and that popular belief had some basis in fact. Militant Secularists who were at war with organized religion for social reasons attempted to recruit science as an ally. More importantly, Victorian evangelicalism, the most popular religious mode of the period, was anti-intellectual and committed to the rigid belief that every word in the Bible was inspired by God and true in a plain sense. Evangelicals, quite rightly, regarded science as an enemy.

From the end of the Napoleonic Wars until Darwin published *On The Origin of Species* (1859), geology was the queen of the sciences. During this time geology came into conflict with the Bible, at least with the Bible interpreted literally. Geologists, of whom a surprising proportion in England were clergymen, demonstrated that the world could not have been created in six days, and that Archbishop Ussher's seventeenth century calculation that creation took place in 4004 B.C. was wildly inaccurate, and that the flood probably did not take place. Those views created no sensation until they were popularized in Robert Chamber's journalistic *Vestiges of Creation* (1844).

With the publication of Darwin's *On The Origin of Species*, biology took over the position formerly held by geology, and the sense of warfare between science and religion grew sharper. Darwin's theory of evolution through natural selection seemed impossible to reconcile with the Biblical account of creation, and the implication that man might not be a direct creation of God shocked many people.

At the same time that geology and biology were challenging the Biblical version of creation, there were emerging, particularly in Germany, scientific historical methods and principles of literary criticism that might be applied to the Bible and the period in which it was written. *The Life of Jesus,* published in German by David Strauss in 1835 and translated by George Eliot in 1846, created some stir among intellectuals, but the publication of *Essays and Reviews* (1860) by seven English Churchmen brought about public uproar. The essayists advocated subjecting the Bible to scholarly criticism like any other book, they explained away the miracles described in the Bible, and they publicized the science of Biblical criticism that had been developed in Germany. Their approach to the Bible was decidedly antagonistic to the simplistic literalism of the evengelicals, but among the general public Biblical criticism, like science, seemed a threat to Christianity, not just evengelicalism.

More intellectual Churchmen and Dissenters, untrammelled by the inflexible obscurantism of the evangelicals, were able to come to terms surprisingly quickly with developments in physical science and Biblical criticism. These men, who included most of the leading figures in both the Church and Nonconformity by the late 1880s, accepted geological time and the theory of evolution as part of the coventional wisdom of their time, and some of them were eminent Biblical critics. For them, the idea that science and religion were at war had little meaning.

By the 1880s rigid evangelicalism was finished as the dominant religious mode in England. No longer did it attract men and women sensitive to the strongest intellectual currents of their time. At the same time the Secularists, whose tradition was rooted in the French Revolution and the anti-clericalism of English working class radicalism, were coming to seem old fashioned as well.

Guide To Further Reading

Serious reading or research in the area of religion and science must now begin with the splendid bibliography edited by Sydney Eisen and Bernard V. Lightman, *Victorian Science and Religion: A Bibliography with Emphasis on Evolution, Belief, and Unbelief, Comprised of Works Published from C. 1900-1975* (1984).

The best and most comprehensive general treatment of Victorian religious thought is B.M.G. Reardon, *From Coleridge to Gore: A Century of Religious Thought in England* (1971). Reardon deals with science and Biblical criticism as they fit into the shifting framework of Victorian theology. Owen Chadwick discusses the challenge of science more directly, and at considerable length, in *The Victorian Church* (1966; 1970), Volume I, chapter 8, and the first three chapters of Volume II. Chadwick emphasizes the importance of Biblical criticism in shaking the foundations of mid-Victorian orthodoxy. Willis B. Glover traces the crumbling of narrow evangelicalism among scholarly Dissenters in *Evangelical Nonconformity and Higher Criticism in the Nineteenth Century* (1954). Margaret Anne Crowther denounces the harsh mid-century treatment of liberal Anglicans in *Church Embattled: Religious Controversy in Mid-Victorian England* (1970).

Charles C. Gillespie, *Genesis and Geology: A Study in the Relations of Scientific Thought, Natural Theology and Social Opinion in Great Britain 1790-1850* (1951) is now considered a classic work. Gertrude Himmelfarb, *Darwin and the Darwinian Revolution* (1959) cannot be considered authoritative on the scientific significance of Darwin's work, but does an excellent job of assessing Darwin's impact on the intellectual and religious world of the mid nineteenth century. *Darwin and the General Reader* (1958), by Alvar Ellegard systematically surveys the reception of Darwin's theory of evolution in the popular periodical press during the decade following the publication of *On the Origin of Species*. Robert Young explores the complex web of tensions between religion and science in "The Impact of Darwin on Conventional Thought", in *The Victorian Crisis of Faith* (1970), edited by Anthony Symondson.

In "Natural Theology, *Victorian Periodicals* and the Fragmentation of a Common Context," in Colin Chant and John Fauvel, eds., *Darwin to Einstein : Historical Studies on Science and Belief* (1980), Robert Young explores the fate of natural theology in the face of the Darwinian challenge. Frank Turner makes a stimulating attempt to explore why science and religion seemed at war in *Between Science and Religion* (1974). In "The Victorian Conflict Between Science and Religion: A Professional Dimension,"

Isis (1978), Frank Turner develops a powerful case for understanding that conflict, at least in part, as a product of professional ambition and frustration. The context for the professional rise of science is established in T.W. Heyck, *The Transformation of Intellectual Life in Victorian England* (1982). Sheridan Gilley and Ann Loades emphasize conflict in "Thomas Henry Huxley: The War Between Science and Religion," *Journal of Religion* (1981). On Huxley, see also James Paradis, *T.H. Huxley* (1978).

The strongest statement for the view that the military metaphor is inappropriate, that the relation between science and religion in late Victorian England should not be viewed as warfare, is James R. Moore, *The Post Darwinian Controversies: A Study of the Protestant Struggle to Come to Terms with Darwin in Great Britain and America, 1870-1900* (1979).

The Secularist movement and its leaders is thoroughly treated by Edward Royle in his excellent study, *Victorian Infidels 1791-1866* (1974) and in *Radicals, Socialists and Secularists* (1980). F.B. Smith concentrates on the movement at mid-century in his chapter, "The Atheist Mission, 1840-1890", in *Ideas and Institutions of Victorian Britain* (1967), edited by Robert Robson. Susan Budd argues that social discontent lay at the base of working-class unbelief in *Varieties of Unbelief: Atheists and Agnostics in English Society, 1850-1960* (1977). Walter Arnstein in his thoroughly researched work on *The Bradlaugh Case: A Study in Late Victorian Opinion and Politics* (1965), describes the public estimation of atheism in the 1880's.

Sydney Eisen explores a different tradition of secularism, more intellectual and middle class, in "Huxley and the Positivists", *Victorian Studies* (1964); "Frederick Harrison and the Religion of Humanity", *South Atlantic Quarterly* (1967); and "Herbert Spencer and the Spectre of Comte", *Journal of British Studies* (1967).

Natural Theology (1802), by William Paley. Selection.

William Paley (1743-1805), Anglican priest and Archdeacon of Carlisle, was a masterful writer of textbooks on moral philosophy and natural theology. His *Principles of Morals and Political Philosophy* (1785), a lucid statement of Christian utilitarianism, was for many years required reading for undergraduates at Cambridge, Paley's university. Cambridge also adopted as a textbook his most widely acclaimed work, *A View of the Evidences of Christianity* (1794), in which Paley set out in clear prose and well ordered form the principal arguments that defenders of orthodoxy had developed against the sceptical rationalism of the deists. Paley's *Natural Theology* (1802), his last major work, was enormously influential throughout the English-speaking world until Darwin published *On the Origin of Species* in 1859. In *Natural Theology* Paley presented in its fullest and most carefully systematic form, the argument that the laws of nature implied design by an intelligent, beneficent Creator. Within Paley's natural theology there could be no conflict between science and religion, no opposition between nature and God. Each new scientific discovery illustrated and confirmed the rational orderliness of nature, and therefore each new scientific discovery constituted evidence for the Divine Intelligence that had created the world.

Chapter One
State of the Argument

In crossing a heath, suppose I pitched my foot against a *stone* and were asked how the stone came to be there, I might possibly answer that for anything I know to the contrary it had lain there forever; nor would it, perhaps, be very easy to show the absurdity of this answer. But suppose I had found a *watch* upon the ground, and it should be inquired how the watch happened to be in that place, I should hardly think of the answer which I had before given, that for anything I knew the watch might have always been there. Yet why should not this answer serve for the watch as well as for the stone; why is it not as admissible in the second case as in the first? For this reason, and for no other, namely, that when we come to inspect the watch, we perceive — what we could not discover in the stone — that its several parts are framed and put together for a purpose, e.g., that they are so formed and adjusted as to produce motion, and that motion so regulated as to point out the hour of the day; that if the

different parts had been differently shaped from what they are, or
placed after any other manner or in any other order than that in which
they are placed, either no motion at all would have been carried
on in the machine, or none which would have answered the use that
is now served by it. To reckon up a few of the plainest of these parts
and of their offices, all tending to one result: we see a cylindrical box
containing a coiled elastic spring, which, by its endeavor to relax itself,
turns round the box. We next observe a flexible chain — artificially
wrought for the sake of flexure — communicating the action of the
spring from the box to the fusee. We then find a series of wheels,
the teeth of which catch in and apply to each other, conducting the
motion from the fusee to the balance and from the balance to the
pointer, and at the same time, by the size and shape of those wheels,
so regulating that motion as to terminate in causing an index, by an
equable and measured progression, to pass over a given space in a
given time. We take notice that the wheels are made of brass, in order
to keep them from rust; the springs of steel, no other metal being
so elastic; that over the face of the watch there is placed a glass, a
material employed in no other part of the work, but in the room of
which, if there had been any other than a transparent substance, the
hour could not be seen without opening the case. This mechanism
being observed — it requires indeed an examination of the instrument,
and perhaps some previous knowledge of the subject, to preceive and
understand it; but being once, as we have said, observed and
understood — the inference we think is inevitable, that the watch
must have had a maker — that there must have existed, at some time
and at some place or other, an artificer or artificers who formed it
for the purpose which we find it actually to answer, who completely
comprehended its construction and designed its use.

I. Nor would it, I apprehend, weaken the conclusion, that we had
never seen a watch made — that we had never known an artist
capable of making one — that we were altogether incapable of
executing such a piece of workmanship ourselves, or of understanding
in what manner it was performed; all theis being no more than what
is true of some exquisite remains of ancient art, of some lost arts,
and, to the generality of mankind, of the more curious productions
of modern manufacture. Does one man in a million know how oval

frames are turned? Ignorance of this kind exalts our opinion of the unseen and unknown artist's skill, if he be unseen and unknown, but raises no doubt in our minds of the existence and agency of such an artist, at some former time and in some place or other. Nor can I perceive that it varies at all the inference, whether the question arise concerning a human agent or concerning an agent of a different species, or an agent possessing in some respects a different nature.

II. Neither, secondly, would it invalidate our conclusion, that the watch sometimes went wrong or that it seldom went exactly right. The purpose of the machinery, the design, and the designer might be evident, and in the case supposed, would be evident, in whatever way we accounted for the irregularity of the movement, or whether we could account for it or not. It is not necessary that a machine be perfect in order to show with what design it was made: still less necessary, where the only question is whether it were made with any design at all.

III. Nor, thirdly, would it bring any uncertainty into the argument, if there were a few parts of the watch, concerning which we could not discover or had not yet discovered in what manner they conduced to the general effect; or even some parts, concerning which we could not ascertain whether they conduced to that effect in any manner whatever. For, as to the first branch of the case, if by the loss, or disorder, or decay of the parts in question, the movement of the watch were found in fact to be stopped, or disturbed, or retarded, no doubt would remain in our minds as to the utility or intention of these parts, although we should be unable to investigate the manner according to which, or the connection by which, the ultimate effect depended upon their action or assistance; and the more complex the machine, the more likely is this obscurity to arise. Then, as to the second thing supposed, namely, that there were parts which might be spared without prejudice to the movement of the watch, and that we had proved this by experiment, these superfluous parts, even if we were completely assured that they were such, would not vacate the reasoning which we had instituted concerning other parts. The indication of contrivance remained, with respect to them, nearly as it was before.

IV. Nor, fourthly, would any man in his senses think the existence of the watch with its various machinery accounted for, by being told that it was one out of possible combinations of material forms; that whatever he had found in the place where he found the watch, must have contained some internal configuration or other; and that this configuration might be the structure now exhibited, namely, of the works of a watch, as well as a different structure.

V. Nor, fifthly, would it yield his inquiry more satisfaction, to be answered that there existed in things a principle of order, which had disposed the parts of the watch into their present form and situation. He never knew a watch made by the principle of order; nor can he even form to himself an idea of what is meant by a principle of order distinct from the intelligence of the watchmaker.

VI. Sixthly, he would be surprised to hear that the mechanism of the watch was no proof of contrivance, only a motive to induce the mind to think so:

VII. And not less surprised to be informed that the watch in his hand was nothing more than the result of the laws of *metallic* nature. It is a perversion of language to assign any law as the efficient, operative cause of a thing. A law presupposes an agent, for it is only the mode according to which an agent proceeds: it implies a power, for it is the order according to which that power acts. Without this agent, without this power, which are both distinct from itself, the *law* does nothing, is nothing. The expression, "the law of metallic nature," may sound strange and harsh to a philosophic ear; but it seems quite as justifiable as some others which are more familiar to him, such as "the law of vegetable nature," "the law of animal nature," or, indeed, as "the law of nature" in general, when assigned as the cause of phenomena, in exclusion of agency and power, or when it is substituted into the place of these.

VIII. Neither, lastly, would our observer be driven out of his conclusion or from his confidence in its truth by being told that he knew nothing at all about the matter. He knows enough for his argument; he knows the utility of the end; he knows the subserviency and adaptation of the means to the end. These points being known, his ignorance of other points, his doubts concerning other points affect not the certainty of his reasoning. The consciousness of knowing little need not beget a distrust of that which he does know.

****

Chapter Five
Application of the Argument Continued

Every observation which was made in our first chapter concerning the watch may be repeated with strict propriety concerning the eye, concerning animals, concerning plants, concerning, indeed, all the organized parts of the works of nature. As,

I. When we are inquiring simply after the *existence* of an intelligent Creator, imperfection, inaccuracy, liablility to disorder, occasional irregularities may subsist in a considerable degree without inducing any doubt into the question; just as a watch may frequently go wrong, seldom perhaps exactly right, may be faulty in some parts, defective in some, without the smallest ground of suspicion from thence arising that it was not a watch, not made, or not made for the purpose asscribed to it. When faults are pointed out, and when a question is started concerning the skill of the artist or the dexterity with which the work is executed, then, indeed, in order to defend these qualities from accusation, we must be able either to expose some intractableness and imperfection in the materials or point out some invincible difficulty in the execution, into which imperfection and difficulty the matter of complaint may be resolved; or, if we cannot do this, we must adduce such specimens of consummate art and contrivance proceeding from the same hand as may convince the inquirer of the existence, in the case before him, of impediments like those which we have mentioned, although, what from the nature of the case is very likely to happen, they be unknown and unperceived by him. This we must do in order to vindicate the artist's skill, or at least the perfection of it; as we must also judge of his intention and of the provisions employed in fulfilling that intention, not from an instance in which they fail but from the great plurality of instances in which they succeed. But, after all, these are different questions from the question of the artist's existence; or, which is the same, whether the thing before us be a work of art or not; and the questions ought always to be kept separate in the mind. So likewise it is in the works of nature. Irregularities and imperfections are of little or no weight in the consideration when that consideration relates simply to the existence of a Creator. When the argument respects his attributes, they are of weight; but are then to be taken in conjunction — the attention is not to rest upon them, but they are to be taken in conjunction with the unexceptional evidences which we possess of skill, power, and benevolence displayed in other instances; which evidences may, in strength, number, and variety, be such and may so overpower apparent blemishes as to induce us, upon the most reasonable ground, to believe that these last ought to be referred to some cause, though we be ignorant of it, other than defect of knowledge or of benevolence in the author.

II. There may be also parts of plants and animals, as there were supposed to be of the watch, of which in some instances the operation, in others the use, is unknown. These form different cases; for the operation may be unknown, yet the use be certain. Thus it is with the lungs of animals. It does not, I think, appear that we are acquainted with the action of the air upon the blood, or in what manner that action is communicated by the lungs; yet we find that a very short suspension of their office destroys the life of the animal. In this case, therefore, we may be said to know the use, nay, we experience the necessity of the organ though we be ignorant of its operation. Nearly the same thing may be observed of what is called the lymphatic system. We suffer grievous inconveniences from its disorder, without being informed of the office which it sustains in the economy of our bodies. There may possibly also be some few examples of the second class in which not only the operation is unknown, but in which experiments may seem to prove that the part is not necessary; or may leave a doubt how far it is even useful to the plant or animal in which it is found. This is said to be the case with the spleen, which has been extracted from dogs without any sensible injury to their vital functions. Instances of the former kind, namely, in which we cannot explain the operation, may be numerous; for they will be so in proportion to our ignorance. They will be more or fewer to different persons, and in different stages of science. Every improvement of knowledge diminishes their number. There is hardly, perhaps, a year passes that does not in the works of nature bring some operation or some mode of operation to light, which was before undiscovered — probably unsuspected. Instances of the second kind, namely, where the part appears to be totally useless, I believe to be extremely rare; compared with the number of those of which the use is evident, they are beneath any assignable proportion and perhaps have been never submitted to trial and examination sufficiently accurate, long enough continued, or often enough repeated. No accounts which I have seen are satisfactory. The mutilated animal may live and grow fat — as was the case of the dog deprived of its spleen — yet may be defective in some other of its functions, which whether they can all, or in what degree of vigor and perfection, be performed, or how long preserved without the extirpated organ, does not seem to be ascertained by experiment. But to this case, even were it fully made out, may be applied the consideration which we suggest concerning the watch, namely, that these superfluous parts do not negative the reasoning which we instituted concerning those parts which are useful, and of which we know the use; the indication of contrivance with respect to them remains as it was before.

Father and Son: A Study of Two Temperaments (1907), by Edmund
Gosse. Selections.

Sir Edmund Gosse (1849-1928) was a distinguished literary critic and
man of letters. In *Father and Son* Edmund Gosse describes his
changing relations with his father, Philip Henry Gosse, the well
known naturalist. Philip Henry Gosse (1810-1888) was a gifted
observer and popular writer on botanical and zoological subjects,
highly respected by his comtemporaries for his work on marine
invertebrates. He was a devout Christian, an adherent of the
Plymouth Brethren, whose religion rested upon a simple,
straightforward acceptance of the Bible as the word of God.
Committed both to scientific accuracy and to a literal reading of the
Bible, the elder Gosse was deeply troubled in the 1850s by the
apparent conflict between Genesis and geology, and by the theory
of evolution. In the following selection Edmund Gosse describes how
his father attempted to deal with these difficulties.

So, through my Father's brain, in that year of scientific crisis, 1857,
there rushed two kinds of thought, each absorbing, each antagonistic
to the other. It was this discovery, that there were two theories of
physical life, each of which was true, but the truth of each
incompatible with the truth of the other, which shook the spirit of
my Father with perturbation. It was not, really, a paradox, it was
a fallacy, if he could only have known it, but he allowed the turbid
volume of superstition to drown the delicate stream of reason. He
took one step in the service of truth, and then he drew back in an
agony, and accepted the servitude of error.

　　This was the great moment in the history of thought when the
theory of the mutability of species was preparing to throw a flood
of light upon all departments of human speculation and action. It was
becoming necessary to stand emphatically in one army or the other.
Lyell was surrounding himself with disciples, who were making
strides in the direction of discovery. Darwin had long been collecting
facts with regard to the variation of animals and plants. Hooker and
Wallace, Asa Gray and even Agassiz, each in his own sphere, were
coming closer and closer to perception of that secret which was first
to reveal itself clearly to the patient and humble genius of Darwin.
In the year before, in 1856, Darwin, under pressure from Lyell, had

begun that modest statement of the new revelation, that "abstract of an essay," which developed so mightily into "The Origin of Species."Wollaston's "Variation of Species" had just appeared, and had been a nine days' wonder in the wilderness.

On the other side, the reactionaries, although never dreaming of the fate which hung over them, had not been idle. In 1857 the astounding question had for the first time been propounded with contumely, "What, then, did we come from an orang-outang?" The famous "Vestiges of Creation" had been supplying a sugar-and-water panacea for those who could not escape from the trend of evidence, and who yet clung to revelation. Owen was encouraging reaction by resisting, with all the strength of his prestige, the theory of the mutability of species.

In this period of intellectual ferment, as when a great political revolution is being planned, many possible adherents were confidentially tested with hints and encouraged to reveal their bias in a whisper. It was the notion of Lyell, himself a great mover of men, that, before the doctrine of natural selection was given to a world which would be sure to lift up at it a howl of execration, a certain body-guard of sound and experienced naturalists, expert in the description of species, should be privately made aware of its tenour. Among those who were thus initiated, or approached with a view towards possible illumination, was my Father. He was spoken to by Hooker, and later on by Darwin, after meetings of the Royal Society in the summer of 1857.

My Father's attitude towards the theory of natural selection was critical in his career and oddly enough, it exercised an immense influence on my own experience as a child. Let it be admitted at once, mournful as the admission is, that every instinct in his intelligence went out at first to greet the new light. It had hardly done so, when a recollection of the opening chapter of "Genesis" checked it at the outset. He consulted with Carpenter, a great investigator, but one who was fully as incapable as himself of remodelling his ideas with regard to the old, accepted hypotheses. They both determined, on various grounds, to have nothing to do with the terrible theory, but to hold steadily to the law of the fixity of species. It was exactly at this juncture that we left London, and the slight and occasional, but

always extremely salutary personal intercourse with men of scientific
leading which my Father had enjoyed at the British Museum and at
the Royal Society come to an end. His next act was to burn his ships,
down to the last beam and log out or which a raft could have been
made. By a strange act of wilfulness, he closed the doors upon himself
for ever.

My Father had never admired Sir Charles Lyell. I think that the
famous "Lord Chancellor manner" of the geologist intimidated him,
and we undervalue the intelligence of those whose conversation puts
us at a disadvantage. For Darwin and Hooker, on the other hand,
he had profound esteem, and I know not whether this had anything
to do with the fact that he chose, for his impetuous experiment in
reaction, the field of geology, rather than that of zoology or botany.
Lyell had been threatening to publish a book on the geological history
of Man, which was to be a bomb-shell flung into the camp of the
catastrophists. My Father, after long reflection, prepared a theory
of his own, which, as he fondly hoped, would take the wind out of
Lyell's sails, and justify geology to godly readers of "Genesis." It
was, very briefly, that there had been no gradual modification of the
surface of the earth, or slow development of organic forms, but that
when the catastrophic act of creation took place, the world presented,
instantly, the structural appearance of a planet on which life had long
existed.

The theory, coarsely enough, and to my Father's great
indignation, was defined by a hasty press as being this — that God
hid the fossils in the rocks in order to tempt geologists into infidelity.
In truth, it was the logical and inevitable conclusion of accepting,
literally, the doctrine of a sudden act of creation; it emphasised the
fact that any breach in the circular course of nature could be conceived
only on the supposition that the object created bore false witness to
past processes, which had never taken place. For instance Adam
would certainly possess hair and teeth and bones in a condition which
it must have taken many years to accomplish, yet he was created full-
grown yesterday. He would certainly — though Sir Thomas Browne
denied it — display an "omphalos," yet no umbilical cord had ever
attached him to a mother.

Never was a book cast upon the waters with greater anticipations of success than was this curious, this obstinate, this fanatical volume. My Father lived in a fever of suspence, waiting for the tremendous issue. This "Omphalos" of his, he thought, was to bring all the turmoil of scientific speculation to a close, fling geology into the arms of Scripture, and make the lion eat grass with the lamb. It was not surprising, he admitted, that there had been experienced an ever-increasing discord between the facts which geology brings to light and the direct statements of the early chapters of "Genesis." Nobody was to blame for that. My Father, and my Father alone, possessed the secret of the enigma; he alone held the key which could smoothly open the lock of geological mystery. He offered it, with a glowing gesture, to atheists and Christians alike. This was to be the universal panacea; this the system of intellectual therapeutics which could not but heal all the maladies of the age. But, alas! atheists and Christians alike looked at it, and laughed, and threw it away.

In the course of that dismal winter, as the post began to bring in private letters, few and chilly, and public reviews, many and scornful, my Father looked in vain for the approval of the churches, and in vain for the acquiescence of the scientific societies, and in vain for the gratitude of those "thousands of thinking persons," which he had rashly assured himself of receiving. As his reconciliation of Scripture statements and geological deductions was welcomed nowhere; as Darwin continued silent, and the youthful Huxley was scornful, and even Charles Kingsley, from whom my Father had expected the most instant appreciation, wrote that he could not "give up the painful and slow conclusion of five and twenty years' study of geology, and believe that God has written on the rocks one enormous and superfluous lie," — as all this happened or failed to happen, a gloom cold and dismal, descended upon our morning teacups. It was what the poets mean by an "inspissated" gloom; it thickened day by day, as hope and self-confidence evaporated in thin clouds of disappointment. My Father was not prepared for such a fate. He had been the spoiled darling of the public, the constant favourite of the press, and now, like the dark angels of old,

> so huge a rout
> Encumbered him with ruin.

He could not recover from amazement at having offended

everybody by an enterprise which had been undertaken in the cause
of universal reconciliation.

****

The key is lost by which I might unlock the perverse malady from
which my Father's conscience seemed to suffer during the whole of
this melancholy winter. But I think that a dislocation of his intellectual
system had a great deal to do with it. Up to this point in his career,
he had, as we have seen, nourished the delusion that science and
revelation could be mutually justified, that some sort of compromise
was possible. With great and ever greater distinctness, his
investigations had shown him that in all departments of organic
nature there are visible the evidences of slow modification of forms,
of the type developed by the pressure and practice of aeons. This
conviction had been borne in upon him until it was positively
irresistible. Where was his place, then, as a sincere and accurate
abserver? Manifestly, it was with the pioneers of the new truth, it
was with Darwin, Wallace and Hooker. But did not the second chapter
of "Genesis" say that in six days the heavens and earth were finished,
and the host of them and, that on the seventh day God ended his work
which he had made?

Here was a dilemma! Geology certainly *seemed* to be true, but
the Bible, which was God's word, *was* true. If the Bible said that all
things in Heaven and Earth were created in six days, created in six
days they were, — in six literal days of twenty-four hours each. The
evidences of spontaneous variation of form, acting, over an immense
space of time, upon ever-modifying organic structures, *seemed*
overwhelming, but they must either be brought into line with the six-
day labour of creation, or they must be rejected. I have already shown
how my Father worked out the ingenious "Omphalos" theory in order
to justify himself as a strictly scientific observer who was also a
humble slave of revelation. But the old convention and the new
rebellion would alike have none of his compromise.

To a mind so acute and at the same time so narrow as that of my
Father — a mind which is all logical and positive without breadth,
without suppleness and without imagination — to be subjected to a
check of this kind is agony. It has not the relief of a smaller nature,
which escapes from the dilemma by some foggy formula; nor the

resolution of a larger nature to take to it wings and surmount the obstacle. My Father although half suffocated by the emotion of being lifted as it were, on the great biological wave, never dreamed of letting go his clutch of the ancient tradition, but hung there, strained and buffeted. It is extraordinary that he — an "honest hodman of science," as Huxley once called him — should not have been content to allow others, whose horizons were wider than his could be, to pursue those purely intellectual surveys for which he had no species of aptitude. As a collector of facts and marshaller of observations, he had not a rival in that age; his very absence of imagination aided him in this work. But he was more an attorney than a philosopher, and he lacked that sublime humility which is the crown of genius. For, this obstinate persuasion that he alone knew the mind of God, that he alone could interpret the designs of the Creator, what did it result from if not from a congenital lack of that highest modesty which replies "I do not know" even to the questions which Faith, with menacing finger, insists on having most positively answered?

A review of Charles Darwin, *On the Origin of Species* (1859),
published by Samuel Wilberforce in the *Quarterly Review*, July 1860.
Selections.

Samuel Wilberforce (1805-1873), bishop of Oxford and then of
Winchester, was a great Victorian churchman. He was the son of
William Wilberforce, the celebrated Evangelical and leader of the
campaign against the slave trade. A man of great energy and ability,
Samuel Wilberforce was educated at Oxford and rose rapibly in power
and influence within the Anglican Church. He was made bishop of
Oxford in 1845, and he governed his diocese with great skill and
success. Active in the House of Lords, prominent in ecclesiastical
politics, acquainted with the royal family, Wilberforce was a
conspicuous public figure when Darwin published *On the Origin of
Species*. Wilberforce had little knowledge of science. His review of the
Origin represents the reaction of a successful and intelligent
ecclesiastic confidently rooted in traditional culture. His religious
convictions and his view of the world remained unshaken by the
discoveries of the geologists and biologists. He became, for a time, the
emblem of ecclesiastical opposition to Darwin's theory of evolution.

Any contribution to our Natural History literature from the pen
of Mr. C. Darwin is certain to command attention. His scientific
attainments, his insight and carefulness as an observer, blended with
no scanty measure of imaginative sagacity, and his clear and lively
style, make all his writings unusually attractive. His present volume
on the 'Origin of Species' is the result of many years of observation,
thought, and speculation; and is manifestly regarded by him as the
'opus' upon which his future fame is to rest. It is true that he
announces it modestly enough as the mere precursor of a mightier
volume. But that volume is only intended to supply the facts which
are to support the completed argument of the present essay. In this
we have a specimen-collection of the vast accumulation; and, working
from these as the high analytical mathematician may work from the
admitted results of his conic sections, he proceeds to deduce all the
conclusions to which he wishes to conduct his readers.

The essay is full of Mr. Darwin's characteristic excellences. It
is a most readable book; full of facts in natural history, old and new,
of his collecting and of his observing; and all of these are told in his

own perspicuous language, and all thrown into picturesque combinations and all sparkle with the colours of fancy and the lights of imagination. It assumes too the grave proportions of sustained argument upon a matter of the deepest interest, not to naturalists only, or even to men of science exclusively, but to every one who is interested in the history of man and of the relations of nature around him to the history and plan of creation.

* * * * * * * * *

We can perhaps best convey to our readers a clear view of Mr. Darwin's chain of reasoning, and of our objections to it, if we set before them, first, the conclusion to which he seeks to bring them; next, the leading propositions which he must establish in order to make good his final inference; and then the mode by which he endeavours to support his propositions.

The conclusion, then, to which Mr. Darwin would bring us is, that all the various forms of vegetable and animal life with which the globe is now peopled or of which we find the remains preserved in a fossil state in the great Earth-Museum around us, which the science of geology unlocks for our instruction, have come down by natural succession of descent from father to son, — 'animals from at most four or five progenitors, and plants from an equal or less number' (p. 484), as Mr. Darwin at first somewhat diffidently suggests; or rather, as, growing bolder when he has once pronounced his theory, he goes on to suggest to us, from one single head: —

'Analogy would lead me one step further, namely, to the belief that ALL ANIMALS and PLANTS have descended from some one prototype. But analogy may be a deceitful guide. Nevertheless, all living things have much in common in their chemical composition, their germinal vesicles, their cellular structure, and their laws of growth and reproduction . . . Therefore I should infer from analogy that probably all the organic beings which have ever lived on this earth' (man therefore of course included) ' have descended from some one primordial form into which life was first breathed by the Creator.' — p. 484.

This is the theory which really pervades the whole volume. Man, beast, creeping thing, and plant of the earth, are all the lineal and direct descendants of some one individual *ens*, whose various progeny have been simply modified by the action of natural and ascertainable conditions into the multiform aspect of life which we see around us. This is undoubtedly at first sight a somewhat startling conclusion to arrive at. To find that mosses, grasses, turnips, oaks, worms, and flies, mites and elephants, infusoria and whales, tadpoles of to-day and venerable saurians, truffles and men, are all equally the lineal descendants of the same aboriginal common ancestor, perhaps of the nucleated cell of some primaeval fungus, which alone possessed the distinguishing honour of being the 'one primordial form into which life was first breathed by the Creator' — this, to say the least of it, is no common discovery — no very expected conclusion. But we are too loyal pupils of inductive philosophy to start back from any conclusion by reason of its strangeness. Newton's patient philosophy taught him to find in the falling apple the law which governs the silent movements of the stars in their courses; and if Mr. Darwin can with the same correctness of reasoning demonstrate to us our fungular descent, we shall dismiss our pride, and avow, with the characteristic humility of philosophy, our unsuspected cousinship with the mushrooms, —

'Claim kindred there, and have our claim allowed,'

— only we shall ask leave to scrutinise carefully every step of the argument which has such an ending, and demur if at any point of it we are invited to substitute unlimited hypothesis for patient observation, or the spasmodic fluttering flight of fancy for the severe conclusions to which logical accuracy of reasoning has led the way.

Now, the main proposition by which Mr. Darwin's conclusion is attained are these: —

1. That observed and admitted variations spring up in the course of descents from a common progenitor.

2. That many of these variations tend to an improvement upon the parent stock.

3. That, by a continued selection of these improved specimens as the progenitors of future stock, its powers may be unlimitedly increased.

4. And, lastly, that there is in nature a power continually and universally working out this selection, and so fixing and augmenting these improvements.

Mr. Darwin's whole theory rests upon the truth of these propositions, and crumbles utterly away if only one of them fail him. These therefore we must closely scrutinise.

* * * * * * * * *

We come then to these conclusions. All the facts presented to us in the natural world tend to show the none of the variations produced in the fixed forms of animal life, when seen in its most plastic condition under domestication, give any promise of a true transmutation of species; first, from the difficulty of accumulating and fixing variations within the same species; secondly, from the fact that these variations, though most serviceable for man, have no tendency to improve the individual beyond the standard of his own specific type, and so to afford matter, even if they were infinitely produced, for the supposed power of natural selection on which to work; whilst all variations from the mixture of species are barred by the inexorable law of hybrid sterility. Further, the embalmed records of 3000 years show that there has been no beginning of transmutation in the species of our most familiar domesticated animals; and beyond this, that in the countless tribes of animal life around us, down to its lowest and most variable species, no one has ever discovered a single instance of such transmutation being now in prospect; no new organ has ever been known to be developed — no new natural instinct to be formed — whilst, finally, in the vast museum of departed animal life which the strata of the earth imbed for our examination, whilst they contain for too complete a representation of the past to be set aside as a mere imperfect record, yet afford no one instance of any such change as having ever been in progress, or give us anywhere the missing links of the assumed chain, or the remains which would enable now existing variations, by gradual approximations, to shade off into unity.

On what then is the new theory based? We say it with unfeigned regret, in dealing with such a man as Mr. Darwin, on the merest hypothesis, supported by the most unbounded assumptions.

* * * * * * * * *

There are no parts of Mr. Darwin's ingenious book in which he gives the reins more completely to his fancy than where he deals with the improvement of instinct by his principle of natural selection. We need but instance his assumption, without a fact on which to build it, that the marvellous skill of the honey-bee in constructing its cells is thus obtained, and the slave-making habits of the Formica Polyerges thus formed. There seems to be no limit here to the exuberance of his fancy, and we cannot but think that we detect one of those hints by which Mr. Darwin indicates the application of his system from the lower animals to man himself, when he dwells so pointedly upon the fact that it is always the *black* ant which is enslaved by his other coloured and more fortunate brethren. 'The slaves are black!' We believe that, if we had Mr. Darwin in the witness-box, and could subject him to a moderate cross-examination, we should find that he believed that the tendency of the lighter-coloured races of mankind to prosecute the negro slave-trade was really a remains, in their more favoured condition, of the 'extraordinary and odious instinct' which had possessed them before they had been 'improved by natural selection' from Formica Polyerges into Homo. This at least is very much the way in which (p. 479) he slips in quite incidentally the true identity of man with the horse, the bat, and the porpoise: —

'The framework of bones being the same in the hand of a man, wing of a bat, fin of a porpoise, and leg of the horse, the same number of vertebrae forming the neck of the giraffe and of the elephant, and innumerable other such facts, at once explain themselves on the theory of descent with slow and slight successive modifications.' — p. 479.

Such assumptions as these, we once more repeat, are most dishonourable and injurious to science.

****

Our readers will not have failed to notice that we have objected to the views with which we have been dealing solely on scientific grounds. We have done so from our fixed conviction that it is thus that the truth or falsehood of such arguments should be tried. We have no sympathy with those who object to any facts or alleged facts in nature, or to any inference logically deduced from them, because they believe them to contradict what it appears to them is taught by Revelation. We think that all such objections savour of a timidity which is really inconsistent   with   a   firm   and   well-instructed   faith: —

'Let us for a moment,' profoundly remarks Professor Sedgwick, 'suppose that there are some religious difficulties in the conclusions of geology. How, then, are we to solve them? Not by making a world after a pattern of our own — not by shifting and shuffling the solid strata of the earth, and then dealing them out in such a way as to play the game of an ignorant or dishonest hypothesis — not by shutting our eyes to facts, or denying the evidence of our senses — but by patient investigation, carried on in the sincere love of truth, and by learning to reject every consequence not warranted by physical evidence.'

He who is as sure as he is of his own existence that the God of Truth is at once the God of Nature and the God of Revelation, cannot believe it to be possible that His voice in either, rightly understood, can differ, or deceive His creatures. To oppose facts in the natural world because they seem to oppose Revelation, or to humour them so as to compel them to speak its voice, is, he knows, but another form of the ever-ready feebleminded dishonesty of lying for God, and trying by fraud or falsehood to do the work of the God of truth. It is with another and a nobler spirit that the true believer walks amongst the works of nature. The words graven on the everlasting rocks are the words of God, and they are graven by His hand. No more can they contradict His Word written in His book, than could the words of the old covenant graven by His hand on the stony tables contradict the writings of His hand in the volume of the new dispensation. There may be to man difficulty in reconciling all the utterances of the two voices. But what of that? He has learned already that here he knows only in part, and that the day of reconciling all apparent contradictions between what must agree is nigh at hand. He rests his mind in perfect quietness on this assurance, and rejoices in the gift of light without a misgiving a to what it may discover: — 'A man of deep thought and great practical wisdom,' says Sedgwick, 'one whose piety and benevolence have for many years been shining before the world, and of whose sincerity no scoffer (of whatever school) will dare to start a doubt, recorded his opinion in the great assembly of the men of the Empire within the walls of this University, "that Christianity had everything to hope and nothing to fear from the advancement of philosophy."

This is as truly the spirit of Christianity as it is that of philosophy. Few things have more deeply injured the cause of religion than the busy fussy energy with which men, narrow and feeble alike in faith and in science, have bustled forth to reconcile all new discoveries in physics with the word of inspiration. For it continually happens that some larger collection of facts, or some wider view of the phenomena of nature, alter the whole philosophic scheme; whilst Revelation has been committed to declare an absolute agreement with what turns out after all to have been a misconception or an error. We cannot, therefore, consent to test the truth of natural science by the Word of Revelation. But this does not make it the less important to point out on scientific grounds scientific errors, when those errors tend to limit God's glory in creation, or to gainsay the revealed relations of that creation to Himself. To both these classes of error, though, we doubt not, quite unintentionally on his part, we think that Mr. Darwin's speculations directly tend.

Mr. Darwin writes as a Christian, and we doubt not that he is one. We do not for a moment believe him to be one of those who retain in some corner of their hearts a secret unbelief which they dare no vent; and we therefore pray him to consider well the grounds on which we brand his speculations with the charge of such a tendency. First, then, he not obscurely declares that he applies his scheme of the action of the principle of natural selection to MAN himself, as well as to the animals around him. Now, we must say at once, and openly, that such a notion is absolutely incompatible not only with single expressions in the word of God on that subject of natural science with which it is not immediately concerned, but, which in our judgment is of far more importance, with the whole representation of that moral and spiritual condition of man which is its proper subjectmatter. Man's derived supremacy over the earth; man's power of articulate speech; man's gift of reason; man's free-will and responsibility; man's fall and man's redemption; the incarnation of the Eternal Son; the indwelling of the Eternal Spirit, — all are equally and utterly irreconcilable with the degrading notion of the brute origin of him who was created in the image of God, and redeemed by the Eternal son assuming to himself his nature. Equally inconsistent, too, not with any passing expressions, but with the whole scheme of God's dealings with man as recorded in His word, is Mr. Darwin's daring notion of man's further development into some unknown extent of powers, and shape, and size, through natural selection acting through that long vista of ages which he casts mistily over the earth upon the most favoured individuals of his species. We care not in these pages to push the argument further. We have done enough for our purpose in thus succinctly intimating its course. If any of our readers doubt what must be the result of such speculations carried to their logical and legitimate conclusion, let them turn to the pages of Oken, and see for themselves the end of that path the opening of which is decked out in these pages with the bright hues and seemingly innocent deductions of the transmutation-theory.

Nor can we doubt, secondly, that this view, which thus contradicts the revealed relation of creation to its Creator, is equally inconsistent with the fulness of His glory. It is, in truth, an ingenious theory for diffusing throughout creation the working and so the personality of the Creator. And thus, however unconsciously to him who holds them, such views really tend inevitably to banish from the mind most of the peculiar attributes of the Almighty.

How, asks Mr. Darwin, can we possibly account for the manifest plan, order, and arrangement which pervade creation, except we allow to it this self-developing power through modified descent?

'As Milne-Edwards has well expressed it, Nature is prodigal in variety, but niggard in innovation. Why, on the theory of creation, should this be so? Why should all the parts and organs of many independent beings, each supposed to have been separately created for its proper place in nature, be so commonly linked together by graduated steps? Why should not Nature have taken a leap from structure to structure? — p. 194.

And again: —

'It is a truly wonderful fact — the wonder of which we are apt to overlook from familiarity — that all animals and plants throughout all time and space should be related to each other in group subordinate to group, in the manner which we everywhere behold, namely, varieties of the same species most closely related together, species of the same genus less closely and unequally related together, forming sections and sub-genera, species of distict genera much less closely related, and genera related in different degrees, forming sub-families, families, orders, sub-classes, and classes.' — pp. 128-29.

How can we account for all this? By the simplest and yet the most comprehensive answer. By declaring the stupendous fact that all creation is the transcript in matter of ideas eternally existing in the mind of the Most High — that order in the utmost perfectness of its relation pervades his works, because it exists as in its centre and highest fountain-head in Him the Lord of all. Here is the true account of the fact which has so utterly misled shallow observers, that Man himself, the Prince and Head of this creation, passes in the earlier stages of his being through phases of existence closely analogous, so far as his earthly tabernacle is concerned, to those in which the lower animals ever remain. At that point of being the development of the protozoa is arrested. Through it the embryo of their chief passes to the perfection of his' earthly frame. But the types of those lower forms of being must be found in the animals which never advance beyond them — not in man for whom they are but the foundation for an afterdevelopment; whilst he too, Creation's crown and perfection, thus bears witness in his own frame to the law of order which pervades the universe.

Life and Letters of Thomas Henry Huxley (1913), by Leonard
Huxley. Selections.

Thomas Henry Huxley (1825-1895) was a biologist and a public
advocate for science. At the time of publication of Darwin's *On the
Origin of Species* (1859), Huxley was already well known in scientific
circles, particularly for his work in comparative anatomy. Soon after
the appearance of the *Origins*, Huxley became the most prominent
and most pugnacious champion of Darwin's theory of evolution.
Huxley seemed to delight in battle, and, particularly in the ten years
following 1859, he spent much of his time speaking and writing on
behalf of science and evolution. The famous encounter between
Huxley and Samuel Wilberforce at the Oxford meeting of the British
Association for the Advancement of Science in 1860 stands at the
beginning of Huxley's career as a defender of freedom of thought and
an enemy of what he considered to be ecclesiastical obscurantism.
Leonard Huxley has put together the following account of the
confrontation between Wilberforce and Huxley from the reports of
several different eye witnesses.

———————————◆———————————

The famous Oxford Meeting of 1860 (of the British Association for
the Advancement of Science) was of no small importance in Huxley's
career. It was not merely that he helped to save a great cause from
being stifled under misrepresentation and ridicule — that he helped
to extort for it a fair hearing; it was now that he first made himself
known in popular estimation as a dangerous adversary in debate —
a personal force in the world of science which could not be neglected.
From this moment he entered the front fighting line in the most
exposed quarter of the field.

Most unluckily, no contemporary account of his own exists of the
encounter. Indeed, the same cause which prevented his writing home
the story of the day's work nearly led to his absence from the scene.
It was known that Bishop Wilberforce, whose first class in
mathematics gave him, in popular estimation, a right to treat on
scientific matters, intended to "smash Darwin"; and Huxley,
expecting that the promised debate would be merely an appeal to
prejudice in a mixed audience, before which the scientific arguments
of the Bishop's opponents would be at the utmost disadvantage,
intended to leave Oxford that very morning and join his wife at
Hardwicke, near Reading, where she was staying with her sister. But

in a letter, quoted below, he tells how, on the Friday afternoon, he chanced to meet Robert Chambers, the reputed author of the *Vestiges of Creation*, who begged him "not to desert them." Accordingly he postponed his departure; but seeing his wife next morning, had no occasion to write a letter.

Several accounts of the scene are already in existence: one in the *Life of Darwin* (vol. ii. p. 320), another in the 1892 *Life*, p. 236 *sq.*; a third that of *Lyell* (vol. ii. p. 335), the slight differences between them representing the difference between individual recollections of eye-witnesses. In addition to these I have been fortunate enough to secure further reminiscences from several other eye-witnesses.

Two papers in Section D, of no great importance in themselves, became historical as affording the opponents of Darwin their opportunity of making an attack upon his theory which should tell with the public. The first was on Thursday, June 28. Dr. Daubeny of Oxford made a communication to the Section, "On the final causes of the sexuality of plants, with particular reference to Mr. Darwin's work on the *Origin of Species*." Huxley was called upon to speak by the President, but tried to avoid a discussion, on the ground "that a general audience, in which sentiment would unduly interfere with intellect, was not the public before which such a discussion should be carried on."

This consideration, however, did not stop the discussion; it was continued by Owen. He said he "wished to approach the subject in the spirit of the philosopher," and declared his "conviction that there were facts, by which the public could come to some conclusion with regard to the probabilities of the truth of Mr. Darwin's theory." As one of these facts, he stated that the brain of the gorilla "presented more differences, as compared with the brain of man, than it did when compared with the brains of the very lowest and most problematical of the Quadrumana."

Now this was the very point, as said above, upon which Huxley had made special investigations during the last two years, with precisely opposite results, such as, indeed, had been arrived at by previous investigators. Hereupon he replied, giving these assertions a "direct and unqualified contradiction," and pledging himself to "justify that unusual procedure elsewhere," — a pledge which was amply fulfilled in the pages of the *Natural History Review* for 1861.

Accordingly it was to him, thus marked out as the champion of the most debatable thesis of evolution, that, two days later, the Bishop addressed his sarcasms, only to meet with a withering retort. For on the Friday there was peace; but on the Saturday came a yet fiercer battle over the "Origin," which loomed all the larger in the public eye, because it was not merely the contradiction of one anatomist by another, but the open clash between Science and the Church. It was, moreover, not a contest of bare fact or abstract assertion, but a combat of wit between two individuals, spiced with the personal element which appeals to one of the strongest instincts of every large audience.

It was the merest chance, as I have already said, that Huxley attended the meeting of the section that morning. Dr. Draper of New York was to read a paper on the "Intellectual Development of Europe considered with reference to the views of Mr. Darwin." "I can still hear," writes one who was present, "the American accents of Dr. Draper's opening address when he asked 'Air we a fortuitous concourse of atoms?' " However, it was not to hear him, but the eloquence of the Bishop, that the members of the Association crowded in such numbers into the Lecture Room of the Museum, that this, the appointed meeting-place of the section, had to be abandoned for the long west room, since cut in two by a partition for the purposes of the library. It was not term time, nor were the general public admitted; nevertheless the room was crowded to suffocation long before the protagonists appeared on the scene, 700 persons or more managing to find places. The very windows by which the room was lighted down the length of its west side were packed with ladies, whose white handkerchiefs, waving and fluttering in the air at the end of the Bishop's speech, were an unforgettable factor in the acclamation of the crowd.

On the east side between the two doors was the platform. Professor Henslow, President of the section, took his seat in the centre; upon his right was the Bishop, and beyond him again Dr. Draper; on his extreme left was Mr. Dingle, a clergyman from Lanchester, near Durham, with Sir J. Hooker and Sir J. Lubbock in front of him, and nearer the centre, Professor Beale of King's

College, London, and Huxley.

The clergy, who shouted lustily for the Bishop, were massed in the middle of the room; behind them in the north-west corner a knot of undergraduates (one of them was T.H. Green, who listened but took no part in the cheering) had gathered together beside Professor Brodie, ready to lift their voices, poor minority though they were, for the opposite party. Close to them stood one of the few men among the audience already in Holy orders, who joined in — and indeed led — the cheers for the Darwinians.

So "Dr. Draper droned out his paper, turning first to the right hand and then to the left, of course bringing in a reference to the Origin of Species which set the ball rolling."

An hour or more that paper lasted, and then discussion began. The President "wisely announced *in limine* that none who had not valid arguments to bring forward on one side or the other would be allowed to address the meeting; a caution that proved necessary, for no fewer than four combatants had their utterances burked by him, because of their indulgence in vague declamation."

"First spoke (writes Professor Farrar) a layman from Brompton, who gave his name as being one of the Committee of the (newly-formed) Economic section of the Association. He, in a stentorian voice, let off his theological venom. Then jumped up Richard Greswell with a thin voice, saying much the same, but speaking as a scholar; but we did not merely want any theological discussion, so we shouted them down. Then a Mr. Dingle got up and tried to show that Darwin would have done much better if he had taken him into consultation. He used the blackboard and began a mathematical demonstration on the question — "Let this point A be man, and let that point B be the mawnkey." he got no further; he was shouted down with cries of "mawnkey." None of these had spoken more than three minutes. It was when these were shouted down that Henslow said he must demand that the discussion should rest on *scientific* grounds only.

Then there were calls for the Bishop, but he rose and said he understood his friend Professor Beale had something to say first. Beale, who was an excellent histologist, spoke to the effect that the new theory ought to meet with fair discussion, but added, with great modesty, that he himself had not sufficient knowledge to discuss the subject adequately. Then the Bishop spoke the speech that you know, and the question about his mother being an ape, or his grandmother."

From the scientific point of view, the speech was of small value. It was evident from his mode of handling the subject that he had been "crammed up to the throat," and knew nothing at first hand; he used no argument beyond those to be found in his *Quarterly* article, which appeared a few days later, and is now admitted to have been inspired by Owen. "He ridiculed Darwin badly and Huxley savagely; but," confesses one of his strongest opponents, "all in such dulcet tones, so persuasive a manner, and in such well-turned periods, that I who had been inclined to blame the President for allowing a discussion that could serve no scientific purpose, now forgave him from the bottom of my heart."

The Bishop spoke thus "for full half an hour with inimitable spirit, emptiness and unfairness." "In a light, scoffing tone, florid and fluent, he assured us there was nothing in the idea of evolution; rock-pigeons were what rock-pigeons had always been. Then, turning to his antagonist with a smiling insolence, he begged to know, was it through his grandfather or his grandmother that he claimed his descent from a monkey?"

This was the fatal mistake of his speech. Huxley instantly grasped the tactical advantage which the descent to personalities gave him. He turned to Sir Benjamin Brodie, who was sitting beside him, and emphatically striking his hand upon his knee, exclaimed, "The Lord hath delivered him into mine hands." The bearing of the exclamation did not dawn upon Sir Benjamin until after Huxley had completed his "forcible and eloquent" answer to the scientific part of the Bishop's argument, and proceeded to make his famous retort.

"On this (continues the writer in *Macmillan's Magazine*) Mr. Huxley slowly and deliberately arose. A slight tall figure, stern and pale, very quite and very grave, he stood before us and spoke those tremendous words — words which no one seems sure of now, nor, I think, could remember just after they were spoken, for their meaning took away our breath, though it left us in no doubt as to what it was. He was not ashamed to have a monkey for his ancestor; but he would be ashamed to be connected with a man who used great gifts to obscure the truth. No one doubted his meaning, and the effect was tremendous. One lady fainted and had to be carried out; I, for one, jumped out of my seat."

The fullest and probably most accurate account of these concluding words is the following, from a letter of the late John Richard Green, then an undergraduate, to his friend, afterwards Professor Boyd Dawkins: —

"I asserted — and I repeat — that a man has no reason to be ahshamed of having an ape for his grandfather. If there were an ancestor whom I should feel shame in recalling it would rather be a *man* — a man of restless and versatile intellect — who, not content with an equivocal success in his own sphere of activity, plunges into scientific questions with which he has no real acquaintance, only to obscure them by an aimless rhetoric, and distract the attention of his hearers from the real point at issue by eloquent digressions and skilled appeals to religious prejudice."

Further, Mr. A.G. Vernon-Harcourt, F.R.S., Reader in Chemistry at the University of Oxford, writes to me: —

"The Bishop had rallied your father as to the descent from a monkey, asking as a sort of joke how recent this had been, whether it was his grandfather or further back. Your father, in replying on this point, first explained that the suggestion was of descent through thousands of generations from a common ancestor, and then went on to this effect — "But if this question is treated, not as a matter for the calm investigation of science, but as a matter of sentiment, and if I am asked whether I would choose to be descended from the poor animal of low intelligence and stooping gait, who grins and chatters as we pass, or from a man, endowed with great ability and a splendid position, who should use these gifts" [here, as the point became clear, there was great outburst of applause, which mostly drowned the end of the sentence] "to discredit and crush humble seekers after truth, I hesitate what answer to make.

"No doubt your father's words were better than these, and they gained effect from his clear, deliberate utterance, but in outline and in *scale* this represents truly what was said."

After the commotion was over, "some voices called for Hooker, and his name having been handed up, the President invited him to give his view of the theory from the Botanical side. This he did, demonstrating that the Bishop, by his own showing, had never grasped the principles of the 'Origin,' and that he was absolutely ignorant of the elements of botanical science. The Bishop made no reply, and the meeting broke up."

****

The result of this encounter, though a check to the other side, cannot, of course, be represented as an immediate and complete triumph for evolutionary doctrine. This was precluded by the character and temper of the audience, most of whom were less capable of being convinced by the arguments than shocked by the boldness of the retort, although, being gentlefolk, as Professor Farrar remarks, they were disposed to admit on reflection that the Bishop had erred on the score of taste and good manners. Nevertheless, it was a noticeable feature of the occasion, Sir M. Foster tells me, that when Huxley rose he was received coldly, just a cheer of encouragement from his friends, the audience as a whole not joining in it. But as he made his points the applause grew and widened, until, when he sat down, the cheering was not very much less than that given to the Bishop. To that extent he carried an unwilling audience with him by the force of his speech. The debate on the ape question, however, was continued elsewhere during the next two years, and the evidence was completed by the unanswerable demonstrations of Sir W.H. Flower at the Cambridge meeting of the Association in 1862.

The importance of the Oxford meeting lay in the open resistance that was made to authority, at a moment when even a drawn battle was hardly less effectual than acknowledged victory. Instead of being crushed under ridicule, the new theories secured a hearing, all the wider, indeed, for the startling nature of their defence.

What would follow on the Effacement of Christianity (1890), by
George Jacob Holyoake. Selections.

George Jacob Holyoake (1817-1906), was Victorian England's most
celebrated Secularist. A tinsmith by training, Holyoakc became a full-
time Owenite Socialist organizer in 1840. He had been active in the
Reform and Chartist agitations of the eighteen-thirties. Among his
various crusades, Holyoake became involved in well-publicized legal
battles for freedom of thought and freedom of the press. After 1846
his main interest was in the development and spread of a positive
philosophy of atheism for the working classes.

This is the creed of the orthodox Churches. They all take the Bible
to be a divinely inspired book of guidance, both as to faith and
practice. They all save one, believe in three co-equal Deities. They
all believe that one of them, called Christ, was an actual begotten
son of the Father, and coame on this earth as such for the purpose
of being put to death, that he might appease the anger of his parent,
and thereby induce him to forgive the human family, condemned on
account of sin committed (by one of them) before any of them were
born. They all believe that God has provided a place of torment, wide
enough and deep enough to hold all the human race past, present
and to come, who have not, by a profession of belief in a Crucified
Savior, established exemption from the awful fate of the damned.
They all believe that there is another being, the antagonist of God,
who is the keeper of hell, and who "goes about like a roaring lion,"
snatching at the souls of men, with a view to devour them and cast
them into hell, of which he is the independent, absolute and
irresponsible governor, from whom God does not profess any
intention to deliver them, nor Christ avow any power to save them,
except by faith in him. Yet to appropriate the property of another
is not more disgraceful than to profit by the blood of another, and
seek to escape from your guilt by his sacrifice. They all believe that
prayer is the profitable resource of the saint, "that it will," as Mr.
Spurgeon asserts, "fill the meal barrel, or save the sinking ship."
They all believe that no one in this life can be sure of exemption form
eternal perdition, since his future lot will not be determined until the
arrival of a day of judgment, to which the living may be summoned
to attend, and the dead be brought again to life, to undergo trial and

sentence, a hundred or a thousand centuries after their decease. All these things the orthodox Churches believe and teach, all these astounding tenets are held by Dissenters and Roman Catholics alike; the Catholics holding this belief in a more intense and horrible form than the Church of England. It is true that many members of the Church of England, and a few of its ministers, profess to hold some of these doctrines in another sense, or in a less fearful form; but even they *preach the doctrine.* They read the services of the Church which contain the terrible tenets, in the most solemn manner, and do not so far think them untrue as to make open protest against them, and all sign the Thiry-nine Articles which contain them, professing, in good faith, solemnly to hold and teach and maintain them.

A gentleman having come into possession of an old-established inn, and finding it well built, well placed and commodious, converted it into a residence, but left outside the old sign. A traveler arriving rang the bell. On the footman appearing, he said, "Take my horse, and order me a beefsteak, sharp." "You mistake this place, sir. It is no longer a hostelry it is a private home," was the answer given the traveler. He, irritated, indignant and irreverent, at having dismounted in vain, answered: "If you have gone into a new business, why the devil do you not take down the old sign?" This is the way with modern theologians. They have new doctrines and interpretations, which they call "developments," to the perplexity and confusion of all honest travelers.

* * * * * * * *

The "social and moral effects of the discontinuance of Christian teaching and the abolition of its institutions" would soon be seen to be advantageous to society. Tenets of Christianity clearly subversive of progress being withdrawn, it must follow that the natural forces of humanity would be set free and have fuller scope. For instance, the tenet of the inherent depravity of all human beings, and the teaching that this hereditary corruption can only be counteracted by "saving grace," is a direct disencouragement of improvement by education. No mother can believe in her heart in the inherent badness of her child. How could she contemplate with pleasure or kiss the "depraved" little thing which the holiest instinct of her nature teaches her to love and trust? This doctrine, if fully and intelligently believed, would discourage all education of a secular description. This is known to be so. The greatest opposition and the strongest endeavors are continually made to prevent any education from being attempted which is not based on the doctrine of inherent baseness. The effacement of this tenet of depravity would be a new impetus to all kinds of educational effort and inspire it with confidence. Therefore, this tenet alone being effaced, the forces of intelligence and morality would be enormously increased.

Again, the tenets of the Bible being taken as the standard to which all experiences of truth and science must conform has been in every age, since Christianity was propagated, a formidable impediment to progress. It is impossible to estimate what improvement the world would have seen, had Freethought not been thus coerced and intimidated. Were the repressive tenet of Biblical infallibility effaced in the millions of minds over which it still dominates, the resources of intellect and morality, founded on nature and experience, would soon be sufficient to run the world.

Were the tenets and institutions of Christianity, with the ethically deterrent influence they exercise, once withdrawn from society, the instinct of self-preservation, the passion for progress, the natural love of morality, the necessity of honor and justice and truth, would not only be still in force, but would become more active and energetic than heretofore. Then the sense of secular responsibility, which is now obscured by Christian tenets and discouraged by Christian agencies, and defamed by all Christian preachers, who more or less teach the distrust of natural morality and deride its efficacy or persistent force, would have full effect. The case of the world will not be so bad as is supposed were the effects of Christianity to cease. Already and for years past, natural and scientific influences have done much to advance and sustain society. But Christianity is very egotistical and claims to have done and to do everything, the credit of which belongs to other forces and other principles.

It does not follow, nor is it pretended in these pages, that because Christianity might now be dispensed with, that it has not been in many ways a force for good in the world. Paganism, with all its moral deficiency, was doubtless a nobler religion than the superstitions it effaced. In like manner Christianity has been an influence for good in earlier, dark and ignorant ages. Even now over minds brutish, untaught and suffering, and over whom nobler secular forces are prevented from operating, Christianity often exercises a beneficial influence. So far as its wiser and advanced preachers keep alive a sentiment of reverence for ideals of Love and Truth for their own sake, their work is to be valued. Many Christian ministers and Christian believers make noble sacrifices for duty — as they understand it — and may be rightly honored by those who deem their cardinal doctrines erroneous. Were the thousand pulpits of Great Britain silenced suddenly and altogether the public sentiment in favor of humanity, purity of life and justice, would for a time be lowered. At the same time it is conceivable that if the same tongues proclaimed, with the same earnestness and eloquence, the moralities of life according to nature, and proclaim them without the dogmas and tenets of Christian theology, public sentiment in favor of truth and progress would be far higher than it is.

It may be admitted that Christianity, by superseding superstitions grosser than its own, has paved the way, in some respects, to the present ascendency of science, though it has in so many other ways retarded its growth. But now that Science has established itself in spite of Christianity — has attained an authority of its own, and occupies ground independently of Christianity, owing nothing to it, nor yielding it allegiance, the world is better enabled to do without Christianity than otherwise would be the case. Science has disclosed the true grounds of morality, resting on ethical laws and not on Biblical dogmas. The moralities of science are universal in their nature and in their general acceptance. A nobler morality prevails now which gives laws to Religion, instead of Religion, as formerly, giving laws to morality. "The secret of genius," said one distinguished by its possession, "is to suffer no fiction to exist. To demand in all things good faith, reality, and a purpose: and first, last, midst, and without end, to honor every truth by use." Therefore morality would continue, social improvement would progress, notwithstanding that the tenets and institutions of Christianity should be effaced. We are not without singular historic proof that this will be so.

Voltaire who personated the Skepticism of the last century: Paine, who according to all priests, personated the Infidelity of England at the beginning of this century; William Lloyd Garrison, denounced by every orthodox pulpit in America, openly rejected every Christian tenet which interfered with human liberty. Yet these men did nore for morality and humanity than all the preachers of Christianity in their day. Voltaire, at the peril of his liberty and life, rescued a friendless family from the fire and the wheel, when the priests were murdering them, and delivered the intellect of France forever from the rack of the Church. The pen of Paine accomplished more for the independence of America than the sword of Washington, for he inspired the patriots who gave their lives for it; and Garrison gave liberty to the Slaves whose bondage the Clergy defended. The Christianity of three nations produced no three men in their day who did anything comparable to the achievement of these three Skeptics, who wrought this splendid good not only without Christianity, but in opposition to it. Had Christian tenets and institutions been effaced in their day, they had accomplished still greater good without the peril they had to brave.

Thus, the complacent saying, "Christ or Chaos," is a mistake contrary to history and experience. Were Christianity effaced the liberated forces of Science and morality would take its place. The world is tired of the cry of the Saints, "We are the salt of the earth, after us putrefaction." It is the salt of Science and morality which has permeated Christianity, which has of late years preserved *it* from putrefaction.

Besides, attention is necessary to the remarkable alacrity with which Christian preachers are themselves effacing Christianity. It has been said that priests, like wild beasts, retreat before the approach of civilization. Certainly they efface their own tenets in the presence of Science and ethical criticism. The days of creation have been expanded into millions of years — Hell has become Sheol, and the old cardinal doctrines are receiving new interpretations which explain them away. Men who a few years ago were denounced as "Infidels," for not believing the accepted tenets of that time, are now described as ignorant and as caricaturing Christianity if they cite the same tenets as representing Biblical faith. Christianity is effacing itself by incapacity, or policy.

The two most influential ideas which in every age, since it arose, have given Christianity currency among the ignorant and the credulous have been the ideas of Hell and Prayer. Hell had been the *Terror*, and Prayer the *Bribe*, which have won the allegiance of the timid and the needy. These two master passions of Terror and Despair have brought the ignorant, the shrinking and the unfortunate portions of mankind, to the foot of the Cross. Even these are being effaced by new and better teaching of the Priests and by the silent forces of Humanity and Fact.

The vice, fraud, injustice and disease which exist in the world after eighteen centuries of Christianity, show that it is time it gave place to something else. Society is parched by the arid tenets of deterrent faith and futile prayer. There can be little misgiving at the removal of an obstruction which prevents the influx of the refreshing and irrigating waters of reason and truth.

The salutary forces of the world are secular. Christianity is receding, Science is advancing: Christianity is being explained away, Science is being explained into potent existence.

My Apprenticeship (1926), by Beatrice Webb. Selections.

Beatrice Webb (1858-1943), was the daughter of a successful industrialist. She became an eminent Fabian socialist, historian and political strategist. She collaborated with her husband Sidney in formulating policy for the early Labour Party, and helped to found the London School of Economics and the *New Statesman*.

Looking back from the standpoint of to-day (1926), it seems to me that two outstanding tenets, some would say, two idols of the mind, were united in this mid-Victorian trend of thought and feeling. There was the current belief in the scientific method, in that intellectual synthesis of observation and experiment, hypothesis and verification, by means of which alone all mundane problems were to be solved. And added to this belief in science was the consciousness of a new motive; the transference of the emotion of self-sacrificing service from God to man.

In these latter days of deep disillusionment, now that we have learnt, by the bitter experience of the Great War, to what vile uses the methods and results of science may be put, when these are inspired and directed by brutal instinct and base motive, it is hard to understand the naive belief of the most original and vigorous minds of the 'seventies and 'eighties that it was by science, and by science alone, that all human misery would be ultimately swept away. This almost fanatical faith was perhaps partly due to hero-worship. For who will deny that the men of science were the leading British intellectuals of that period; that it was they who stood out as men of genius with international reputations; that it was they who were the self-confident militants of the period; that it was they who were routing the theologians, confounding the mystics, imposing their theories on philosophers, their inventions on capitalists, and their discoveries on medical men; whilst they were at the same time snubbing the artists, ignoring the poets and even casting doubts on the capacity of the politicians? Nor was the cult of the scientific method confined to intellectuals. "Halls of Science" were springing up in crowded working-class districts; and Bradlaugh, the fearless exponent of scientific materialism and the "Fruits of Philosophy", was the most popular demagogue of the hour. Persecuted, proscribed and denounced by those who stood in the high places of Church and State, he nevertheless, by sheer force of character and widespread popular support, imposed himself on the House of Commons, and compelled it finally to abandon its theological test for membership. Indeed, in the 'seventies and 'eighties it looked as if whole sections of the British proletariat — and these the élite — would be swept, like the corresponding class on the Continent, into a secularist movement. To illustrate this idolisation of science, I give one quotation from a widely read little book published in 1872, [Winwood Reade, *The Martyrdom of Man*], which, on account of the broad culture and passionate sincerity with which the author idenrifies science with the intellect of man, has become a classic, and which foreshadows a universe over which the human intellect will reign as the creator and moulder of all things, whether on earth or in heaven.

"His triumph [the triumph of man regarded as pure intellect], indeed, is incomplete; his Kingdom has not yet come. The Prince of Darkness is still triumphant in many regions of the world; epidemics still rage; death is yet victorious. But the God of Light, the Spirit of Knowledge, the Divine Intellect, is gradually spreading over the planet, and upwards to the skies . . . Earth, which is now a purgatory, will be made a paradise, not by idle prayers and supplications, but by the efforts of man himself, and by mental achievements analogous to those which have raised him to his present state. Those inventions and discoveries which have made him, by the grace of God, king of animals, lord of the elements, and sovereign of steam and electricity, were all founded on experiment and observation . . . When we have ascertained, by means of Science, the methods of Nature's operation, we shall be able to take her place and to perform them for ourselves. When we understand the laws which regulate the complex phenomena of life, we shall be able to predict the future as we are already able to predict comets and eclipses and the planetary movements . . . Not only will man subdue the forces of evil that are without; he will subdue those that are within. He will repress the base instincts and propensities which he has inherited from the animals below him; he will obey the laws written in his heart; he will worship the divinity that is within him . . . Idleness and stupidity will be regarded with abhorrence. Women will become the companions of men, and the tutors of their children. The whole world will be united by the same sentiment which united the primeval clan, and which made its members think, feel and act as one . . . These bodies which now we wear belong to the lower animals; our minds have already outgrown them; already we look upon them with contempt. A time will come when Science will transform them by means which we cannot conjecture, and which if explained to us we could not now understand, just as the savage cannot understand electricity, magnetism, steam. Disease will be extirpated; the causes of decay will be removed; immortality will be invented. And then the earth being small, mankind will emigrate into space and will cross airless Saharas which separate planet from planet, and sun from sun. The earth will become a Holy Land which will be visited by pilgrims from all the quarters of the universe. Finally, men will master the forces of Nature; they will become themselves architects of systems, manufacturers of worlds. Man will then be perfect; he will be a creator; he will therefore be what the vulgar worship as God."

This unhesitating reliance on the particular type of mental activty, which is always associated with modern, or shall I call it Western science, was by far the most potent ferment at work in the mental environment in which I was reared, whether in the books I read or the persons with whom I associated on terms of intimacy. When the brain is young there are written words which serve as master-keys to unlock the mind. Long abstracts of, and extracts from, George Henry Lewes's *History of Philosophy* appear in my diary in the autumn of 1881. The gist of Lewes's argument is a contemptuous dismissal of all metaphysics "as condemned, by the very nature of its method, to wander forever in one tortuous labyrinth, within whose circumscribed and winding spaces weary seekers are continually finding themselves in the trodden tracks of predecessors who could find no exit". In contrast with this tragic failure of metaphysical speculation the progress of modern science is eulogised in glowing phrases; "Onward and ever onward, mightier and forever mightier, rolls this wondrous tide of discovery".

****

So much for the belief in science and the scientific method, which was certainly the most salient, as it was the most original, element of the mid-Victorian Time-Spirit. But the scientific method of reasoning, so it seemed to my practical mind, was not an end in itself; it was the means by which a given end could be pursued. It did not, and as I thought could not, yield the purpose of life. What it did was to show the way, and the only way, in which the chosen purpose could be fulfilled. To what end, for what purpose, and therefore *upon what subject-matter* was the new faculty of the intellect to be exercised? And here I come to the second element of the mid-Victorian Time-Spirit: the emotion, which like the warp before the woof, gives strength and direction to the activities of the intellect. I suggest it was during the middle decades of the nineteenth century that, in England, the impulse of selfsubordinating service was transferred, consciously and overtly, from God to man. It would be interesting to trace the first beginnings of this elusive change of feeling. How far was it latent in the dogma that underlay the rise of American Democracy, that all men are born free and equal, with equal rights to life, liberty and the pursuit of happiness? I recall the saying of a well-known leader of the American ethical movement: "As a free-born citizen, I deny the existence of an autocratic Supreme Being to whom I, and all other men, owe obedience and worship; it offends my American sense of independence and equality!" How far was the passing of the Kingdom of God and the coming of the Kingdom of Man implicit in the "Liberty, Equality, and Fraternity" of the French Revolution, with its worship of the Goddess of Reason? We certainly find this new version of "the whole duty of man" in the characteristic political maxim of the British Utilitarians, which prescribed, as the object of human effort, the greatest happiness of the greatest number. With a more romantic content we see it in the life and work of Robert Owen, with his "worship of the supremely good principle in human nature", which became a "social bible", promulgated by "social missionaries" in a "social cathedral".

In the particular social and intellectual environment in which I lived, this stream of tendencies culminated in Auguste Comte's union of the "religion of humanity" with a glorification of science, in opposition to both theology and metaphysics, as the final stage in the development of the human intellect. And once again I note that the reading of books was in my case directed and supplemented by friendly intercourse with the men and women most concerned with the subject matter of the books. As a student I was familiar with the writings, of the most famous of the English disciples and admirers of Auguste Comte. I had learned my lesson from George Henry Lewes. I delighted in John Stuart Mill's *Autobiography*, and had given to his *System of Logic* and *Principles of Political Economy* an assiduous though somewhat strained attention. Above all, the novels of George Eliot had been eagerly read and discussed in the family circle. But I doubt whether my sister Margaret and I would have ordered from the London Library all the works of Comte himself if it had not been for a continuously friendly intercourse with the Frederic Harrisons, at reciprocal dinner-parties in London, picnics in the Cliveden Woods and week-end parties in our respective country homes. In after years the Frederic Harrisons stand out from a host of former London acquaintances as loyal friends, encouraging me in my first attempt at authorship, and in due course welcoming as another friend The Other One. But in those early days they appeared to me as "society folk". For, in spite of heterodox opinions and courageous association with men and women deemed to be undesirable and even pernicious, this accomplished couple, possibly because they were at once well-to-do and personally attractive, were full-fledged members of political society, as distinguished from the narrower Court circle and the more fashionable sporting set. At the social functions of the Gladstonian Administration of 1880-1886 they were much in evidence; more especially were they on terms of intimate comaradeship with the rising group of Radical statesmen and journalists. Unlike the ruck of clever authors, successful barristers, and minor politicians on the make, they selected their acquaintances according to their own scale of values; and, once chosen, they stood through good and evil repute by those whom they deemed to be friends. A brilliant publicist, and insisten lecturer, a most versatile and sympathetic conversationalist, Frederic Harrison had also the greater distinction of being an original thinker and a public-spirited citizen, always eager to appreciate new ideas and encourage unrecognised intellectuals. It was he who first explained to me the economic validity of trade unionism and factory legislation; who taught me to resist the current depreciation of the mediaeval social organisation; and who, in spite of his extreme "positivism", emphasised the real achievements in their own time of the Catholic Church and the craft gilds.

****

Notwithstanding our friendship with the Frederic Harrisons and other leading Comtists, it certainly never occurred to me to join the Church of Humanity. Yet five years afterwards I find, as the prefacing text to a new MS. book, copied out in large letters for my own edification, the following quotation from Auguste Comte:

"Our harmony as moral beings is impossible on any other foundation but altruism. Nay more, altruism alone can enable us to live in the highest and truest sense. To live for others is the only means of developing the whole existence of man.

"Towards humanity, whom is the only true great Being, we, the conscious elements of whom She is the compound, shall henceforth direct every aspect of our life, individual and collective. Our thoughts will be devoted to the knowledge of Humanity, our affections to the love, our actions to her service." [MS. diary, March 15, 1889.]

****

"Social questions [I write in the MS. Diary of 1884] are the vital questions of to-day: they take the place of religion. I do not pretend to solve them. Their solution seems largely a matter of temperament. Still, the most insignificant mind has a certain bias, has an intellectual as well as moral conscience. If we wilfully defy the laws of our special mental constitution we must suffer the penalty of a diseased and twisted nature, and must leave life conscious of faithlessness to the faith that is in us . . . A higher standard of motive is asked for in social action than in any other . . . The social reformer professes to be an uncompromising idealist; he solemnly declares that he is working for the public weal. His whole authority, derived from public opinion, arises from the faith of the people in his honesty of purpose and strength of understanding. If he uses his mind to manipulate facts, and twist them so that they shall serve his own personal interests, if the craving for power is greater than the desire for truth, he is a traitor to the society towards which he professes loyal service." [MS. diary, April 22, 1884]

****

Now, without pretending to sum up the influence of the time-spirit on the social activities of the last quarter of the nineteenth century, what is clear is that upon me — in 1883, a woman of twenty-five — it lead to a definite conclusion. From the flight of emotion away from the service of God to the service of man, and from the current faith in the scientific method, I drew the inference that the most hopeful form of social service was the craft of a social investigator. And some such conclusion seems to have been reached by many of my contemporaries. For detailed descriptions of the life and labour of the people in all its various aspects, sensational or scientific, derived from personal observation or statistical calculation, become a characteristic feature of the publications of this period, whether newspapers or magazines, plays or novels, the reports of philanthropic organisations or the proceedings of learned societies. It may be said that this novel concentration of attention on the social condition of the people was due neither to intellectual curiosity nor to the spirit of philanthropy, but rather to a panic fear of the newly enfranchised democracy. But this is looking at the same fact from another standpoint. For even the most fanatical Socialist asserted that his hopes for the future depended on a deliberately scientific organisation of society, combined with the growth among the whole body of the people of the desire and capacity for disinterested social service.

Chapter X

The New Social Conscience

Introduction

During the decade of the 1880s there developed in the middle and upper classes, particularly among the young and intellectually aware, a sharpened sensitivity towards the problems of the poor. This quickened awareness of poverty coloured the public mood of the decade, and helped create an atmosphere in which the near-sacred conventions of mid-Victorian liberalism — self-help and laissez-faire — could be openly questioned. Sir William Harcourt summed up the new climate of sympathy for the working classes and the willingness to consider new solutions to social problems when he said, in 1889, "We are all socialists now".

On the left wings of both major political parties there emerged in the 80s programs for positive social action on the part of the state, and Salisbury, the Tory leader, took significant steps towards establishing an active role for the state in providing housing for the very poor. The socialist roots of the Labour Party, the Fabian Society and the Social Democratic Federation, were established in the 80s, and the first English translation of *Das Kapital* by Karl Marx appeared in 1887. Political action at the parliamentary level, however, or genuine socialist activity, were not the most characteristic reflections of the social conscience of the decade. The crowds who flocked to hear the attacks on political economy delivered by Henry George, the American author of *Progress and Poverty* (1879), had no clearly formed ideas about how to reform society. Nor did the young men from the public schools and universities who hoped to bring civilization and Christianity to the slums of London by establishing "settlements" there. Neither did those men who were inspired by T.H. Green at Oxford to commit their lives to social service individualism in the social sphere was reinforced by the crumbling of evangelical certainties at the same time. During the 80s the leading theologians among Nonconformists and Churchmen attempted to shift attention in their churches away from the old evangelical by helping those whom they now recognized could not help themselves. But all of these people helped to bring about a climate of public opinion in which, a little later on, positive state action to improve the welfare of the poor seemed not only possible, but necessary.

The churches made a major contribution to this shift in public opinion. In the 80s Christian socialist groups were organized in all the major denominations. While none of these groups developed clearly conceived innovative solutions to the problems they publicized, they clearly both reflected and helped to disseminate sympathy for the poor. The Christian socialists, moreover, were not considered peculiar or relegated to the fringes of their denominations. Some of them were among the leading clergymen of the time, occupying positions of honour and influence in their churches.

What caused the shift in public opinion in the 80s? There is as yet no satisfactory answer to that difficult question. Certainly the mere existence of more information about poverty cannot be the basic cause, for the conditions of slum life were constantly reported from the late 1830s. It is easier to describe than explain the vague sense among many men and women that social theories which emphasized individualism were no longer adequate. This de-emphasis of individualism in the social sphere was reinforced by the crumbling of evangelical certainties at the same time. During the 80s the leading theologians among Nonconformists and Churchmen attempted to shift attention in their churches away from the old evangelical concentration on Christ's life and its implications for contemporary behaviour. Emphasis on God's merciful Fatherhood replaced stress on the eternal punishment of the wicked. A corollary of this Incarnationist theology was recognition of the importance of social action.

The collapse of evangelicalism among men of weight and influence, important as this may have been for the religious life of the nation, cannot explain the new mood of the 80s. By that time religion had become more reflector than a prime mover of intellectual currents. The prime mover for the 1880s is not yet adequately understood.

Guide To Further Reading

Helen M. Lynd, *England in the Eighteen-Eighties* (1945) treats the decade as a time when public opinion was moving rapidly towards accepting new conceptions of social justice. The development of socialism is discussed in Henry Pelling, *Origins of the Labour Party, 1880-1900* (1954), and the impact of religion on socialist thought is stressed in Willard Wolfe's study of Fabian ideas, *From Radicalism to Socialism* (1975). The nature of T.H. Green's commitment to social action is probed in Melvin Richter's penetrating study of his religion and philosophy, *The Politics of Conscience* (1964).

The Christian Socialist Revival, 1877-1914 (1968), by Peter d'A. Jones is a good detailed account of the movement and is unlikely to be superseded. The social views of leading Anglicans throughout the century are studied in G. Kitson Clark, *Churchmen and the Condition of England* (1973). Octavia Barnett's memorial to her husband, *Canon Barnett, His Life, Work and Friends* (2 vols., 1918) is a fascinating memoir of a man deeply involved in the changing social attitudes of the late Victorian Church. David Newsome examines the links between Anglo-Catholicism and social reform in "The Assault on Mammon: Charles Gore and John Neville Figgis", *Journal of Ecclesiastical History* (1966). K.S. Inglis does the same for Dissent in "English Nonconformity and Social Reform, 1880-1900", *Past and Present* (1958). Geoffrey Best emphasizes the theoretical weakness and immediate ineffectuality of Christian socialists in his published lecture, *Bishop Westcott and the Miners* (1968). Anthony Wohl, in "The Bitter Cry of Outcast London", *International Review of Social History* (1968), attempts to explain why poverty attracted so much middle-class attention in the 1880s. He suggests many factors that should be taken into account. Gareth Stedman Jones's excellent book, *Outcast London* (1971), provides a good description of changes in philanthropic styles and a brilliant picture of the structure of London's economy in the second half of the nineteenth century. Writing from a Marxist perspective, he interprets the aroused social conscience of the middle classes as fear of rebellion.

The Bitter Cry of Outcast London (1883), by Andrew Mearns.
Complete text.

The *Bitter Cry* first appeared as an anonymously written pamphlet
in 1883. Its principal author was the Reverend Andrew Mearns,
secretary of the London Congregational Union. Neither the
conceptual framework nor the research for the pamphlet were
particularly original. There had been many similar studies by various
groups and individuals. What was extraordinary was the immense
reaction to its publication. The *Bitter Cry* undoubtedly was
responsible for the renewed interest in housing for the poor.
Conservative and Liberal politicians read and discussed Mearns'
work. Even Queen Victoria was deeply moved by it. "Outcast
London" became an everyday expression.

It is noteworthy that the pamphlet had perhaps more of an impact
in secular than religious circles. Sections of the *Bitter Cry* clearly
indicate the failure of the older evangelical Christian efforts to help
the downtrodden. It also accepts the notion that poverty might be
out of the control of the individual whatever his desire for
self-improvement.

There is no more hopeful sign in the Christian Church of today than
the increased attention which is being given by it to the poor and
outcast classes of society. Of these it has never been wholly neglectful,
if it had it would have ceased to be Christian. But it has, as yet, only
imperfectly realised and fulfilled its mission to the poor. Until recently
it has contented itself with sustaining some outside organisations,
which have charged themselves with this special function, or what
is worse, has left the matter to individuals or to little bands of
Christians having no organisation. For the rest it has been satisfied
with a superficial and inadequate district visitation, with the more
or less indiscriminate distribution of material charities, and with
opening a few rooms here and there into which the poorer people
have been gathered, and by which a few have been rescued. All this
is good in its way and has done good; but by all only the merest edge
of the great dark region of poverty, misery, squalor and immorality
has been touched. We are not losing sight of the London City Mission,
whose agents are everywhere, and whose noble work our
investigations have led us to value more than ever, but, after all has
been done the churches are making the discovery that seething in
the very centre of our great cities, concealed by the thinnest crust

of civilization and decency, is a vast mass of moral corruption, of heart-breaking misery and absolute godlessness, and that scarcely anything has been done to take into this awful slough the only influences that can purify or remove it.

Whilst we have been building our churches and solacing ourselves with our religion and dreaming that the millennium was coming, the poor have been growing poorer, the wretched more miserable, and the immoral more corrupt; the gulf has been daily widening which separates the lowest classes of the community from our churches and chapels, and from all decency and civilization. It is easy to bring an array of facts which seem to point to the opposite conclusion — to speak of the noble army of men and women who penetrate the vilest haunts, carrying with them the blessings of the gospel; of the encouraging reports published by Missions, Reformatories, Refuges, Temperance Societies; of Theatre Services, Midnight Meetings and Special Missions. But what does it all amount to? We are simply living in a fool's paradise if we suppose that all these agencies combined are doing a thousandth part of what needs to be done, a hundredth part of what *could* be done by the Church of Christ. We must face the facts; and these compel the conviction that THIS TERRIBLE FLOOD OF SIN AND MISERY IS GAINING UPON US. It is rising every day. This statement is made as the result of a long, patient and sober inquiry, undertaken for the purpose of discovering the actual state of the case and the remedial action most likely to be effective. Convinced that it is high time some combined and organized effort was made by all demominations of Christians, though not for denominational purposes, the London Congregational Union have determined to open in several of the lowest and most needy districts of the metropolis, suitable Mission Halls, as a base of operations for evangelistic work. They have accordingly made this diligent search, and some of the results are set forth in the following pages, in the hope that all who have the power may be stimulated to help the Union in the great and difficult enterprise which they have undertaken.

Two cautions it is important to bear in mind. First, the information given *does not refer to selected cases*. It simply reveals a state of things which is found in house after house, court after court, street after street. Secondly, there *has been absolutely no* exaggeration. It is a plain recital of plain facts. Indeed, no respectable printer would print, and certainly no decent family would admit even the driest statement of the horrors and infamies discovered in one brief visitation from house to house. *So far from making the worst of our facts for the purpose of appealing to emotion, we have been compelled to tone down everything, and wholly to omit what most needs to be known, or the ears and eyes of our readers would have been insufferably outraged.* Yet even this qualified narration must be to every Christian heart a loud and bitter cry, appealling for the help which it is the supreme mission of the Church to supply. It should be further stated that our investigations were made in the summer. The condition of the poor during the winter months must be very much worse.

NON-ATTENDANCE AT WORSHIP

It is perhaps scarcely necessary to say of the hundreds of thousands who compose the class referred to, that very few attend any place of worship. It is a very tame thing to say, and a very little thing compared with what must follow, but it is needful to proper statement of our case. Before going to the lower depths, where our investigations were principally carried on, we find in the neighbourhood of Old Ford, in 147 consecutive houses, inhabited for the most part by the respectable working class, 212 families, 118 of which never, under any circumstances, attend a place of worship. Out of 2,290 persons living in consecutive houses at Bow Common, only 88 adults and 47 children ever attend, and as 64 of these are connected with one Mission Hall, only 24 out of the entire number worship elsewhere. One street off Leicester Square contains 246 families, and only 12 of these are ever represented at the house of God. In another street in Pentonville, out of 100 families only 12 persons attend any sanctuary, whilst the number of attendants in one district of St. George's-in-the-East is 39 persons out of 4,235. Often the numbers given of those who do attend include such as only go once or twice a year, at some charity distribution, so that our figures are more favourable than the actual facts. Constantly we come across persons who have never been to church or chapel for 20 years, 28 years, more than 30 years; and some persons as old as 64 never remember having been in a place of worship at all. Indeed, with the exception of a very small proportion, the idea of going has never dawned upon these people. And who can wonder? Think of

THE CONDITION IN WHICH THEY LIVE

We do not say the condition of their homes, for how can those places be called homes, compared with which the lair of a wild beast would be a comfortable and healthy spot? Few who will read these pages have any conception of what these pestilential human rookeries are, where tens of thousands are crowded together amidst horrors which call to mind what we have heard of the middle passage of the slave ship. To get into them you have to penetrate courts reeking with poisonous and malodorous gases arising from accumulations of sewage and refuse scattered in all directions and often flowing beneath your feet; courts, many of them which the sun never penetrates, which are never visited by a breath of fresh air, and which rarely know the virtues of a drop of cleansing water. You have to ascend rotten staircases, which threaten to give way beneath every step, and which, in some places, have already broken down, leaving gaps that imperil the limbs and lives of the unwary. You have to grope your way along dark and filthy passages swarming with vermin. Then, if you are not driven back by the intolerable stench, you may gain admittance to the dens in which these thousands of beings who belong, as much as you, to the race for whom Christ died, herd together. Have you pitied the poor creatures who sleep under railway arches, in carts or casks, or under any shelter which they can find in the open air? You will see that they are to be envied in comparison with those whose lot it is to seek refuge here. Eight feet square — that is about the average size of very many of these rooms. Walls and ceiling are black with the accretions of filth which have gathered upon them through long years of neglect. It is exuding through cracks in the boards overhead; it is running down the walls; it is everywhere. What goes by the name of a window is half of it stuffed with rags or covered by boards to keep out wind and rain; the rest is so begrimed and obscured that scarcely can light enter or anything be seen outside.

Should you have ascended to the attic, where at least some approach to fresh air might be expected to enter from open or broken window, you look out upon the roofs and ledges of lower tenements, and discover that the sickly air which finds its way into the room has to pass over the putrefying carcases of dead cats or birds, or viler abominations still. The buildings are in such miserable repair as to suggest the thought that if the wind could only reach them they would soon be toppling about the heads of their occupants. As to furniture — you may perchance discover a broken chair, the tottering relics of an old bedstead, or the mere fragment of a table; but more commonly you will find rude substitutes for these things in the shape of rough boards resting upon bricks, an old hamper or box turned upside down, or more frequently still, nothing but rubbish and rags.

Every room in these rotten and reeking tenements houses a family, often two. In one cellar a sanitary inspector reports finding a father, mother, three children, and four pigs! In another room a missionary found a man ill with small-pox, his wife just recovering from her eighth confinement, and the children running about half naked and covered with dirt. Here are seven people living in one underground kitchen, and a little dead child lying in the same room. Elsewhere is a poor widow, her three children, and a child who had been dead thirteen days. Her husband, who was a cabman, had shortly before committed suicide. Here lives a widow and her six children, including one daughter of 29, another of 21, and a son of 27. Another apartment contains father, mother, and six children, two of whom are ill with scarlet fever. In another nine brothers and sisters, from 29 years of age downwards, live, eat and sleep together. Here is a mother who turns her children into the street in the early evening because she lets her room for immoral purposes until long after midnight, when the poor little wretches creep back again if they have not found some miserable shelter elsewhere. Where there are beds they are simply heaps of dirty rags, shavings or straw, but for the most part these miserable beings find rest only upon the filthy boards. The tenant of this room is a widow, who herself occupies the only bed, and lets the floor to a married couple for 2s. 6d. per week. In many cases matters are made worse by the unhealthy occupations followed by those whom dwell in these habitations. Here you are choked as you enter by the air laden with particles of the superfluous fur pulled from the skins of rabbits, rats, dogs and other animals in their preparation for the furrier. Here the smell of paste and of drying match-boxes, mingling with other sickly odours, overpowers you; or it may be the fragrance of stale fish or vegetables, not sold on the previous day, and kept in the room overnight. Even when it is possible to do so the people seldom open their windows, but if they did it is questionable whether much would be gained, for the external air is scarcely less heavily charged with poison than the atmosphere within.

Wretched as these rooms are they are beyond the means of many who wander about all day, picking up a living as they can, and then take refuge at night in one of the common lodging-houses that abound. These are often the resorts of thieves and vagabonds of the lowest type, and some are kept by receivers of stolen goods. In the kitchen men and women may be seen cooking their food, washing their clothes, or lolling about smoking and gambling. In the sleeping room are long rows of beds on each side, sometimes 60 or 80 in one room. In many cases both sexes are allowed to herd together without any attempt to preserve the commonest decency. But there is a lower depth still. Hundreds cannot even scrape together the two pence required to secure them the privilege of resting in those sweltering common sleeping rooms, and so they huddle together upon the stairs and landings, where it is no uncommon thing to find six or eight in the early morning.

That people condemned to exist under such conditions take to drink and fall into sin is surely a matter for little surprise. We may rather say, as does one recent and reliable explorer, that they are "entitled to credit for not being twenty times more depraved than they are." One of the saddest results of this over-crowding is the inevitable association of honest people with criminals. Often is the family of an honest working man compelled to take refuge in a thieves' kitchen; in the houses where they live their rooms are frequently side by side, and continual contact with the very worst of those who have come out of our gaols is a matter of necessity. There can be no question that numbers of habitual criminals would never have become such, had they not by force of circumstances been packed together in these slums with those who were hardened in crime. Who can wonder that every evil flourishes in such hotbeds of vice and disease? Who can wonder that little children taken from these hovels to the hospital cry, when they are well, through dread of being sent back to their former misery? Who can wonder that young girls wander off into a life of immorality, which promises release from such conditions? Who can wonder that the public-house is "the Elysian field of the tired toiler?"

IMMORALITY

is but the natural outcome of conditions like these. "Marriage," it has been said, "as an institution, is not fashionable in these districts." And this is only the bare truth. Ask if the men and women living together in these rookeries are married, and your simplicity will cause a smile. Nobody knows. Nobody cares. Nobody expects that they are. In exceptional cases only could your question be answered in the affirmative. Incest is common; and no form of vice and sensuality causes surprise or attracts attention. Those who appear to be married are often separated by a mere quarrel, and they do not hesitate to form similar companionships immediately. One man was pointed out who for some years had lived with a woman, the mother of his three children. She died and in less than a week he had taken another woman in her place. A man was living with a woman in the low district called "The Mint." He went out one morning with another man for the purpose of committing a burglary and by that other man was murdered. The murderer returned saying that his companion had been caught and taken away to prison; and the same night he took the place of the murdered man. The only check upon communism in this regard is jealousy and not virtue. The vilest practices are looked upon with the most matter-of-fact indifference. The low parts of London are the sink into which the filthy and abominable from all parts of the country seem to flow. Entire courts are filled with thieves, prostitutes and liberated convicts. In one street are 35 houses, 32 of which are known to be brothels. In another district are 43 of these houses, and 428 fallen women and girls, many of them not more than 12 years of age. A neighbourhood whose populataion is returned at

10,100, contains 400 who follow this immoral traffic, their ages varying from 13 to 50; and of the moral degradation of the people, some idea may be formed from an incident which was brought to our notice. An East-end missionary rescued a young girl from an immoral life, and obtained her a situation with people who were going abroad. He saw her to Southampton, and on his return was violently abused by the girl's grandmother, who had the sympathy of her neighbours, for having taken away from a poor old woman her means of subsistence.

The misery and sin caused by drink in these districts have often been told, but these horrors can never be set forth either by pen or artist's pencil. In the district of Euston Road is one publichouse to every 100 people, counting men, women and children. Immediately around our chapel in Orange Street, Leicester Square, are 100 gin-palaces, most of them very large; and these districts are but samples of what exists in all the localities which we have investigated. Look into one of these glittering saloons, with its motley, miserable crowd, and you may be horrified as you think of the evil that is nightly wrought here there; but contrast it with any of the abodes which you find in the fetid courts behind them, and you will wonder no longer that it is crowded. With its brightness, its excitement, and its temporary forgetfulness of misery, it is a comparative heaven to tens of thousands. How can they be expected to resist its temptations? They could not live if they did not drink, even though they know that by drinking they do worse than die. All kinds of depravity have here their schools. Children who can scarcely walk are taught to steal, and mercilessly beaten if they come back from their daily expeditions without money or money's worth. Many of them are taken by the hand or carried in the arms to the gin-palace, and not seldom may you see mothers urging and compelling their tender infants to drink the fiery liquid. Lounging at the doors and lolling out of windows and prowling about street corners were pointed out several well-known members of the notorious band of "Forty Thieves," who, often in conspiracy with abandoned women, go out after dark to rob people in Oxford Street, Regent Street, and other thoroughfares. Here you pass a coffee-house, there a wardrobe shop, there a tobacconists's, and there a grocers', carrying on a legitimate trade no doubt, but a far different and more remunerative one as well, especially after evening sets in, — all traps to catch the unwary. These particulars indicate but faintly the moral influences from which the dwellers in these squalid regions have no escape, and by which is bred "infancy that knows no innocence, youth without modesty or shame, maturity that is mature in nothing but suffering and guilt, blasted old age that is a scandal on the name we bear."

Another difficulty with which we have to contend, and one in large measure the cause of what we have described, is the

POVERTY

of these miserable outcasts. The poverty, we mean, of those who try to live honestly; for notwithstanding the sickening revelations of immorality which have been disclosed to us, those who endeavour to earn their bread by honest work far outnumber the dishonest. And it is to their infinite credit that it should be so considering that they are daily face to face with the contrast between their wretched earnings and those which are the produce of sin. A child seven years old is known easily to make 10s. 6d. a week by thieving, but what can he earn by such work as match-box making, for which 2¼d. a gross is paid, the maker having to find his own fire for drying the boxes, and his own paste and string? Before he can gain as much as the young thief he must make 56 gross of match-boxes a week, or 1,296 a day. It is needless to say that this is impossible, for even adults can rarely make more than an average of half that number. How long then must the little hands toil before they can earn the price of the scantiest meal! Women, for the work of trousers finishing (*i.e.,* sewing in linings, making button-holes and stitching on the buttons) receive 2½d. a pair, and have to find their own thread. We ask a woman who is making tweed trousers, how much she can earn in a day, and are told one shilling. But what does a day mean to this poor soul? *Seventeen hours!* From five in the morning to ten at night — no pause for meals. She eats her crust and drinks a little tea as she works, making in very truth, with her needle and thread, not her living only, but her shroud. For making men's shirts these women are paid 10d. a dozen; lawn tennis aprons, 3d. a dozen; and babies' hoods, from

1s. to 2s. 6d. a dozen. In St. George's-in-the-East large numbers of women and children, some of the latter only seven years old, are employed in sack-making, for which they get a farthing each. In one house was found a widow and her half-idiot daughter making palliasses at 1¼d. each. Here is a woman who has a sick husband and a little child to look after. She is employed at shirt finishing at 3d. a dozen, and by the utmost effort can only earn 6d. a day, out of which she has to find her own thread. Another, with a crippled hand, maintains herself and a blind husband by match-box making, for which she is remunerated of the liberal scale mentioned above; and out of her 2¼d. a gross she has to pay a girl a penny a gross to help her. Others obtain at Covent Garden in the season 1d. or 2d. a peck for shelling peas, or 6d. a basket for walnuts; and they do well if their labour brings them 10d. or a shilling a day. With men it is comparatively speaking no better. "My master," says one man visited by a recent writer in the *Fortnightly Review,* "gets a pound for what he gives me 3s. for making." And this it is easy to believe, when we know that for a pair of fishing boots which will be sold at three guineas, the poor workman receives 5s. 3d, if they are made to order, or 4s. 6d. if made for stock. An old tailor and his wife are employed in making policemen's overcoats. They have to make, finish, hot-press, put on the buttons, and find their own thread, and for all this they receive 2s. 10d. for each coat. This old couple work from half-past six in the morning until ten at night, and between them can just manage to make a coat in two days. Here is a mother who has taken away whatever articles of clothing she can strip from her four little children without leaving them absolutely naked. She has pawned them, not for drink, but for coals and food. A shilling is all she can procure, and with this she has bought seven pounds of coals and a loaf of bread. We might fill page after page with these dreary details, but they would become sadly monotonous, for it is the same everywhere. And then it should not be forgotten how hardly upon poverty like this must press the exorbitant demand for rent. Even the rack-renting of Ireland, which so stirred our indignation a little while ago, was merciful by comparison. If by any chance a reluctant landlord can be induced to execute or pay for some long-needed repairs, they become the occasion for new exactions. Going through these rooms we come to one in which a hole as big as a man's head, has been roughly covered, and how? A piece of board, from an old soap-box, has been fixed over the opening by one nail, and to the tenant has been given a yard and a half of paper with which to cover it; and for this expenditure — perhaps 4d. at the outside — *threepence a week has been put upon the rent.* If this is enough to arouse our indignation, what must be thought of the following? The two old people just mentioned have lived in one room for 14 years, during which time it has only once been partially cleansed. The landlord has undertaken that it shall be done shortly, and for the past three months has been taking 6d. a week extra for rent for what he is thus *going to do.* This is what the helpless have to submit to; they are charged for these pestilential dens a rent which consumes half the earnings of a family, and leaves them no more than from 4d. to 6d. a day for food, clothing, and fire; a grinding of the faces of the poor which could scarcely be parallelled in lands of slavery and of notorious oppression. This, however, is not all; for even these depths of poverty and degradation are reached by the Education Act, and however beneficent its purpose, it bears with cruel weight upon the class we have described, to whom twopence or a penny a week for the school fees of each of three or four children, means so much lack of bread.

Amidst such poverty and squalor it is inevitable that one should be constantly confronted with scenes of

HEART-BREAKING MISERY —

misery so pitiful that men whose daily duty it has been for years to go in and out amongst these outcasts, and to be intimately acquainted with their sufferings, and who might, therefore, be supposed to regard with comparatively little feeling that which would overwhelm an unaccustomed spectator, sometimes come away from their visits so oppressed in spirit and absorbed in painful thought, that they know not whither they are going. How these devoted labourers can pursue their work at all is a marvel, especially when it is remembered that the misery they actually see suggests to them the certain existence of so much more which no human eye discovers. Who can even imagine the suffering which lies behind a case like the following? A poor woman in an advanced stage of consumption, reduced almost to a skelton, lives in a single room with a drunken husband and five children. When visited she was eating a few green peas. The children were gone to gather some sticks wherewith a fire might be made to boil four potatoes which were lying on the table, and which would constitute the family dinner for the day. Or, take another case related by Rev. Archibald Brown, who, with his missionaries, is doing a noble work amongst the poor in the East of London. People had doubted the accuracy of reports presented by the missionaries, and he accordingly devoted a considerable time to personal visitation and inquiry. He found case after case proving that but little of the wretchedness had been told, and here is a *fair specimen*. At the top of an otherwise empty house lived a family; the husband had gone to try and find some work. The mother, 29 years of age, was sitting on the only chair in the place in front of a grate destitute of any fire. She was nursing a baby six weeks old, that had never had anything but one old rag around it. The mother had nothing but a gown on, and that dropping to pieces; it was all she had night or day. There were six children under 13 years of age. They were barefooted, and the few rags on them scarcely covered their nakedness. In this room, where was an unclothed infant the ceiling was in holes. An old bedstead was in the place, and seven sleep in it at night, the eldest girl being on the floor.

This is bad, but it is not the worst. In a room in Wych Street, on the third floor, over a marine store dealer's, there was, a short time ago, an inquest as to the death of a little baby. A man, his wife and three children were living in that room. The infant was the second child who had died, poisoned by the foul atmosphere; and this dead baby was cut open in the one room where its parents and brothers and sisters lived, ate and slept, *because the parish had no mortuary and no room in which post mortems could be performed!* No wonder that the jurymen who went to view the body sickened at the frightful exhalations. This case was given by Mr. G.R. Sims, in his papers on "How the Poor live" but all the particulars are found in the dry newspaper reports of the inquest. In another miserable room are eight destitute children. Their father died a short time ago, and "on going into the house today" says the missionary, "the mother was lying in her coffin." Here is a filthy attic, containing only a broken chair, a battered saucepan and a few rags. On a dirty sack in the centre of the room sits a neglected, ragged, bare-legged little baby girl of four. Her father is a militiaman, and is away. Her mother is out all day and comes home late at night more or less drunk, and this child is left in charge of the infant that we see crawling about the floor; left for six or eight hours at a stretch — hungry, thirsty, tired, but never daring to move from her post. And this is the kind of sight which may be seen in a Christian land where it is criminal to ill-treat a horse or an ass.

The child-misery that one beholds is the most heart-rending and appalling element in these discoveries; and of this not the least is the misery inherited from the vice of drunken and dissolute parents, and manifest in the stunted, misshapen, and often loathsome objects that we constantly meet in these localities. From the beginning of their lives they are utterly neglected; their bodies and rags alive with vermin; they are subjected to the most cruel treatment; many of them have never seen a green field, and do not know what it is to go beyond the streets immediately around them, and they often pass the whole day without a morsel of food. Here is one of three years old picking up some dirty pieces of bread and eating them. We go in at the doorway where it is standing and find a little girl twelve years old. "Where is your mother?" "In the madhouse." "How long has she been there?" "Fifteen months." "Who looks after you?" The child, who is sitting at an old table making match-boxes, replies, "I look after my little brothers and sisters as well as I can." "Where is your father? Is he in work?" "He has been out of work three weeks, but he has gone to a job of two days this morning." Another house visited contains nine motherless children. The mother's death was caused by witnessing one of her children being run over. The eldest is only fourteen years old. All live in one small room, and there is one bed for five. Here is a poor woman deserted by her husband and left with three little children. One met with an accident a few days ago, and broke his arm. He is lying on a shake-down in one corner of the room, with an old sack round him. And here, in a cellar kitchen, are nine little ones. You can scarcely see across the room for smoke and dirt.

They are without food and have scarcely any clothing.

It is heart crushing to think of the misery suggested by such revelations as these; and there is something unspeakably pathetic in the brave patience with which the poor not seldom endure their sufferings, and the tender sympathy which they show toward each other. Where, amongst the well-conditioned, can anything braver and kinder be found than this? A mother, whose children are the cleanest and tidiest in the Board School which they attend, was visited. It was found that, though she had children of her own, she had taken in a little girl, whose father had gone off tramping in search of work. She was propped up in a chair, looking terribly ill, but in front of her, in another chair, was the wash-tub, and the poor woman was making a feeble effort to wash and wring out some of the children's things. She was dying from dropsy, scarcely able to breathe and enduring untold agony, but to the very last striving to keep her little ones clean and tidy. A more touching sight it would be difficult to present; we might, however, unveil many more painful ones, but must content ourselves with saying that the evidence we have gathered from personal observation more than justifies the words of the writer before referred to, that "there are (*e.g.*, in addition to those who find their way to our hospitals) men and women who lie and die day by day in their wretched single rooms, sharing all the family trouble, enduring the hunger and the cold, and waiting without hope, without a single ray of comfort, until God curtains their staring eyes with the merciful film of death."

WHAT IT IS PROPOSED TO DO

That something needs to be done for this pitiable outcast population must be evident to all who have read these particulars as to their condition — at least, to all who believe them. We are quite prepared for incredulity. Even what we have indicated seems all too terrible to be true. But we have sketched only in faintest outline. Far more vivid must be out colours, deeper and darker far the shades, if we are to present a truthful picture of "Outcast London;" and so far as we have been able to go we are prepared with evidence, not only to prove every statement, but to show that these statements represent the general condition of thousands upon thousands in this metropolis. Incredulity is not the only difficulty in the way of stirring up Christian people to help. Despair of success in any such undertaking may paralyse many. We shall be pointed to the fact that without State interference nothing effectual can be accomplished upon any large scale. And *it is* a fact. These wretched people must live somewhere. They must live near the centres where their work lies. They cannot afford to go out by train or tram into the suburbs; and how, with their poor emaciated, starved bodies, can they be expected — in addition to working twelve hours or more, for a shilling, or less, — to walk three or four miles each way to take and fetch? It is notorious that the Artizans' Dwellings Act has, in some respects, made matters worse for them. Large spaces have been cleared of fever-breeding rookeries to make way for the building of decent habitations, but the rents of these are far beyond the means of the abject poor. They are driven to crowd more closely together in the few stifling places still left to them; and so Dives makes a richer harvest out of their misery, buying up property condemned as unfit for habitation, and turning it into a gold mine because the poor must have shelter somewhere, even though it be the shelter of a living tomb.

The State must make short work of this iniquitous traffic, and secure for the poorest the rights of citizenship; the right to live in something better than fever dens; the right to live as something better than the uncleanest brute beasts. This must be done before the Christian missionary can have much chance with them. But because we cannot do all we wish, are we to do nothing? Even as things are something can be accomplished. Is no lifeboat to put out and no life-belt to be thrown because only half-a-dozen out of the perishing hundreds can be saved from the wreck? The very records which supply the sad story we have been telling, give also proofs of what can be done by the Gospel and by Christian love and tact and devotion. Gladly do many of these poor creatures receive the Gospel. Little match-box makers are heard singing at their toil, "One more day's work for Jesus." "If only mother was a Christian we should all be happy," said one; and on his miserable bed, amidst squalor and want and pain, a poor blind man dies with the prayer upon his lips, "Jesus, lover of my soul, Let me to thy bosom fly." Another writes, "You have filled my heart with joy, and my little room with sunshine." A second, who now regularly attends a place of worship, says, speaking of the visits of the missionary, "Before he came to visit me I used to sit and make match-boxes on Sunday, but a word now and then has enabled me to look up to the Lord. I don't feel like the same person." Another who himself became a missionary to his own class, and exercised great power over them whenever he spoke, was able to say, "I was as bad as any of you, but the Lord Jesus had mercy upon me, and has made me better and so happy." This man had been a "coal-whipper" of notoriously evil life, and was rescued through his casually going into a room in one of the courts of which we have spoken, where a missionary was holding a meeting. Such results should rebuke our faithlessness. Even in these dark and noisome places the lamp of Life may be kindled; even from these miry spots bright gems may be snatched, worth all the labour and all the cost.

It is little creditable to us that all our wealth and effort should be devoted to providing for the spiritual needs of those who are comfortably conditioned, and none of it expended upon the abject poor. It is true that we have not half done our duty to any class, but this fact is no justification of our having wholly neglected this rescue work. To shut up our compassion against those who need it most, because we have not yet done our duty to those who need it less, is a course that we should find it hard to justify to our Master and Lord. His tones were ever those of pitying love even to the most sinful outcast, but would they not gather sternness as He met us with the rebuke: "This ought ye to have done, and not to have left the other undone"? An "exceeding bitter cry" is that which goes up to heaven from the misery of London against the apathy of the Church. It is time that Christians opened their ears to it and let it sink down into their hearts. Many pressing needs are taxing the resources of the London Congregational Union, but the Committee feel that this work amongst the poor must no longer be neglected, and that they must do all they can to arouse the Churches of their order to undertake their share of responsibility. They have determined to take immediate action. Having selected three of the very worst districts in London, from which many of the foregoing facts have been gathered, they have resolved at once to begin operations in the very heart of them. No denominational purpose will sway them, except that they will try to awaken their own denomination to a sense of its duty; there will be no attempt to make Congregationalists or to present Congregationalism. Deeper, broader and simpler must this work be than any which can be carried on upon denominational lines. In such a forlorn hope there is no room for sectarianism. The Gospel of the love of Christ must be presented in its simplest form, and the one aim in everything must be to rescue and not to proselytise. Help will be thankfully welcomed from whatever quarter it may come, and help will be freely given to other workers in the same field, if only by any means some may be saved. It is impossible here, and yet, to give details as to the methods which it is proposed to pursue; suffice it to say that in each district a Mission Hall will be erected, or some existing building transformed into a Hall having appliances and conveniences requisite for the successful prosecution of the Mission. Services and meetings of all kinds will be arranged, and, as far as possible, an agency for house to house visitation organised. An attempt must be made to relieve in some wise and practical, though very limited way, the abounding misery, whilst care is taken to prevent the abuse of charity. In this matter the injudicious and inexperienced may easily do more harm than good, pauperising the people whom they wish to help, and making hypocrites instead of Christians. To indicate what we mean we may mention one case pointed out to us of a woman who attended three different places of worship on the Sunday and some others during the week, because she obtained charitable help from all. But we cannot on this account refuse to try some means of mitigating the suffering with which we come into contact. Therefore this must be attempted along with whatever other means the Committee, in conference with those who have had long experience of this work, may think likely to answer the end they have before them. Their hope is that at least some, even of the lowest and worst, may be gathered in; and their aim will be to make as many of these as they can missionaries to the others; for manifestly those who have been accustomed to speak to and work amongst a somewhat better section of the community will not be so likely to labour successfully amongst these outcasts as will those who have themselves been of their number. The three districts already fixed upon are, as it will be understood, intended only to afford a field for the immediate commencement of this beneficent work. Other districts will be occupied as funds come in and the resources of the Committee are enlarged: but even the comparatively limited operations already undertaken will necessitate so great an expenditure and require so much aid from those who are qualified for the work, that they cannot wisely attempt more at present. For not only will the cost and furnishing of Halls and of carrying on the work be very large, but a relief fund will be needed as indicated above. The Committee, therefore, can only hope to carry forward with any success the project to which they have already put their hands, by the really devoted help of the churches which they represent.

DESCRIPTION OF THE DISTRICTS.

The district known as Collier's Rents, is one of the three to which attention will first be given, and the old chapel, long disused, is now in the builder' hands and will soon be ready for opening, not as a chapel, but as a bright, comfortable, and in every way suitable Hall. It would be impossible to find a building better situated for working among the very poor and degraded than this. It stands in a short street, leading out of Long Lane, Bermondsey, the locality in which were recently found the bodies of nine infants, which had been deposited in a large box at the foot of some stairs in an undertaker's shop. There are around the Hall some 650 families, or 3,250 people, living in 123 houses. The houses are largely occupied by costermongers, bird catchers, street singers, liberated convicts, thieves, and prostitutes. There are many low lodging-houses in the neighbourhood of the worst type. Some of them are tenanted chiefly by thieves, and one was pointed out which is kept by a receiver of stolen goods. In some cases two of the houses are united by means of a passage, which affords a ready method of escape in case of police interference.

Turning out of one of these streets you enter a narrow passage, about ten yards long and three feet wide. This leads into a court eighteen yards long and nine yards wide. Here are twelve houses of three rooms each, and containing altogether 36 families. The sanitary condition of the place is indescribable. A large dust-bin charged with all manner of filth and putrid matter stands at one end of the court, and four water-closets at the other. In this confined area all the washing of these 36 families is done, and the smell of the place is intolerable. Entering a doorway you go up six or seven steps into a long passage, so dark that you have to grope your way by the clammy, dirt-encrusted wall, and then you find a wooden stair, some of the steps of which are broken through. Ascending as best you can, you gain admission to one of the rooms. You find that although the front and back of the house are of brick, the rooms are separated only by partitions of boards, some of which are an inch apart. There are no locks on the doors, and it would seem that they can only be fastened on the outside by padlock. In this room to which we have come an old bed, on which are some evil-smelling rags, is with the exception of a broken chair, the only article of furniture. Its sole occupant just now is a repulsive, half-drunken Irish-woman. She is looking at some old ragged garments in hope of being able to raise something upon them at the pawnshop, and being asked if she is doing this because she is poor, she gets into a rage and cries, "Call me poor? I have got half a loaf of bread in the house, and a little milk;" and then from a heap of rubbish in one corner she pulls out a putrid turkey, utterly unfit for human food, which she tells us she is going to cook for dinner. This woman has just "done seven days" for an assault upon a police officer. We find that she has a husband, but he spends almost all his money at the public-house. Rooms such as this are let furnished (!) at 3s. 6d. and 4s. a week, or 8d. a night, and we are told that the owner is getting from 50 to 60 per cent. upon his money.

And this is a specimen of the neighbourhood. Reeking courts, crowded public-houses, low lodging-houses, and numerous brothels are to be found all around. Even the cellars are tenanted. Poverty, rags, and dirt everywhere. The air is laden with disease-breeding gases. The missionaries who labour here are constantly being attacked by some malady or other resulting from blood poisoning, and their tact and courage are subjected to the severest tests. In going about these alleys and courts no stranger is safe if alone. Not long ago a doctor on his rounds was waylaid by a number of women, who would not let him pass to see his patient until he had given them money; and a Bible-woman, visiting "Kent Street," was robbed of most of her clothing. Even the police seldom venture into some parts of the district except in company. Yet bad as it is there are elements of hopefulness which encourage us to believe that our work will not be in vain. Many of its denizens would gladly break away from the dismal, degrading life they are leading, if only a way were made for them do so; as it is they are hemmed in and chained down by their surroundings in hopeless and helpless misery.

Such is Collier's Rents. To describe the other two localities where our work is to be commenced, in Ratcliff and Shadwell, would, in the main, be but to repeat the same heart-sickening story. Heart-sickening but soul-stirring. We have opened but a little way the door that leads into this plague-house of sin and misery and corruption, where men and women and little children starve and suffer and perish, body and soul. But even the glance we have got is a sight to make one weep. We shall not wonder if some, shuddering at the revolting spectacle, try to persuade themselves that such things cannot be in Christian England, and that what they have looked upon is some dark vision conjured by a morbid pity and a desponding faith. To such we can only say, Will you venture to come with us and see for yourselves the ghastly reality? Others looking on, will believe, and pity, and despair. But another vision will be seen by many, and in this lies our hope — a vision of Him who had "compassion upon the multitude because they were as sheep having no shepherd," looking with Divine pity in His eyes, over this outcast London, and then turning to the consecrated host of His Church with the appeal, "Whom shall we send and who will go for us?"

October, 1883.

Wesleyan Methodist Magazine (1884): "Outcast London; Or Wealth, Want, and Crime", by the Rev. W.J. Dawson. Selections.

W.J. Dawson (1854-1928), entered the Wesleyan Methodist ministry in 1875, and resigned in 1892 after holding appointments in London, Glasgow and Southport. He then became pastor of a Congregational church in London until 1906, when he moved to the pastorate of a Presbyterian church in Newark, New Jersey. He published a very great deal throughout his life, including poetry, novels, and literary essays. The *Wesleyan Methodist Magazine* was the official journal of the denomination.

DURING the last few months general public attention has been called to the condition of the London poor, and perhaps it may be fair to assume that this sudden burst of widespread interest marks the culmination of many efforts, spread through many years, to draw attention to the problems of social reform. The suddenness with which this question has assumed commanding proportions is curious, and is probably explained by the political conditions of the hour. Had there been no prospect of a Municipal Bill for London, it is probable that Mr. Peek's admirable book on *Social Wreckage,* and the Congregational Union's pamphlet, *The Bitter Cry of Outcast London,* would have passed into the swift oblivion of a hundred similar appeals published during the last ten years. Indeed, it is a fine satire upon English philanthropy that the condition of outcast London should attract little attention till it has become a political question.

For it is essential in the discussion of this question to remember that it is by no means a new one. The bitter satire of the whole business lies in the spasmodic horror with which the great bulk of the London Christian world has awakened to the sense of the festering mass of infamy and vice which it has tolerated for years upon the very thresholds of its churches. The London City Mission has been nobly grappling with this very problem for years; meetings have been held and reports published — we dare not say circulated — *ad libitum;* Methodism has published its modest account of Christian revolution in Chequer Alley, and within the last few months even, from the very quarters mentioned by the Congregational Union, — the Mint and Collier's Rents, both within a stone's-throw of the Southwark Chapel, — startling appeals have been made by the Rev.

Forster Crozier, to the Methodist public. Christian men and women
have applauded Home Missionary speakers; have duly received and
forgotten City Mission reports; have read stories of how the poor live
and die, with some degree of quickened emotional interest; have in
some cases, few comparatively, spared a guinea or two for this true
rescue work of society, and in the main have satisfied themselves with
the mere sentiment of not unreal pity which has possessed them.

More than twenty years ago Mrs. Browning put all her passion
and pathos into the very same plea, and writing in Rome told us how
we had

'ruins worse than Rome's
In our pauper men and women.
Women leering through the gas
(Just such bosoms used to nurse you).
Men turned wolves by famine — pass!
These can speak themselves and curse you.

But these others, children small,
Spilt like blots about the city,
Quay and street and palace wall,
Take them up into your pity.

Ragged children with bare feet,
Whom the angels in white raiment
Know the name of, to repeat
When they come on you for payment.'

And as many years ago Charles Mackay struck the same chord,
crying:

'They swarm in the streets to pilfer,
They plague the broad highway,
Till they grow too old for pity,
And ripe for the law to slay.'

Indeed, stifled wails of the bitter cry of outcast London have been
heard at any time during the last quarter of a century; or rather, the
full volume of that terrible cry has been heard in all its intense
bitterness by some who have troubled themselves to listen, as a
constant undertone of anguish, yearning up through all our triumphs
and splendours, our anthems and happy psalms, for much longer than
a quarter of a century, but in the main few have believed the report.

The public have been contented to know that there *were* missionaries in Blue Anchor Alley, and Bible-women in St. Giles's, and have taken it for granted that all that could be done was being done. There is a natural selfish tendency in human nature to dismiss the distasteful, and more evil is thus 'wrought by want of thought' than 'want of heart.' We are reminded of a newspaper statement a few days ago that some of the finest mansions of the West End look down upon purlieus as infamous and foul as the worst East-end rookery; but that a window judiciously painted, or artistically draped, usually shuts out the vision of this corrupting and putrescent misery. At last the drapery is torn away, and the outer woe has corroded through the paint wherewith selfish indolence has hid the want and squalor crying vainly to it from without; and the result is a shock of universal surprise. And we cannot help adding, that this very horrified surprise is the sternest condemnation of that section of the Christian public from whom it springs. Let them measure what degree of rebuke there is implied in the fact, that what the statement and appeal of philanthropists and churches for many years could not accomplish, has been suddenly achieved by a political movement and a penny tract!

There are other significant signs that the questions involved in this revelation of vice and misery are destined to obtain a yet wider and indeed a dangerous consideration. Many years ago a brilliant essayist reminded us that under the very shadow of our Houses of Parliament we were fostering a haggard army of thieves and felons, whose united malice would sap and overwhelm the empire. But the warnings of political and literary Cassandras are usually received with a very slight flutter of momentary alarm. The immense growth and consolidation of the empire, and the corresponding growth of wealth, have blinded us to the portents of the times, and apparently have given the lie to our prophets of disaster. We were told the other day by Lord Shaftesbury that London is kept in order by fewer policemen and soldiers than any city in the world: and this happily is true. But it is possible for the most dangerous revolutions of sentiment and opinion to be worked out without challenging either policeman's truncheon or soldier's sword. And such appears to be the case. Socialism is full of intense activity and hope: and in the misery of the poor it seeks its justification, and among the less degraded poor finds its converts; and not only among the poor, as may be ascertained by a cursory acquaintance with the daily papers. There are societies of educated and brilliant men which hold their meetings in the mansions of Belgravia itself, where Communistic theories are eagerly discussed and adopted. There are even clergymen who openly avow their belief in Socialism as the only remedy for the poor man's wrong.

* * * * * * * * *

But it is from the people and the Churches that the real help must come. It remains to indicate in a few sentences the outlines of such a remedy.

In the first place, it is evident that the combined mission agencies of all the Churches are incompetent to grapple with this difficulty. As the author of the *Bitter Cry* says: 'The flood of sin and misery is steadily gaining on us!' We fear two new Mission-halls are not likely to effectually check it, and a similar conviction must have oppressed the author of the pamphlet in the course of his investigations. There is even reasonable ground to suppose that many districts are over-missioned. 'May I pray and read with you?' said a City Missionary not long since to a poor woman who was forced to stop her work to receive him. 'You may read as much as you like,' she replied; 'but you are the fourth missionary as has come this morning, and I hav'n't any more time for praying.'

Dr. Chalmers found the same state of affairs when he undertook to visit the wynds of Edinburgh, and said he could not go into a house without meeting another of his fraternity coming out. A friend of the present writer's filled with a conviction of the moral destitution of the families inhabiting one of the huge flats in his neighbourhood, at length resolved to visit every room regularly. To his surprise he found that every church in the neighbourhood had apparently come to the same conclusion, for the stairs swarmed with visitors. Nor can it be said that the Churches of London have drawn the purse-strings against the cry of the poor; for Mr. Peek tells us that the charity of London may be estimated at between four and five million pounds a year. We may as well acknowledge frankly that these evils cannot be eradicated by the unaided efforts of the Churches. The marvel is that men who are starving, and women who are worn to the bone by ill-paid drudgery, have had the patience to listen to the exhortations of their well-fed visitors. It must surely often have seemed a mockery to the missionary himself to offer spiritual advice to those who wanted bread; and when he has looked round the filthy and over-crowded room, where decency and cleanliness were impossible, he must have often realized, with heart-breaking intensity, the huge difficulties which bar his progress; and he must have felt, with bitter yearning, what bright victories were his, if once these difficulties were swept away. There can be no grander testimony to the power of the Gospel than that in this heathendom light has shone: the lily has bloomed out of corruption, and amid the slime and vileness of the very sewers of society, the saint has flourished fair and strong.

It is to the Government we must look, in the first place, for help. Already great schemes have been drafted, and the politicians are astir. One thing no government ought to do, namely, to build houses for the poor out of the public funds; and the demand that many people are making in this direction is simply foolish. 'To attempt to do so would be the introduction of practical Communism; and, as it would necessarily encourage improvidence, the result would be, in the long run, only to aggravate the evil to a terrible extent. But there are certain things that the Government can do, and should do at once. Government can prevent a landlord's letting a house unfit for human habitation; and Government can also appoint sanitary inspectors, who are in their own service, and who are in no way paid by a vestry, or under the control of a vestry; and in this way strict justice might be done in the condemnation of unfit habitations. It is for the Christian sentiment of the country to take the lead in this crusade, and it may do so with well-founded hopes of victory.

But supposing Government to have done all that is demanded, there then remains a further difficulty. Things might be much the worse: for, in proportion as houses were demolished, over-crowding would increase; and it is usually found that houses of an increased rental are erected on the sites thus opened. Here, then, public philanthropy must step in; and companies should be formed for the erection of houses for the poor at the lowest remunerative rentals.

It is not to be expected that such companies would pay large dividends; but between nothing per cent. and the landlord's present per-centage there is surely a fair halting-point; and the probability is that such companies, commenced in benevolence, would soon find themselves in receipt of very fair returns.

Another suggestion, which, however, we admit is full of danger, is the formation of a central fund for the relief of the abject poor. Mr. Peek objects strongly to the alms-giving of missionaries and sick-visitors, as tending to pauperise the poor; but if no help were rendered to the poor in this way, from what source would it come? There are constant cases of real and terrible distress; there are such long martyrdoms of privation, such unavailing and bitter struggles with want, everywhere existing among the poor, that those who visit them must often be miserably conscious of the insufficiency of any help which they may offer. Alms-giving thus becomes rather a token of sympathy, than a means of effectual relief. And a fund of this kind, placed in competent hands, and carefully administered, by money-grants or gifts of clothes, and medicine in time of sickness; of a sewing-machine to a sempstress whose sight is failing, or other similar benevolence, or by adding shilling for shilling to any scanty savings which might be accumulated, would be of incalculable benefit; and we think it would not be difficult to prevent its abuse.

Public philanthropy, again, could do much in the erection of baths, recreation rooms, and coffee-houses in these localities. It may of course be said that this has been already done for the working-classes: but upon examination it will be found that here, as with the Peabody mansions, it is the aristocracy of the working-classes who have reaped the benefit, while the abject poor have remained untouched. Coffee-houses are usually found in the better streets, and here not infrequently they are failures. But the public-house is found everywhere, and thrives best in the foulest neighbourhoods. Until public philanthropy is prepared to place the coffee-house *wherever* the public-house is found, until it is prepared to sink money in pure benevolence for the maintenance of such houses in rookeries themselves, our temperance reformers must be content to postpone their Elysium of a sober London. Enough has been said, too, to show that the filth in which the people live is not merely an outcome, but also a cause of their misery, and anything that would teach cleanliness would be at least a valuable auxiliary to godliness. If we may sketch an ideal Mission, we should endeavour to forget the dingy and often dilapidated erection which often bears the name of *hall;* and substitute a plain and commodious building, where the Gospel should be preached in its simplest form, but by its best living exponents, with plenty of thoroughly good singing and music, which might easily be supplied by the ladies of our wealthy congregations, if only an organised appeal were made to them.

But beyond all this, we should like to see social reform associated with every Mission: bath rooms, in which the poor might be taught cleanliness; recreation rooms, through which they might be weaned from the gin-palace; and simple cookery-schools, in which they might learn how to make the most wholesome and economical use of the commonest articles of diet. One of the greatest sources of failure in such Missions hitherto has been, that they have been looked upon as inferior work, and have been left to individuals of humble capacity: whereas they afford the grandest field of labour that the English Churches can offer their most capable and brilliant members. Another great error is, that such Missions have been left wholly unconnected with such social reforms as we have indicated, and what good the missionary has done in the mission-hall, has been greatly counteracted by the foul conditions of his convert's homes. It is time that social reform was married to Christian zeal; and if Sir Samuel Morley, for instance, really means what he says, and is anxious to spend his money upon philanthropy, but cannot discover a sufficiently rational object of benevolence, let him consider what might be accomplished by a series of mission-centres on the lines we have ventured to indicate.

And what is there to prevent such a reformation, save the selfishness and inertness of the Churches? It is true that the poor themselves are beginning to protest against improvement; but their attitude is only too sadly intelligible: they know by experience the more demolition of rookeries there is, the more overcrowding there will be. Let them once see that reform is to be constructive as well as destructive, and it will be hailed as bond-slaves hail liberty. Outcast London has assured us in many ways that it is not beyond redemption. Whenever a true-hearted man has gone down into its horrible pit and miry clay to save men, whenever it has been taught self-help and righteousness, as by Mr. Charrington in the East-End, and the late Mr. Lloyd Harris of the Southwark Help-myself Society in the South-East — it has responded nobly and by thousands. It is not the policemen and the soldiers of London who have kept these hungry thousands from revolt: it is rather the men and women who are the heroic advance-guard of the Churches, who are content to spend their lives in carrying the Gospel to those who need it most; and the words uttered by Baby Chandra in Calcutta, may be applied with splendid force to these devoted toilers in London: ' If to any army appertains the honour of holding India for England, that army is the army of Christian missionaries, headed by their invincible Captain Jesus Christ!' But how small is this army which is hurling its thin, forlorn-hope against these citadels of shame; and how crippled is it in resource through the selfishness of those who have sent it out! Is it to be left to struggle on, or is the word to be passed along the whole line that a movement to front must be effected? This is the question English Christians have now to consider. It is the Christian sentiment of the country which has demanded and obtained a hearing for this 'Bitter Cry;' and having done so much, there are now two dangers that menace the successful issue of the movement. The first is that the daily revelation of horrors which the papers bid us sup upon, may satiate the public taste, and public interest and feeling may die down before anything is done. The second and more real danger is that having become a political question it may cease to be a Christian one, and its effectual solution would be thus rendered impossible. For the only hope of a permanent settlement lies in the combined action of enlightened statesmanship and Christian charity and toil.

The Official Report of the Church Congress (1884): "The Duty of
the Church with regard to the Overcrowded Dwellings of the Poor,
In Towns", by the Rt. Rev. Dr. Walsham How. Selections.

Walsham How (1823-1897), after twenty-eight successful years as
Rector of Whittington, an obscure Shropshire parish, became in 1879
suffragan to the Bishop of London with supervision of the poverty-
stricken East End. As suffragan, with the title of Bishop of Bedford,
he publicized the plight of the slum dwellers among the rich. His
drawing-room meetings, his appearance at public schools and
universities, as well as his sermons and publications were effective
in helping to arouse a social conscience among the middle and upper
classes. From 1888 until his death he was the first Bishop of
Wakefield.

I SUPPOSE we cannot, in the title of our subject, take the word
"Church" in its larger and truer sense, as embracing all the Church's
lay members, because it is obvious that owners of property, and others
in positions of responsibility, are not bound to the duty which may
lie upon them *quâ* Churchpeople, but *quâ* Citizens. "The Church,"
then, must mean either the Church in her corporate capacity, as
expressing herself in her Convocations and Diocesan Conferences or
Synods; or the Church as represented by the clergy in their several
parishes. These are not days when one need to stop to argue that
such a subject as that of the dwellings of the poor is a fitting one,
either for the grave deliberation of the Church's representative
assemblies, or for the active personal interest of her ministers. Were
it only for the intimate connection between the home life of the people
and their moral and spiritual well-being, the subject is one the Church
cannot afford to neglect. But, however much her first thought and
interest must centre round the higher life, it is becoming daily more
and more certain that she cannot neglect the wider and more varied
phases of national life without cramping her usefulness, and alienating
the sympathy of the people. A Church, which teaches about another
world, but does not seem to take much interest in this, is one which
will embrace within its fold a limited number of the working class.
The mistake has been made on times past, and we are reaping the
fruit of it now. Working-men will smile incredulously if told that
Christianity, or the Church, aims at helping them to live better truer

happier lives here. They have never heard of a *present* kingdom of heaven.

I do not know that the Church could have done, or can do, much in her corporate capacity in the matter of housing the people. It is true that some years ago the Convocation of Canterbury issued a most valuable and exhaustive report in the subject of Intemperance, practical and very efficient action being taken by the establishment of the Church of England Temperance Society. And no doubt it would have been an excellent thing had a similar course been taken as to the overcrowding and insanitary state of the dwellings of the poor. But the subject was infinitely more difficult; all manner of social and economic questions bristled around it; and, even had public opinion been stirred as it is now, and had the matter been brought before Convocation, it would probably have been felt to belong rather to the politician and the philanthropist than to the ecclesiastic.

We turn then to the clergy in their several parishes. And we should be indeed ashamed if we had to confess that, seeing and knowing the evil as they did, they had never bestirred themselves to remedy it. I imagine there have been very few clergy, of those at least who have been diligent in visiting their flocks, who have not tried to remedy the evils of overcrowding and of unclean or unhealthy surroundings in individual cases. Nor would it be fair to refuse to bear testimony to the willingness of the principal landowners (I speak chiefly here of country districts) to better the state of things when brought to their knowlege. Indirectly also the clergy have done far more than any other class to improve the habits of the people. They have been the pioneers in the education of the poor, and have, often amidst much dislike and opposition on the part of the employers of labour, often with far larger pecuniary sacrifices than they could well afford, laboured to elevate the condition of the people, and through their schools to carry lessons of order and cleanliness and comfort to the homes of their scholars.

But direct efforts on a larger scale and of a more systematic character have not been lacking. I am not going to pretend that the clergy have done all they could, or that they, like the rest of the world, were not often too reluctant to meddle with a very difficult and thorny question, pehaps too tender of the feelings and intersts of those more directly responsible. It wants a brave man to deliberately pull down a hornet's nest about his ears. Besides, clergymen are but men after all, and, though I allow that they ought to lead rather than to follow public opinion, yet it would have been a miracle if they had not more or less partaken of that acquiescence in a state of things supposed to be inevitable, which was so general, and in that belief in the gradual action of the law of supply and demand, which political economists taught them to look upon as too sacred for interference. Still, if you look back over the last quarter of a century, and ask what names stand out as those of men who have laboured most earnestly for the bettering of the dwellings of the poor, you will find not a few of the clergy in the forefront of the band. Many in East London can recollect the self-denying energy of the Rev. W. Queckett, the first Vicar of Christ Church, St. George's-in-the-East, of whom it was said that he knew every drain in the parish. Nor will the labours and zeal of the Rev. W. Denton, who in 1862 appealed to the House of Lords to take up the subject which at last was taken up warmly by the late Lord Derby, and there was a two days' debate in the House of Lords upon Mr. Denton's representation; but, alas, with no practical results, public opinion not being then sufficiently instructed and excited in the matter. Mr. Denton's labours, however, were crowned with more success than the oratory of the Upper House, for to his suggestion and patient care is really owing the system of reformatory schools. Again, no one who knows anything at all about the matter is ignorant of Canon Girdlestone's strenuous exertions to better the condition of the labourers in the South by arranging for their migration to the North of England, where they could obtain far larger wages, for which action he was promptly "boycotted" by the farmers of his neighbourhood, who, perhaps not unnaturally, disliked a process which resulted in the necessity for the payment of higher wages. Again, let anyone compare the state of Gravel Lane, in the parish of St. Peter's, London Docks, as it was before Charles Lowder came there, and as it is now. Or ask about the labour for bettering the homes of the poor undertaken by a former Rector of Spitalfields, Mr. Stone, or by the present Rector, Mr. Billing. Or see with what untiring patience Mr. Barnett, of St. Jude's, Whitechapel, has fought against the wretched misery of the houses in his parish, until they have finally been swept away, and only the miserable official delays and the extreme cost of the cleared site have hindered a large provision of better dwellings, now happily just about to be built. I have ventured to name these instances, to which it would not be difficult to add largely, because a supposition has got abroad that the Church has been exceptionally supine and apathetic in the presence of a gigantic evil, brought of necessity prominently before the eyes of her ministers; clergy, next to medical men, seeing more of the misery of unhealthy and insufficient housing of the people than any others. This supposition is not true. It is the reverse of true. The whole nation has been backward in the matter. We are all to blame, some more and some less. But certainly, if any have been bestirring themselves, the clergy have. Suffer me to remind you that the great efforts made by many of our East London clergy — notably Mr. Kitto, the present rector of Stepney — to promote emigration, efforts which have resulted in wonderful happiness and prosperity in all but a very small minority of cases, have had for their main object the relief of the overcrowding so destructive of health and morality, and the bettering the condition of the working classes.

And now what more can we do? I have not mentioned the past action of some of the clergy in this cause as if it were something to boast of and to be contented with. I have mentioned it in order to refute an unjust accusation of apathy. We are in reality only at the beginning of an enormous question. What has been done, however much in itself, is nothing to what remains to be done. The Peabody, Waterlow, and other trusts providing model lodging-houses, have done, and are doing, admirable work. For, although it is true that they do not provide for the same *stratum* of the working-class as that displaced by the destruction of condemned dwellings, yet indirectly they make room for these by housing a class a little above them. The working men's trains from the suburban towns of working men's houses have also been of great use, many being thus able to live in purer air and better surroundings, and to save in rent more than they expend in travelling to and fro. But though the relief secured by blocks of model lodging-houses and by the workmen's trains is not inconsiderable, yet it is very trifling compared with what is really required for the decent housing of the working classes in London.

The problem is not so difficult of solution in other towns, where the suburbs are within easy walking distance of the main centres of work, and where sites are not so costly. In London, while vast numbers must live near the place of their employment, the absolute impossibility of finding room for fresh buildings within a circuit of many miles, and the extreme costliness of such sites as can be obtained by demolition of condemned houses, produce their inevitable consequences of high rents and overcrowding. As things are at present, a very large proportion of our population is compelled to be content with a single room for each family.

What can the Church do to remedy this state of things?

1. She must create and direct public opinion. She must not be silent, as though she cared not, in the face of the grievous state of things which she witnesses. Even if she lacks power to point to the remedy, she can at least expose the evil. There is no doubt that the machinery necessary for remedying the worst evils, for enforcing attention to sanitary matters, and for the destruction of unhealthy dwellings, is sufficient. Mr. Torrens's Acts and Sir Richard Cross's Acts are very drastic remedies. But we want the impetus of an awakened and enlightened public opinion to put them in force. That impetus is at present supplied in a large measure owing to the attention now directed to the subject, but the danger is lest this impetus should quickly expend itself and subside. The Church should see that no slackness and apathy supervene upon the present outburst of energy.

2. The Church should enlist and encourage workers in the cause. The best work hitherto done has undoubtedly been done by Miss Octavia Hill and her band of trained ladies. Probably most know the plan Miss Octavia Hill has worked out. She buys — i.e., she gets various wealthy people to buy — blocks of poor and wretched houses, and then sets to work to improve the houses and their inhabitants together. Lady collectors collect the rents from room to room weekly, and their mission is to win the people to cleaner and better habits, and, as they do so, to improve and repair the houses. The success of this simple plan has been enormous, and so much has Miss Hill been encouraged in her self-denying efforts, that she has told us she does not consider any, however bad, incapable of improvement. There

is no demolition, no turning out of some hundreds of wretched beings to find shelter by overcrowding some already well-filled region. It is a real work of noble philanthropy, full of happy promise for the future. Surely the Church ought to welcome and foster and encourage such work as this. And surely she ought to feel that in such work she has the very best and truest help to her own more directly spiritual work. For my part, I should despair of doing much for the souls of these poor people if I had not such allies as these.

3. I think, thirdly, the Church should strive to stir up the owners of property to a higher conception of their responsibilities. Is there an end of all duty in respect of property when an owner has granted a long lease, and so has (legally) no more to do with it except to receive his rent from his lessee? Well, thank God, all owners of property do not take this view, and there is rising among us a strong feeling that the ground-landlord has his duties and repsonsibilities still. Some of you will remember a fine passage of Carlyle upon "rights." A man's "rights," he declares, are what it is *right* he should do.

4. Next I would urge that the Church, through her clergy and various agents, should teach the people to care for better homes and purer surroundings. It is very sad to hear in some cases that the people are too well content, if only they are allowed to live herded together without regard to decency or morality, in places a gentleman would not think fit for his dogs, so that only the rents are low, and they can spend more in gin. If we are to get the people to care for a home above, we must first teach them to care for a home below. And we are glad to be told (as we have been told in our Royal Commission) that in many parts the people are grievously discontented with the state in which they are living.

5. Is it quite beyond the province of the Church to teach people how to help themselves, and to make their own houses more pure and healthful? Surely the Church might do much (I believe already her clergy, district visitors, sisters, deaconesses, and mission women, *are* doing much) to encourage better and more cleanly habits, and to discourage overcrowding and idleness.

6. Lastly, I would urge that we should in every way in our power foster the great movements for promoting temperance and purity.

If sins against the one are slaying their thousands, I am not sure that sins against the other are not slaying their tens of thousands. Anyhow, if our people once learn the priceless blessings of temperance and purity, I believe that problem would be more than half solved. For after all, far the larger part of the solution must lie with the people themselves. We want to help them in every way, but we cannot help them if they will not help themselves. Let them as a body resolve that their houses shall no longer be the horrible dens they have been content to inhabit, but so far as they can make them so, pure and clean, and healthy; let them resolve to cast out from among them the terrible curse of drunkenness; and then we shall no longer have to couple thoughts of shame with that word which is to many of us so dear — the word "home"!

*Social Christianity: Sermons Delivered in St. James's Hall,
London* (1890), by Hugh Price Hughes. Complete text of the sermon
"Jesus Christ And Social Distress".

Hugh Price Hughes (1847-1902), was a prominent Wesleyan
Methodist minister. From its foundation in 1885 he edited the
Methodist Times to support his "forward movement", a program of
energetic social and ecclesiastical action for the denomination. In 1886
he began his West London mission where he remained until his death.
A radical in politics and a preacher of great power, he was one of
the most conspicuous figures on the religious scene during the last
fifteen years of the century.

Last Monday I received a letter from an excellent Christian
gentleman, who said that he went away from this Hall last Sunday
afternoon "very much grieved." He was delighted to see so large a
congregation; he rejoiced at the opportunity which was given me of
preaching the Gospel. But instead of "preaching the Gospel," I talked
about the duty of citizens to elect vestrymen who would close
unsanitary dwellings, and otherwise discharge their public functions:
and as the result he adds that it is only too possible that some who
heard me, and might have been saved, are now "in hell suffering the
torments of the damned." I feel extremely thankful to that good man
for giving me such sincere advice, and I have the deepest sympathy
with him. Twenty years ago I should have said just the same thing
if I had come to this Hall and heard any minister talk as I talked last
Sunday. There is no doubt that my correspondent, who is probably
a much better Christian than I am, represents thousands of some of
the best Christians in England; and yet I say deliberately that I come
here, on Sunday afternoon, to argue before you, before the open Bible,
and before Jesus Christ, that the view which my correspondent holds
is *one of the most dangerous ever entertained by Christian men;* that
it was the main reason why the French Revolution became a Reign
of Terror; and that it is now the principal cause of the menacing
advance of atheistic Socialism, Communism, and Nihilism in Europe.

Not that I under-estimate the importance of the kind of preaching
that he wishes to have on every occasion that a Christian minister
opens his mouth. Once only during the whole week do I propose to
deal specially with the Social aspects of Christianity. If every day

of the week and twice on Sunday we preach the Gospel even to his satisfaction, may I not be permitted for this one brief hour, without neglecting any other duty of my sacred office, to deal with that public application of the Gospel which has been so long and so perilously neglected by those who are the followers of Jesus Christ? Ever since I was a boy one fact has distressed me more than any other — the fact that the masses of the European peoples are alienated from the Gospel, and that the men on the Continent do not go to any place of worship. When I have contemplated the extraordinary career of such men as Garibaldi, who excited boundless enthusiasm among the masses of the people wherever he went, I have said to myself: How is it that this boundless enthusiasm is directed towards Garibaldi and not towards Jesus Christ? I hold that eveything that was true and helpful in the teaching of Garibaldi may be found in the teaching of Jesus Christ; and that all his sympathy with the masses of the people and his desire to promote the progress of the human race are to be found in the teaching of the Prophet of Galilee.

I have long been persuaded that the reason why the masses of the people have to so great an extent failed to realize that their best friend is Jesus Christ, is the fact that we ministers of religion have taken the very course which my excellent correspondent urged upon me last Monday. We have dealt too exclusively with the individual aspect of the Christian faith. We have constantly acted as if Christianity had nothing to do with business, with pleasure, and with politics; as if it were simply a question of private life and of prayer-meetings. It is because the spirit of Christ has not been introduced into public life that Europe is in a perilous condition to-day. I have often thought how distressing it was that so great and illustrious a man, and so devout a believer in God, as Mazzini should have deliberately rejected the Christian religion on this ground: That he believed Christianity taught men to be selfish; that it taught them to be so absorbed in their own individual salvation, and to be so wrapped up in thoughts of the future that they neglected their duty on earth. Now, I absolutely deny that this is the case. I protest that it is contradicted by history. I contend that everything that is best in Mazzini himself is due to Christ. We have been so accustomed to breathe a Christian atmosphere that very few of us have any conception of the intolerable condition of the human race when Jesus Christ came. But so gifted a man as Mazzini would never have made such a terrible mistake unless we Christians had neglected to declare that the teaching of Christ was applicable to every phase of life.

I recently received an excellent letter from a member of the Society of Friends, and you will not be surprised to hear that he wishes me to speak on the subject of war. Most assuredly I shall on no distant occasion. I was very much struck by one remark in that letter. This good man said he thought it was high time that Christianity should become "an applied science." My wish is to apply Christianity to every aspect of life. Christianity is not something that has to do with a mere fragment of our existence. It has to do with us as men of business and as citizens quite as much as it has to do with us in our private life; and there are endless ways in which we can preach the Gospel in addition to holding prayer-meetings and delivering what may be called sermons. In *The Methodist Times* this week there is published a remarkable communication with respect to some heroic work that my truly Christian friend, Mr. Frederick N. Charrington, has been doing in the East End of London. He began his career as a thorough-going Christian in a very remarkable way. When he was converted to God he was a brewer. He started a Bible-class, and one day it occurred to him that it was very inconsistent that he should try to reclaim with a Bible-class on Sunday the men who were made drunk with his beer on Saturday. Thereupon, without hesitation, that brave young man, for the sake of Christ and the human race, sacrificed £80,000.

Now, it seems to me that this was a far finer exhibition of true Christianity than the exhibition that took place in London some time ago, when citizens of this so-called Christian city were rushing furiously through the streets of London, terribly afraid that they would be too late to secure shares in Allsopp's Brewery. Having surrendered that £80,000, Mr. Charrington began his heroic work in the Mile End Road. Within the last few weeks he has deemed it to be part of his duty as a Christian man to put the Criminal Law Amendment Act in force, and he has closed forty of the most imfamous houses in that part of London. Now, I say that by closing all these houses Mr. Carrington has done much more good than if he had merely held numerous prayer-meetings. While referring to this Act, let me remind you that it is a mighty weapon which we owe to those fearless Christians, Mr. W.T. Stead and Rev. Benjamin Waugh, and it is a weapon which any man may take into his own hand, and use with decisive effect. Let everybody know that under this Act the landlord, the owner, the manager, and the keeper of bad houses are all liable to imprisonment; and wherever you have a few brave Christians prepared to put the new law in force the vestibules of hell may be closed.

Mr. Charrington told my representative that the Vestry of Mile End had refused to enforce the law. If the excellent Christian who wrote to me is present, I beg his special attention to that fact. Here is an illustration of the importance of putting Christian men in the Vestry. There are a number of publicans in that Vestry; and, as everybody knows, the unhappy harlots are the best customers of the publicans. There have been, in all parts of the country, instances where infamous houses have actually belonged to town councillors and vestrymen. Is it not time, I ask, that a Christian minister should say it is a part of our duty as citizens to see that in all our Vestries and other local assemblies men are elected who do not fear the face of man, and who are ready to do their duty loyally to their country and to their God? Let me give another illustration of the necessity of including the Vestry in our conception of Christianity as an applied science. That zealous philanthropist, Mr. Arnold White, has interested himself very much in the condition of the London poor. He made some investigations a few months ago with respect to the sugar, the tea, and the butter with which the East End poor are supplied, often at a very much greater cost than we pay for ours in the West End. The result of his investigations was that in some instances the sugar was not sugar, the tea was not tea, and the butter was not butter. I bring no sweeping charges against small tradesmen as a class, but I do say that the Adulteration Acts are not enforced. Mr. White states in print that in some cases the reason is that the vestrymen are themselves interested in preventing those Acts from being enforced.

The Royal Commission which sat a short time ago, with the Prince of Wales as its President, to consider the condition of the poor, reporting with respect to unsanitary houses, stated that we actually had in existence to-day, laws under which every miserable tenement in London might be closed. Why are they not closed? Because the Christians have not looked after the Vestries: and the time has come, and more than come, when we must pray God to give us grace to discharge our duty in public as well as to say out prayers in private. If we needed any proof that Christians should give their attention to these duties as well as to prayer-meetings and to holiness meetings, we might find it in the career of one of the most illustrious evangelical Christians that ever adorned the pages of Christian history — the late much lamented Lord Shaftesbury. Only the other day I came across a very remarkable sentence in the first speech he ever delivered in proposing his first Factory Act in 1833. If there ever was a devoted, evangelical Christian who cared for the souls of men, Lord Shaftesbury did. The gentleman who wrote me, I may here mention, talked throughout his letter about "souls," "dealing with souls," "saving souls," and so on. I might have settled the matter by saying that I had no disembodied "souls" in my congreation, but that I had souls incarnate, souls attached to bodies, and that we must deal with man as a complex being. If I had a congregation of disembodied souls who had no physical wants and no connection with London, I might take a very different course. But there is too much truth in the saying I have often quoted of late that "some very earnest Christians are so diligently engaged in saving *souls* that they have no time to save *men* and *women*."

But to return to Lord Shaftesbury. On that memorable occasion he said: "The Ten Hours Bill is a great religious question, for it involves the means of thousands and tens of thousands being brought up in the faith and fear of the God who created them. I have read of those who sacrifice their children to Moloch, but they were merciful people compared with the Englishmen of the nineteenth century. So long as these facts were not known the guilt attached to the proprietors; but if this terrible system is permitted to continue any longer, the guilt will descend on the whole nation." So said Lord Shaftesbury, and I echo his words. Now that the social misery of the people has been once more brought home to us all by the invaluable service of the public press, we are all in our degree responsible for it. Who can estimate the blessings that have followed the Factory

Acts? A short time ago I went down to the Pottery district, and was told of the unspeakably degraded condition in which men, women, and children lived before the law of England protected the weak against the greedy and the strong: and I say that when Lord Shaftesbury, as a devout believer in the Lord Jesus Christ, persuaded this country — amid the opposition of John Bright and a great many sincere friends of the people who did not understand the bearings of the question — to decide that all over England the weak and defenceless should be protected by these Acts, he did more to establish the kingdom of Jesus Christ than if he had merely spent his time in preaching thousands of what my critic would call Gospel sermons.

I should like to know, indeed, what is the "good news" of the Gospel? Is it selfish individualism? I emphatically deny it. This afternoon we had occasion to refer to the song with which the angels from heaven saluted the birth of Christ. They sang of "Peace on earth, goodwill among men." They evidently thought Christ had come into this world to reconcile Labour and Capital; and to induce foolish and selfish nations to lay aside their weapons of violence and to dwell together in peace and brotherly love. If my excellent friend who wrote to me on Monday had been with the shepherds on that occasion he would doubtless have rebuked the angels for referring to "Peace on earth" instead of saying something about souls. I need scarcely tell you that the Apostles, however, were of the same mind as the angels. St. James says that an essential part of pure religion is to visit the fatherless and widows; that is, to show kindness and mercy to those who need it. St. Peter tells us that an essential part of true religion is to honour all men. St. Paul says that the very crown and summit of a good life is to love your neighbour. St. John states emphatically that he who does not love his brother cannot love God. He says, further, that the man who does not positively love his brother hates him.

And when we turn to our blessed Lord and Master Himself, you know how He defined the good Samaritan, and the "brother" and the "neighbour." The good Samaritan said nothing at first to the disabled Jew about his soul. He put him on his ass, attended to his wounds, and paid his hotel bill. What has the excellent gentleman who wrote to me to say to that? The Samaritan's first act was to establish friendly relations, to prove that he was the Jew's true brother, and after that the Jew would be willing to hear him on the subject of spiritual religion.

We come, lastly, to the example which is presented to us in the text. If you turn to the chapter from which the Lesson was taken, you find this remarkable passage: "Jesus was moved with compassion towards them, and healed their sick." As I reminded you last Sunday, on nearly every occasion on which Christ saw a multitude He had compassion on them. My excellent friend might have said: "Lord, you are losing a great opportunity. What is the body in comparison with the soul? What is the use of healing their bodies?" But the first thing Christ did was to heal their bodies; then He preached to them; then, after He had preached, and when the evening was come, the disciples came to Him, and said: "This is a desert place, and the time is past; send the multitude away, that they may go into the villages and buy themselves victuals." But Jesus said: "They have no need to go away; give ye them to eat."

And when we are told that there are thousands and tens of thousands of starving men in this country, are not we too ready to say: "Send them away. Let them go to New Zealand or Manitoba. Let them emigrate"? I do not deny that for many emigration is extremely desirable, but not for all. We must not go to sleep on a pillow of that sort, in utter indifference to the social conditions of the masses of our fellow-countrymen. We must not suppose that when we have said the country is overcrowded we can sit down in comfortable despair, and flatter ourselves that we have discharged our duty. Are you quite sure that the country is overcrowded? Perhaps it has never occurred to you that for every mouth God has created two hands. Of one thing I am profoundly convinced, it will be impossible for us to evangelize the starving poor so long as they continue in a starving condition. I have had almost as much experience of evangelistic work as any man in this country, and I have never been able to bring any one who was actually starving to Christ.

Let us turn to the nineteenth chapter of the Book of Kings, where we find Elijah when he was flying from Jezebel. Elijah lay down in a surly and cowardly mood under a juniper tree, and as he slept, an angel touched him and said: "Arise and eat." If the angel had been like our friend who wrote to me on Monday, he would have begun to chide him, and to say: "Now, Elijah, it is very disgraceful to act in that way, and to be cast down, after you have won a glorious victory in the name of the Lord Jehovah. Repent of your sins." That would have been all true. But what the angel did say was: "Arise and eat." It was useless to talk to a starving man in the physical condition in which Elijah was; and so we read that when he looked up "there was a cake baken on the coals, and a cruse of water at his head, and he did eat and drink and laid him down again." The angel of the Lord awoke him a second time. What did he say? Did he say: "You ungrateful wretch! I came and provided you with all your needs here in this wilderness. You are a disgrace to your profession as a prophet"? No; for the second time the angel said: "Arise and eat"; and he did so. Even Elijah was unfit to understand and appreciate the will of God until he had eaten two hearty meals. Now, if that was true of the great prophet of God, is it not even more true of the common-place Londoner, who cannot be expected to have such a conception of his duty as Elijah had? Is it not quite evident that we must deal with every aspect of human nature in order to carry out the teaching of Jesus Christ?

In conclusion, let me ask your attention to an admirable suggestion. A benevolent gentleman, who was here last Sunday, and who is much interested, as I hope we all are, in the social condition of our fellow-citizens, called upon me during the week, and made the following suggestion: Would it not be a blessed thing if we could persuade some of the comfortable and well-to-do classes of the West End to interest themselves personally and directly in some of the honest, sober, and industrious families in the East End who are poverty-stricken and in need of assistance? Would it not be desirable to ask Christian men and women, heads of houses and their families, to volunteer to "patronize" in the ancient sense of that word involving no humiliation on either side, a particular family; instead of subscribing to some charitable fund which others distribute? Money could be given where money was needed, the girls could be assisted into service, and the boys into business. If Christian households are interested in particular families their sympathies will be more drawn forth; different classes will be more promoted than by the vague distribution of gifts.

This gentleman has sent me three specimen families, and if there are three gentlemen here who would be prepared to take up these cases we could supplement them by any number. The first is that of a shipwright, who has worked only four weeks since Christmas. The family at home consists of a boy of fourteen and a girl of ten. Two wretched small rooms are occupied. The rent is 4s. per week; 37s. 6d. rent is due. The wife is consumptive and very ill. The mother and children when visited had not had anything to eat for some time but dry bread. The second case is that of a coachbuilder doing odd jobs. He has a decent-looking wife and five children, the eldest nine years and the youngest fourteen days. The husband is a sober man, and willing to work. The third case is that of a poor widow, whose husband died two years ago of consumption. He had not earned anything for two years before his death. There are three girls and two boys. The eldest girl is too ill to do anything. One of the younger girls is in consumption, and is expected to follow her father soon. She ought to be in a Home. Four rooms are occupied, the rent of which is 7s. 6d. a week. The family are in great distress. The rooms are very clean. If we could get two or three families to interest themselves in such cases as these, we should be conferring untold blessings on the human race; and at the same time illustrating one of the most splendid methods of "preaching the Gospel."

The Official Report of the Church Congress (1890): "Socialism", by the Rt. Rev. Brooke Foss Westcott. Complete text.

Brooke Foss Westcott (1825-1901), was an undergraduate and later a fellow of Trinity College, Cambridge. He became in 1852 headmaster of Harrow, and in 1870 Regius Professor of Divinity at Cambridge. He was consecrated Bishop of Durham in 1890. Westcott was one of the most distinguished Biblical scholars in nineteenth-century England. From its creation in 1889 until his death, he was president of the Christian Social Union and an active spokesman for social reform.

————◆◆◆————

It is not my intention to discuss in this paper any of the representative types of Socialism, the paternal Socialism of Owen, or the state Socialism of Bismarck, or the international Socialism of Marx, or the Christian Socialism of Maurice, or the evolutionary Socialism of the Fabian Essays. I wish rather to consider the essential idea which gave or still gives vitality and force to these different systems; to indicate the circumstances which invest the idea with paramount importance at the present time; and especially to commend it to the careful study of the younger clergy.

I. — The term Socialism has been discredited by its connection with many extravagant and revolutionary schemes; but it is a term which needs to be claimed for nobler uses. It has no necessary affinity with any form of violence, or confiscation, or class selfishness, or financial arrangement. I shall venture therefore to employ it apart from its historical associations as describing a theory of life and not only a theory of economics. In this sense Socialism is the opposite of Individualism; and it is by contrast with Individualism that the true character of Socialism can best be discerned. Individualism and Socialism correspond with opposite views of humanity. Individualism regards humanity as made up of disconnected or warring atoms. Socialism regards it as an organic whole, a vital unity formed by the combination of contributory members, mutually interdependent. It follows that Socialism differs from Individualism both in method and in aim. The method of Socialism is co-operation; the method of Individualism is competition. The one regards man as working with man for a common end; the other regards man as working against man for private gain. The aim of socialism is the fulfilment of service;

the aim of Individualism is the attainment of some personal advantage, riches, or place, or fame. Socialism seeks such an organization of life as shall secure for everyone the most complete development of his powers; Individualism seeks primarily the satisfaction of the particular wants of each one, in the hope that the pursuit of private interests will in the end secure public welfare. If men were perfect, with desires and powers harmoniously balanced, both lines of action would lead to the same end. As it is however, experience shews that limitations must be placed upon the self assertion of the single man; and the growing sense of dependence, as life becomes more and more complex, necessarily increases that feeling of personal obligation which constrains us each to look to the things of others. At the same time in the intercourse of a fuller life we learn that our character is impoverished in proportion as we are isolated; and we learn also that evil or wrong in one part of a society makes itself felt throughout the whole.

But if we admit the central idea of Socialism, that the goal of human endeavour is the common wellbeing of all alike, sought through conditions which provide for the fullest culture of each man, as opposed to the special development of a race or a class by the sacrifice of others, in slavery, or serfdom, or necessary subjection, it does not follow that the end can be reached only in one way. The powers of men are different, and equal development does not involve equality. Experience will direct and confirm reform, for life is manifold. But a common end will hallow individuality for more effective service. The single man will not be sacrificed to the society. He will be enabled to bring to it the offering of his disciplined powers, and so to realize his freedom.

Socialism, as I have defined it, is not, I repeat, committed to any one line of action, but everyone who accepts its central thought will recognize certain objects for immediate effort. He will seek to secure that labour shall be acknowledged in its proper dignity as the test of manhood, and that its reward shall be measured not by the necessities of the indigent, but by its actual value as contributing to the wealth of the community. He will strive to place masses of men who have no reserve of means in a position of stability, and to quicken them by generous ideas. He will be bold to proclaim that the evils of luxury and penury cannot be met by palliatives. He will claim that all should confess in action that every power, every endowment, every possession is not of private use, but a trust to be administered in the Name of the Father for their fellowmen.

II. — Such a view of the social destiny of the individual with all he has, is brought home to us at the present time by the conception which we have gained of the evolution, or rather of the providential ordering, of life. There have been from very early times dreams of ideal states fashioned by great thinkers who felt how far the world in which they lived fell short of the society for which man was made. They looked within for the laws of their imaginary commonwealths. We have at length a surer guide for our hopes in the records of the past. Studying the course which history has taken, we can forecast the future, for the broad outline of human discipline is clear. In the Old World the ruling thought was the dignity of a race or of a class to which all beside in a greater or less degree were made to minister. In the New World — ushered in by the Advent — the ruling thought has been the dignity of man as man, of men as men, and however imperfectly the great truth revealed in the Incarnation has been grasped and embodied, still it has in some sense been now brought home to the West little by little through many lessons. At first in the Middle Ages the society was dominant, ordered in a heirarchy of classes. Then at the Reformation the individual claimed independence, and the voice of authority was followed by the voice of reason. Now, when the complexity of life baffles purely rational analysis, and theoretical freedom has been found to degenerate into anarchy, we catch sight of a fuller harmony, in which the offices of the society and of the citizen, of tradition and conscience, shall be reconciled. Functions which were once combined have been sharply separated as a step towards a more complete union. Here also the law of a higher life has been fulfilled, and the parts of the body have been differentiated so that their dependence one upon another may be seen in its beneficent operation. The modern conception of capital and trade, or rather the isolated facts which foreshadowed them, usury and buying to sell again (regrating), were repugnant to mediaeval religious feeling. Now, when the range of production and distribution has been indefinitely extended, we have to face problems which mediaeval experience could not anticipate, and cannot help us to solve. As late as the last century capitalist, producer, and consumer were not unfrequently united. If each of these three classes has now been sharply distinguished and hitherto kept apart by conflicting material interests, it is, if we may trust the teachings of the past, that they may in due time be brought together again in a full, free, and chosen fellowship. The relations which exist between them at present are modern and transitional. Wage-labour, though it appears to be an inevitable step in the evolution of Society, is as little fitted to represent finally or adequately the connection of man with man in the production of wealth, as at earlier times slavery or serfdom. Our position then is one of expectancy and preparation, but we can see the direction of social movement. We wait for the next stage in the growth of the State, when in free and generous co-operation each citizen shall offer the fulness of his own life that he may rejoice in the fulness of the life of the body.

Such an issue may appear to be visionary. It is, I believe, far nearer than we suppose. It is at least the natural outcome of what has gone before. The society has been organized effectively without regard to the individual. The individual has been developed in his independence. It remains to show how the richest variety of individual differences can be made to fulfil the noblest ideal of the State, when fellow labourers seek in the whole the revelation of the true meaning of their separate offerings. And nothing has impressed me more during my years of work than the rapidity and power with which the thoughts of dependence, solidarity, and brotherhood, of our debt to the past and our responsibility for the future, have spread among our countrymen. Men have grown familiar with the principle of combination for limited objects. Such unions have called out already heroic efforts and heroic sufferings, and are a discipline for a larger fellowship. There is indeed enough to sadden us in the selfishness which too often degrades rich and poor alike; but self-respect has grown widely among those who are poor in material wealth, from the consciousness of a high calling, and self-denial has quickened to a noble activity many who are oppressed with the burden of great possessions. There is on all sides an increasing and glad recognition of duties answering to opportunities, and if education has created or deepened the desire for reasonable leisure, it has also opened springs of enjoyment which riches cannot make more healthy or more satisfying. At the same time our public wealth is quickly accumulating. Buildings, galleries, gardens, bring home to every Englishman that he has an inheritance in the grandeur of his country; and the English family still guards in honour the fundamental types of human communion and fatherhood and brotherhood, which are a sufficient foundation for a Kingdom of God. All things indeed once more are ready, and a clear call is given to us to prove pur faith.

III. — Here then lies the duty of the Christian teacher. The thoughts of a true Socialism — the thoughts that men are "one man" in Christ, touches all and all touch each with an inevitable influence, that, as we live by others, we can find no rest till we live for others — are fundamental thoughts of the Law and the Prophets, of the Gospel and the Epistles, which we are empowered and bound to make effective under the conditions of modern life. The results of reflection and experience have at length made them intelligible. To interpret and embody them in a practical form is the office of believers now.

We must show that Christianity, which has dealt hitherto with the individual, deals also with the State, with classes and not only with men, with social conditions and not only with personal character. In the endeavour to fulfill this duty the past will help us by analogy, but not by example. New questions cannot be settled by tradition. There is an order in the accomplishment of the Divine counsel. Even great evils are not met and conquered at once. Discerning our own work we shall not condemn or blame our fathers that they did not anticipate it. They did more or less perfectly the work which was prepared for them to do. We are required not to repeat their service, but, enriched and strengthened by what they have won, we shall labour to bring the doctrine of the Incarnation to bear upon the dealings of man with man, and of nation with nation, and aim at providing that the opportunities of living worthily of that central fact of existence shall be within the reach of all.

As we strive to do this we shall come to understand the force of the loftiest truths of theology. We shall find that that which is transcendental is indeed practical as a motive, an inspiration, a support. We alone — I do not scruple to affirm it — we alone, who believe that "the Word became flesh," can keep hope fresh in the face of the sorrows of the world, for we alone know that evil is intrusive and remediable; we alone know that the victory over the world has been won, and that we have to gather with patience the fruits of the victory.

Violence can destroy but it cannot construct. Love destroys the evil when it replaces the evil by the good.

But while we affirm the absolute supremacy of the spiritual, and the universal sovereignty of Christ reigning from the Cross, we remember that our work must be done under the conditions of earth, and that it is here, on the sordid field of selfish conflicts, that we must prepare the Kingdom of God. At the same time, we recognize that the social problem of to-day, the relations of capital and labour, belongs especially to Englishmen, who by their national character have ruled the development of modern industry. As Englishmen have set the problem, so on Englishmen lies the responsibility of solving it. And the position of the English clergy gives them peculiar opportunities for moderating with wise faith the discussions which will open the way for the solution. The clergy of the National Church are not a close and isolated caste. They are drawn from every class. They are trained in sympathy with every variety of thought and culture. They are lifted above the influences of party by the greatness of their work. They are enabled to labour for a distant end by the greatness of the faith which they proclaim.

I ask then — I ask myself not without sorrowful perplexity — whether we have, in view of the teaching of present facts, considered what God's counsel for men in Creation and Redemption is? Whether the state of things in our towns and in our villages either answers or tends to answer to the Divine idea? Whether the present distribution of wealth is not perilous alike to those who have and to those who want? Whether we have not accepted the laws of the material order as the laws of all nature? Whether we have pondered over the moral significance of the poor and the weak? Whether we have reflected on the wider application of that principle, which it is the glory of medicine to have guarded, that every discovery affecting man's well-being is the property of the race and not of the finder?

I do not enter now on any questions of detail. I desire simply to direct attention to questions which go to the very heart of the Gospel; and I beg the younger clergy, with whatever strength of persuasion I can command, to think over these things; to discuss them one with another reverently and patiently; to seek to understand and not to silence their adversaries; to win for themselves the truth which gives to error whatever permanence it has; to remember that bold and sweeping statements come more commonly from doubt or ignorance than from just conviction. But I beg them not to improvise hasty judgments. The personal value of an opinion depends for the most part upon the pains which have been spent in forming it. Zeal, enthusiasm, devotion are not enough to guide us in the perplexities of conduct. We need above all knowledge as the basis of action.

As yet we have not mastered the elements of the problems of society. Theories have been formed from the examination of groups of isolated phenomena. But life is one and complex. We must indeed see our end before we begin our work, but it may be that different ways will be found to lead to it; and, as far as I can judge, the social question of our day will finally recieve not one answer but many. But in one respect all the answers will agree: all will be religious.

Meanwhile our office as Christian teachers is to proclaim the ideal of the Gospel, and to form opinion. And if we do this: if we confess that our mission is to hasten a Kingdom of God on earth, and, if we ourselves move resolutely forward as the Spirit guides us, I believe that we shall find through the common offices of our daily intercourse that peace which springs out of the consciousness of common sacrifices made for one end, and the assurance of strength which comes through new victories of faith. We cannot doubt that God is calling us in this age through the characteristic teachings of science and of history to seek a new social application of the Gospel. We cannot doubt therefore, that it is through our obedience to the call that we shall realize its Divine power. The proof of Christianity which is prepared by God, as I believe, for our times, is a Christian Society filled with one Spirit in two forms — righteousness and love.